"X/1999 DEMANDS YOUR ATTENTION...THIS TITLE IS A SELF-CONTAINED, INTELLECTUAL SERIES THAT, WHILE [IT] BEGRUDGINGLY GIVES THE READER PLENTY OF GRATUITOUS ACTION AND VIOLENCE, MANAGES TO STAND APART FROM THAT AND ENTICE READERS WITH THE BEAUTY OF ITS ART AND THE SERIOUSNESS OF THE STORY."

—EX: THE ONLINE WORLD OF ANIME & MANGA

This volume contains the X/1999 installments from Animerica Extra, the Anime Fan's Comic Magazine, Vol. 3, No. 8 through Vol. 4, No. 4 in their entirety.

STORY & ART BY CLAMP

ENGLISH ADAPTATION BY FRED BURKE

Translation/Lillian Olsen
Touch-Up Art & Lettering/Wayne Truman
Cover Design/Hidemi Sahara
Graphics and Layout/Carolina Ugalde

Publisher/Seiji Horibuchi
Editor in Chief/Hyoe Narita
Managing Editor/Annette Roman
Editor/Julie Davis

VP of Sales and Marketing/Rick Bauer

Printed in Canada

Published by Viz Communications, Inc.
P.O. Box 77010 • San Francisco, CA 94107

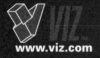

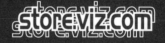

www.viz.com

store.viz.com

10 9 8 7 6 5 4 3 2 1
First printing, August 2002

X/1999 GRAPHIC NOVELS TO DATE

X/1999: PRELUDE
X/1999: OVERTURE
X/1999: SONATA
X/1999: INTERMEZZO
X/1999: SERENADE
X/1999: DUET
X/1999: RHAPSODY
X/1999: CRESCENDO

ANIMERICA EXTRA GRAPHIC NOVEL

X/1999™
CRESCENDO

BY CLAMP

X/1999
THE STORY THUS FAR

The End of the World has been prophesied…and
time is running out. Kamui Shiro is a young man
who was born with a special power—the power to
decide the fate of the Earth itself.

Kamui had grown up in Tokyo, but had fled
with his mother after the suspicious death of a
family friend. Six year later, his mother too, dies
under suspicious circumstances, engulfed in
flames. Her last words to him are that he should
return to Tokyo…that his destiny awaits.

Kamui obeys his mother's words, but almost
immediately upon his arrival, he's challenged to a
psychic duel—a first warning that others know of
his power, and of his return.

Kamui is also reunited with his childhood
friends, Fuma and Kotori Monou. Although
Kamui attempts to push his friends away, hoping
to protect them, they too are soon drawn into the
web of destiny that surrounds him.

Meanwhile, the two sides to the great con-
flict to come are being drawn. On one side is the
dreamseer Hinoto, a blind princess who lives
beneath Japan's seat of government, the Diet
Building. On the other side is Kanoe, Hinoto's
dark sister with similar powers, but a different
vision of Earth's ultimate future. Around these
two women gather the Dragons of Heaven and
the Dragons of Earth, the forces that will fight to
decide the fate of the planet. The only variable in
the equation is Kamui, whose fate it will be to
choose which side he will join.

Although not all of the Dragons have yet
assembled, the battle has already begun. Fuma
and Kotori's father, priest of the Togakushi shrine,
is killed by a Dragon of Earth, Nataku, for the
sacred sword kept in the shrine. Tokiko Magami,
Kamui's aunt, mysteriously disappears before she
can fully explain the secrets of Kamui's birth, only
to reappear just as suddenly, giving bloody birth
to a *second* sacred sword…for Kamui, and his
destiny.

Now, the time of decision has come….

Kamui Shiro
A young man with psychic powers whose destiny will decide the fate of the world.

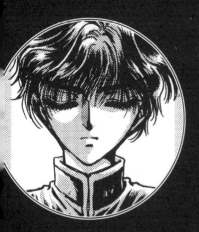

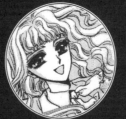

Kotori Monou
A delicate girl with a heart condition, Kotori was Kamui's childhood friend. She is deeply in love with Kamui.

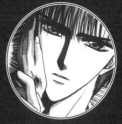

Fuma Monou
Kotori's brother, and Kamui's childhood friend.

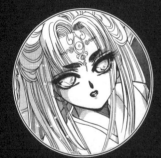

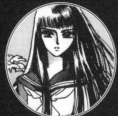

Arashi
Priestess of the Ise Shrine, Arashi can materialize a sword from the palm of her hand.

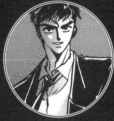

Sorata
A brash, but good-natured young Buddhist priest of the Mt. Koya shrine.

Hinoto
Blind, unable to speak or walk, Hinoto is a fragile, but powerful prophetess, far older than she looks. Attended by her two maidservants, Sohi and Hien, she lives in a secret shrine located beneath Tokyo's Diet Building, and often advises the Japanese government with her visions. She communicates with the power of her mind alone.

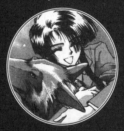

Yuzuriha Nekoi
The 14-year-old Nekoi is the youngest of the Dragons. She is always accompanied by a spirit dog, Inuki, that only she and others with psychic powers can see.

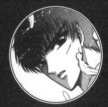

Subaru Sumeragi
Another member of the Seven Seals, Subaru is the 13th family head of a long line of spiritualists and powerful medium and exorcist. He is also the lead character of another Clamp manga series, *Tokyo Babylon*.

Kanoe
Hinoto's sister shares her ability to see the future…but Kanoe has predicted a different final result.

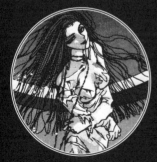

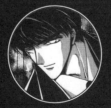

Seishiro Sakurazuka
Also called *Sakurazukamori*, the mysterious Seishiro shares a deep rivalry with the Dragon of Heaven Subaru. He is also a crossover character from *Tokyo Babylon*. He lost his sight in one eye during that series.

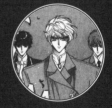

Nokoru, Suoh, and Akira
Three mysterious young men from the Clamp Academy who present Kamui with the deceased Tokiko's recorded message. They are crossover characters from the manga *Clamp Campus Detectives*.

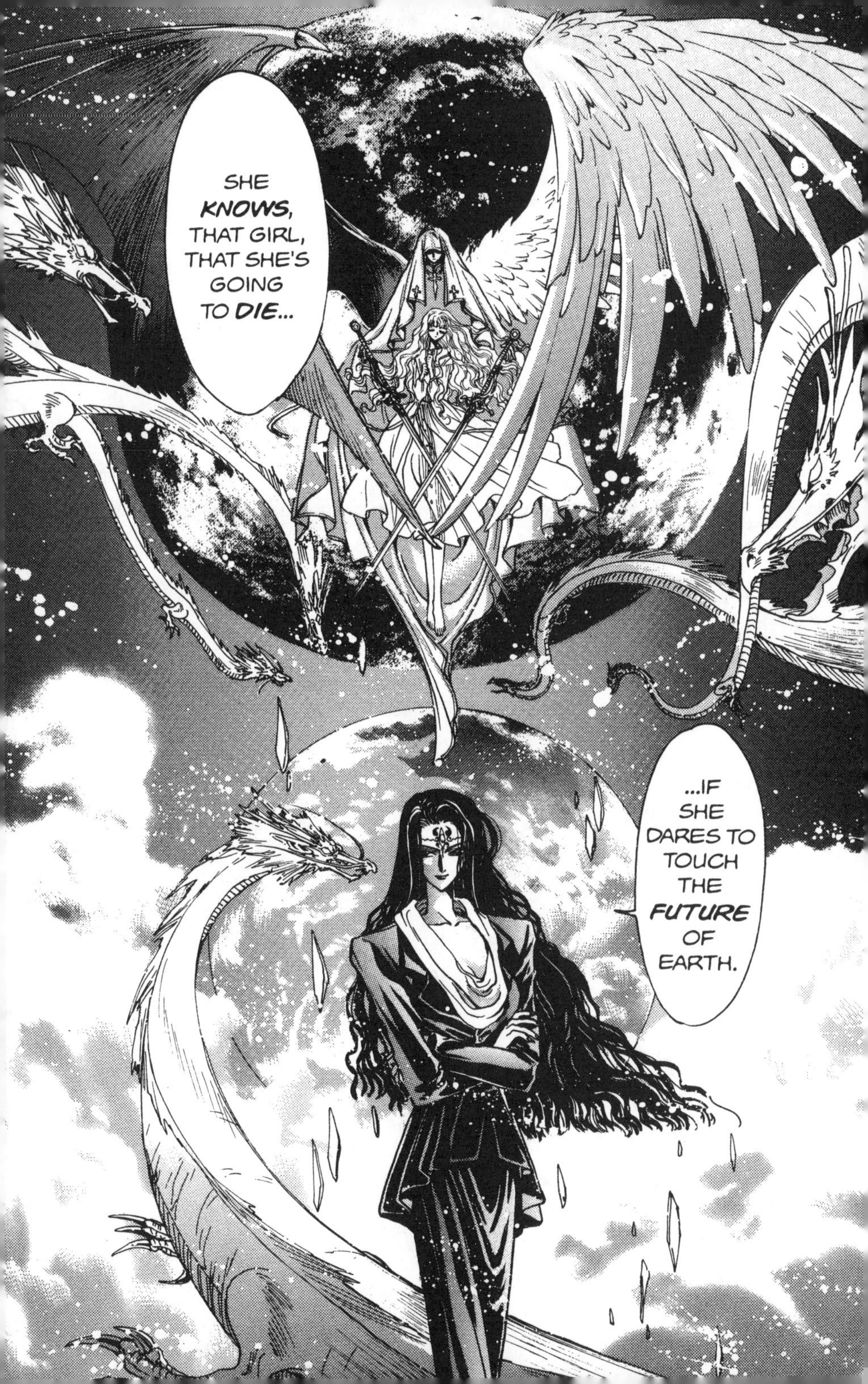
SHE KNOWS, THAT GIRL, THAT SHE'S GOING TO DIE...
...IF SHE DARES TO TOUCH THE FUTURE OF EARTH.

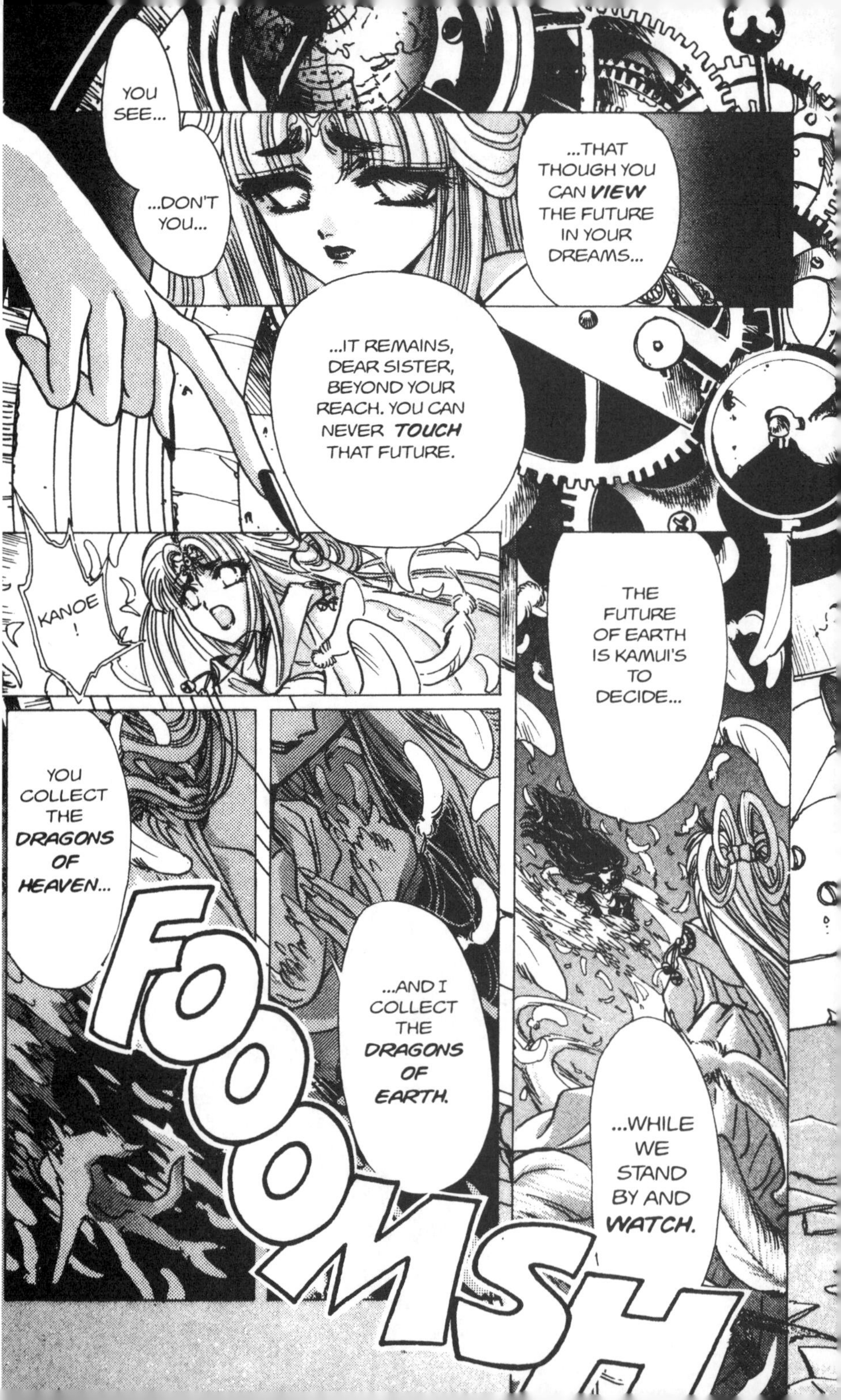
YOU SEE...
...DON'T YOU...
...THAT THOUGH YOU CAN VIEW THE FUTURE IN YOUR DREAMS...
...IT REMAINS, DEAR SISTER, BEYOND YOUR REACH. YOU CAN NEVER TOUCH THAT FUTURE.
KANOE !
THE FUTURE OF EARTH IS KAMUI'S TO DECIDE...
YOU COLLECT THE DRAGONS OF HEAVEN...
...AND I COLLECT THE DRAGONS OF EARTH.
...WHILE WE STAND BY AND WATCH.
FOOOMSH

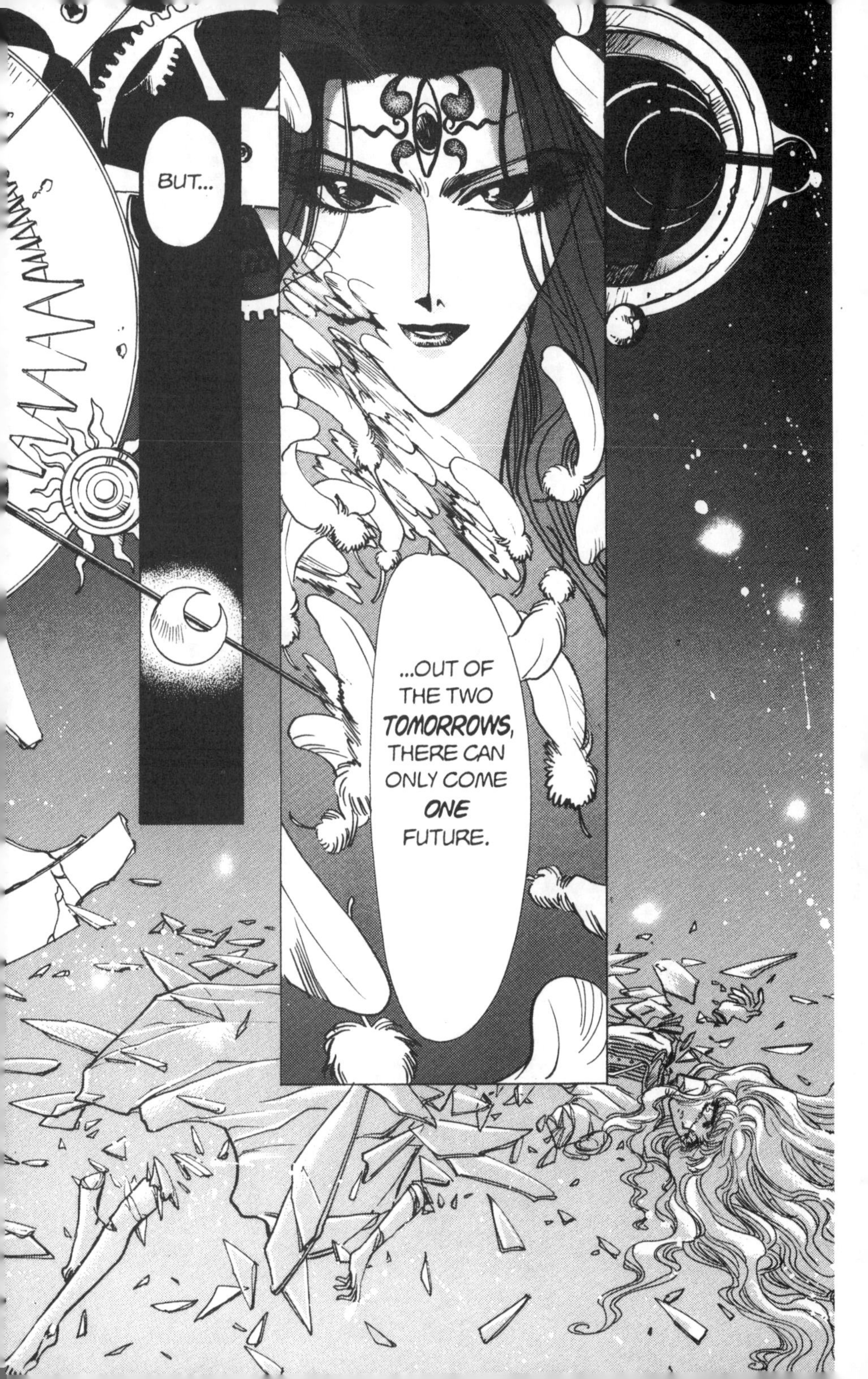
BUT...
...OUT OF THE TWO TOMORROWS, THERE CAN ONLY COME ONE FUTURE.

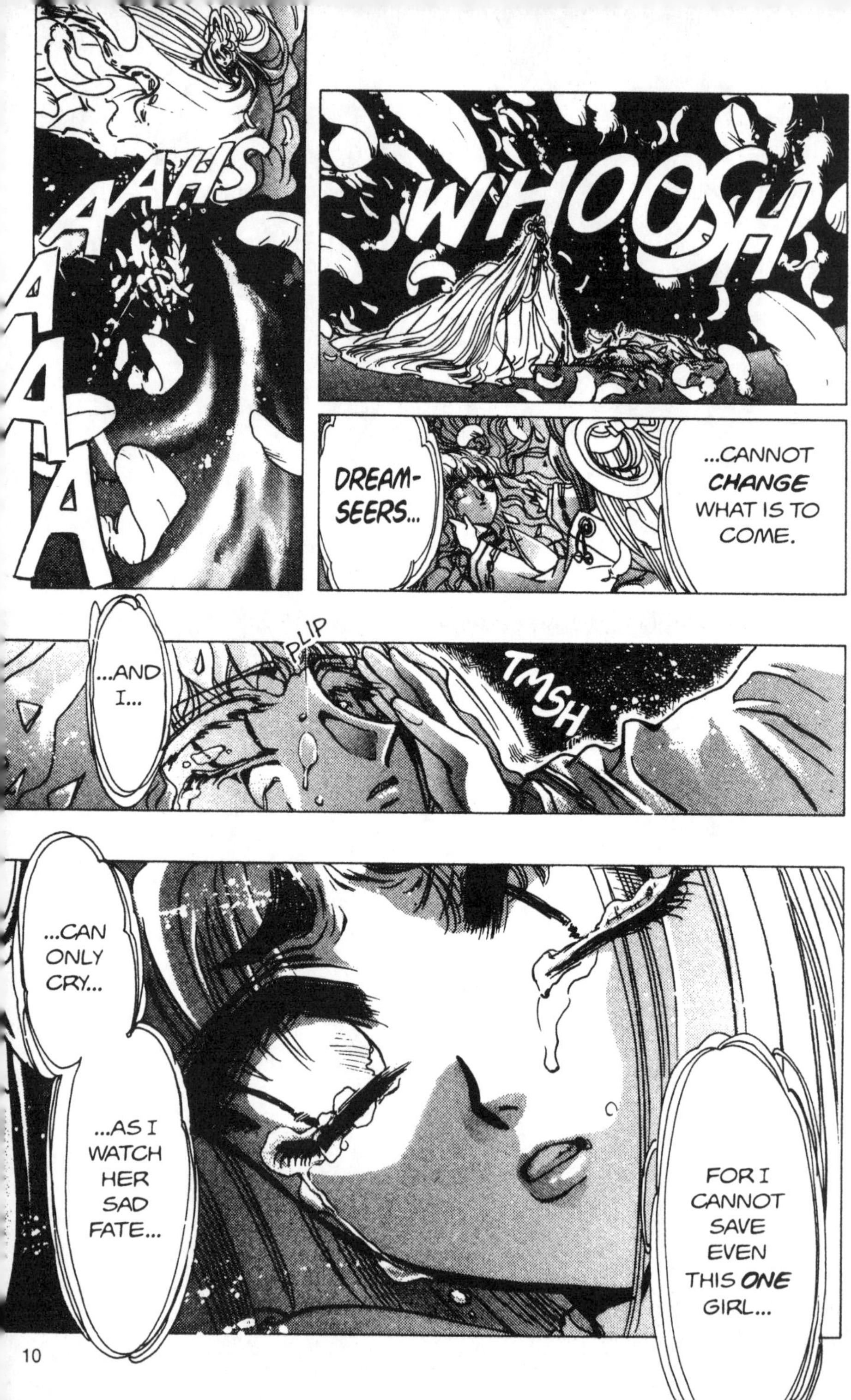
AAHS
AAAA
WHOOSH
DREAM-SEERS...
...CANNOT **CHANGE** WHAT IS TO COME.
...AND I...
PLIP
TMSH
...CAN ONLY CRY...
...AS I WATCH HER SAD FATE...
FOR I CANNOT SAVE EVEN THIS **ONE** GIRL...

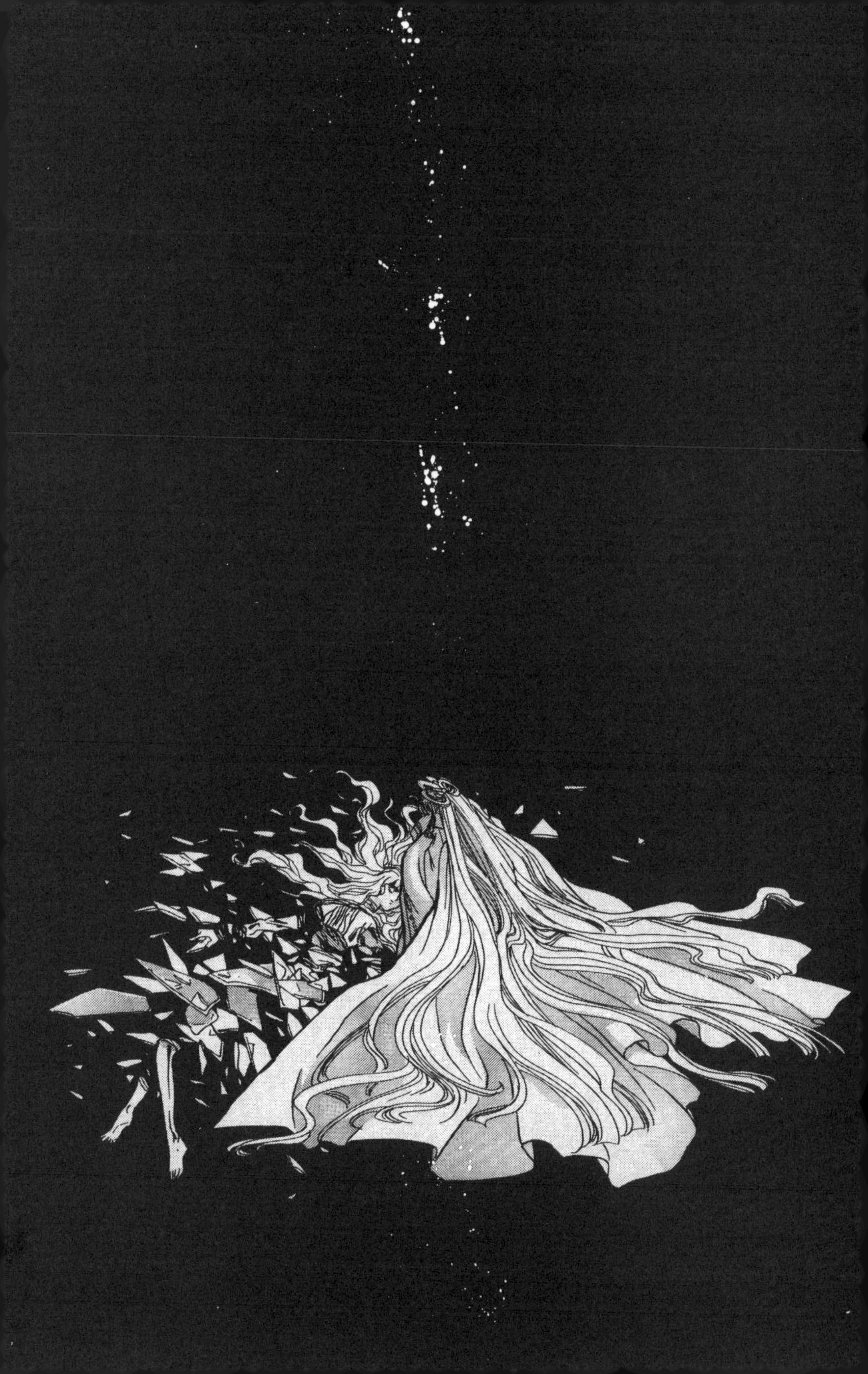

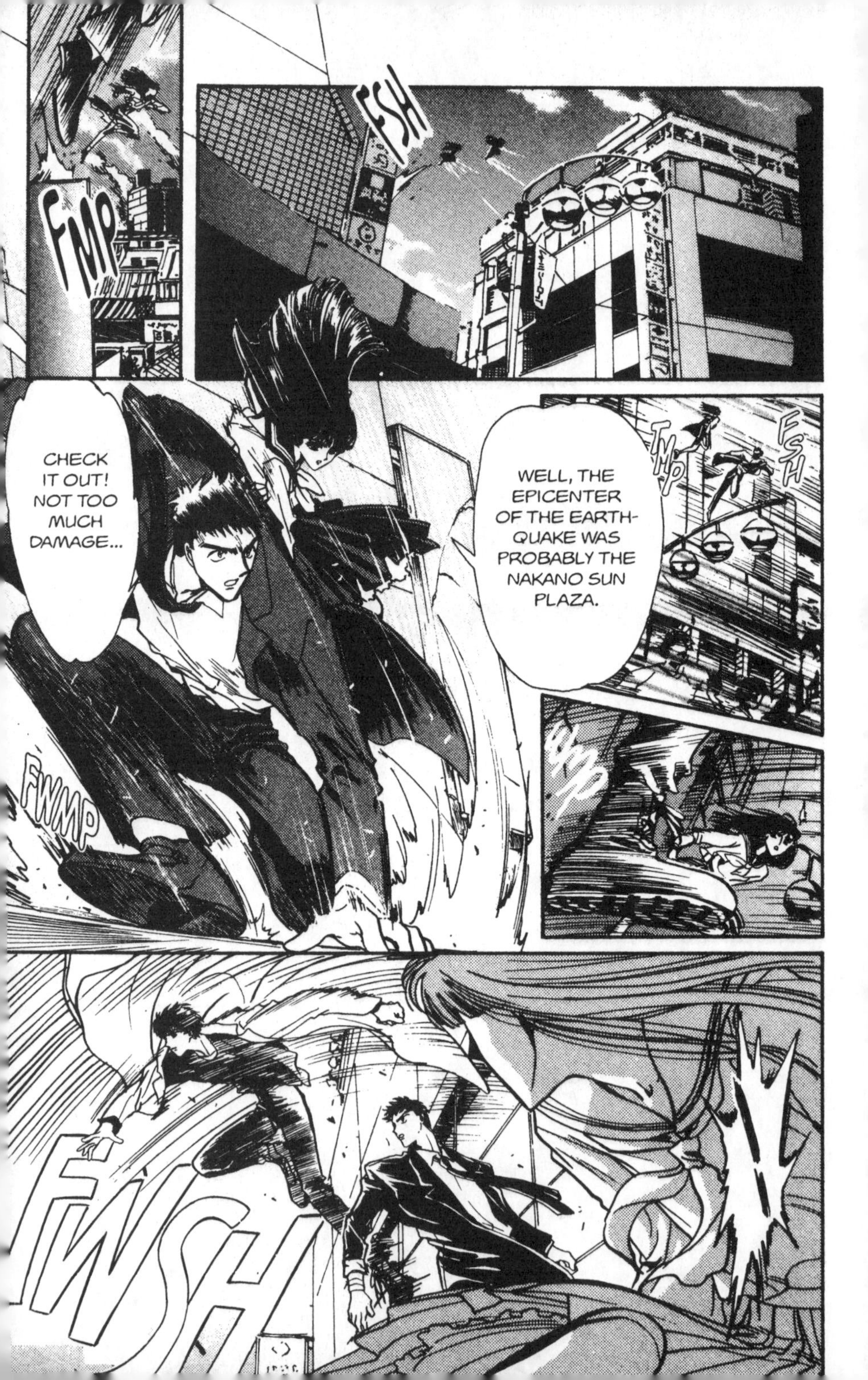
FSH
FMP
TMP
FSH
WMP
CHECK IT OUT! NOT TOO MUCH DAMAGE...
WELL, THE EPICENTER OF THE EARTHQUAKE WAS PROBABLY THE NAKANO SUN PLAZA.
FWMP
FWSH

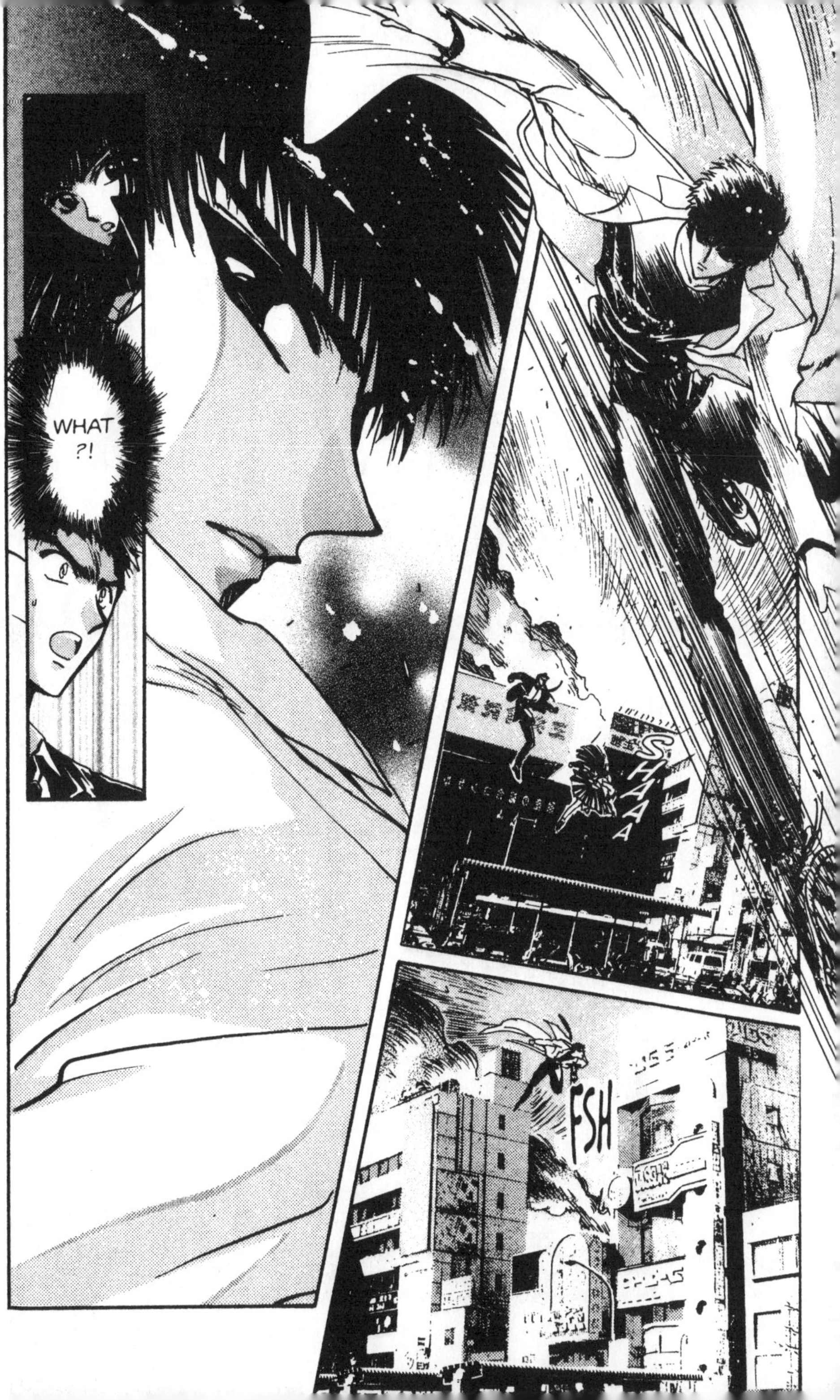
SHAAA
WHAT ?!
FSH

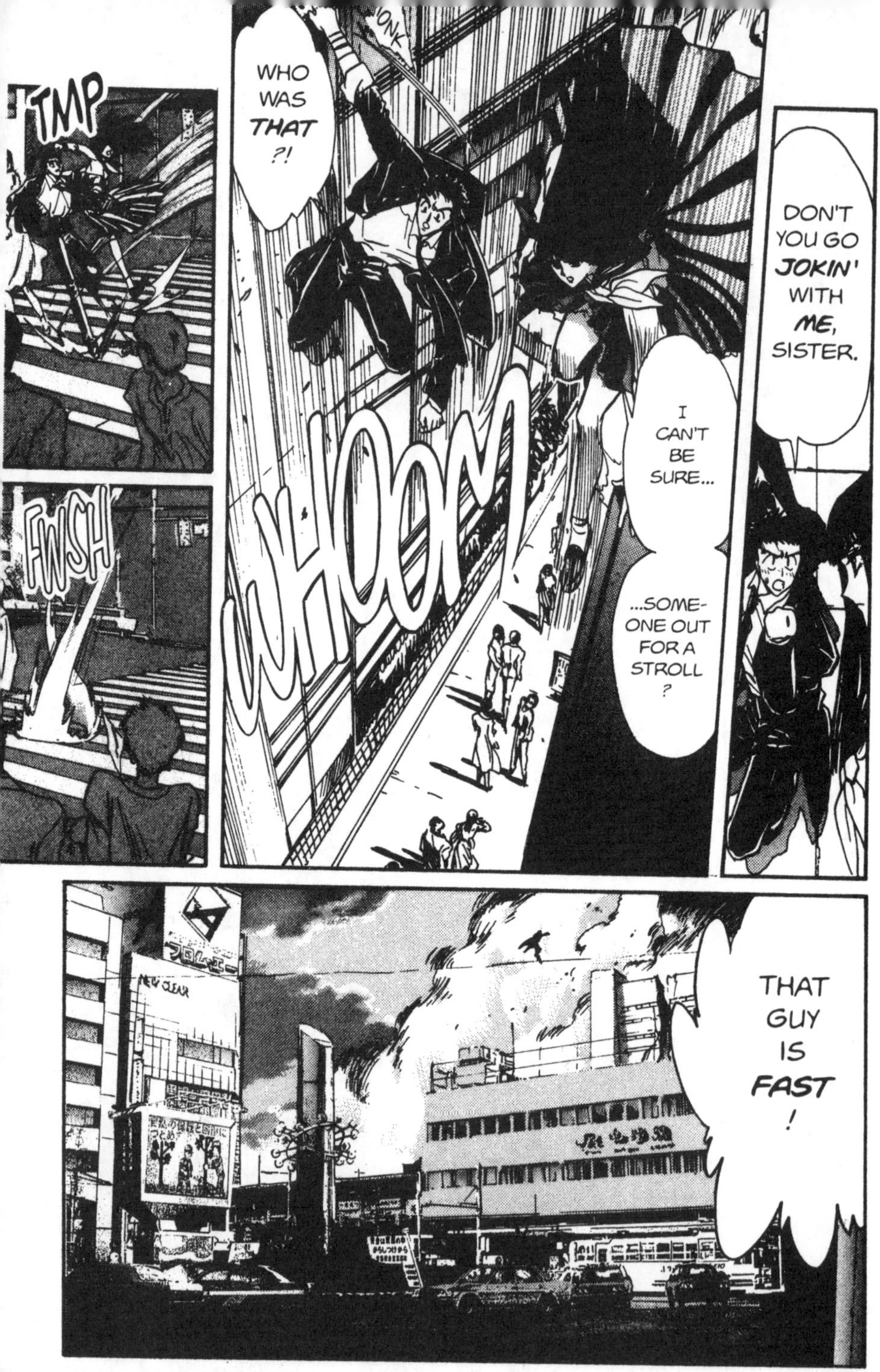
ONK
WHO WAS THAT?!
I CAN'T BE SURE...
...SOMEONE OUT FOR A STROLL?
WHOOM
DON'T YOU GO JOKIN' WITH ME, SISTER.
TMP
FWSH
THAT GUY IS FAST!

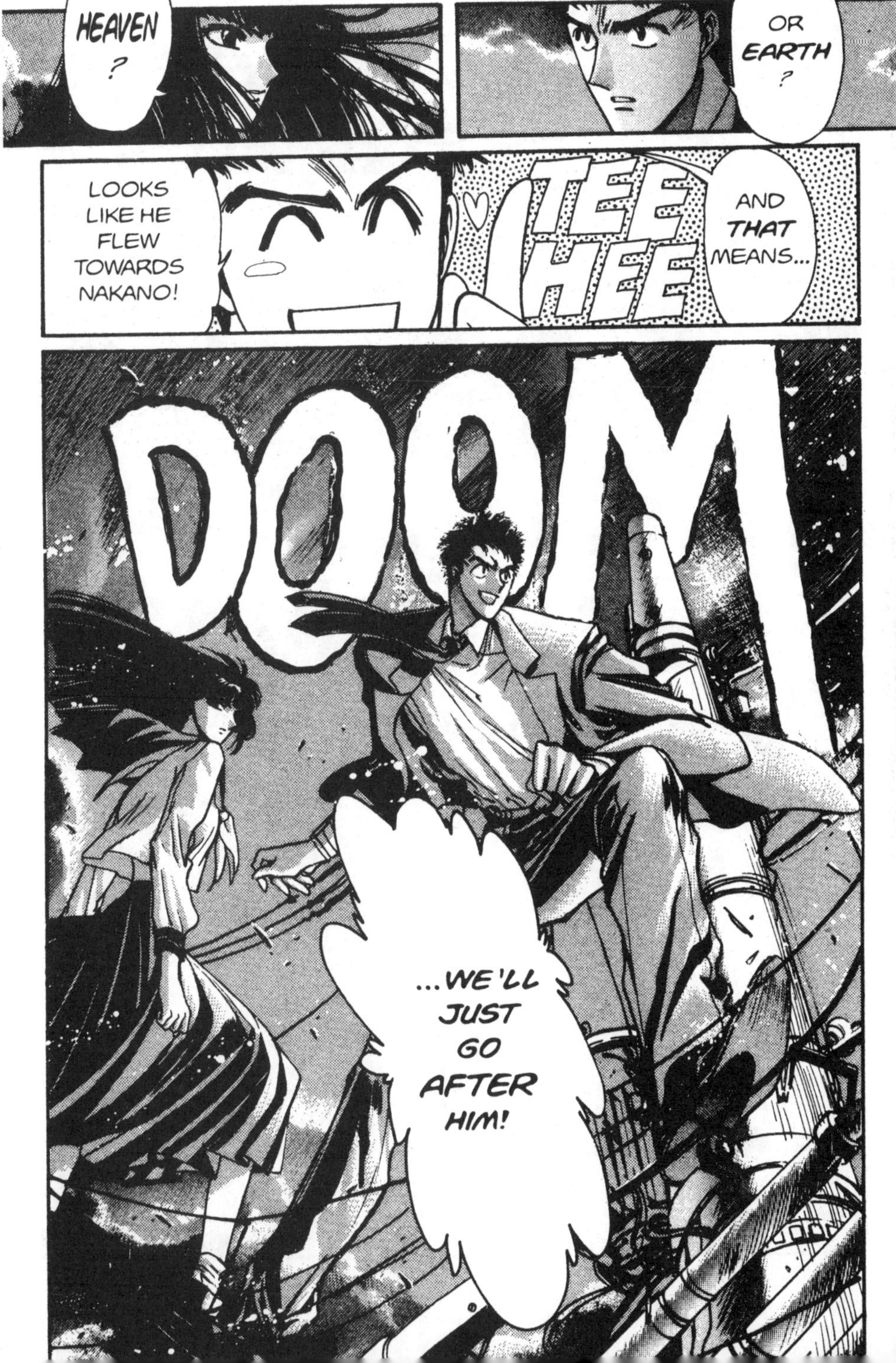
HEAVEN ?
OR EARTH ?
LOOKS LIKE HE FLEW TOWARDS NAKANO!
TEE HEE
AND THAT MEANS...
DOOM
...WE'LL JUST GO AFTER HIM!

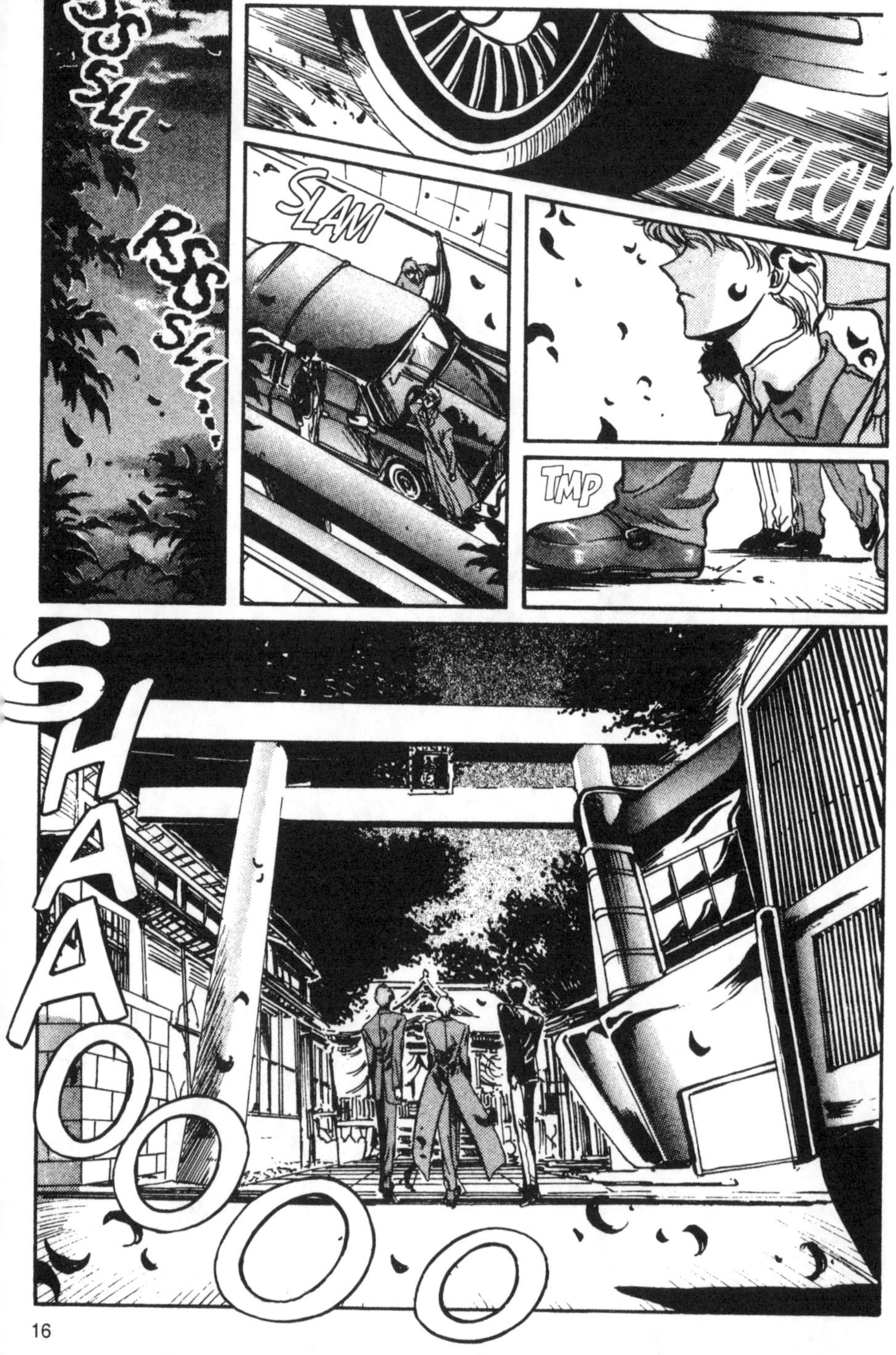
SKECH
TMP
SLAM
STSSSLL
RSSSSLL...
SHAAOOOOO

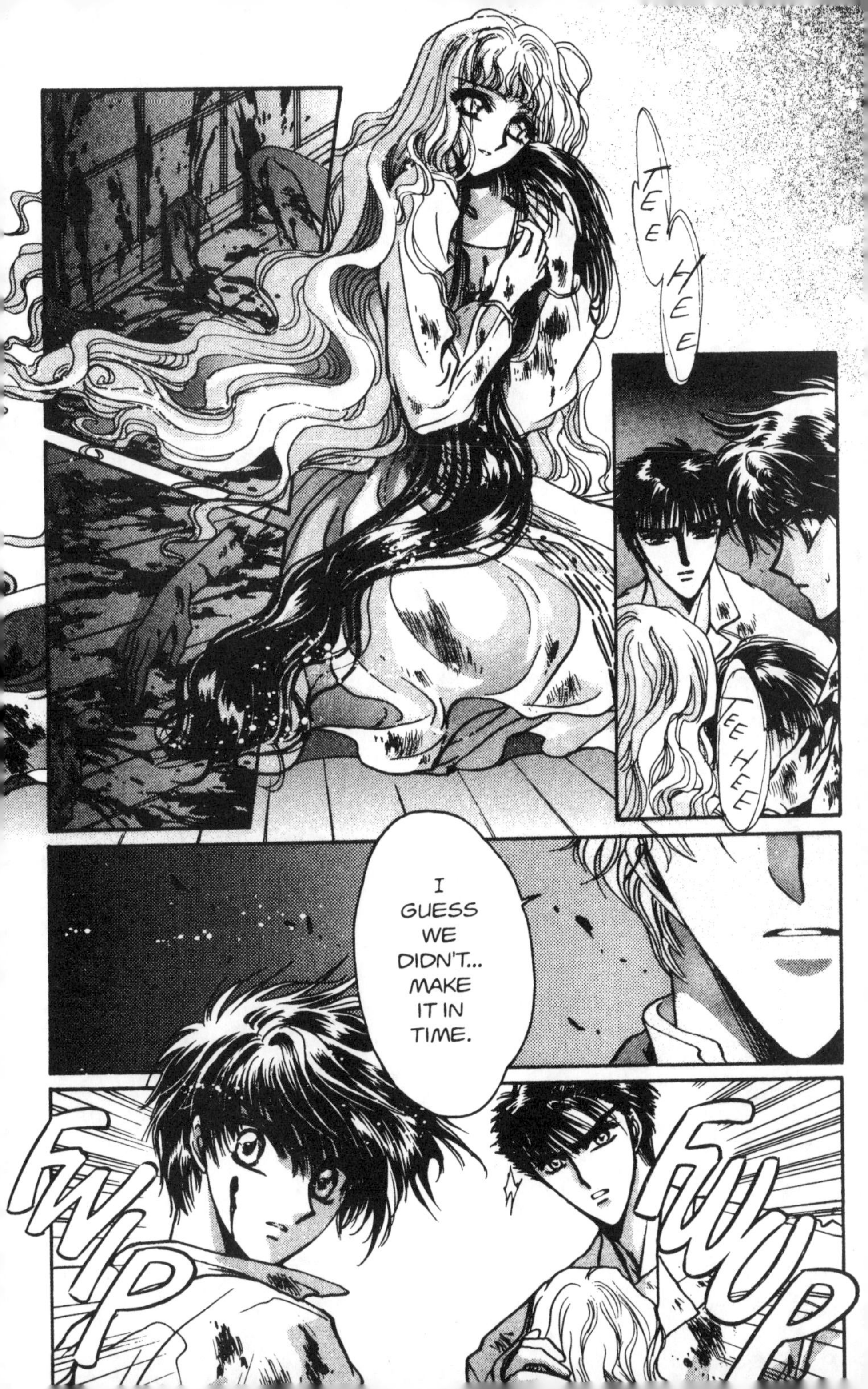
TEE HEE HEE
TEE HEE HEE
I GUESS WE DIDN'T... MAKE IT IN TIME.
FWUP
FWIP

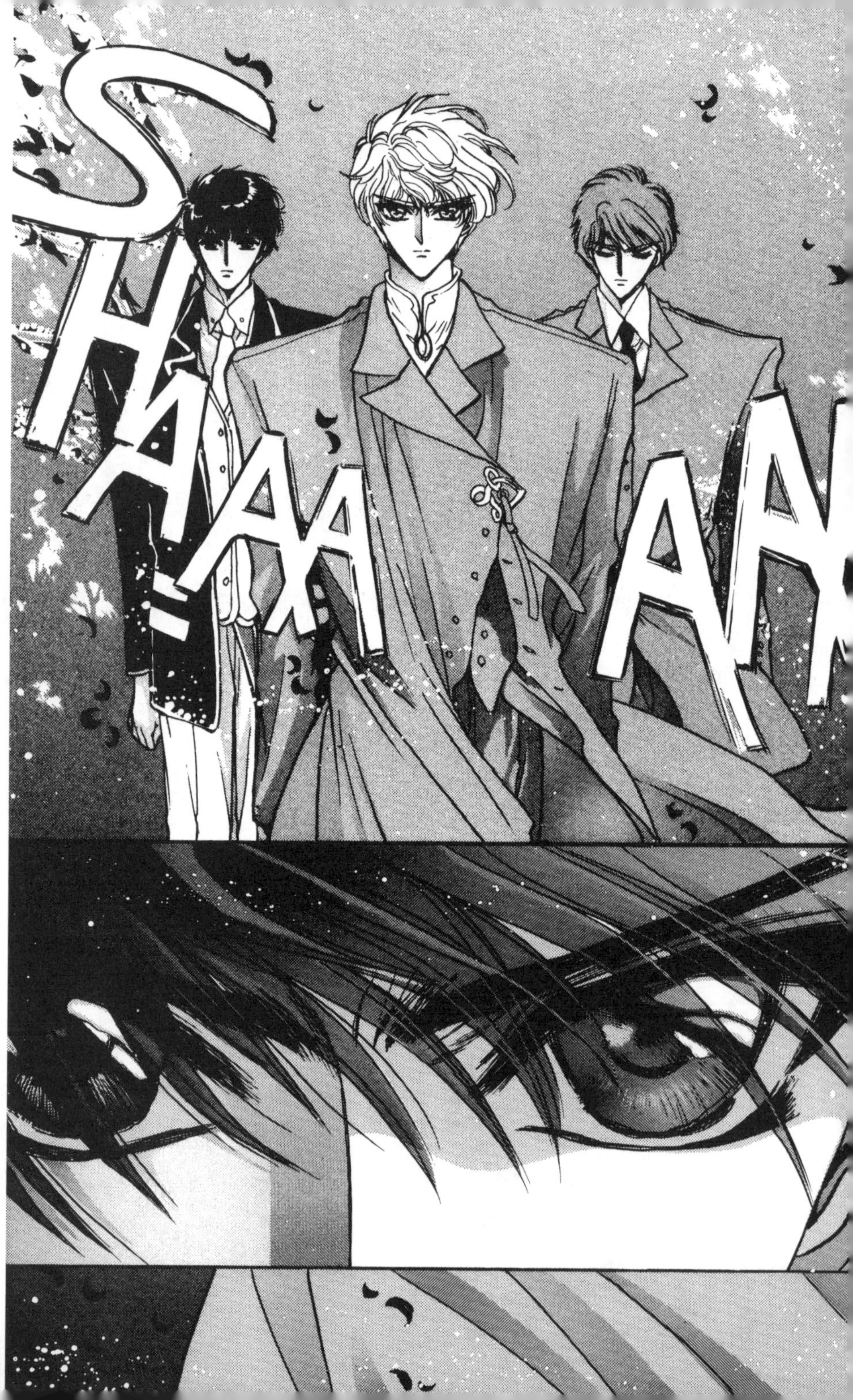
SHAAAAA

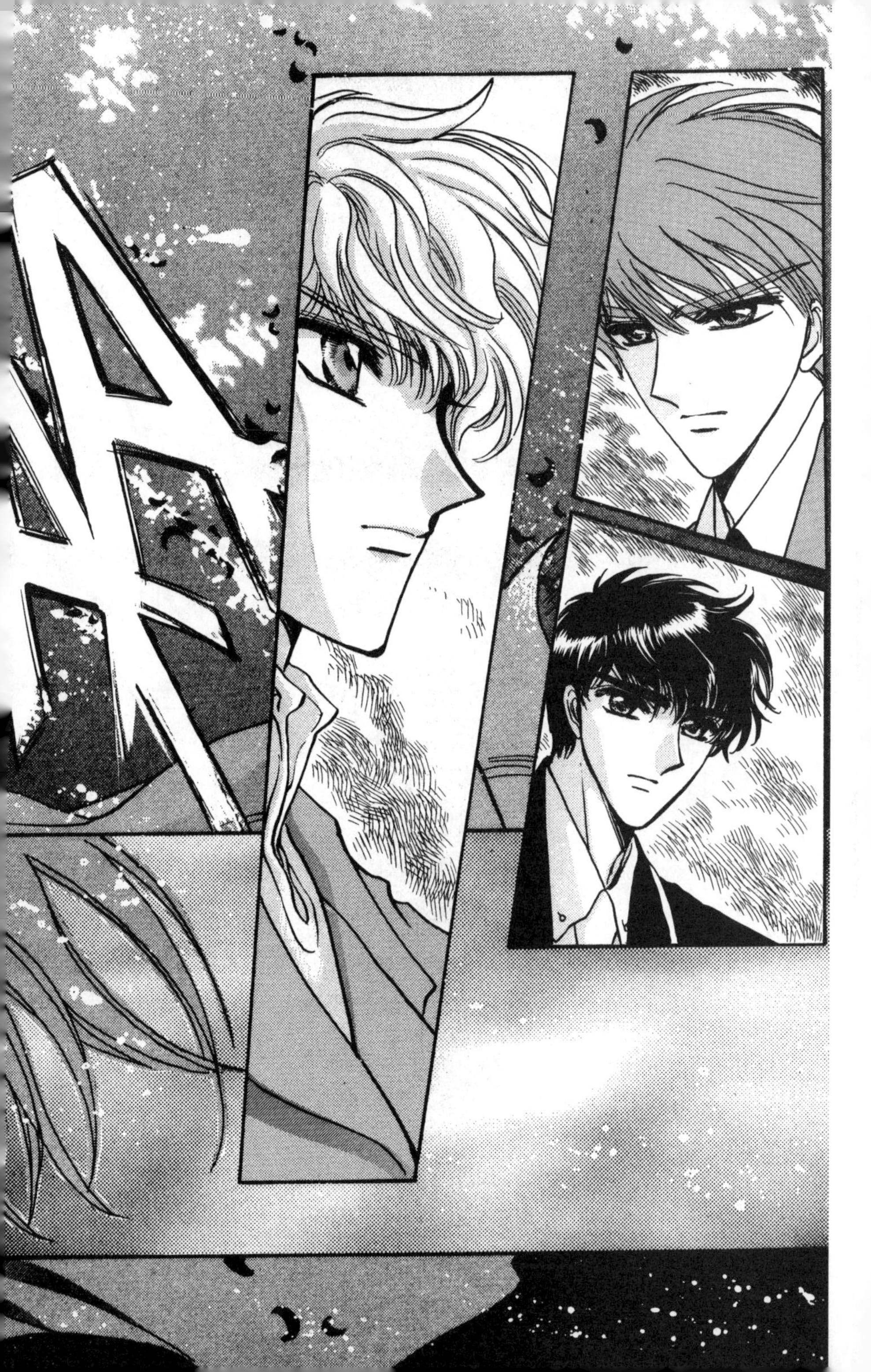

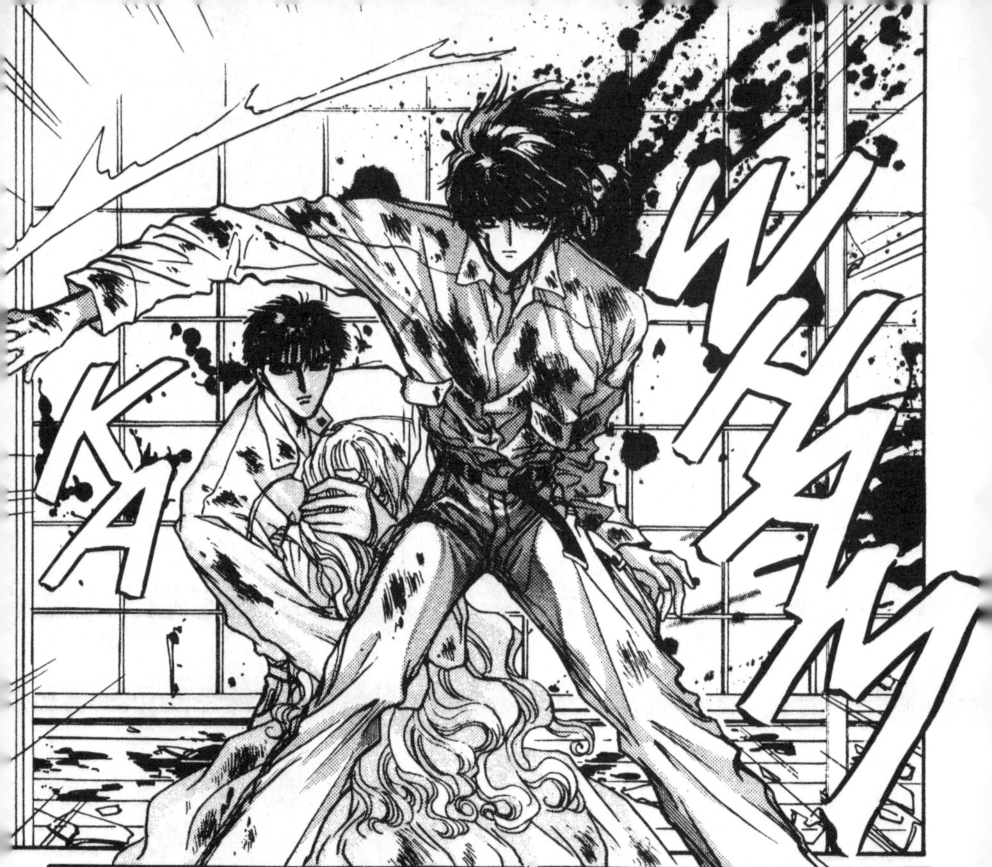
WHAM
KA
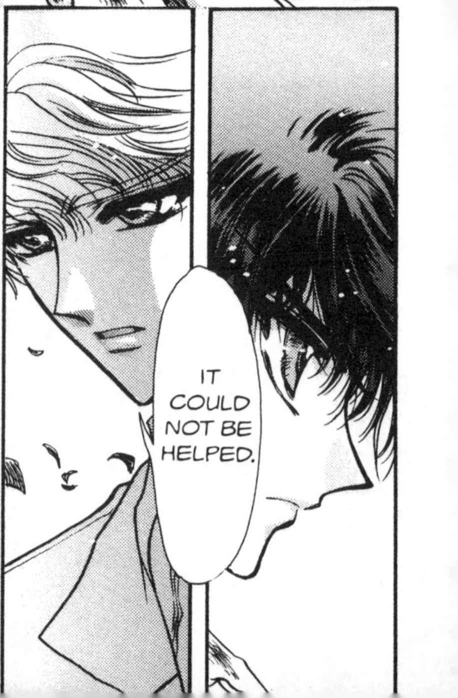
IT COULD NOT BE HELPED.
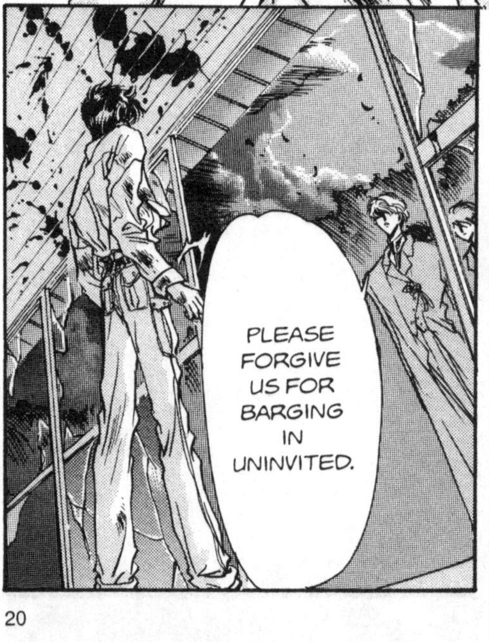
PLEASE FORGIVE US FOR BARGING IN UNINVITED.

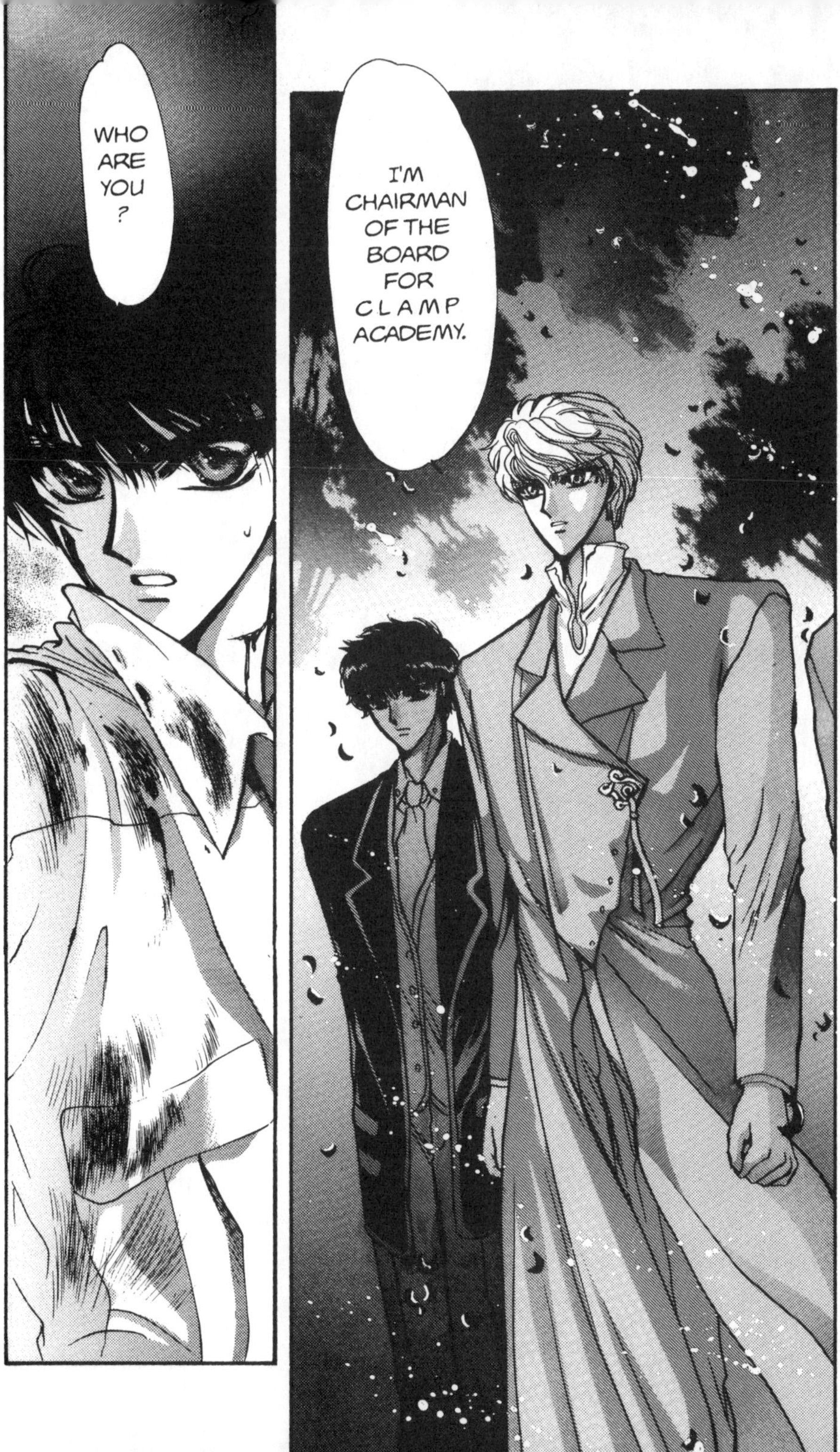
WHO ARE YOU ?
I'M CHAIRMAN OF THE BOARD FOR CLAMP ACADEMY.

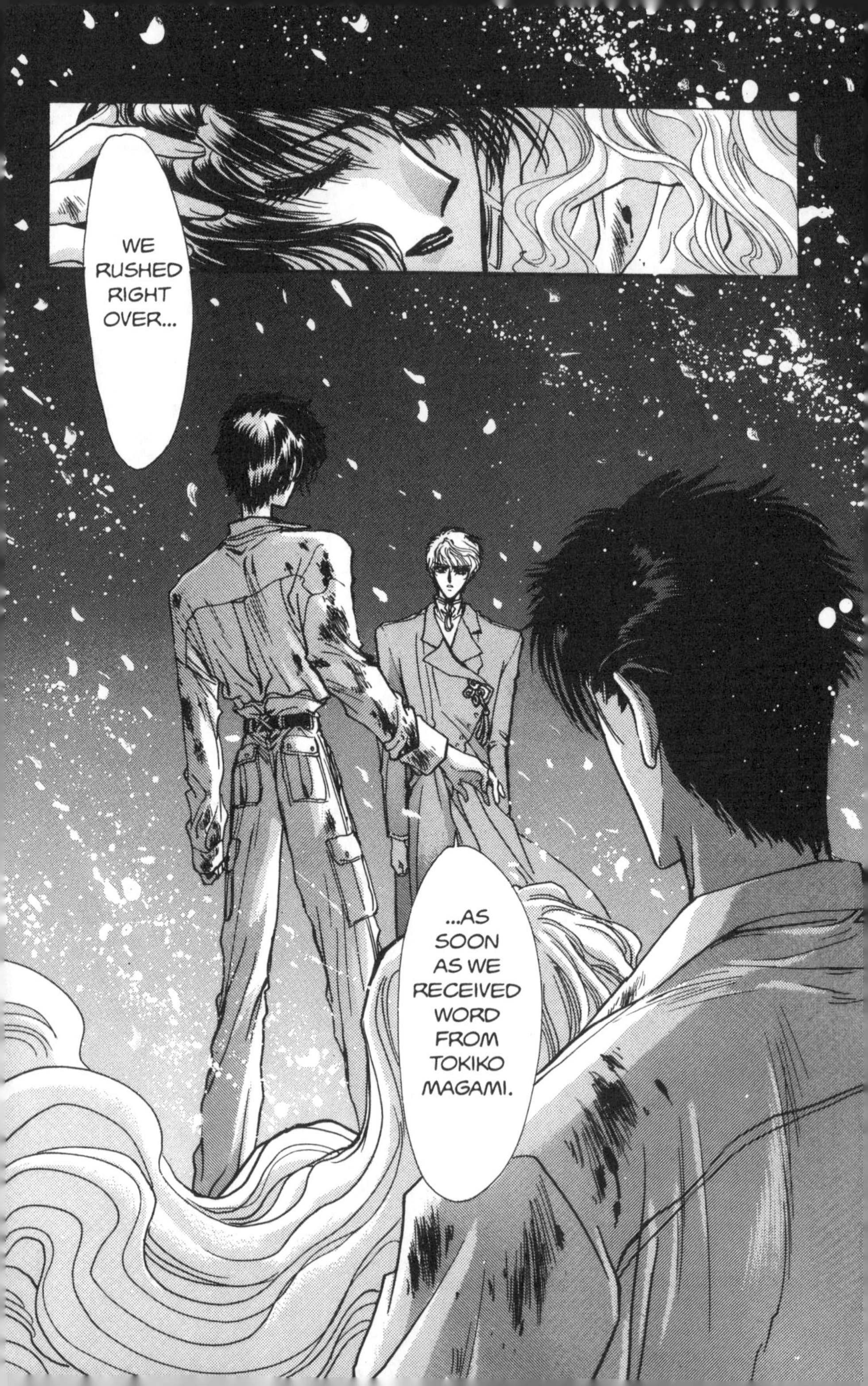
WE RUSHED RIGHT OVER...
...AS SOON AS WE RECEIVED WORD FROM TOKIKO MAGAMI.

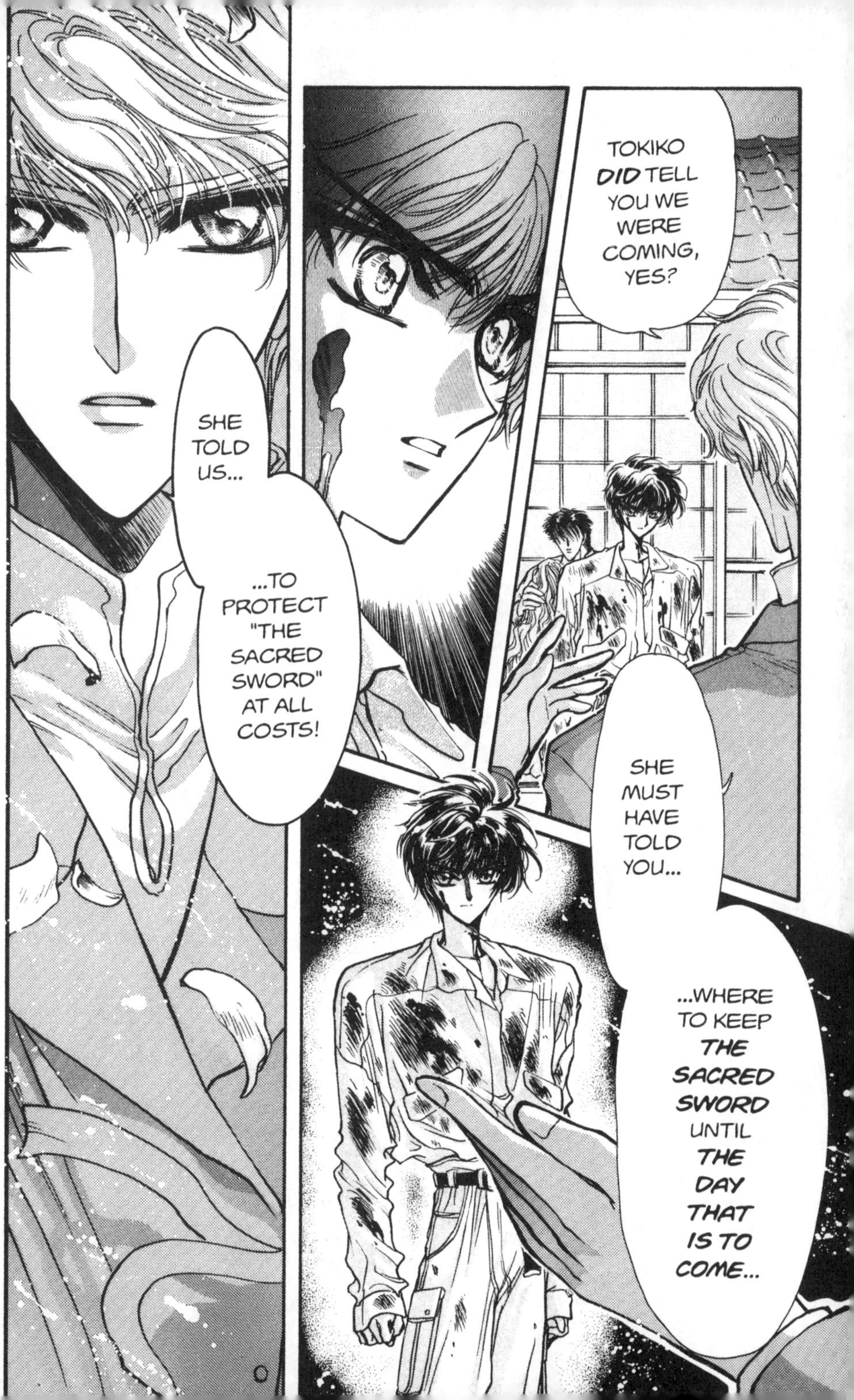
TOKIKO DID TELL YOU WE WERE COMING, YES?
SHE TOLD US...
...TO PROTECT "THE SACRED SWORD" AT ALL COSTS!
SHE MUST HAVE TOLD YOU...
...WHERE TO KEEP THE SACRED SWORD UNTIL THE DAY THAT IS TO COME...

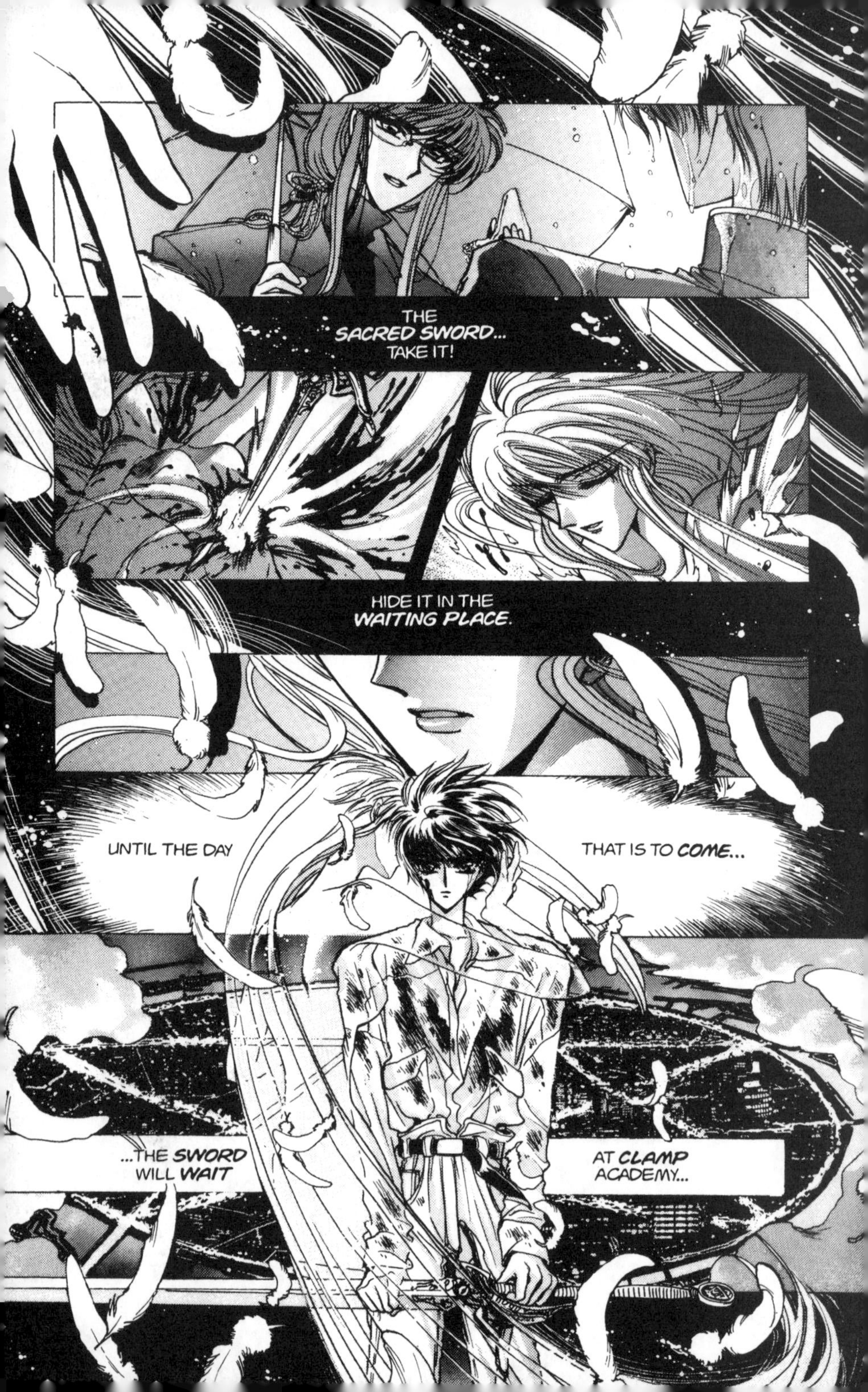
THE SACRED SWORD... TAKE IT!
HIDE IT IN THE WAITING PLACE.
UNTIL THE DAY
THAT IS TO COME...
AT CLAMP ACADEMY...
...THE SWORD WILL WAIT

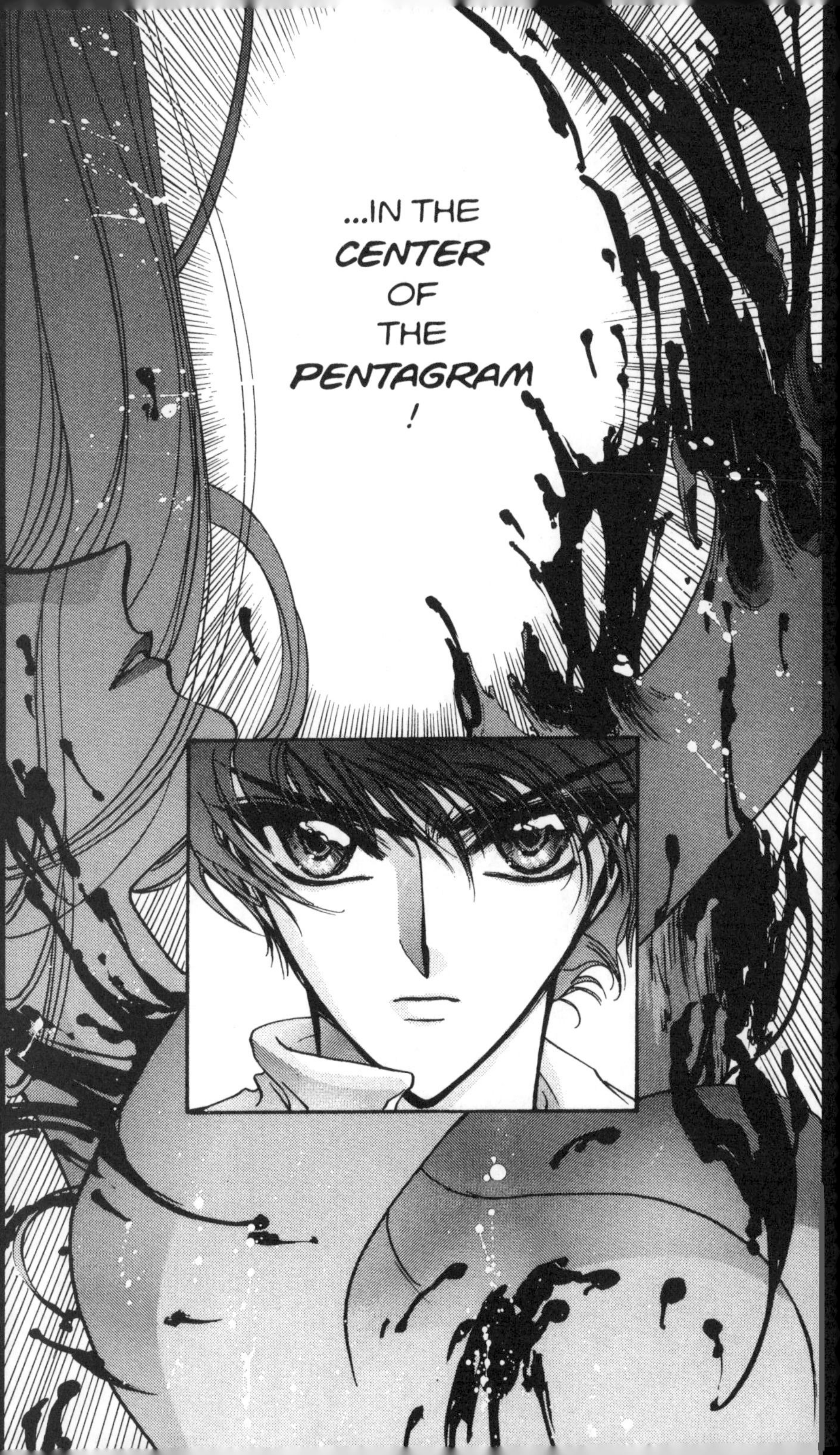
...IN THE CENTER OF THE PENTAGRAM!

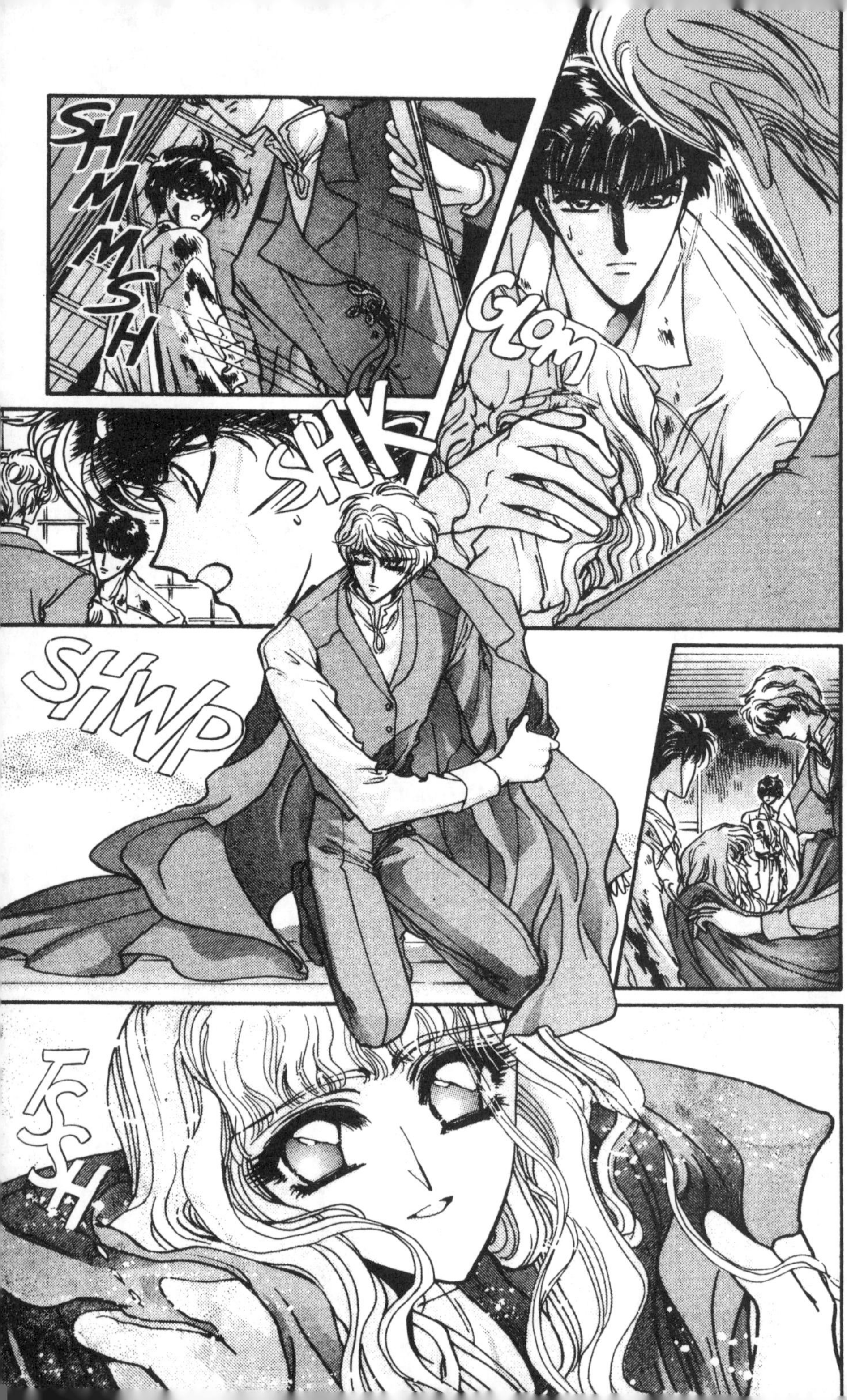
GLOM
SHMMMSH
SHK
SHWP
TSSH

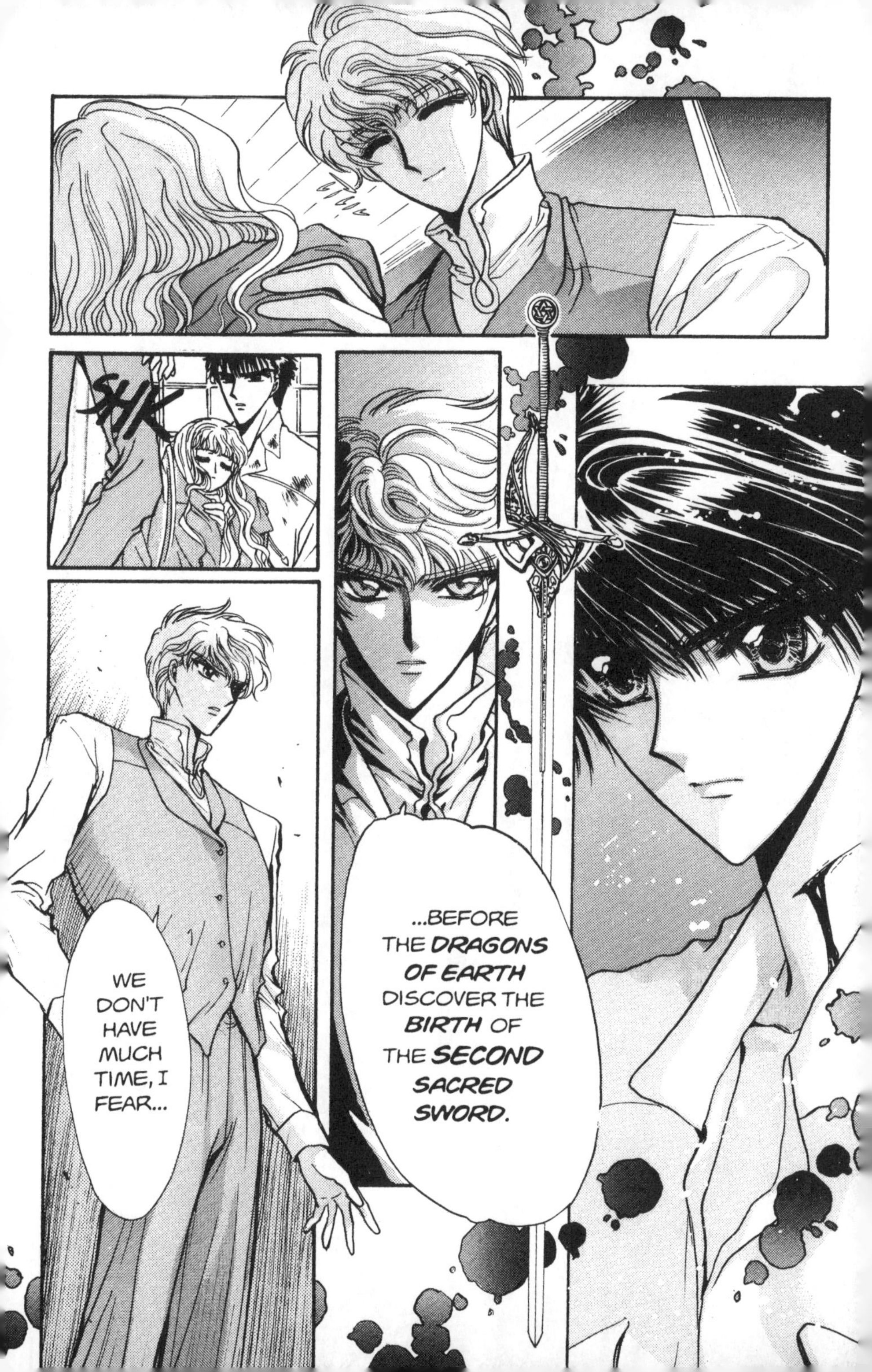
SHK
WE DON'T HAVE MUCH TIME, I FEAR...
...BEFORE THE DRAGONS OF EARTH DISCOVER THE BIRTH OF THE SECOND SACRED SWORD.

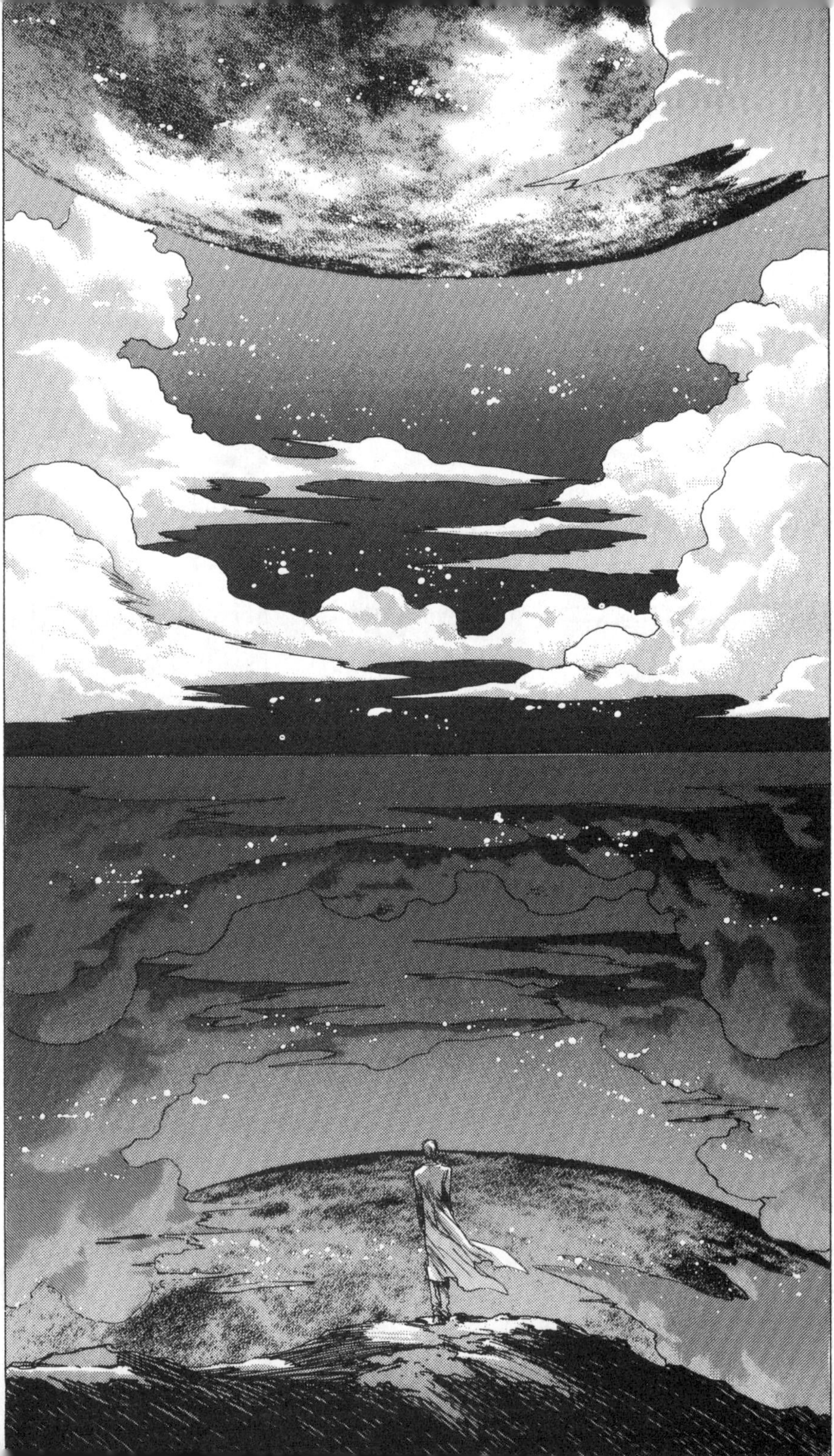

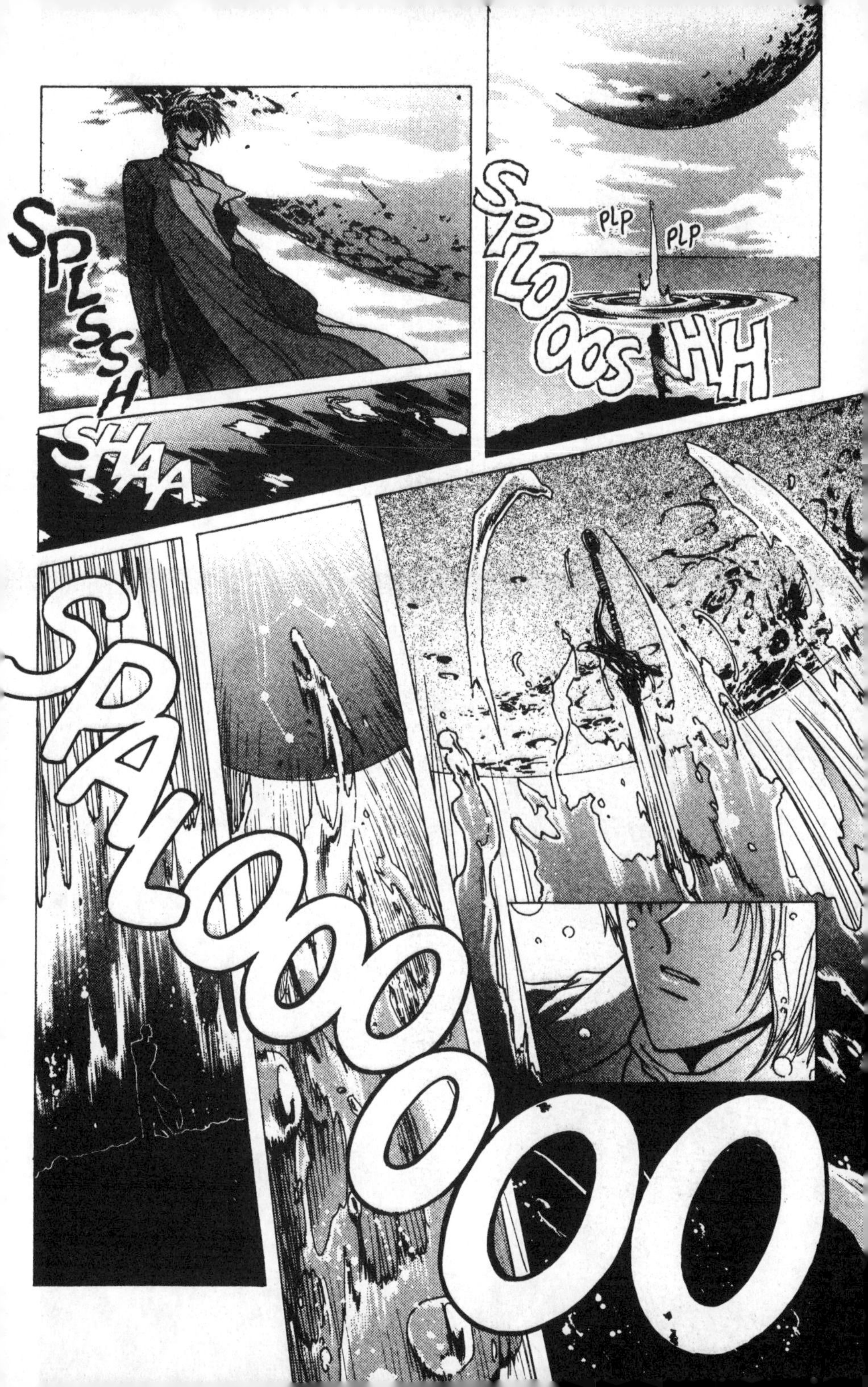
SPLOOOSHHH
PLP
PLP
SPLSSSH
SHAA
SPALOOOOOOO

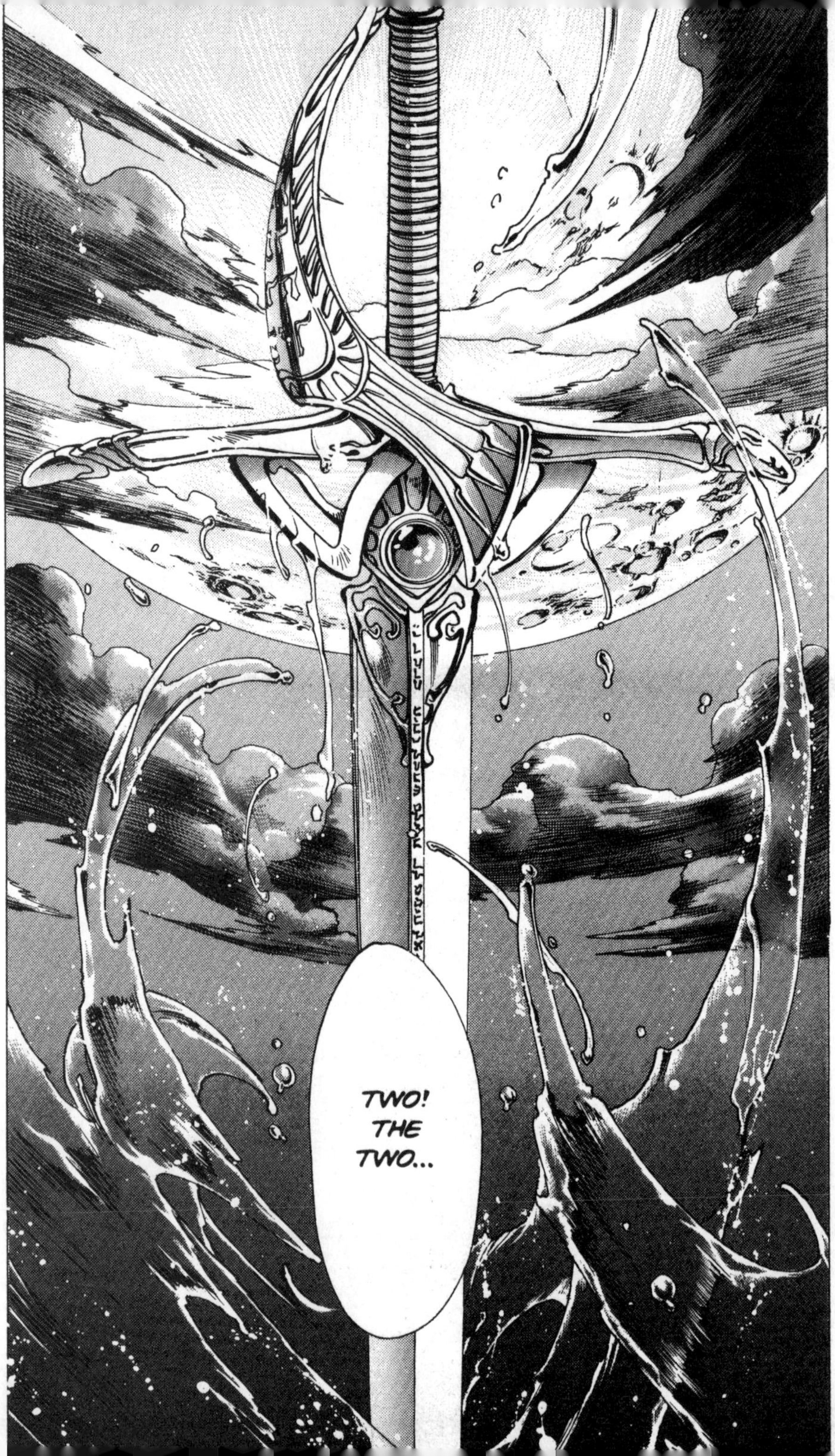
TWO!
THE
TWO...

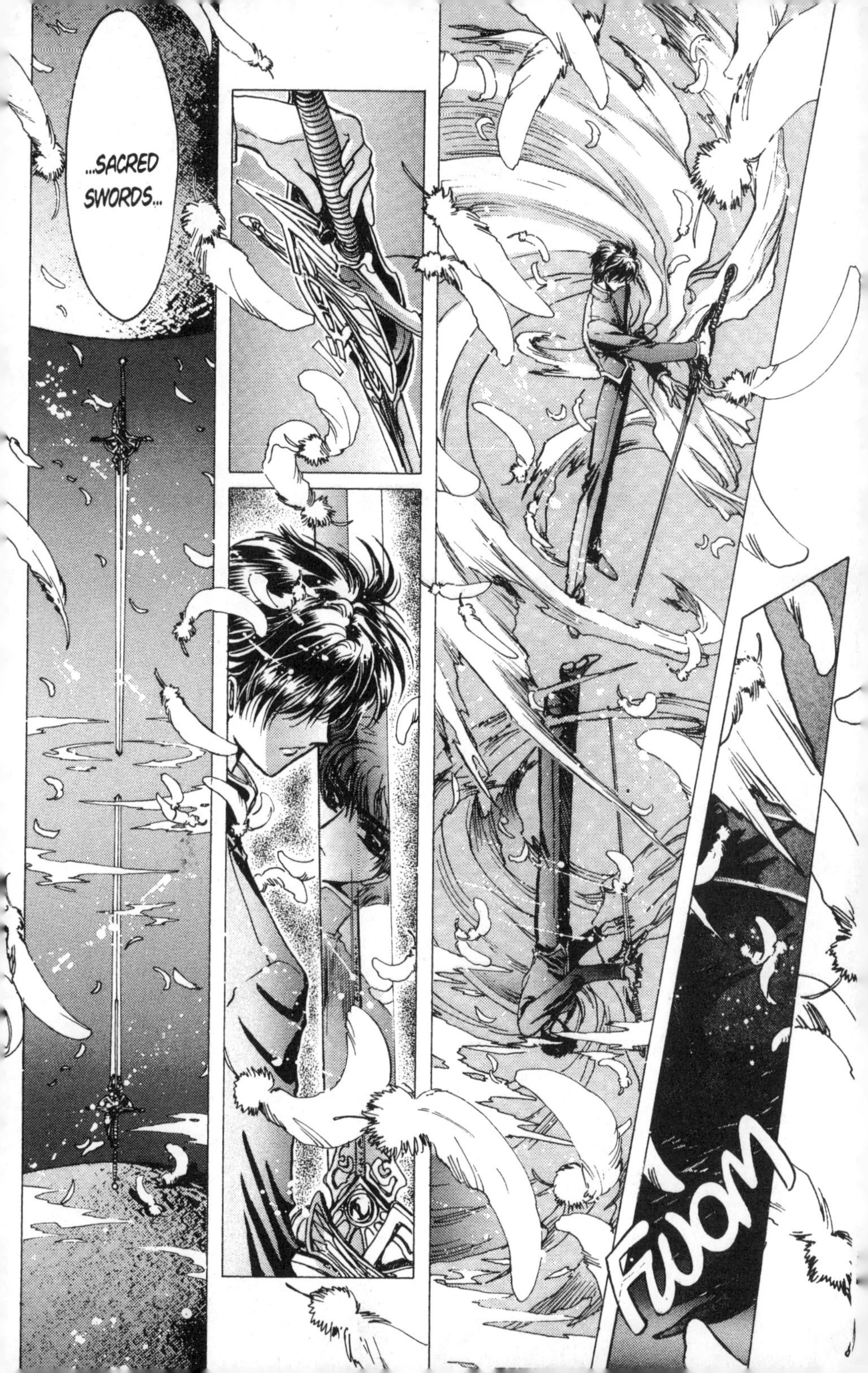
...SACRED SWORDS...
FWOM

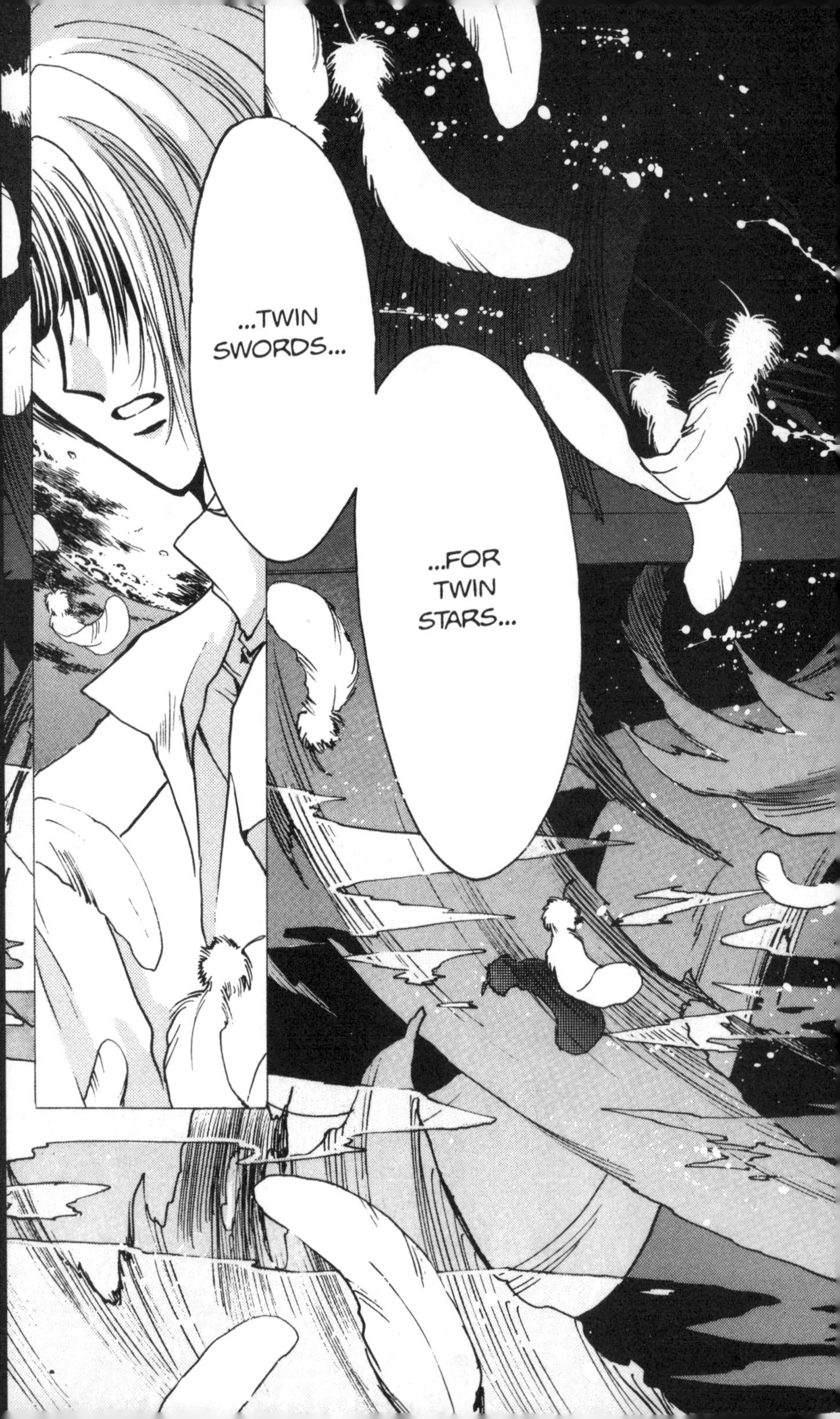
...TWIN SWORDS...
...FOR TWIN STARS...

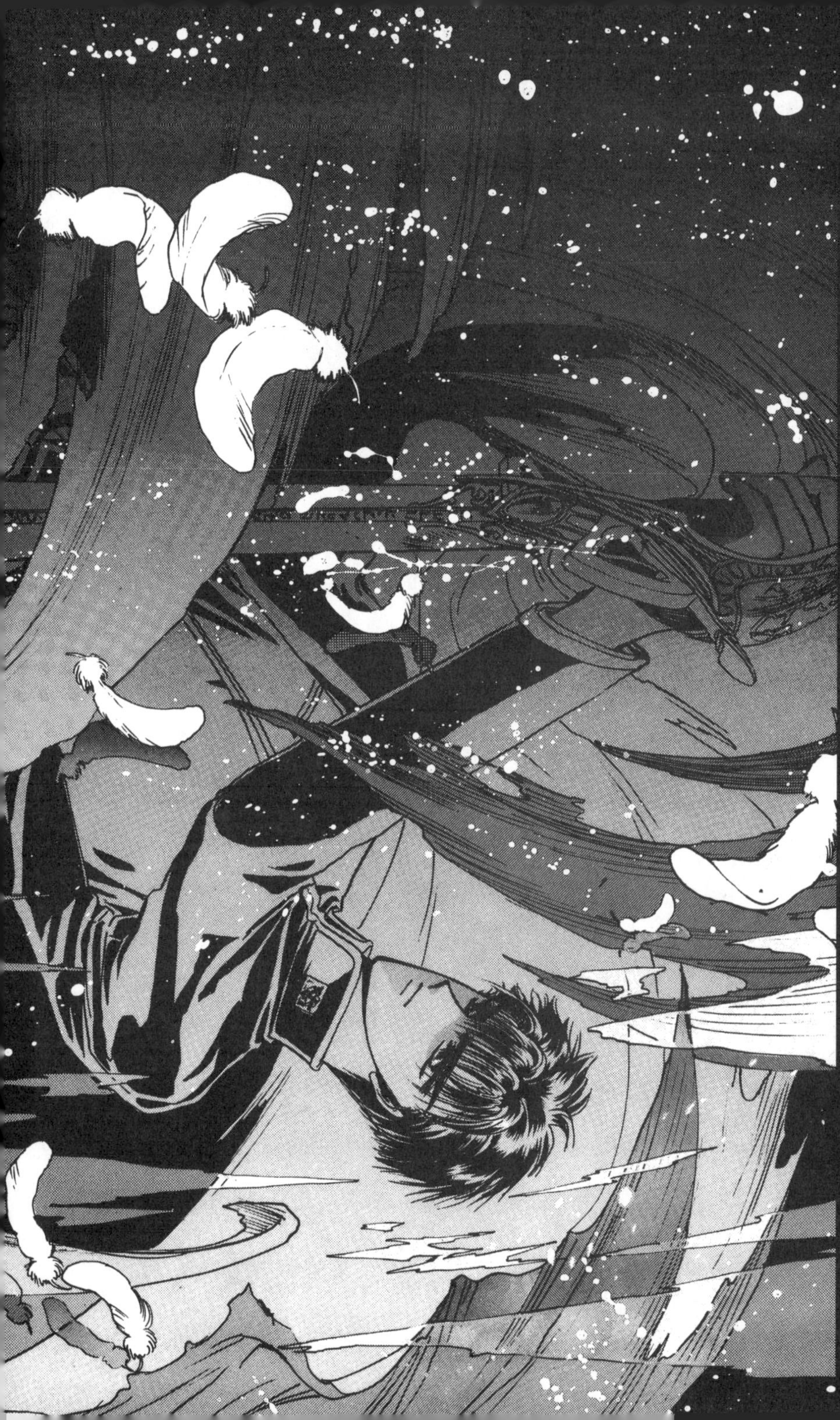

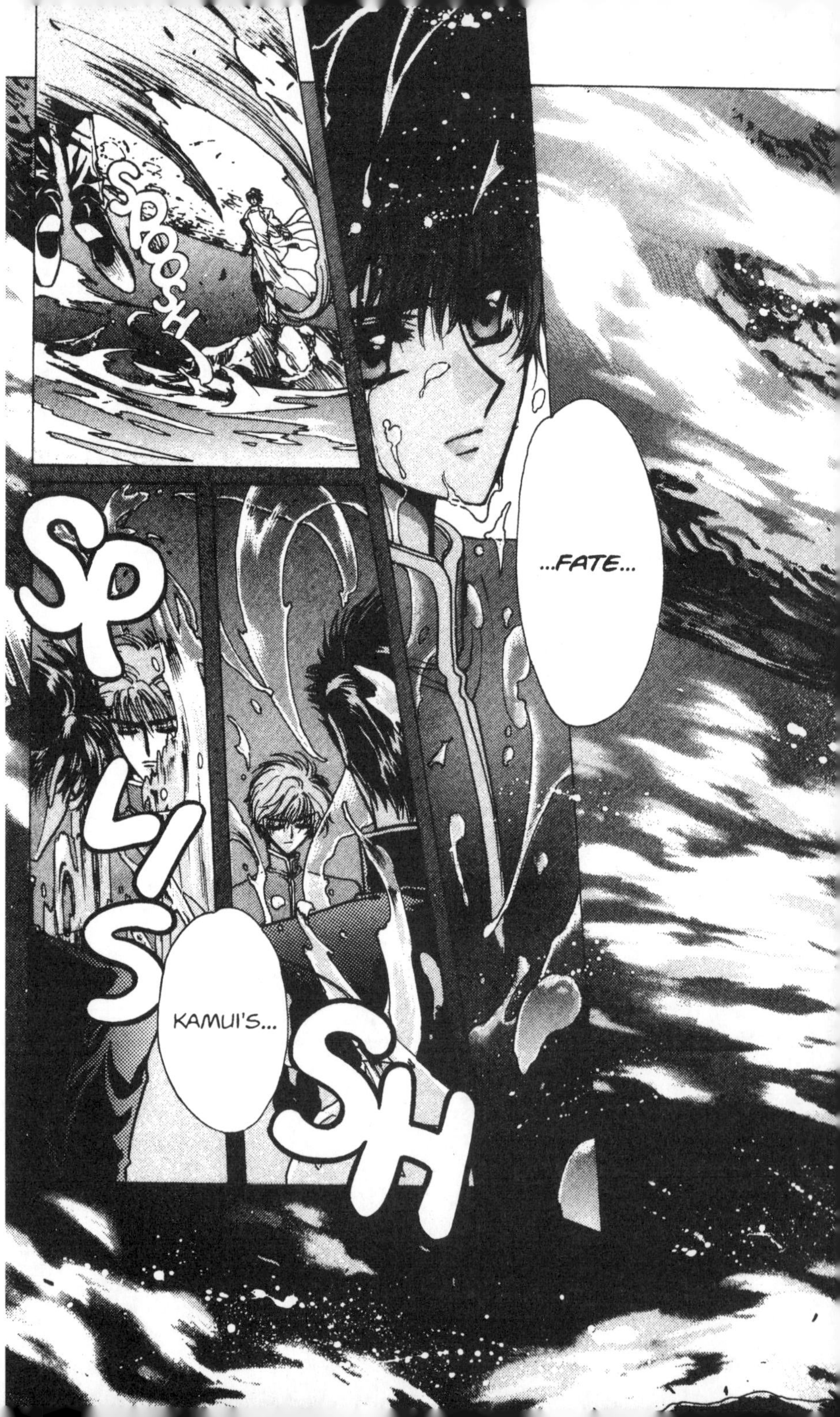
SPROOSH
...FATE...
SPLISSH
KAMUI'S...

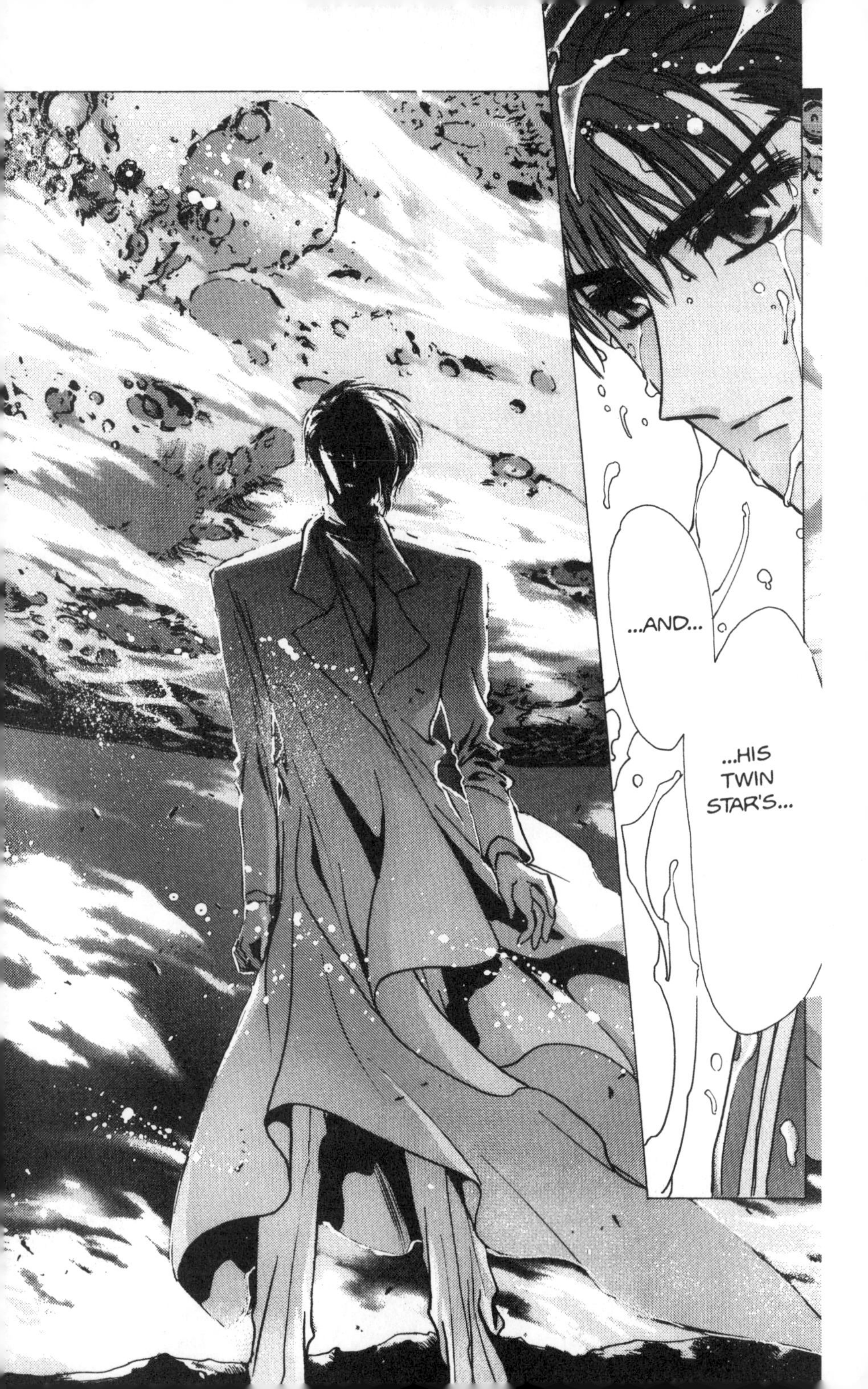
...AND...
...HIS TWIN STAR'S...

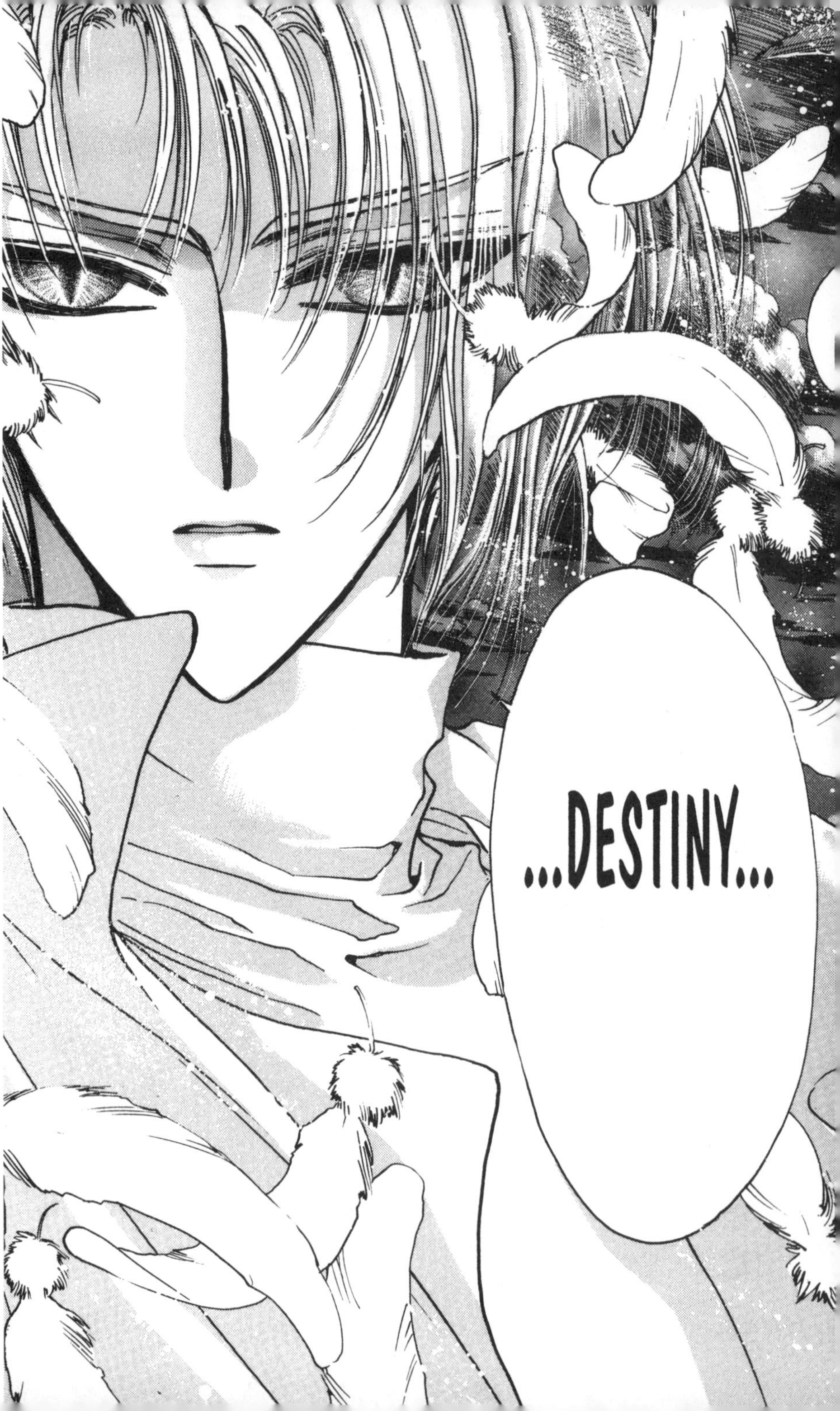
...DESTINY...

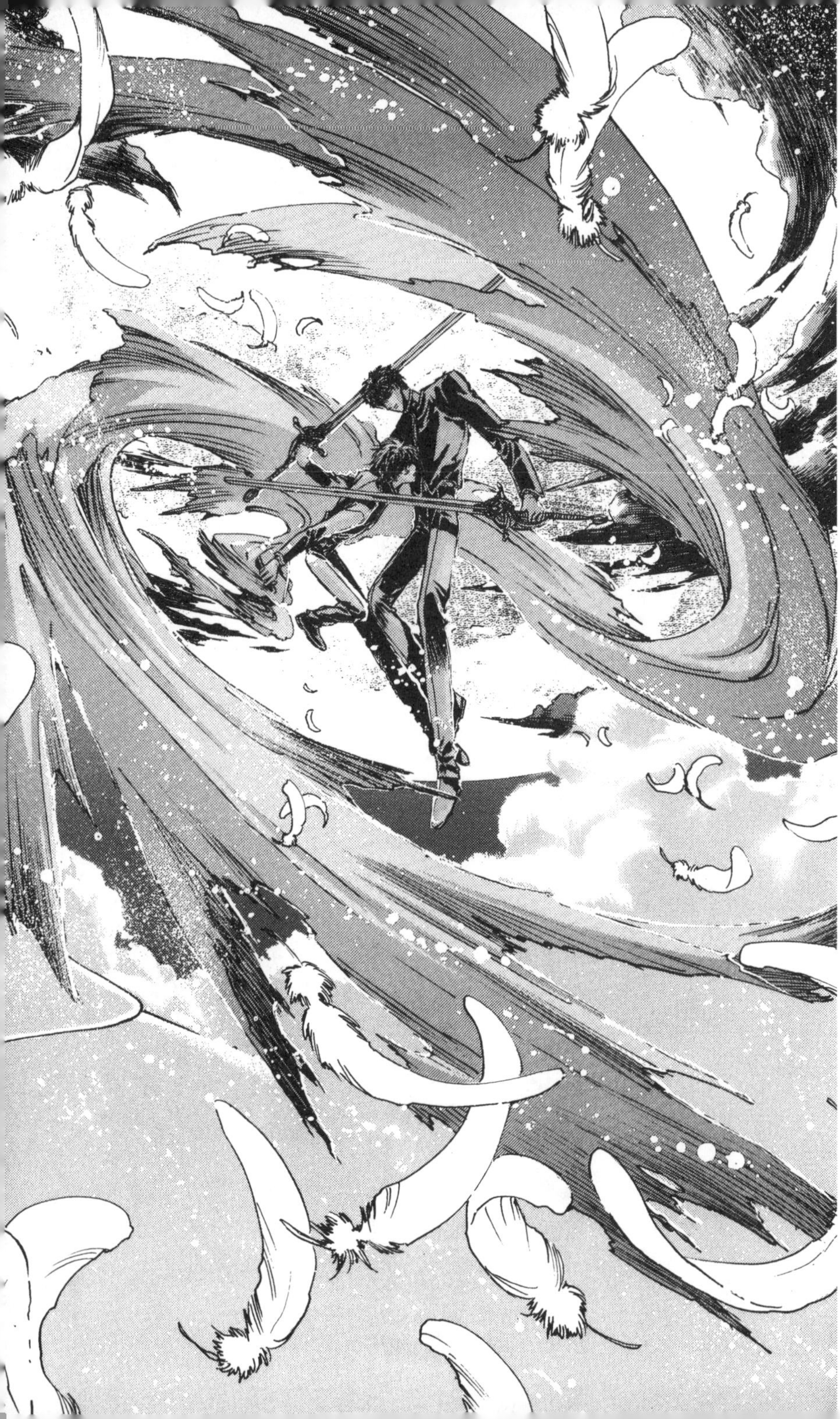

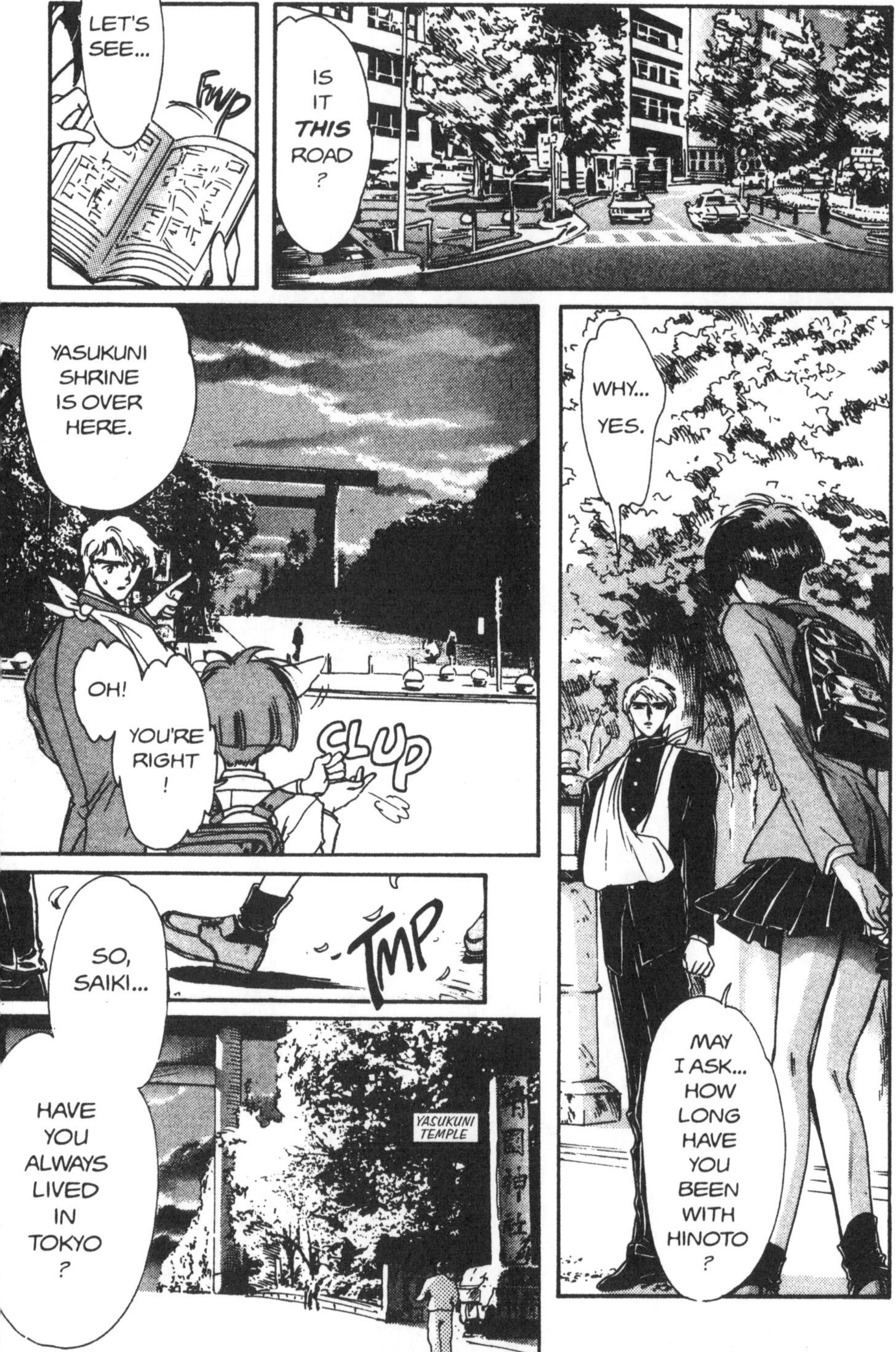
LET'S SEE...
FWP
IS IT THIS ROAD?
YASUKUNI SHRINE IS OVER HERE.
OH!
YOU'RE RIGHT!
CLUP
SO, SAIKI...
TMP
HAVE YOU ALWAYS LIVED IN TOKYO?
YASUKUNI TEMPLE
WHY... YES.
MAY I ASK... HOW LONG HAVE YOU BEEN WITH HINOTO?

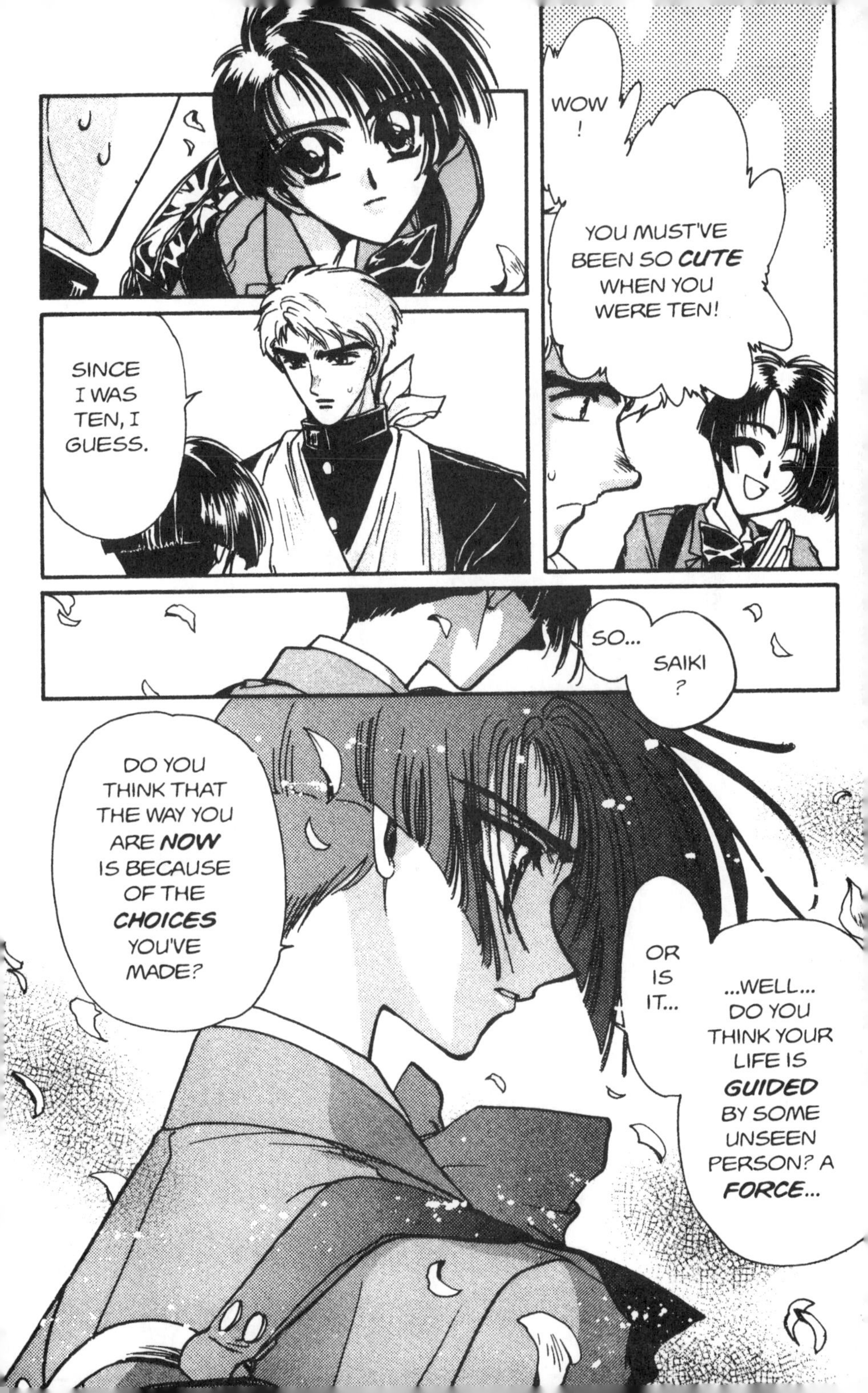
SINCE I WAS TEN, I GUESS.
WOW!
YOU MUST'VE BEEN SO CUTE WHEN YOU WERE TEN!
SO... SAIKI?
DO YOU THINK THAT THE WAY YOU ARE NOW IS BECAUSE OF THE CHOICES YOU'VE MADE?
OR IS IT...
...WELL... DO YOU THINK YOUR LIFE IS GUIDED BY SOME UNSEEN PERSON? A FORCE...

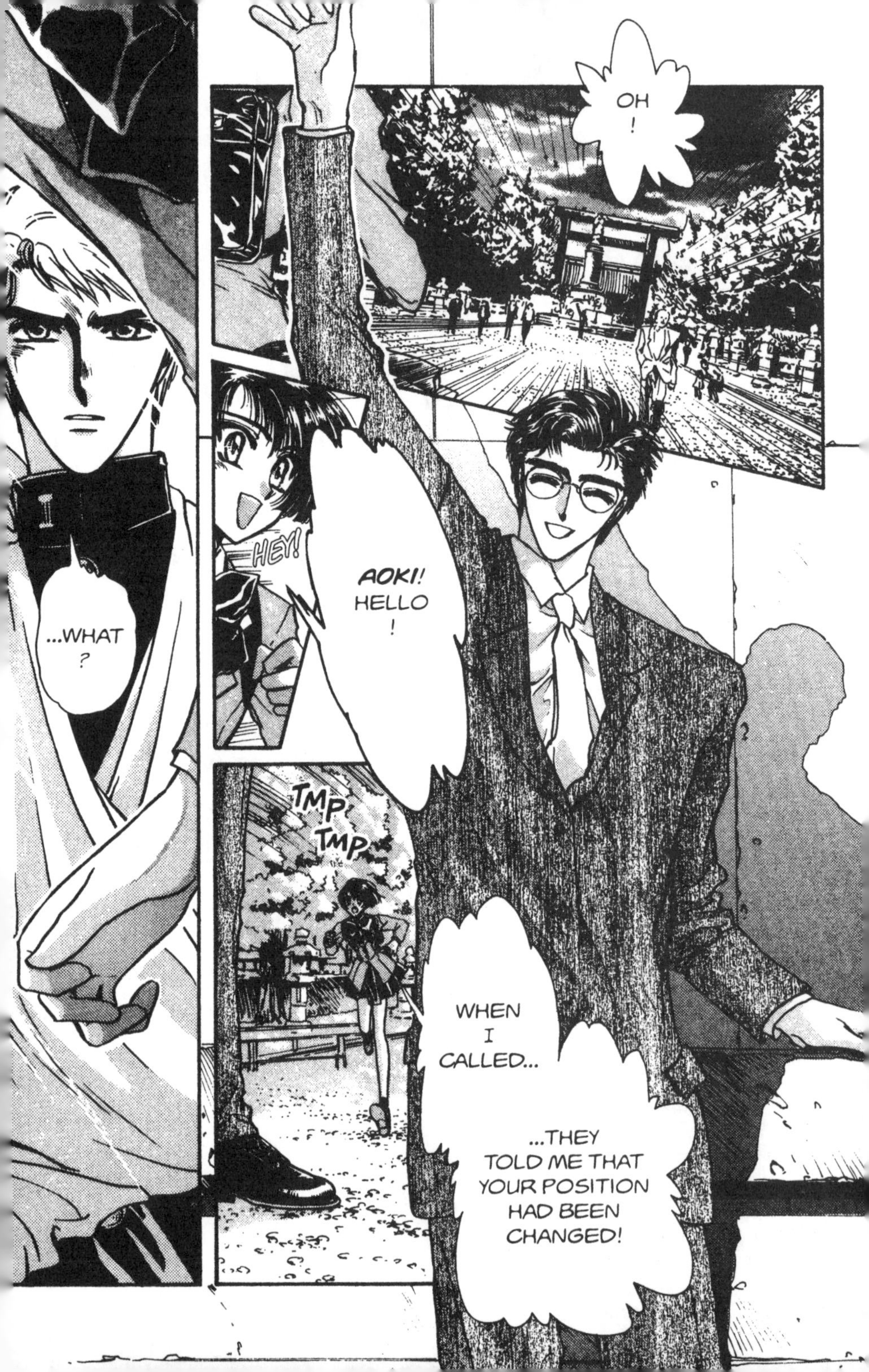
OH!
HEY!
AOKI! HELLO!
TMP TMP
WHEN I CALLED...
...THEY TOLD ME THAT YOUR POSITION HAD BEEN CHANGED!
...WHAT?

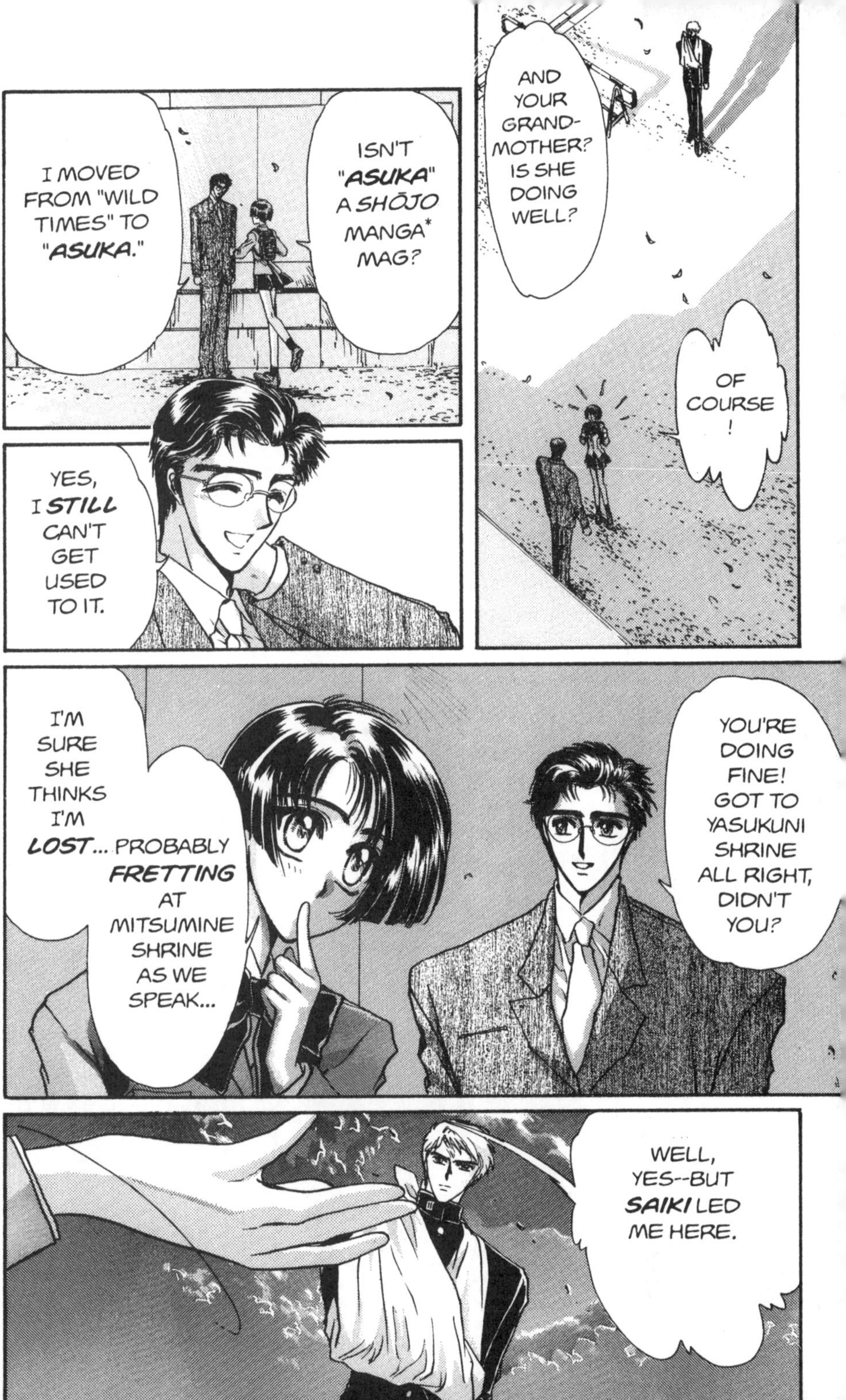
AND YOUR GRANDMOTHER? IS SHE DOING WELL?
OF COURSE!
ISN'T "ASUKA" A SHŌJO MANGA* MAG?
I MOVED FROM "WILD TIMES" TO "ASUKA."
YES, I STILL CAN'T GET USED TO IT.
YOU'RE DOING FINE! GOT TO YASUKUNI SHRINE ALL RIGHT, DIDN'T YOU?
I'M SURE SHE THINKS I'M LOST... PROBABLY FRETTING AT MITSUMINE SHRINE AS WE SPEAK...
WELL, YES--BUT SAIKI LED ME HERE.

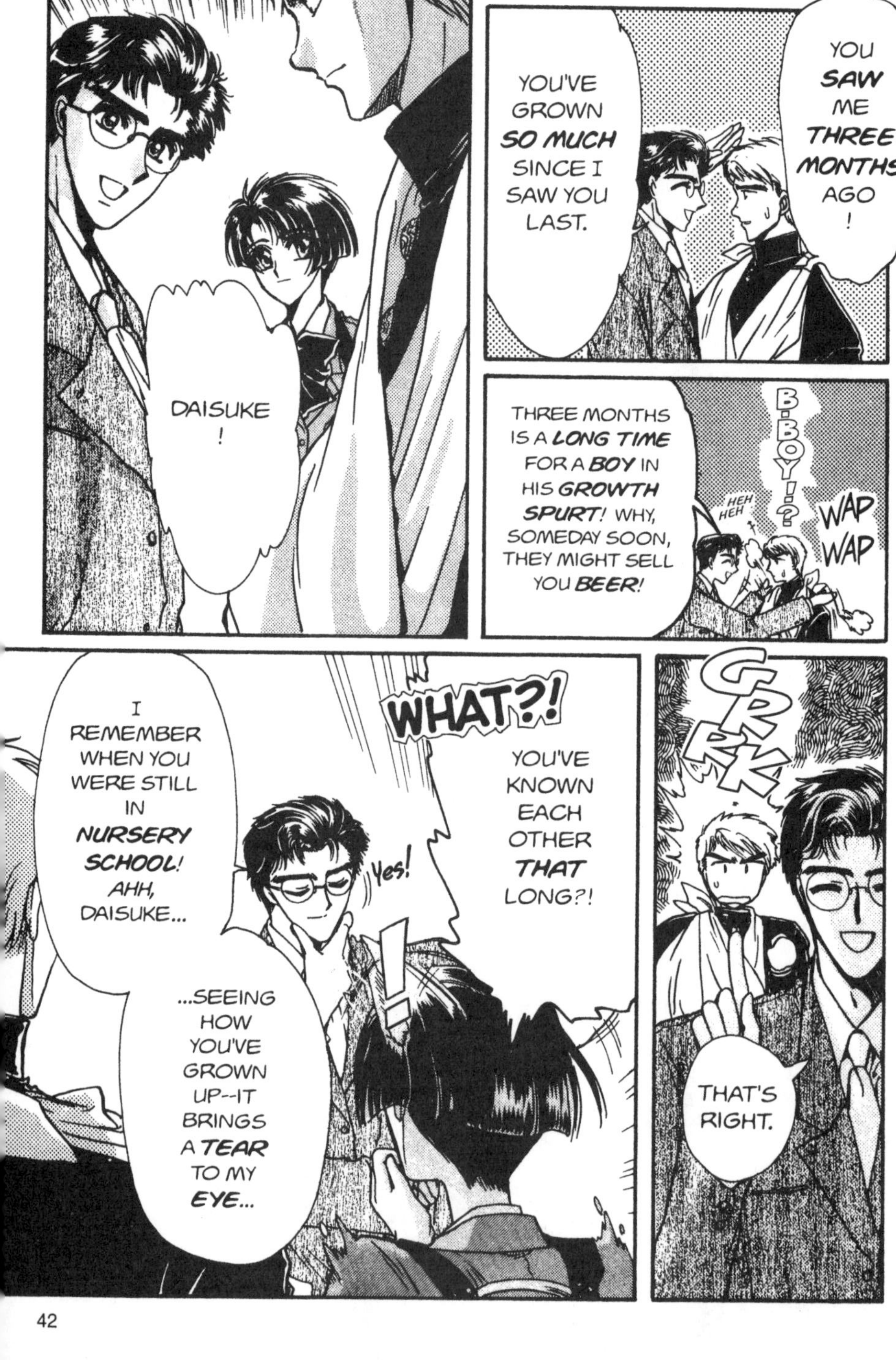
DAISUKE!
YOU'VE GROWN SO MUCH SINCE I SAW YOU LAST.
YOU SAW ME THREE MONTHS AGO!
THREE MONTHS IS A LONG TIME FOR A BOY IN HIS GROWTH SPURT! WHY, SOMEDAY SOON, THEY MIGHT SELL YOU BEER!
HEH HEH
B-BOY!?
WAP WAP
I REMEMBER WHEN YOU WERE STILL IN NURSERY SCHOOL! AHH, DAISUKE...
...SEEING HOW YOU'VE GROWN UP--IT BRINGS A TEAR TO MY EYE...
WHAT?!
YOU'VE KNOWN EACH OTHER THAT LONG?!
Yes!
!
GRRK
THAT'S RIGHT.

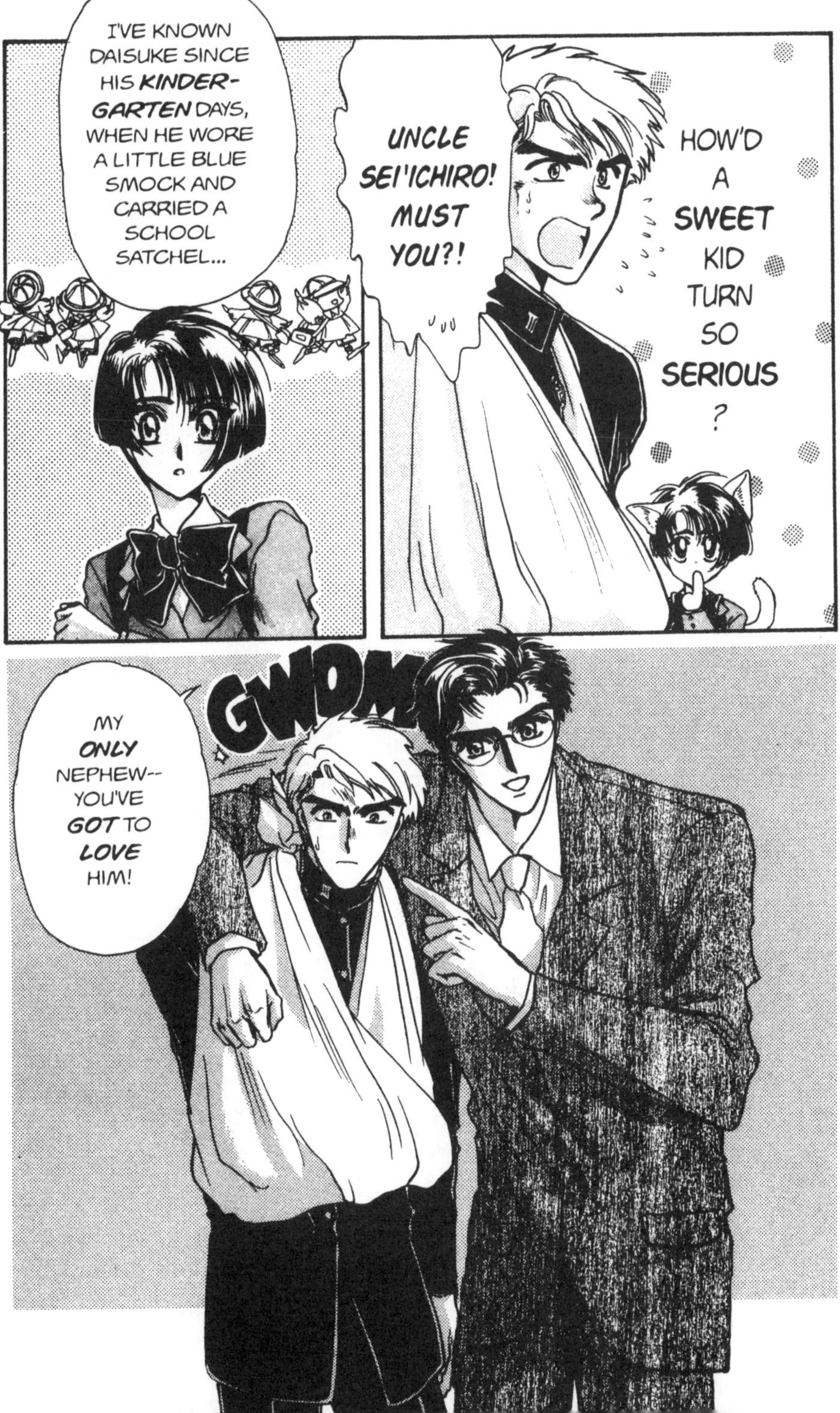
I'VE KNOWN DAISUKE SINCE HIS KINDER-GARTEN DAYS, WHEN HE WORE A LITTLE BLUE SMOCK AND CARRIED A SCHOOL SATCHEL...
UNCLE SEI'ICHIRO! MUST YOU?!
HOW'D A SWEET KID TURN SO SERIOUS?
GWOM
MY ONLY NEPHEW-- YOU'VE GOT TO LOVE HIM!

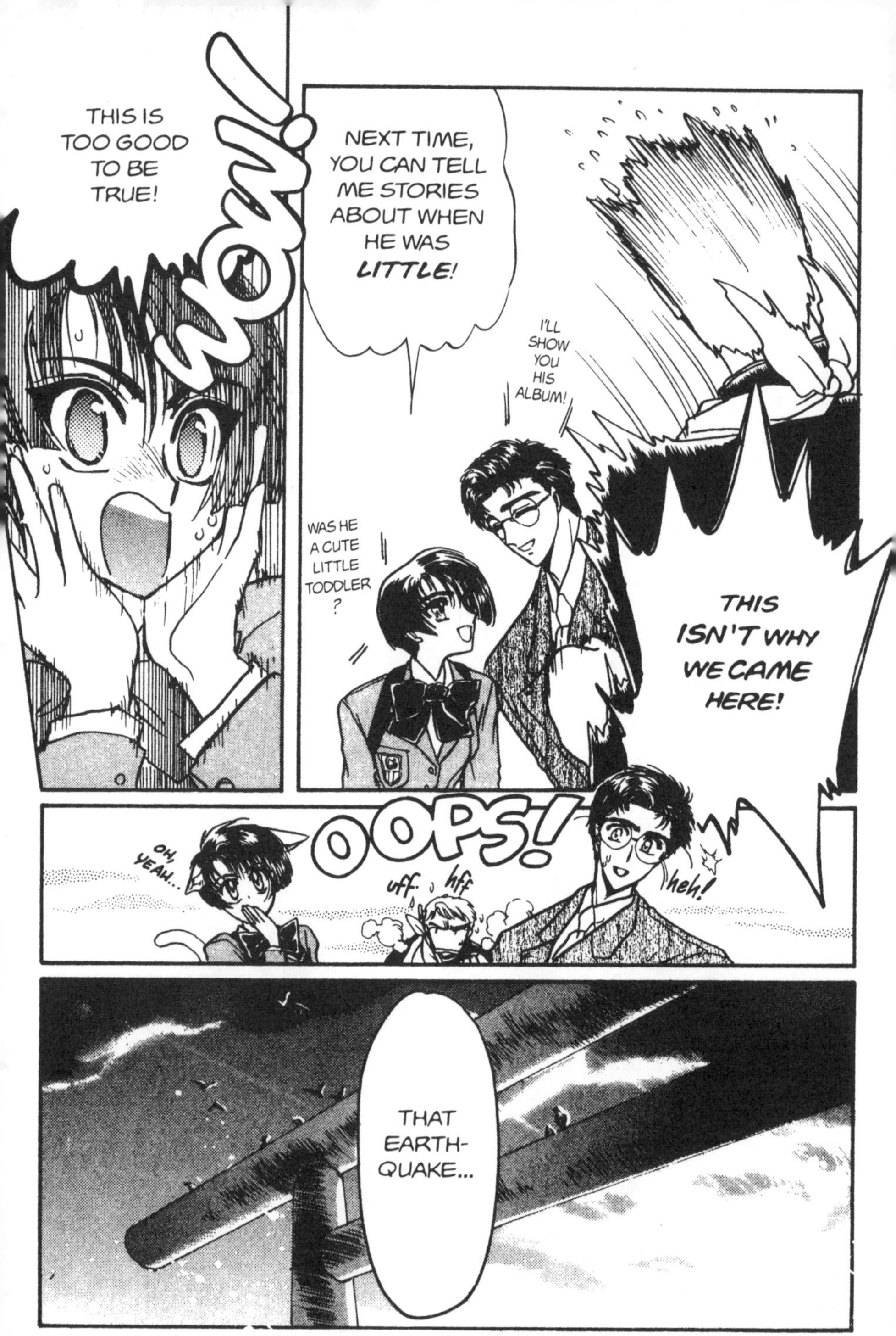

NEXT TIME, YOU CAN TELL ME STORIES ABOUT WHEN HE WAS *LITTLE!*
I'LL SHOW YOU HIS ALBUM!
WAS HE A CUTE LITTLE TODDLER?
WOW!
THIS IS TOO GOOD TO BE TRUE!
THIS ISN'T WHY WE CAME HERE!
heh!
OOPS!
uff. hff
OH, YEAH...
THAT EARTH-QUAKE...

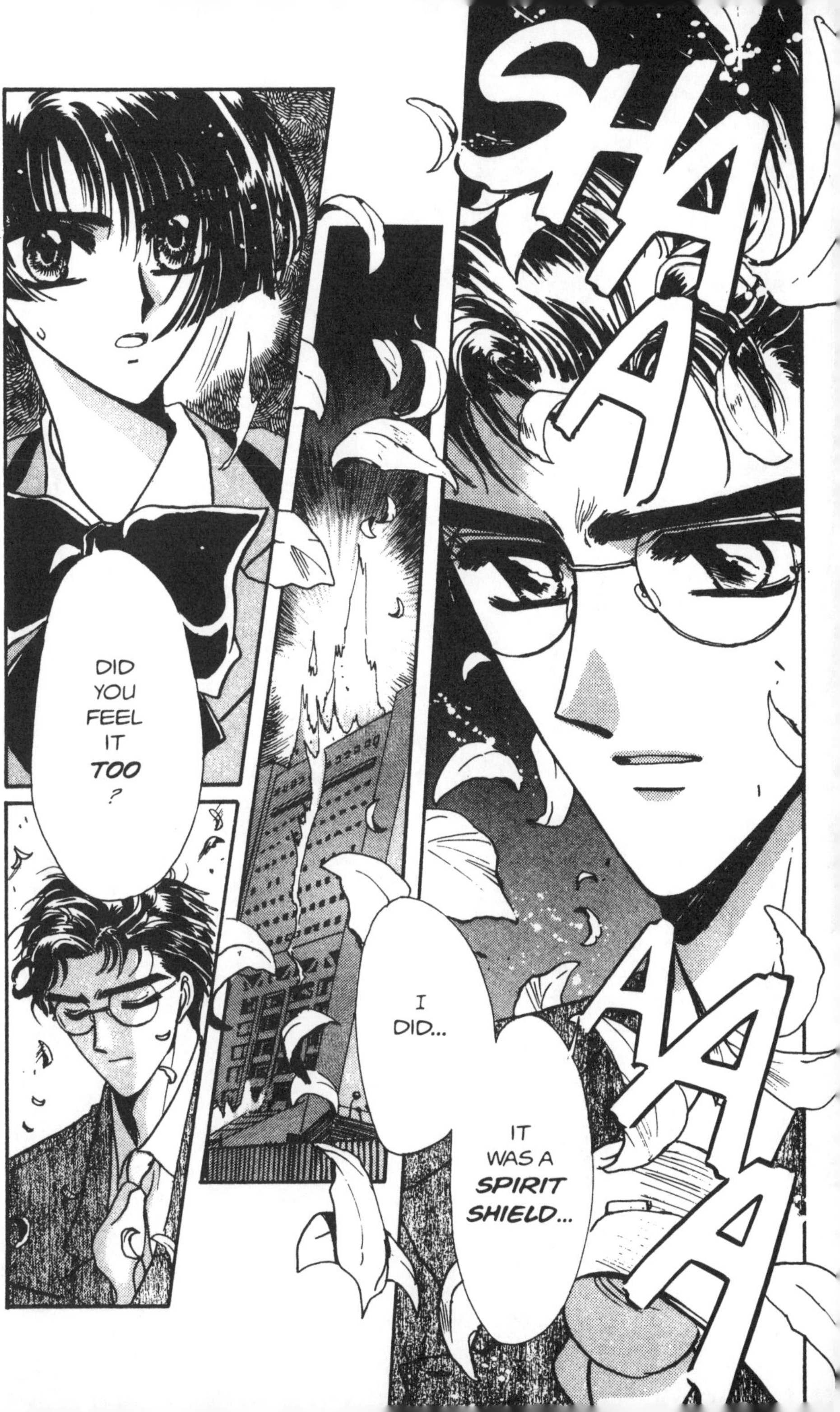
SHAAAAAA
DID YOU FEEL IT *TOO*?
I DID...
IT WAS A **SPIRIT SHIELD**...

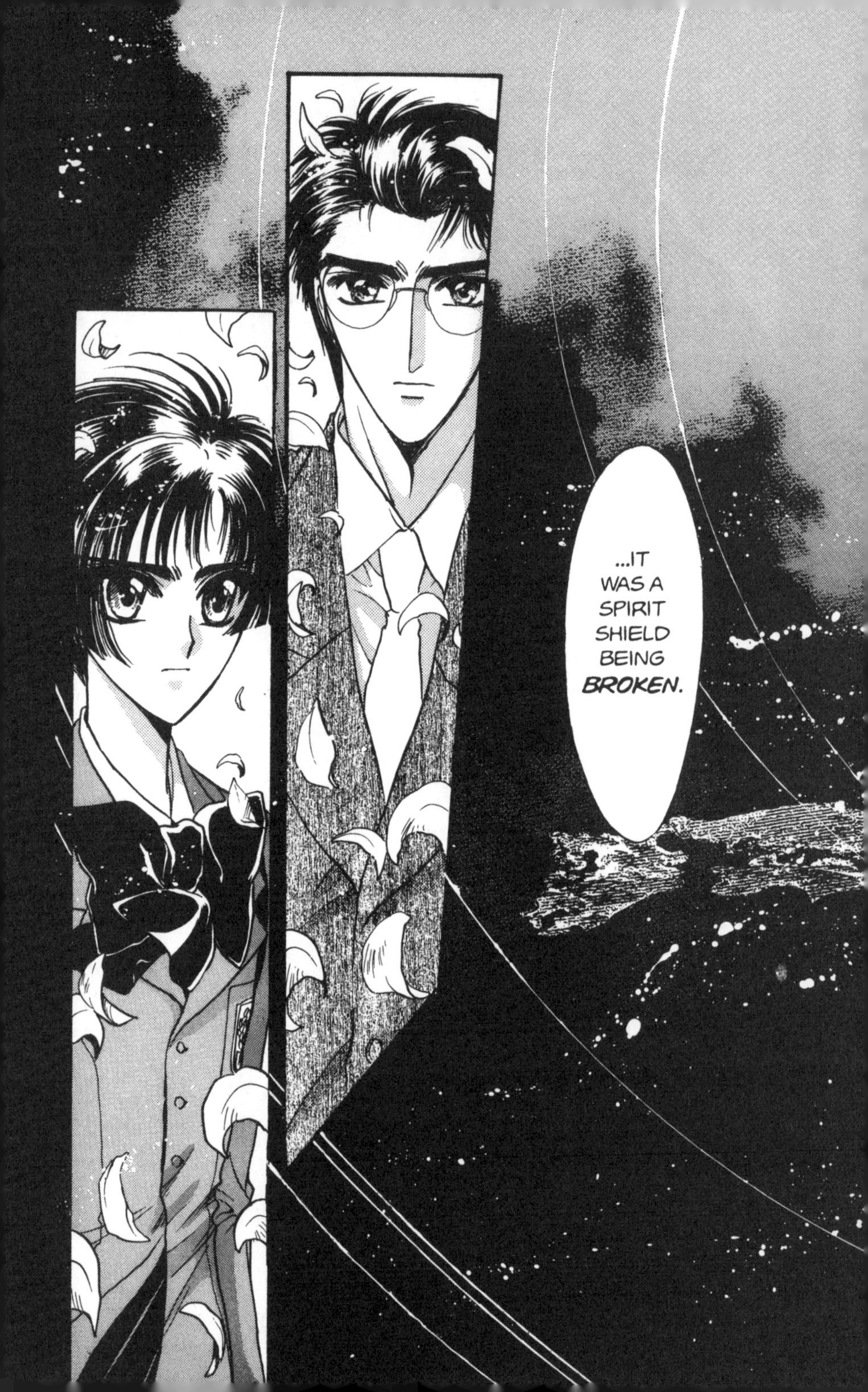
...IT WAS A SPIRIT SHIELD BEING **BROKEN**.

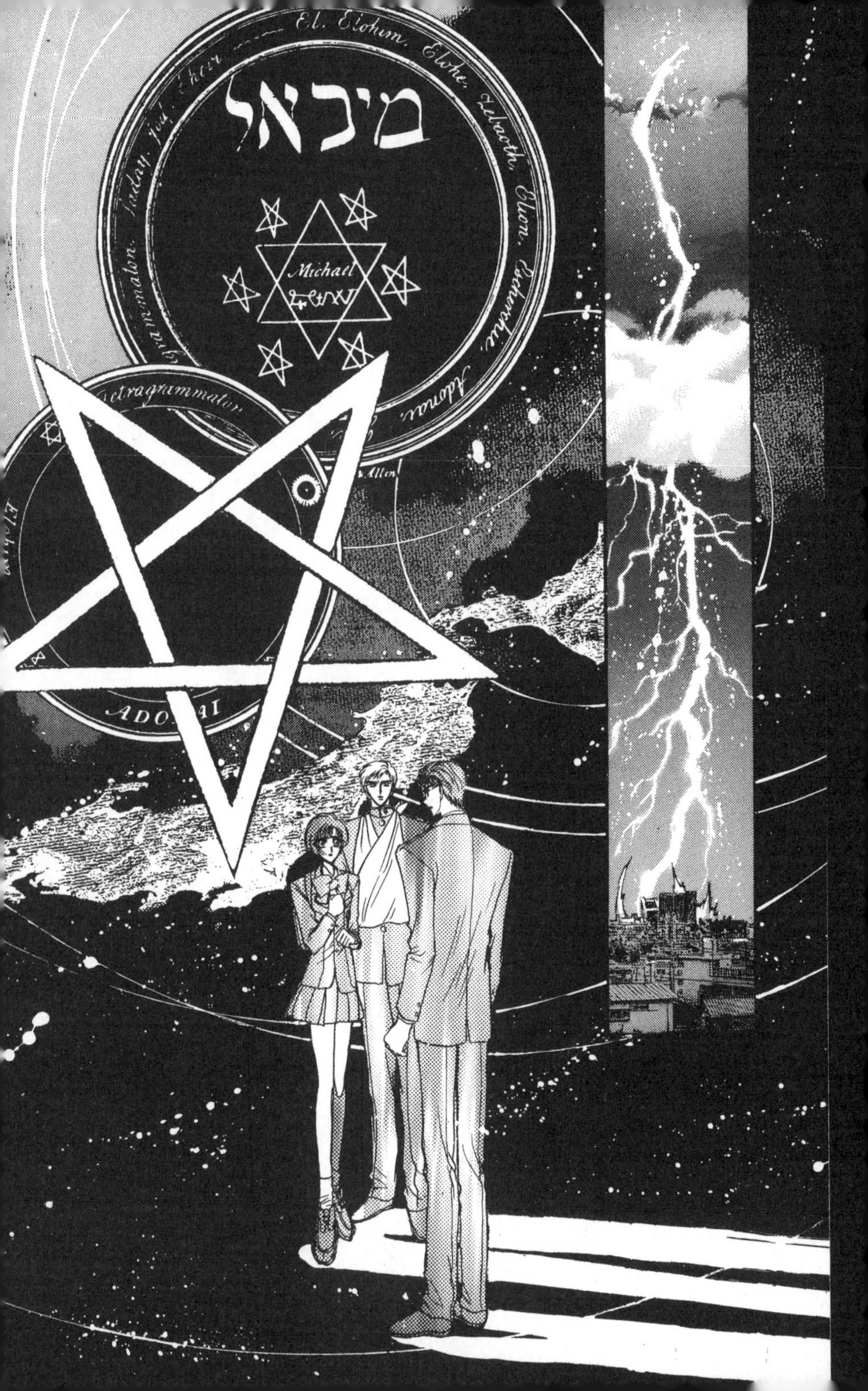
מיכאל
Michael

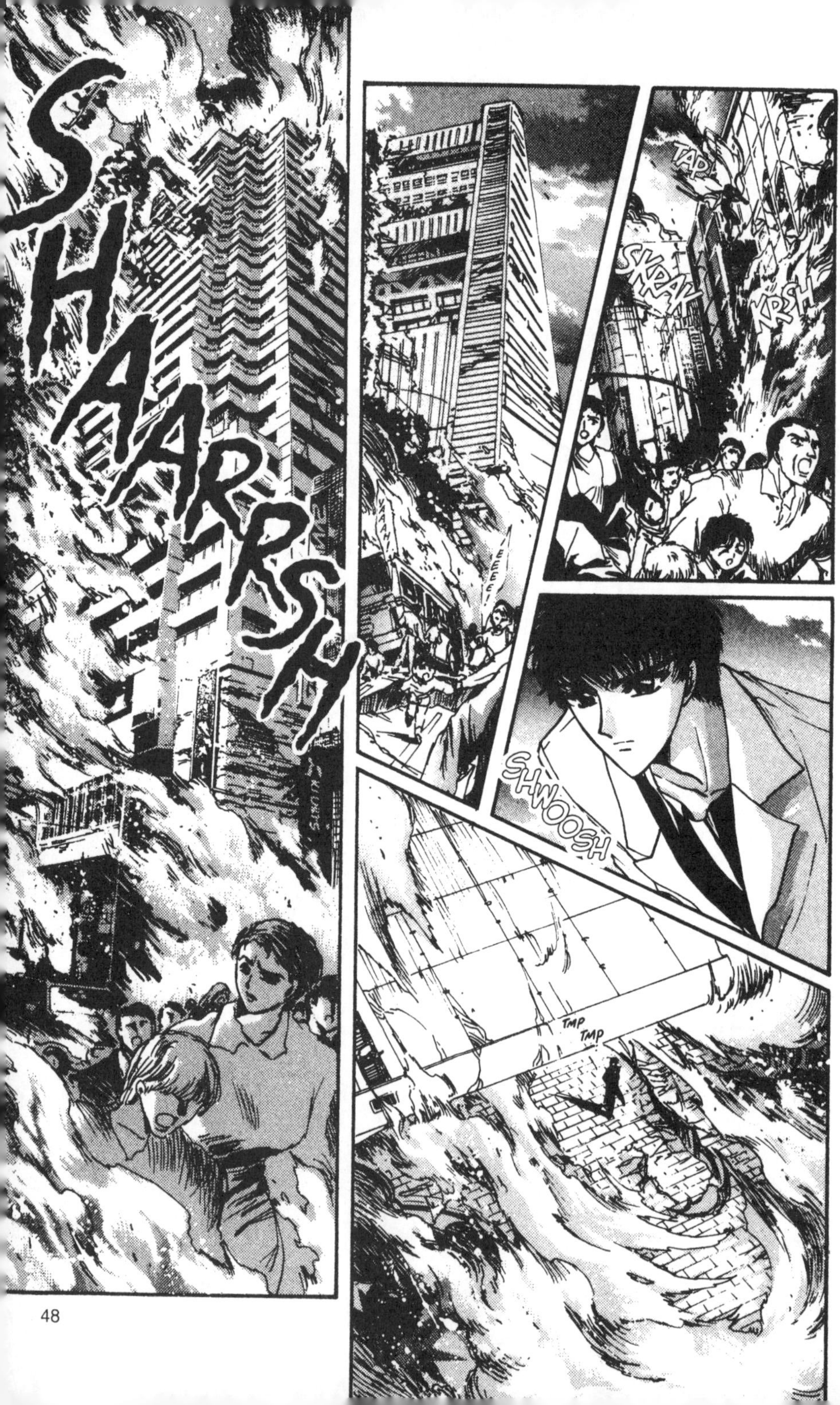
TAP
SKRAK
KRSH
EEEE!
SHWOOSH
TMP TMP
SHAARRSH

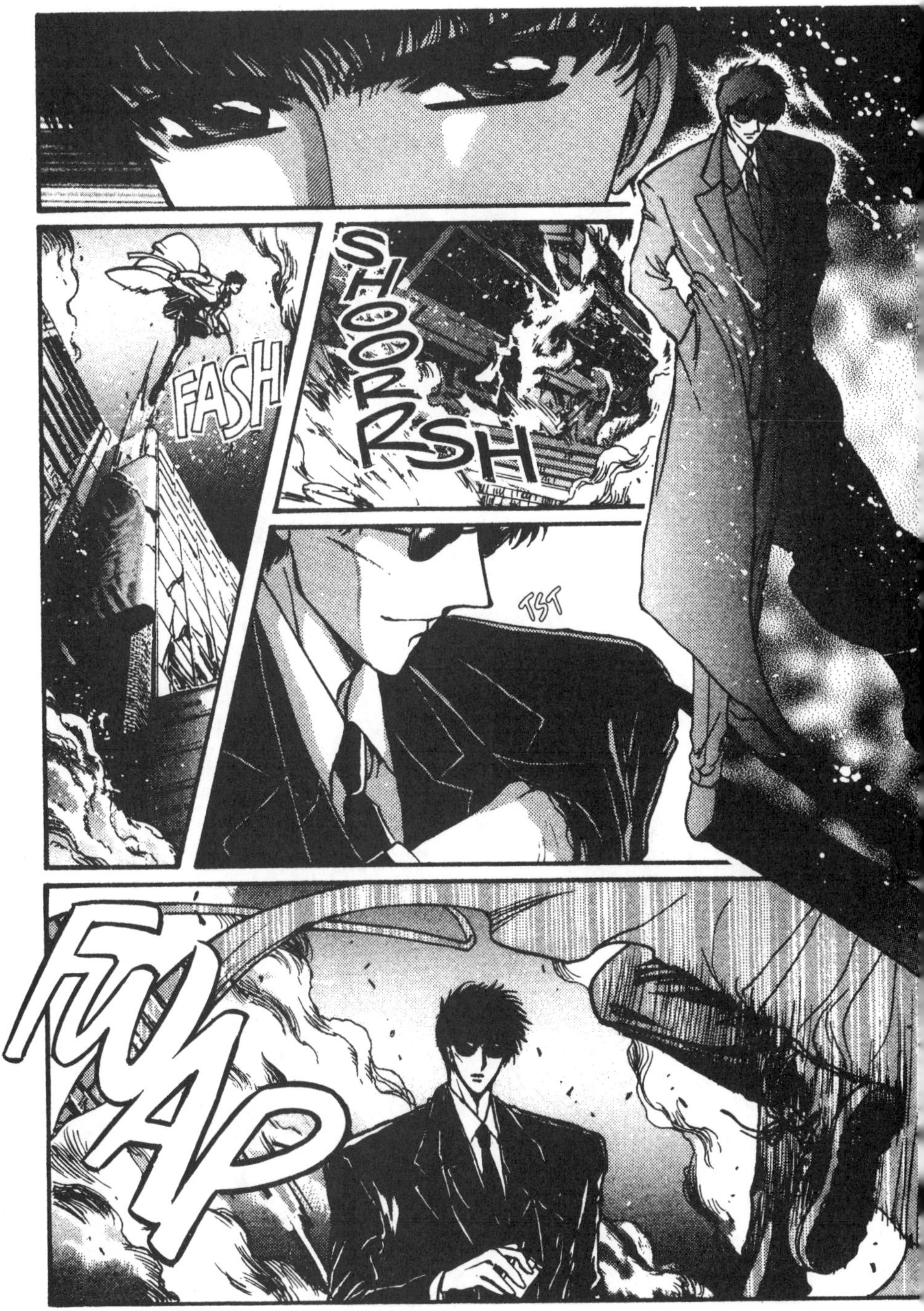
SHOORRSH
FASH
TST
FWAP

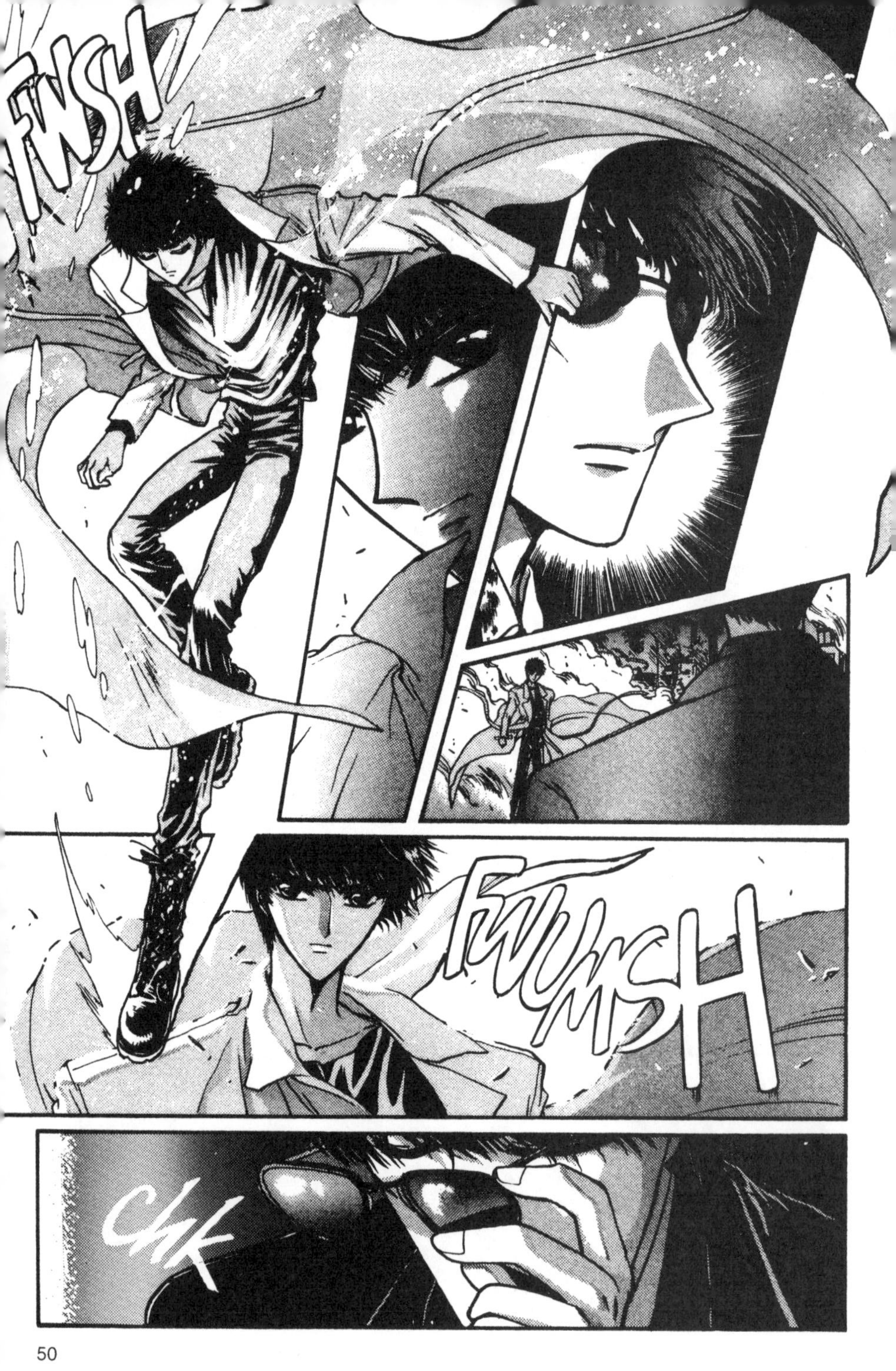
FWSH
FWUMSH
CHK

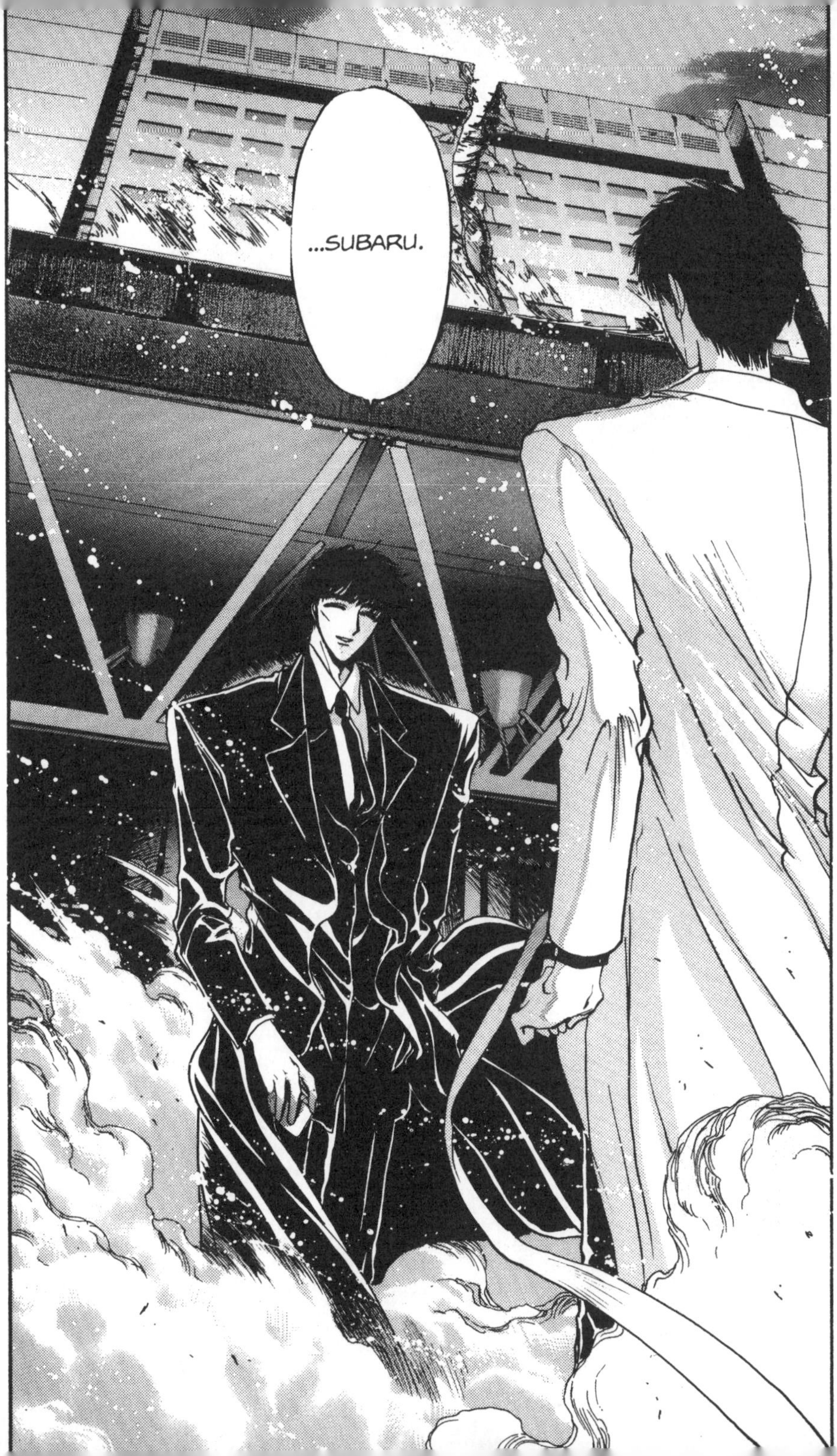
...SUBARU.

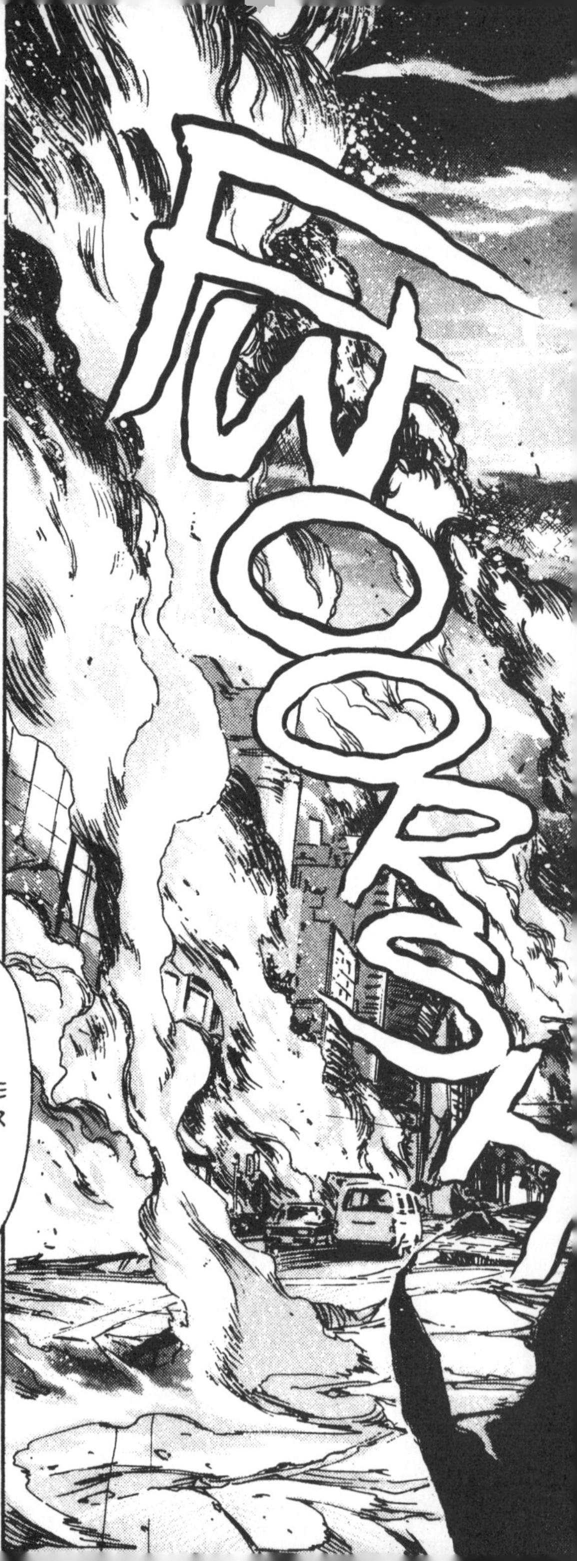
FWOORS

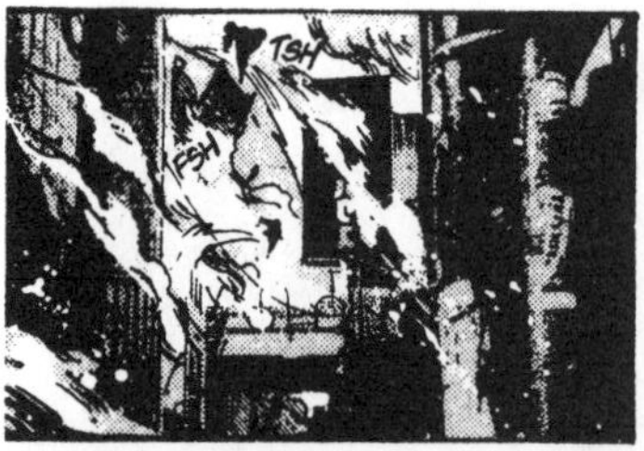
TSH
FSH

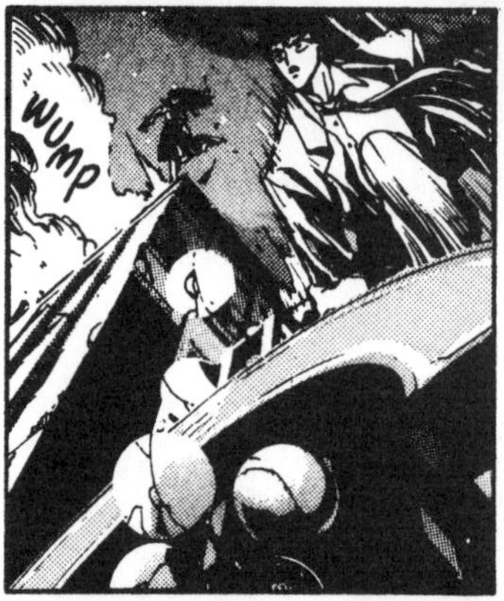
WUMP

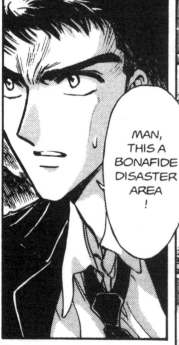

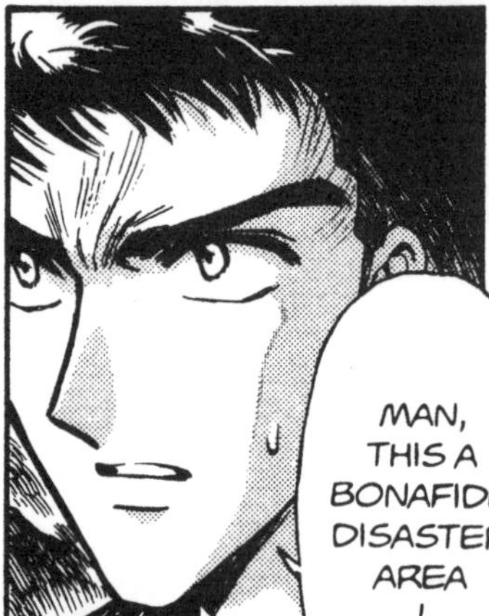
MAN, THIS A BONAFIDE DISASTER AREA !

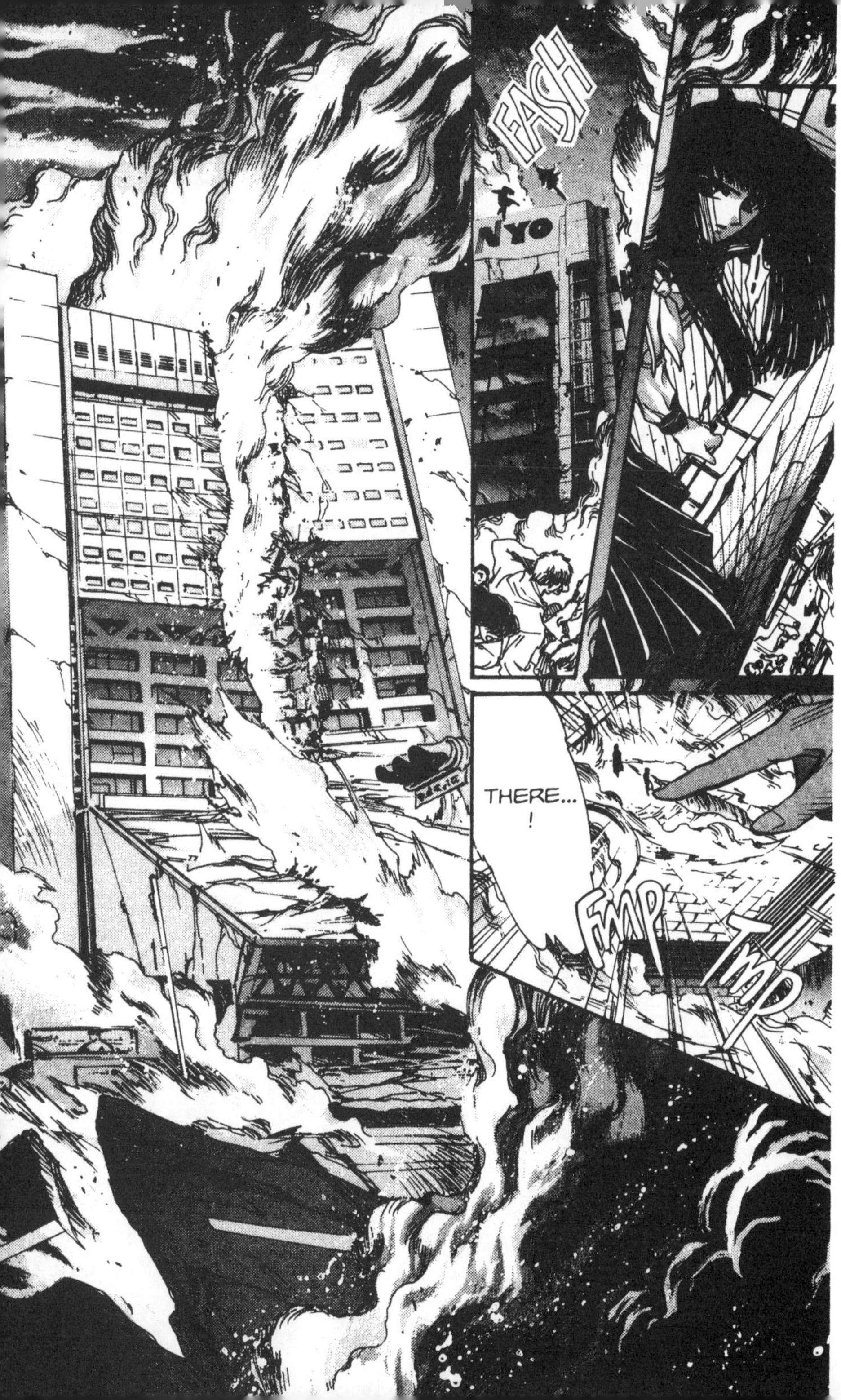
FASH
THERE... !
FMP
TMP

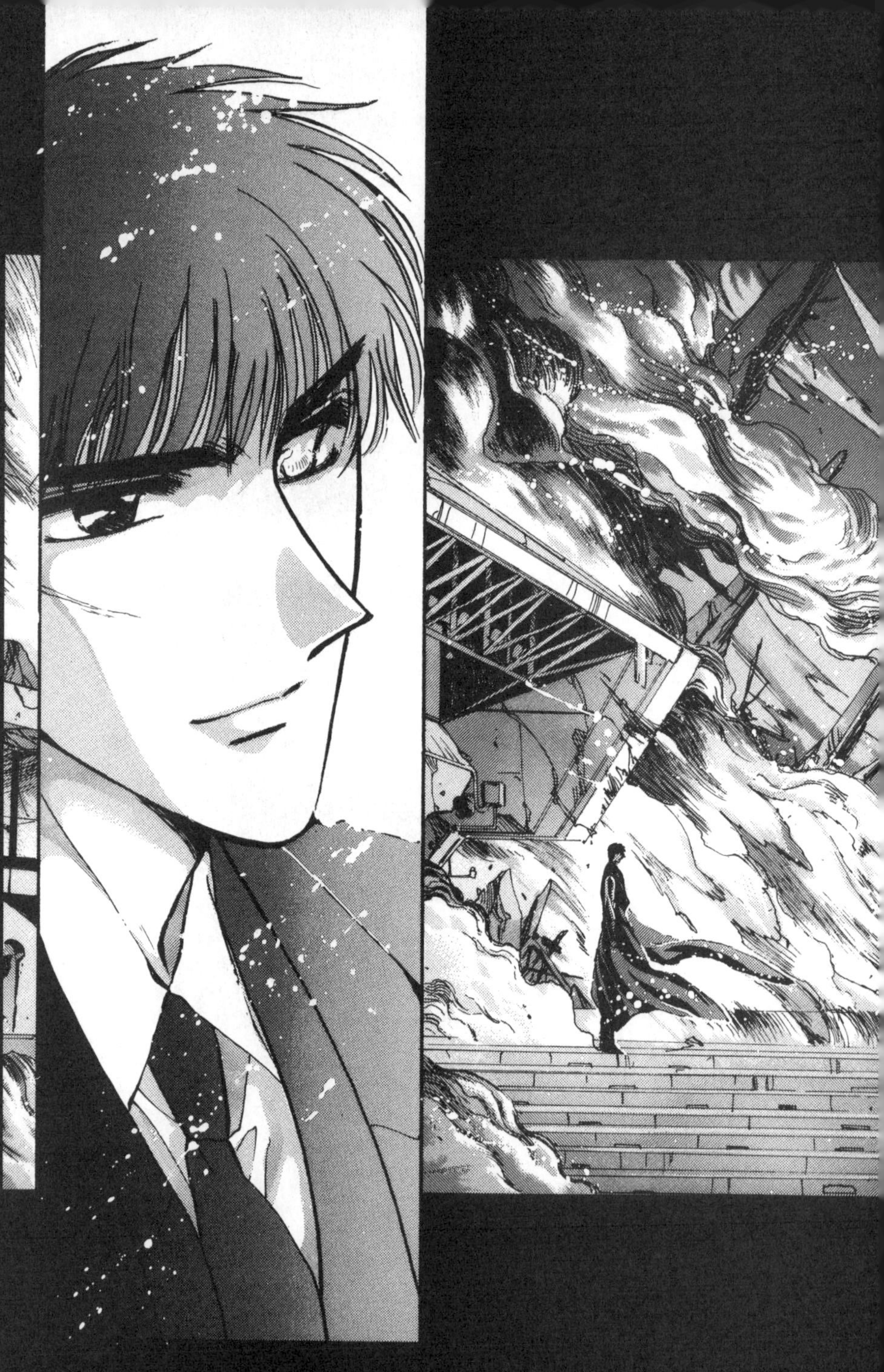

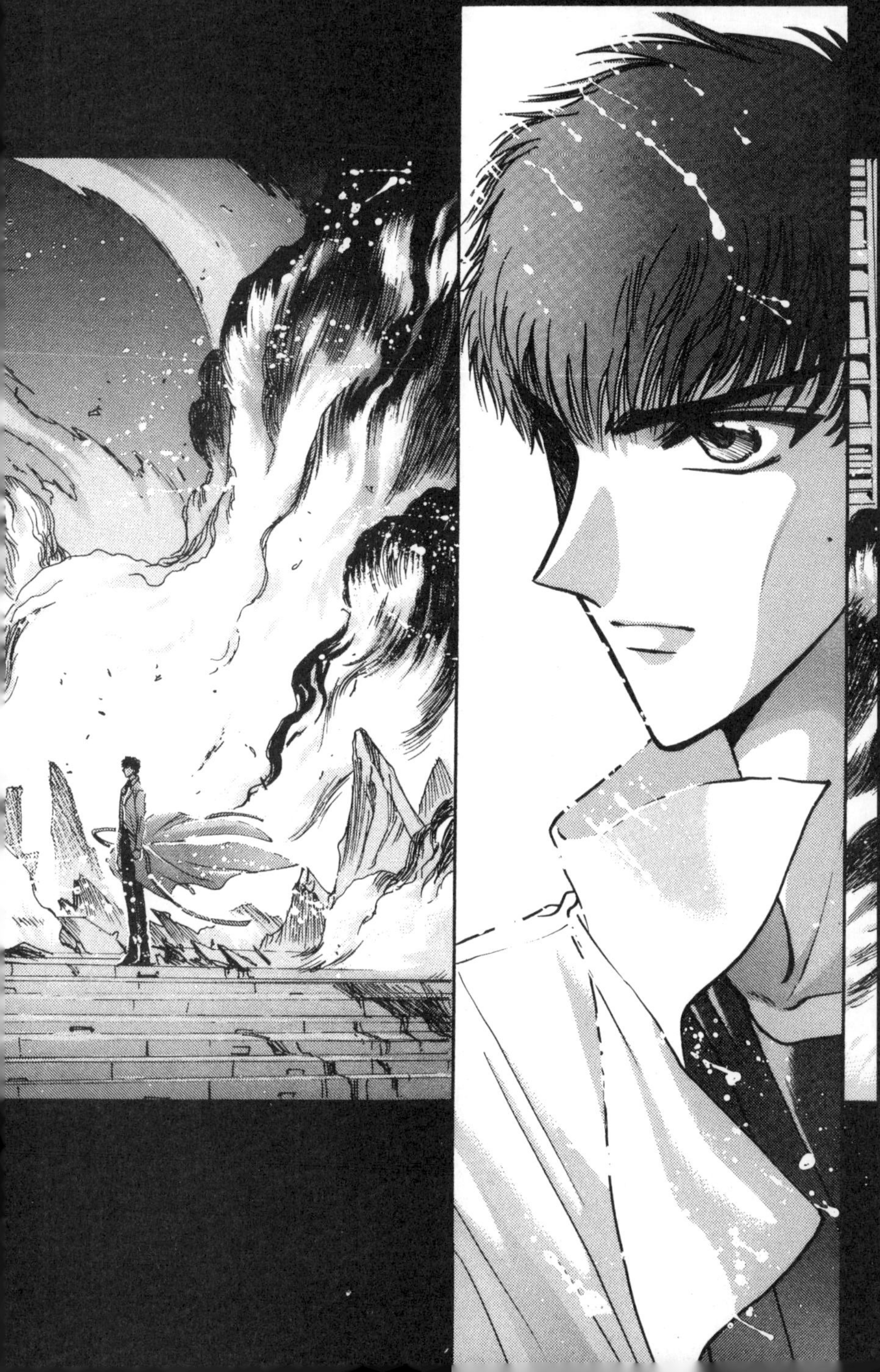

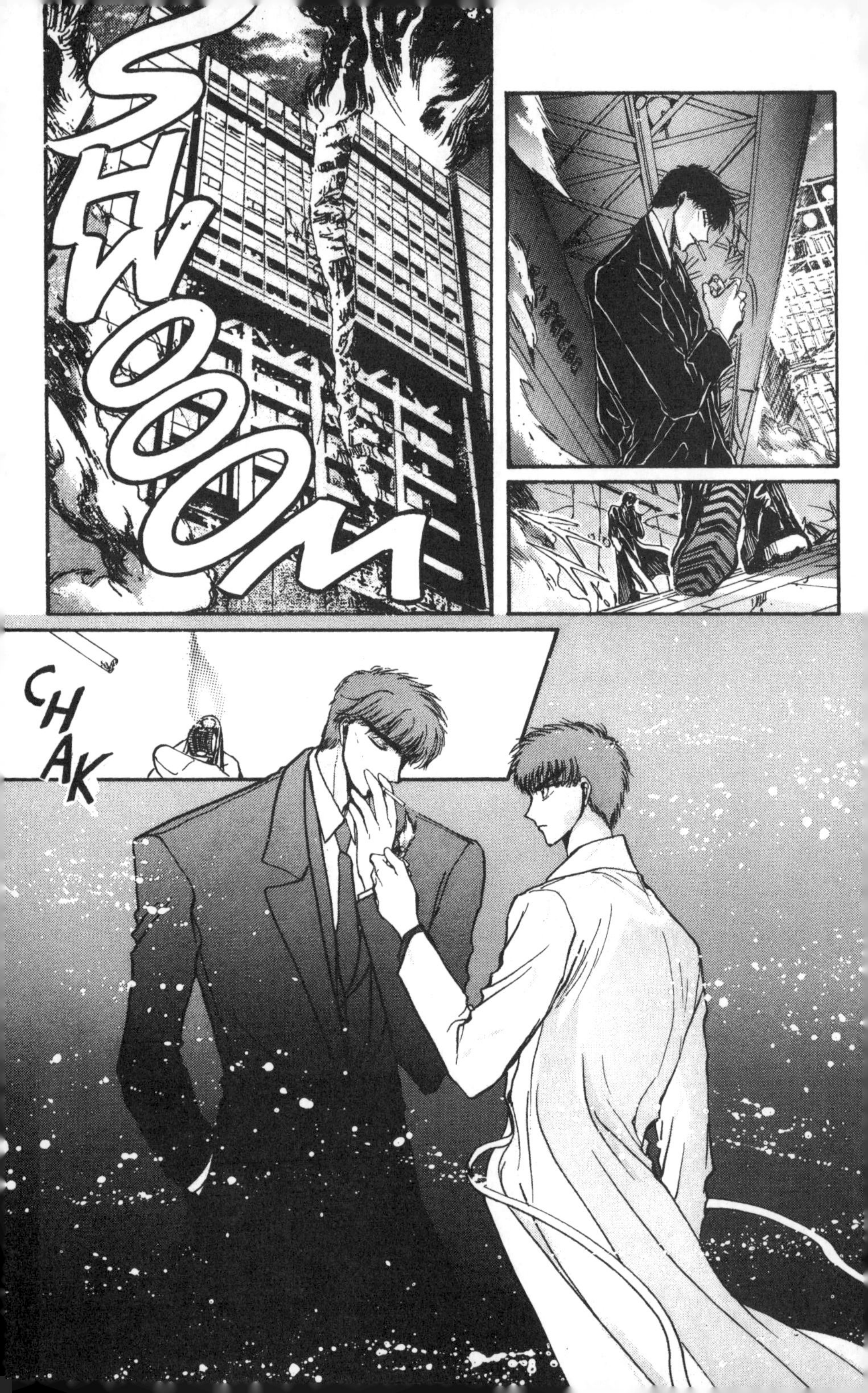
SHWOOOM
CHAK

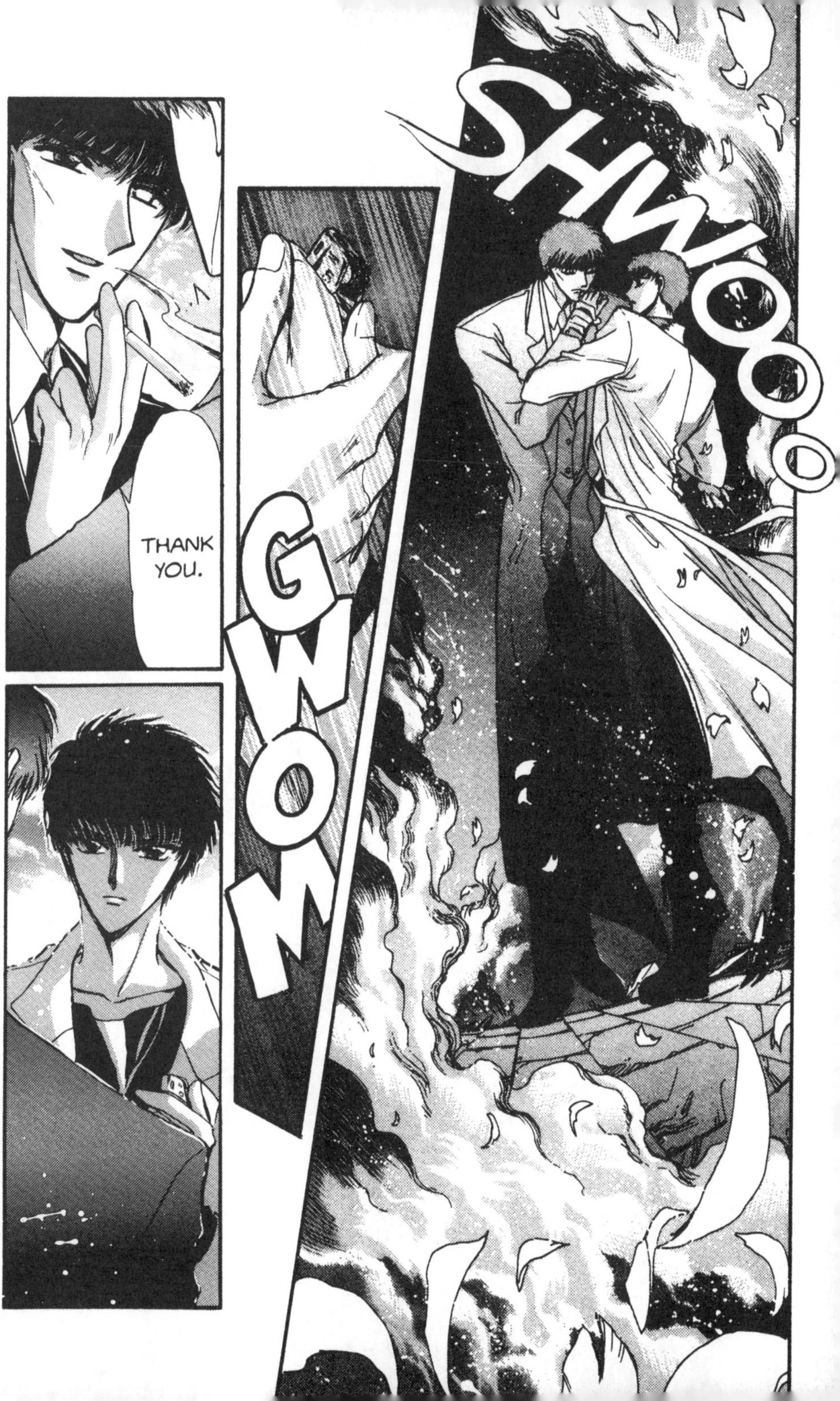SHWOOOO
GWOM
THANK YOU.

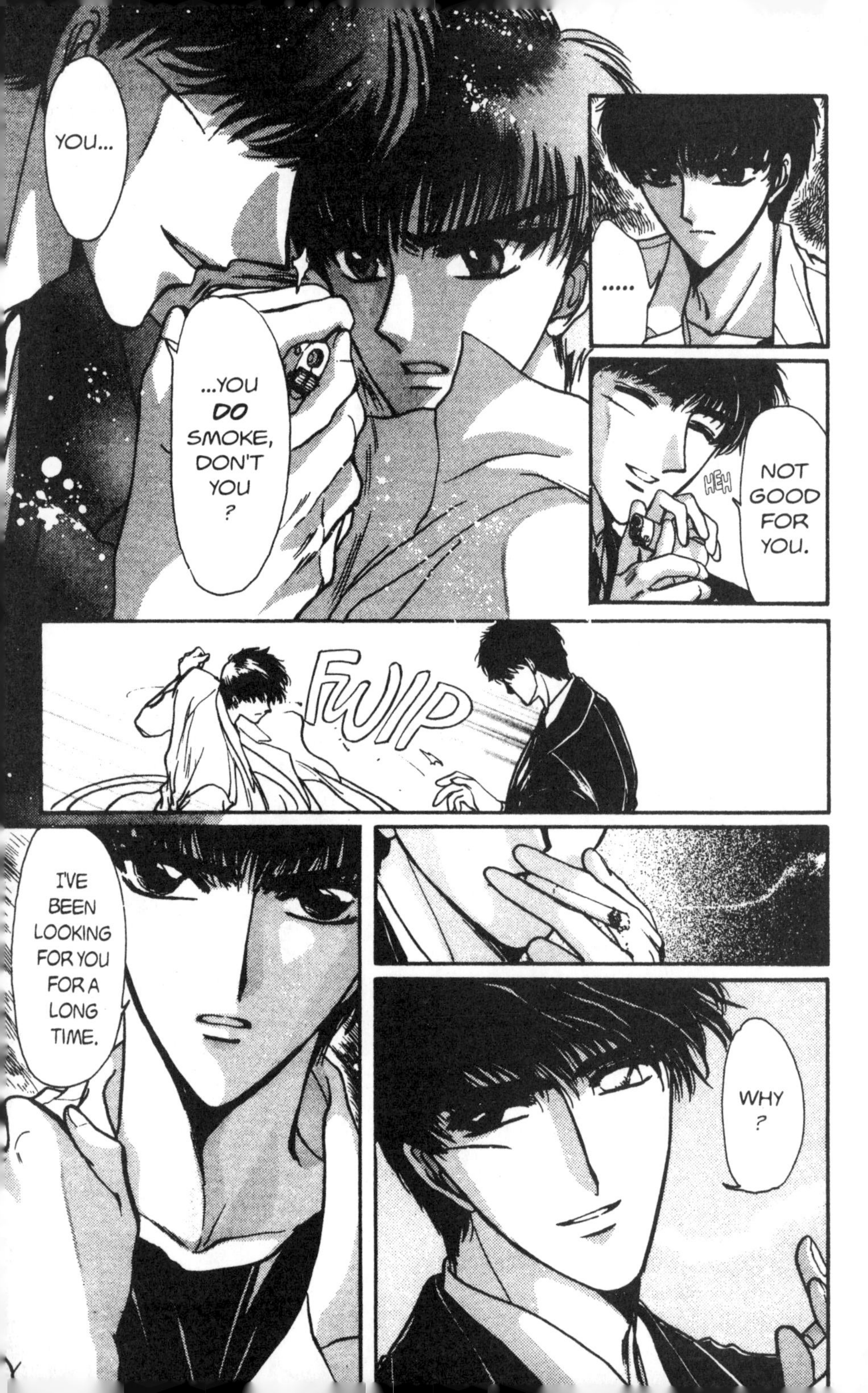

YOU...
...YOU DO SMOKE, DON'T YOU?
.....
HEH
NOT GOOD FOR YOU.
FWIP
I'VE BEEN LOOKING FOR YOU FOR A LONG TIME.
WHY?

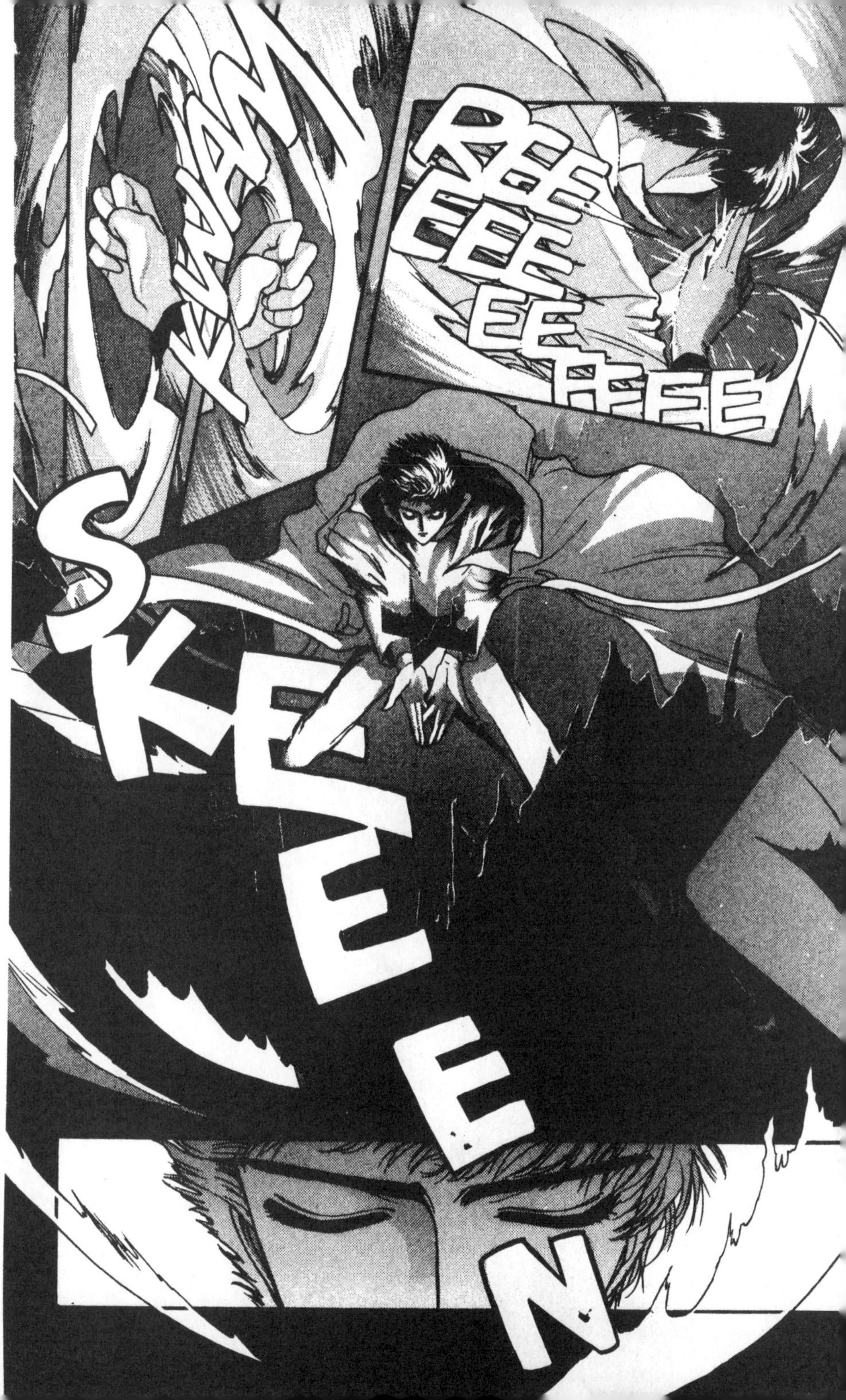
REEEEEEEEEEEE
SKEEEN

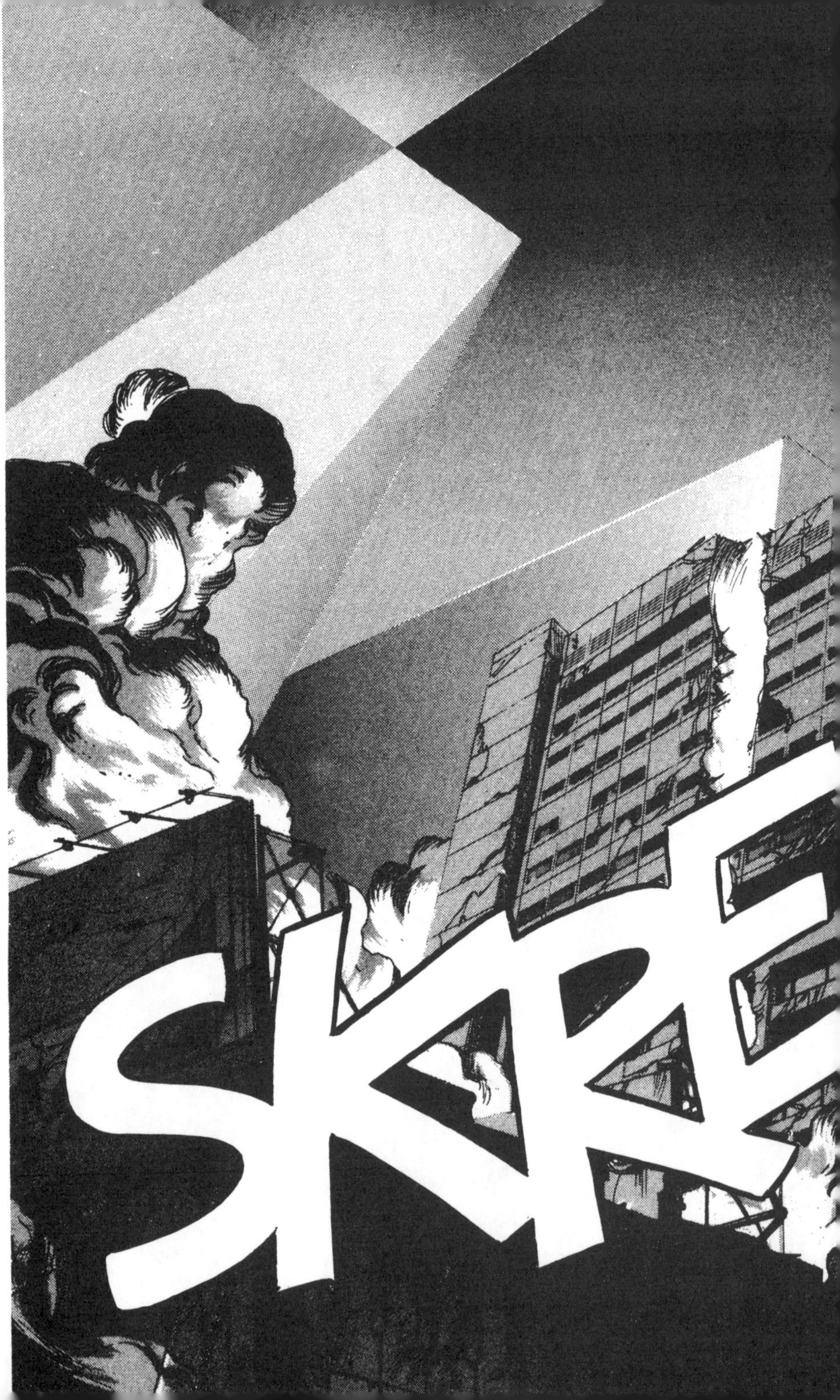
SKR

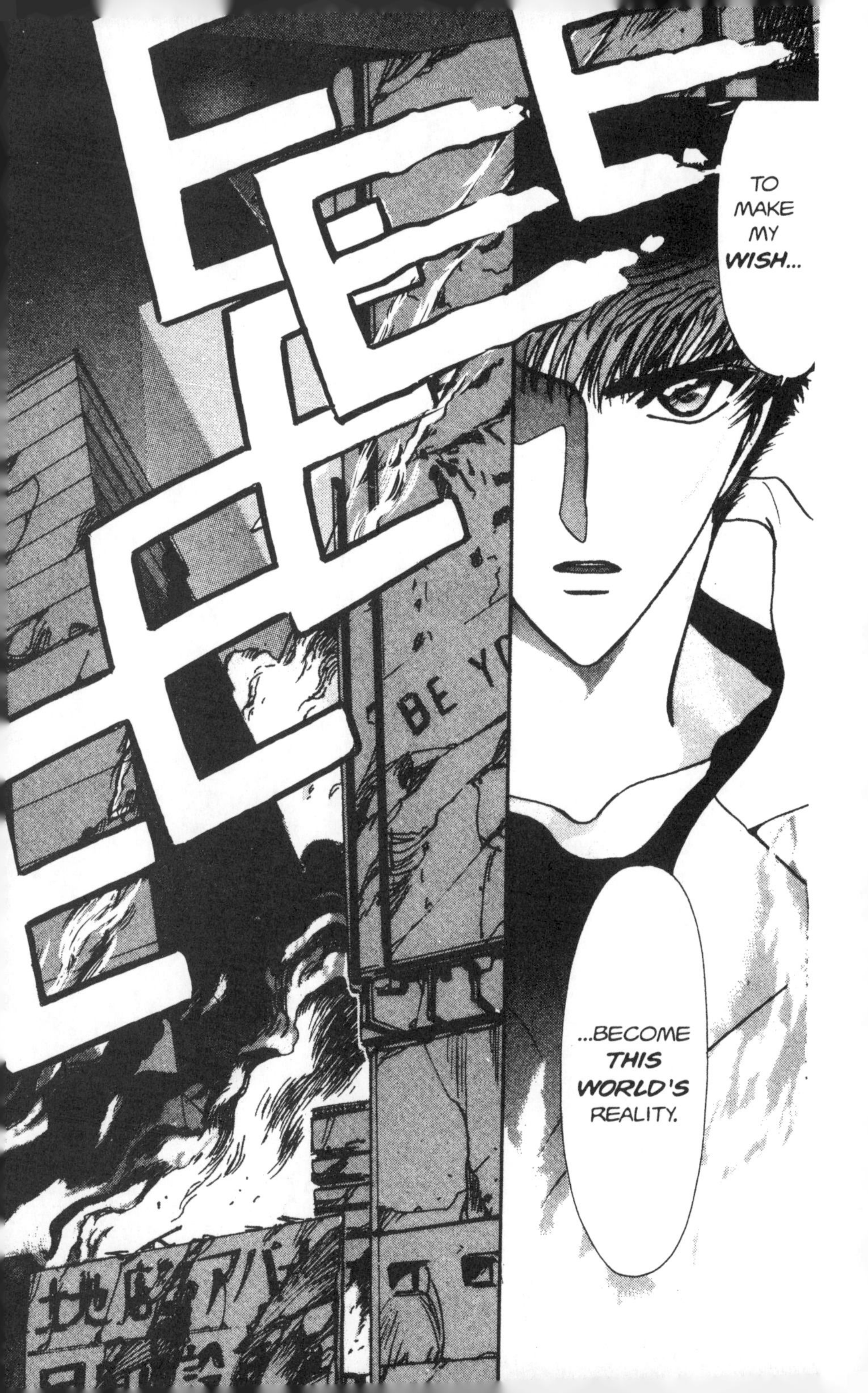
TO MAKE MY WISH...
...BECOME THIS WORLD'S REALITY.

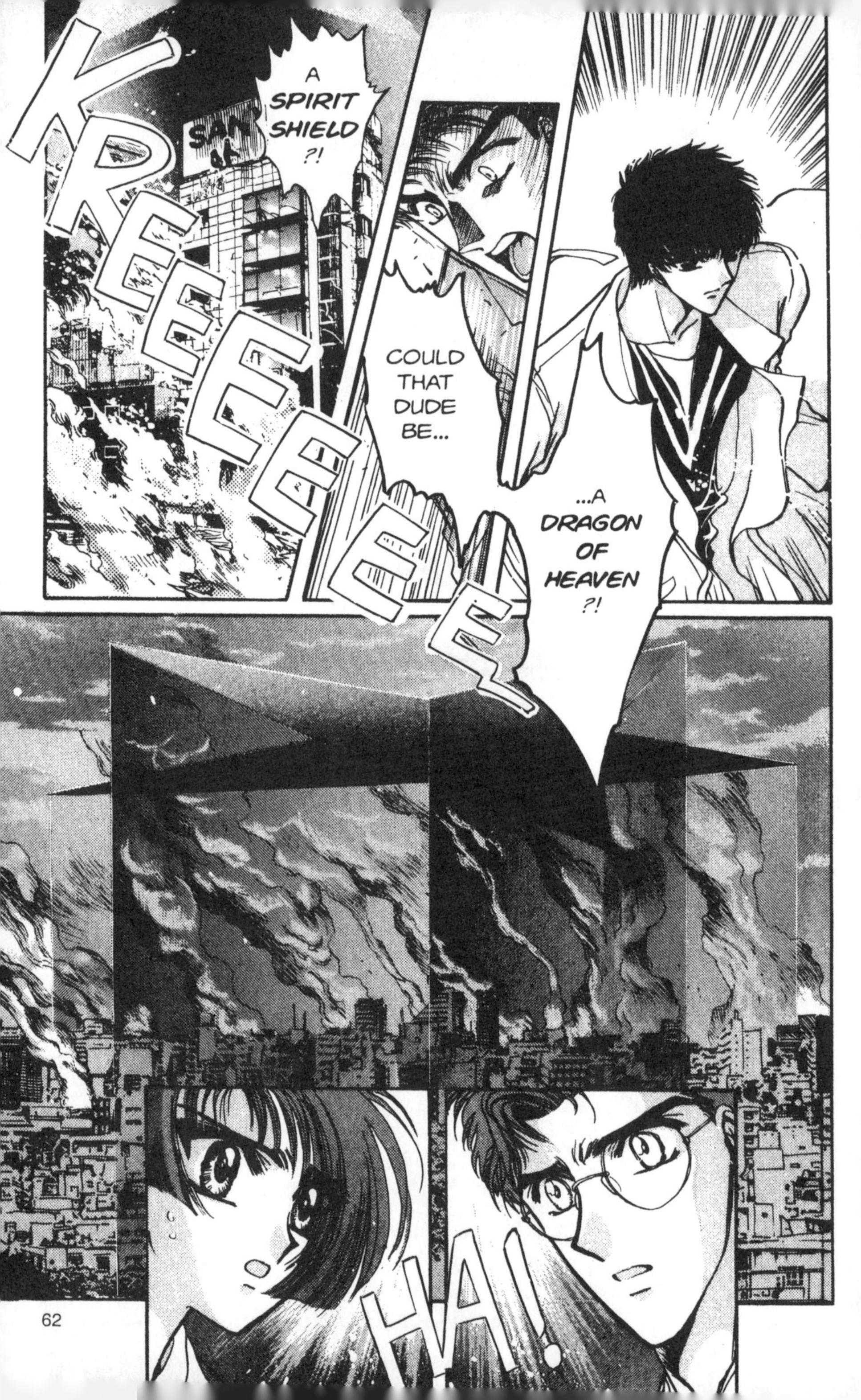
KREEEEEEEE
A SPIRIT SHIELD ?!
COULD THAT DUDE BE...
...A DRAGON OF HEAVEN ?!
HA!

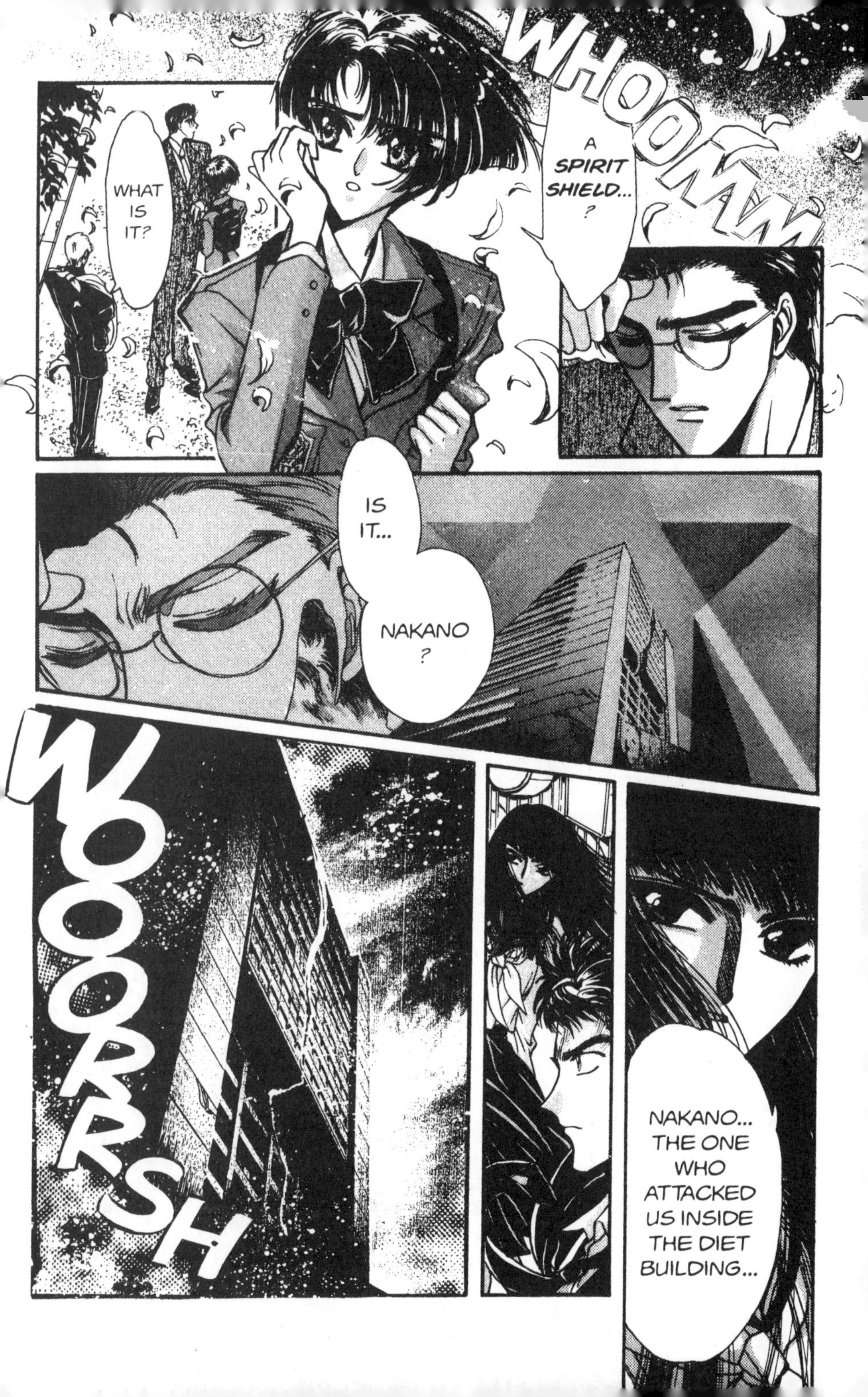
WHOOMMM
A SPIRIT SHIELD...?
WHAT IS IT?
IS IT... NAKANO?
NAKANO... THE ONE WHO ATTACKED US INSIDE THE DIET BUILDING...
WOOORRSH

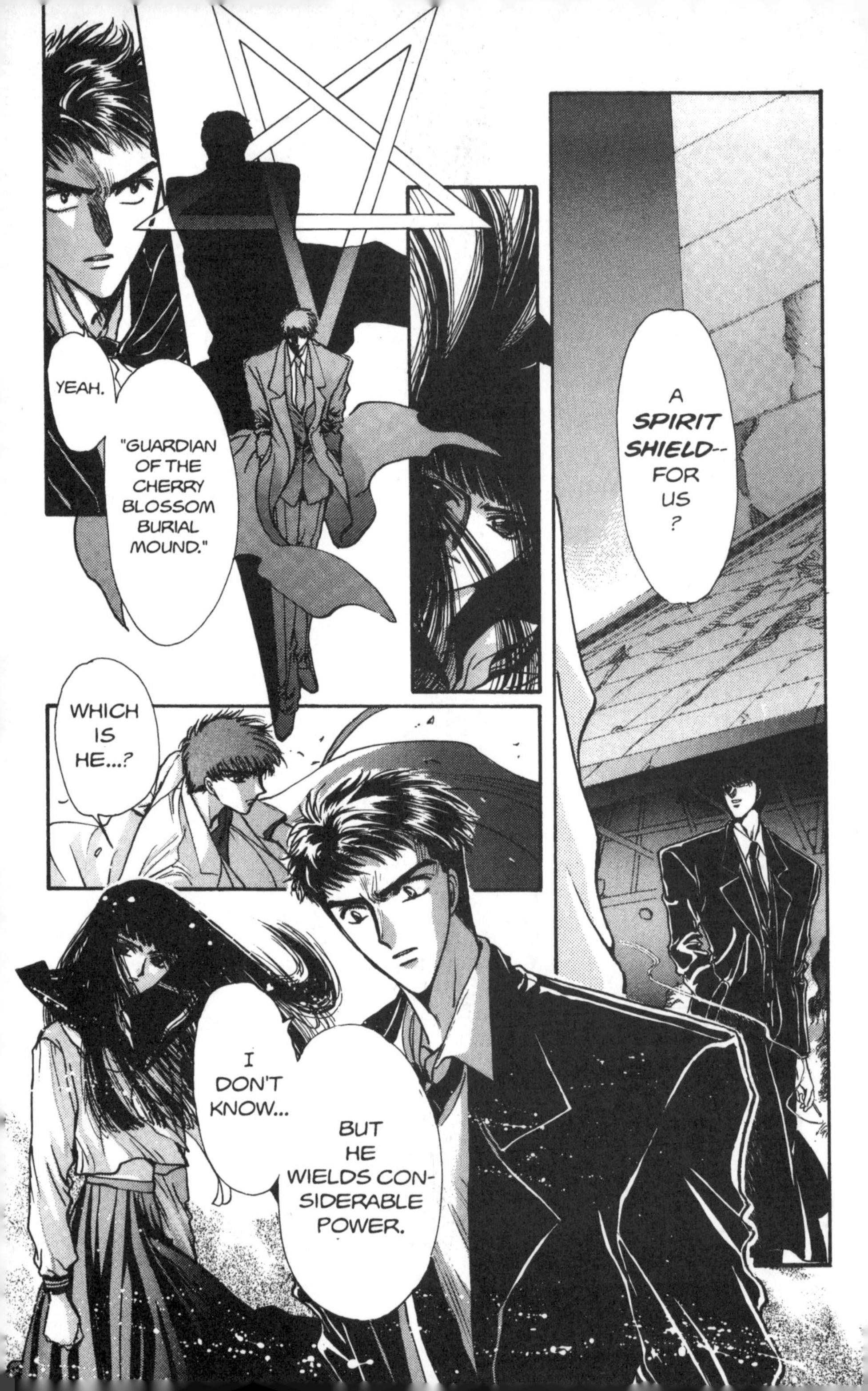
A SPIRIT SHIELD-- FOR US ?
YEAH.
"GUARDIAN OF THE CHERRY BLOSSOM BURIAL MOUND."
WHICH IS HE...?
I DON'T KNOW...
BUT HE WIELDS CON-SIDERABLE POWER.

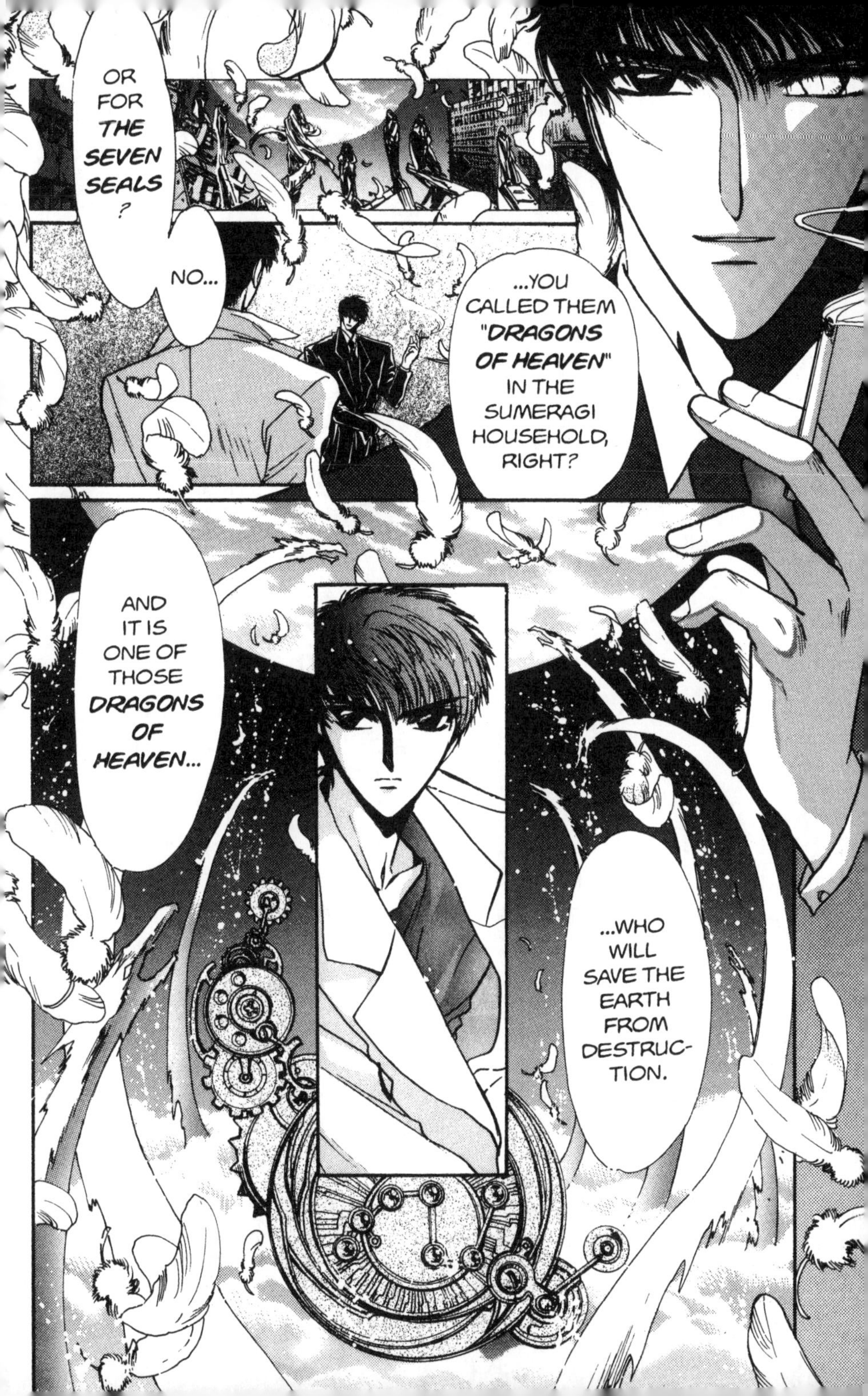
OR FOR THE SEVEN SEALS?
NO...
...YOU CALLED THEM "DRAGONS OF HEAVEN" IN THE SUMERAGI HOUSEHOLD, RIGHT?
AND IT IS ONE OF THOSE DRAGONS OF HEAVEN...
...WHO WILL SAVE THE EARTH FROM DESTRUC-TION.

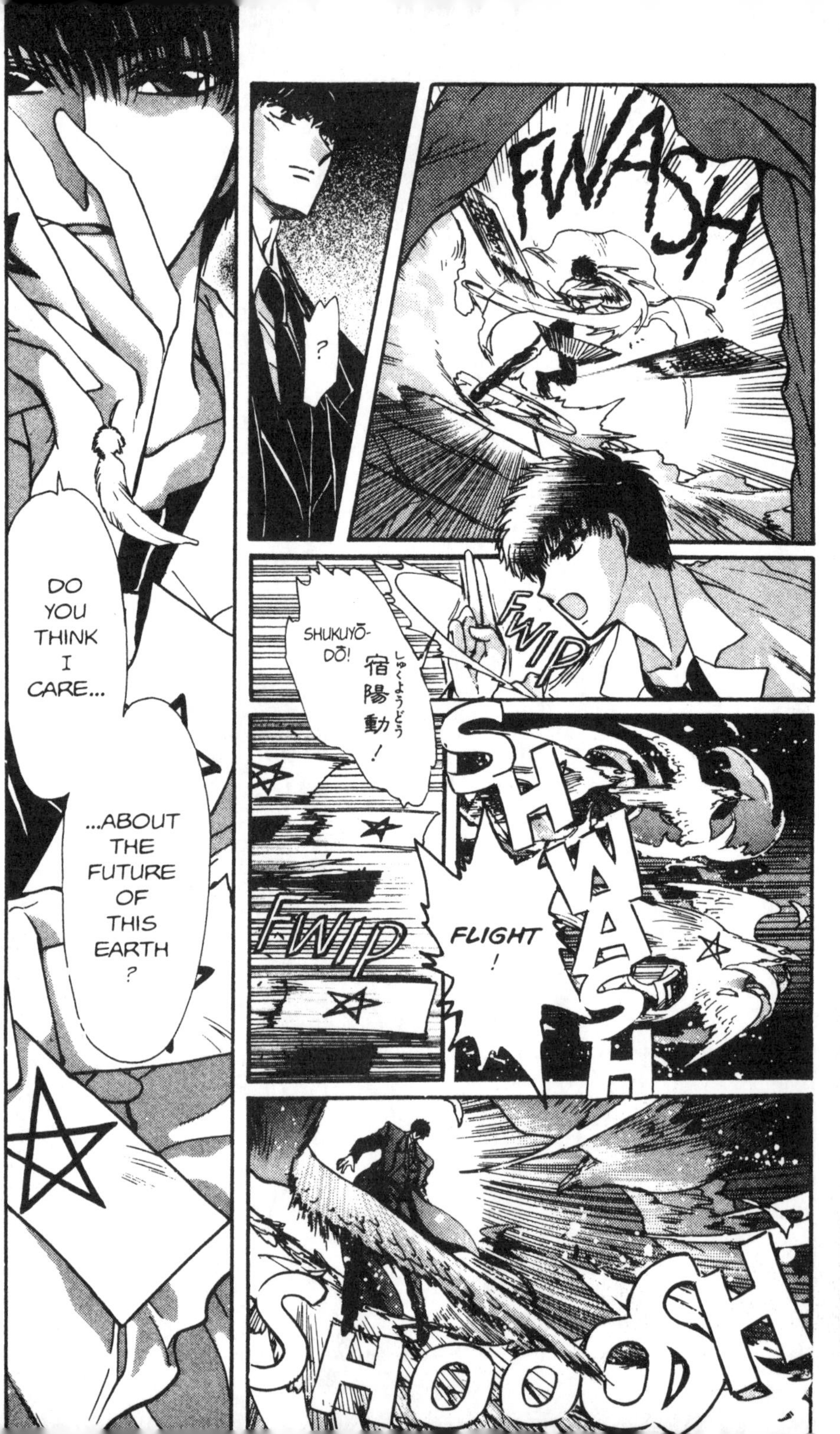
FWASH
?
FWIP
SHUKUYŌ-DŌ!
しゅくようどう
宿陽動!
SHWASH
FWIP
FLIGHT!
SHOOOSH
DO YOU THINK I CARE...
...ABOUT THE FUTURE OF THIS EARTH?

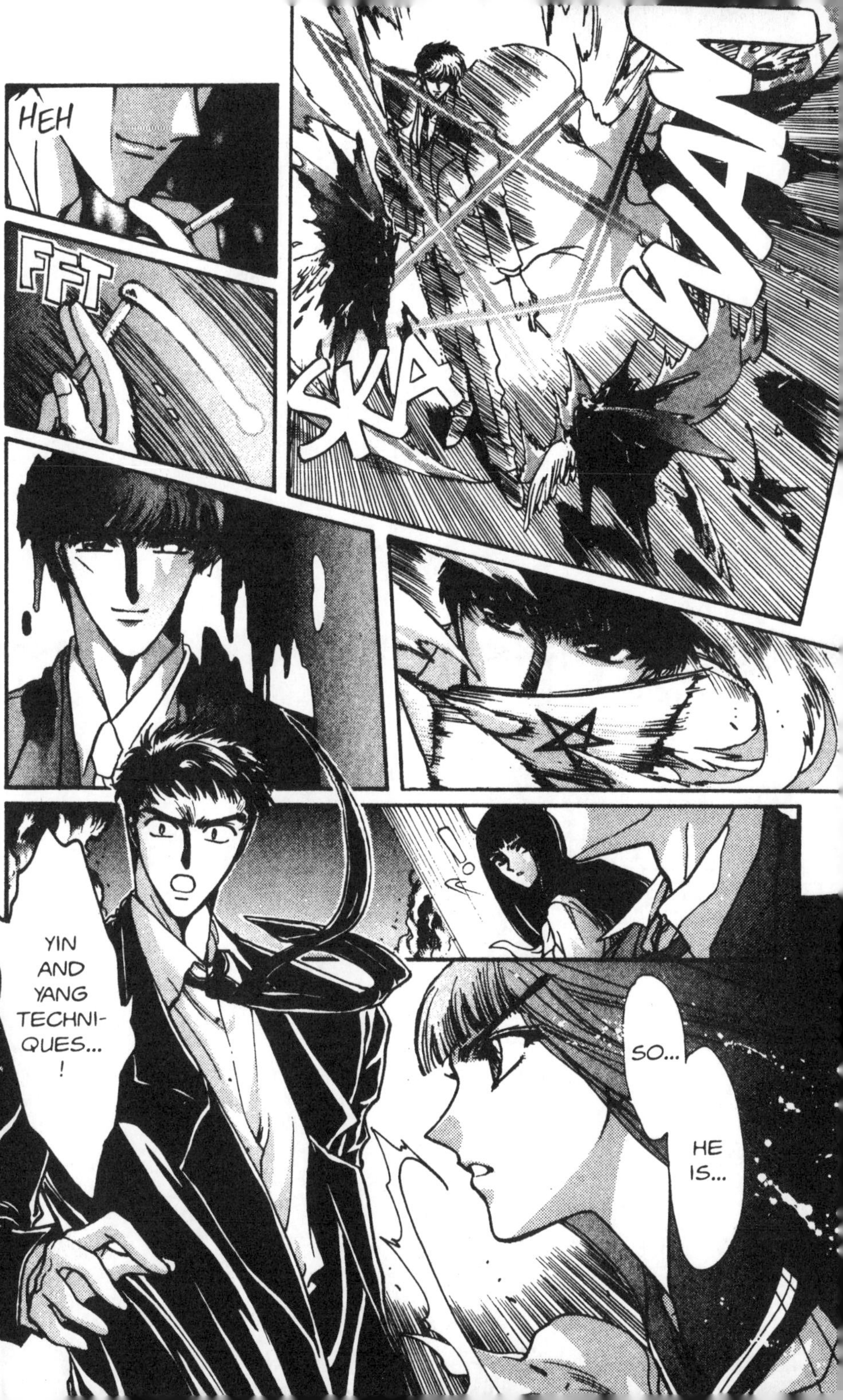
SKA
WA
HEH
FFT
!
SO...
HE IS...
YIN AND YANG TECHNIQUES...!

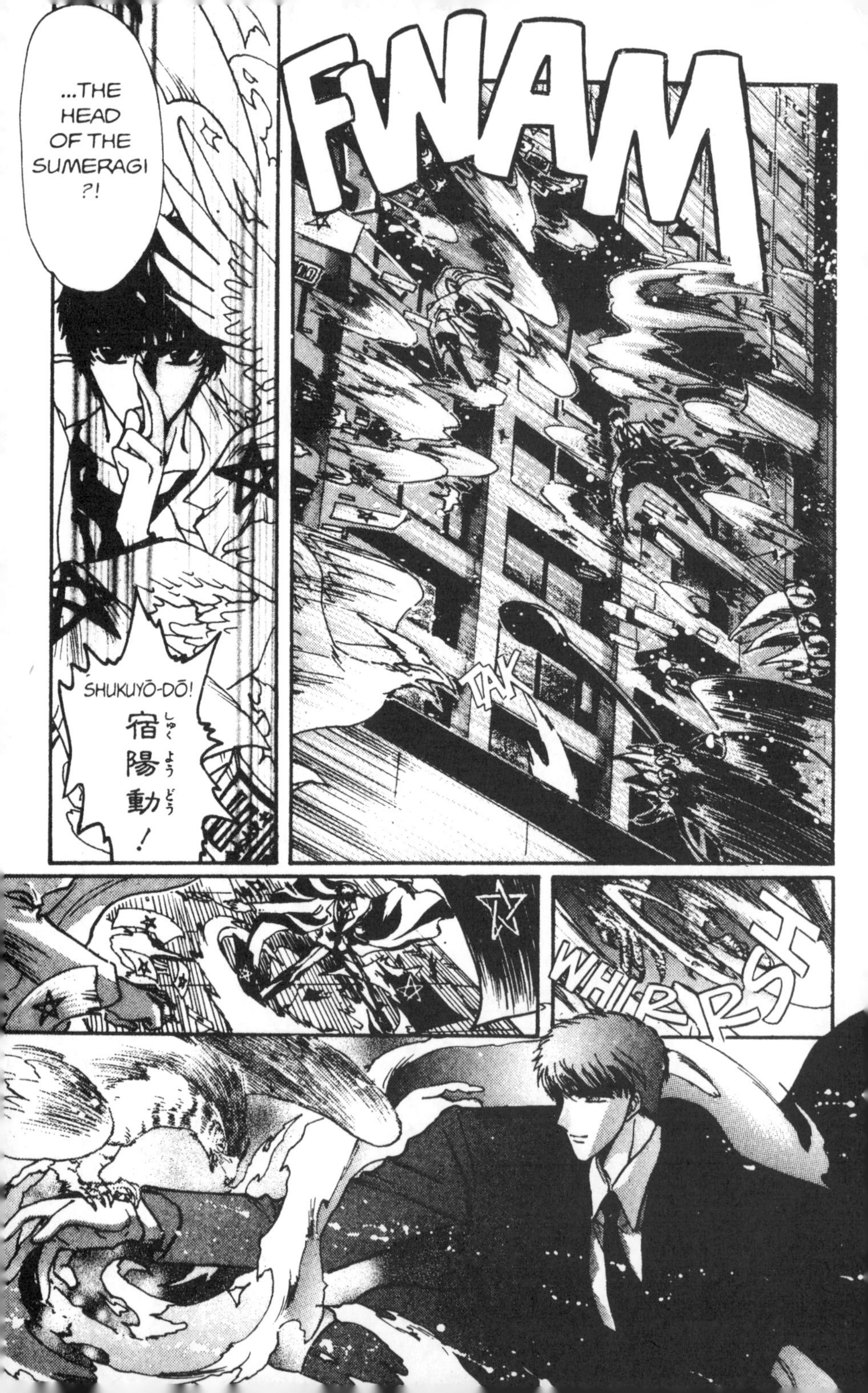
FWAM
TAK
...THE HEAD OF THE SUMERAGI ?!
SHUKUYŌ-DŌ!
宿陽動！
WHIRRSH

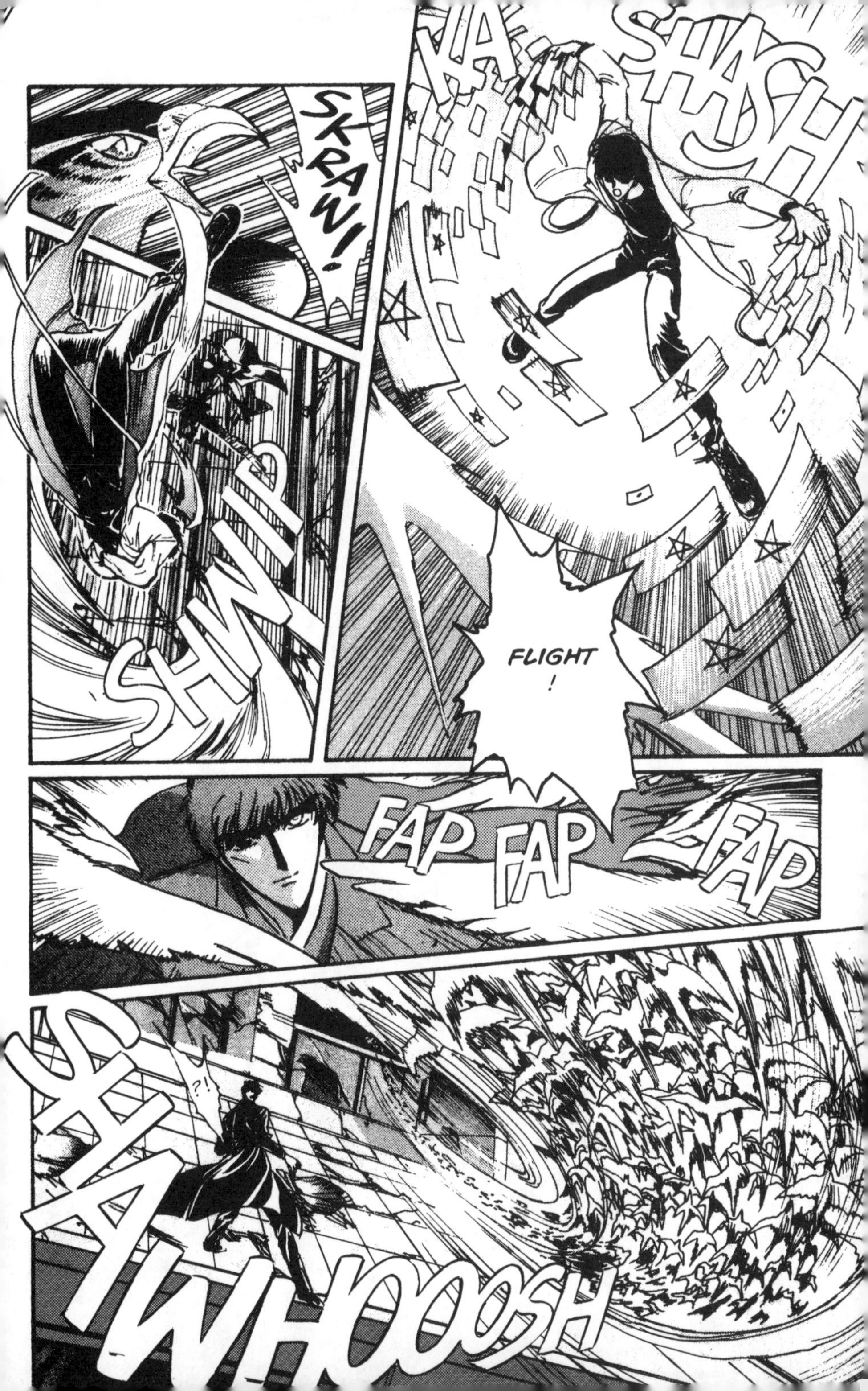
SHASH
FLIGHT!
SKRAW!
SHWIP
FAP FAP FAP
?!
SHA WHOOOSH

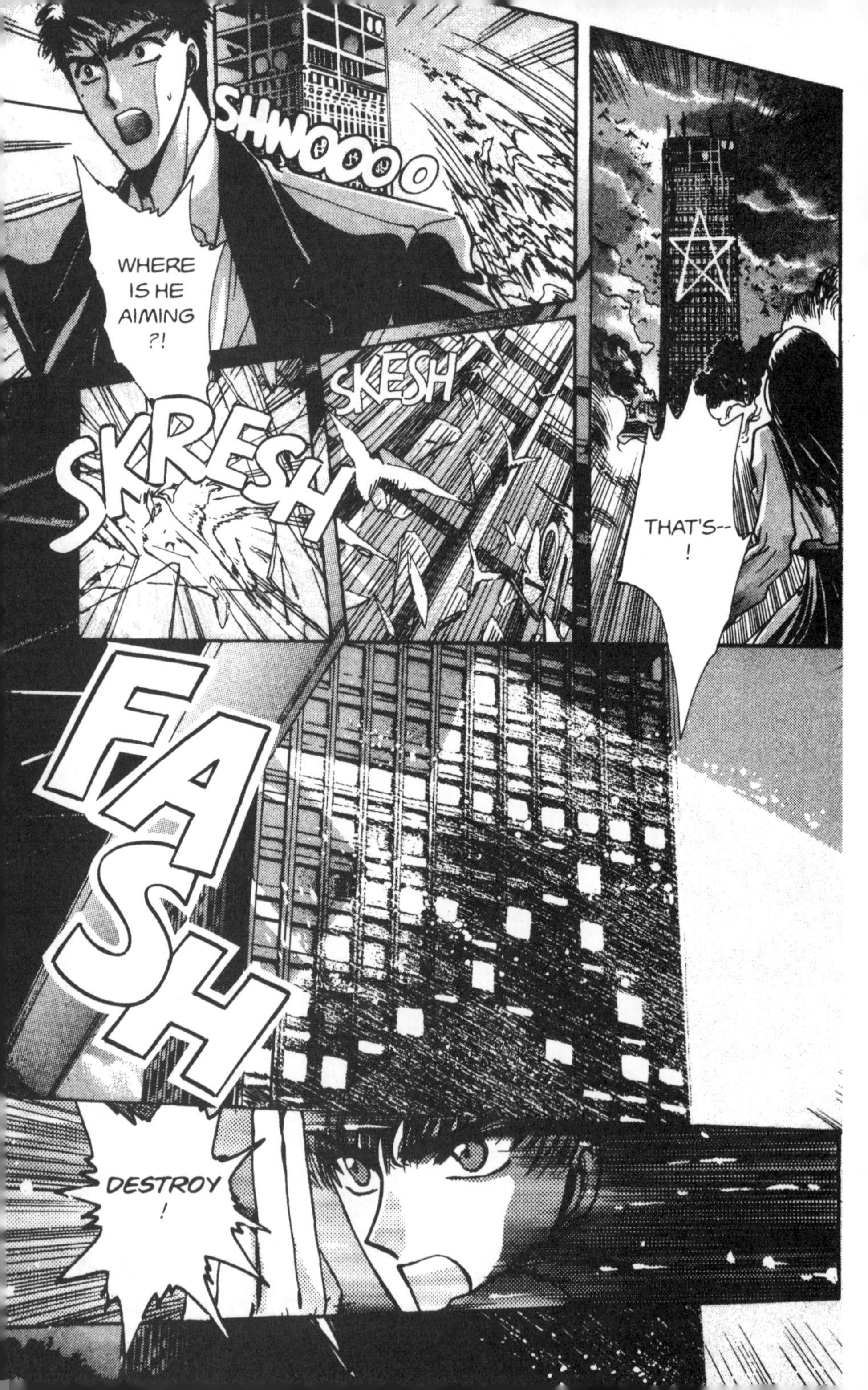
THAT'S--!
SHWOOOO
WHERE IS HE AIMING?!
SKESH
SKRESH
FASH
DESTROY!

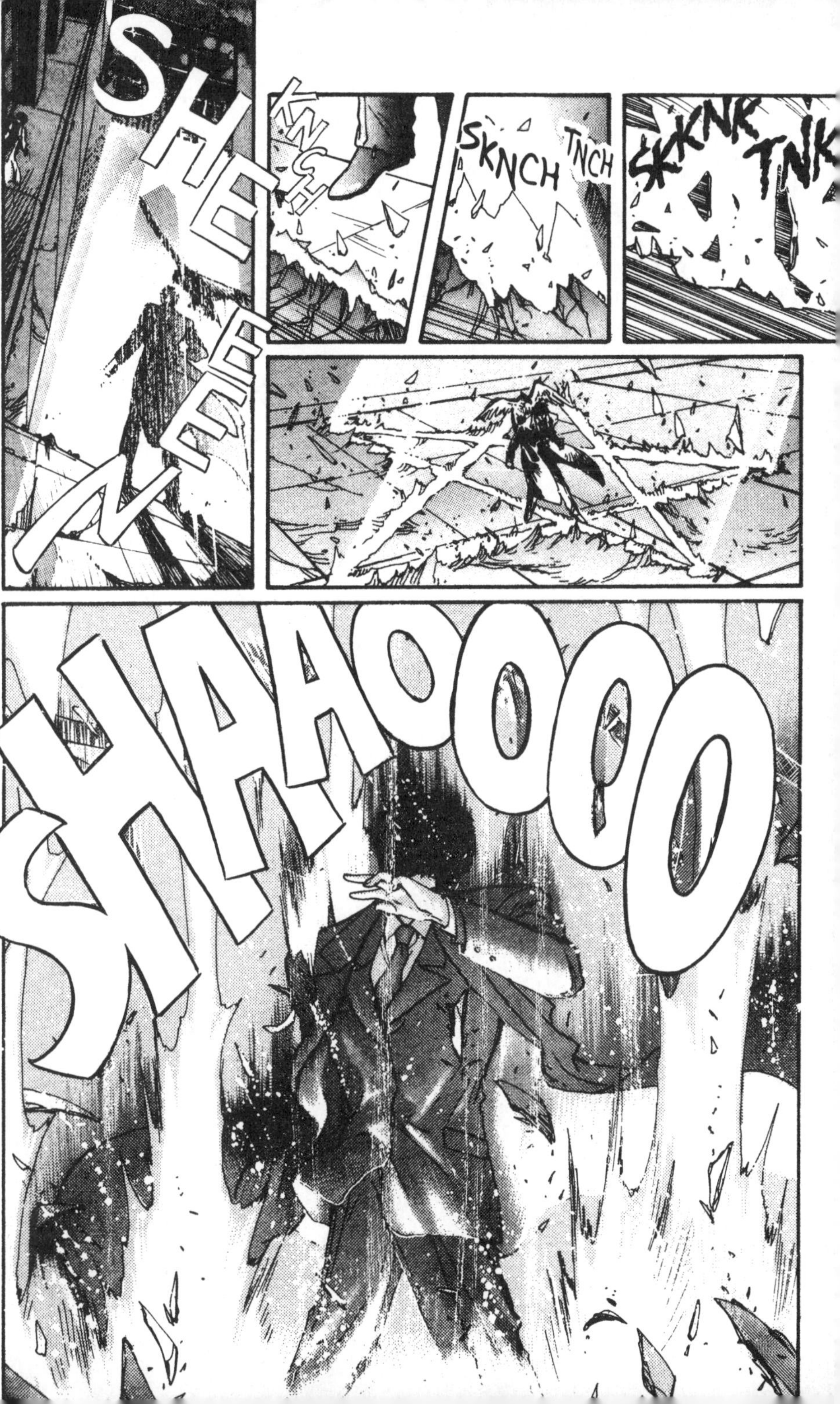
SKKNK
TNK
SKNCH
TNCH
KNCH!
SHEEEN
SHAOOOO

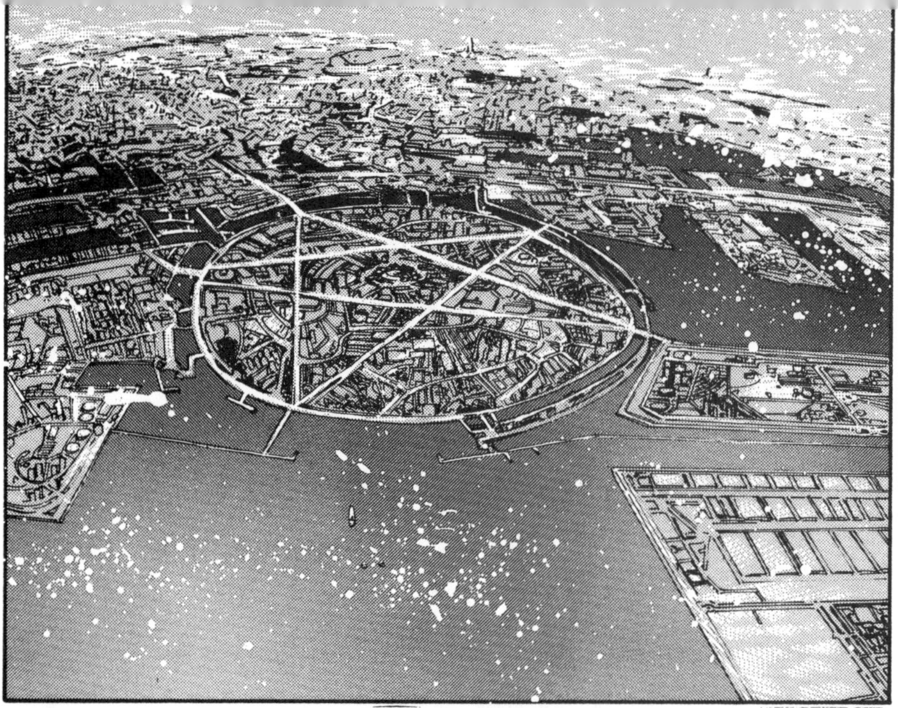

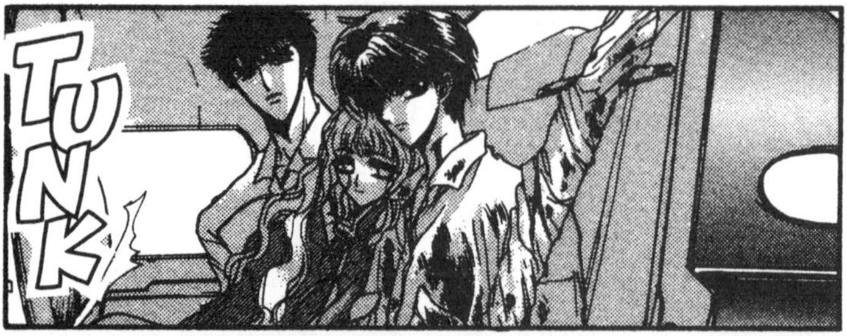
TUNK

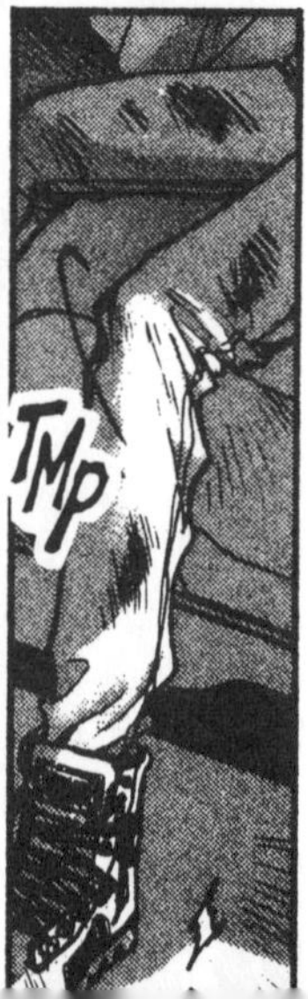
TMP

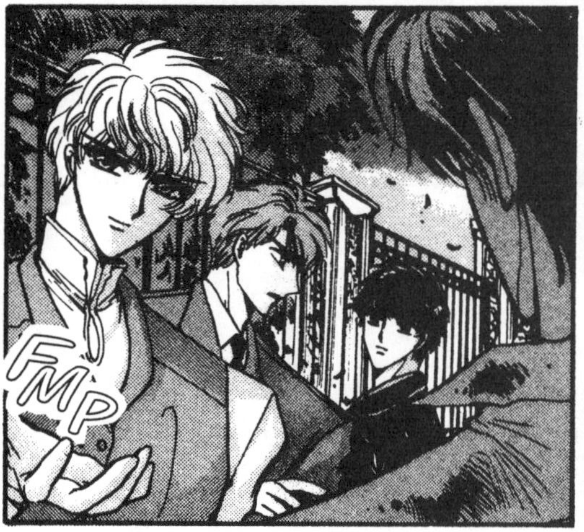
FMP

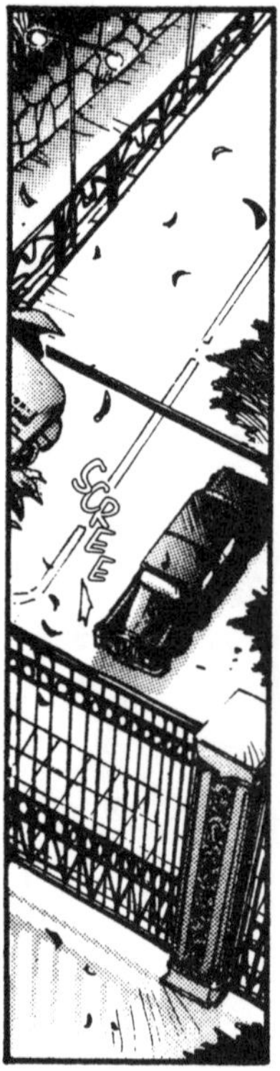
SCREE

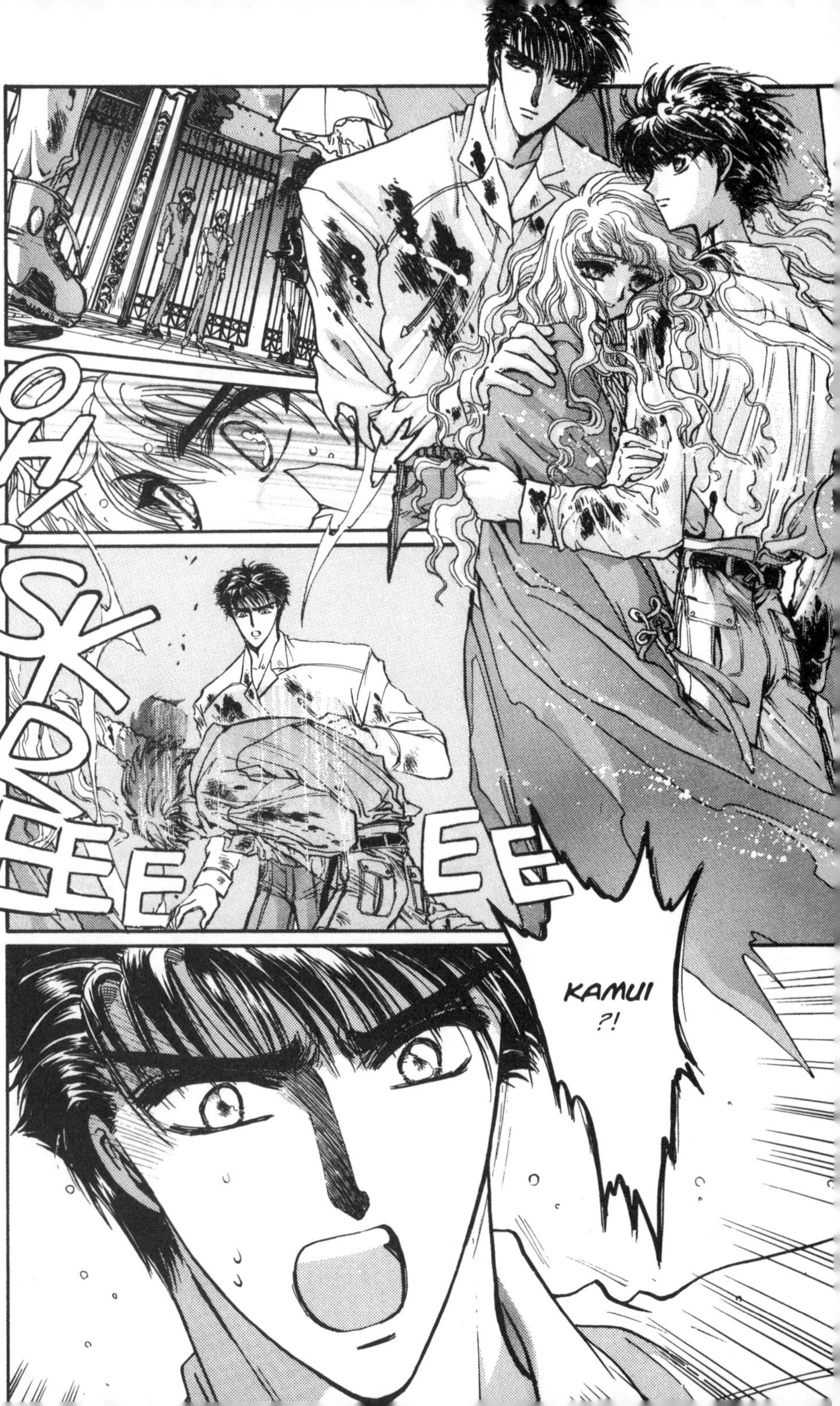
OH! SKREEEE
KAMUI ?!

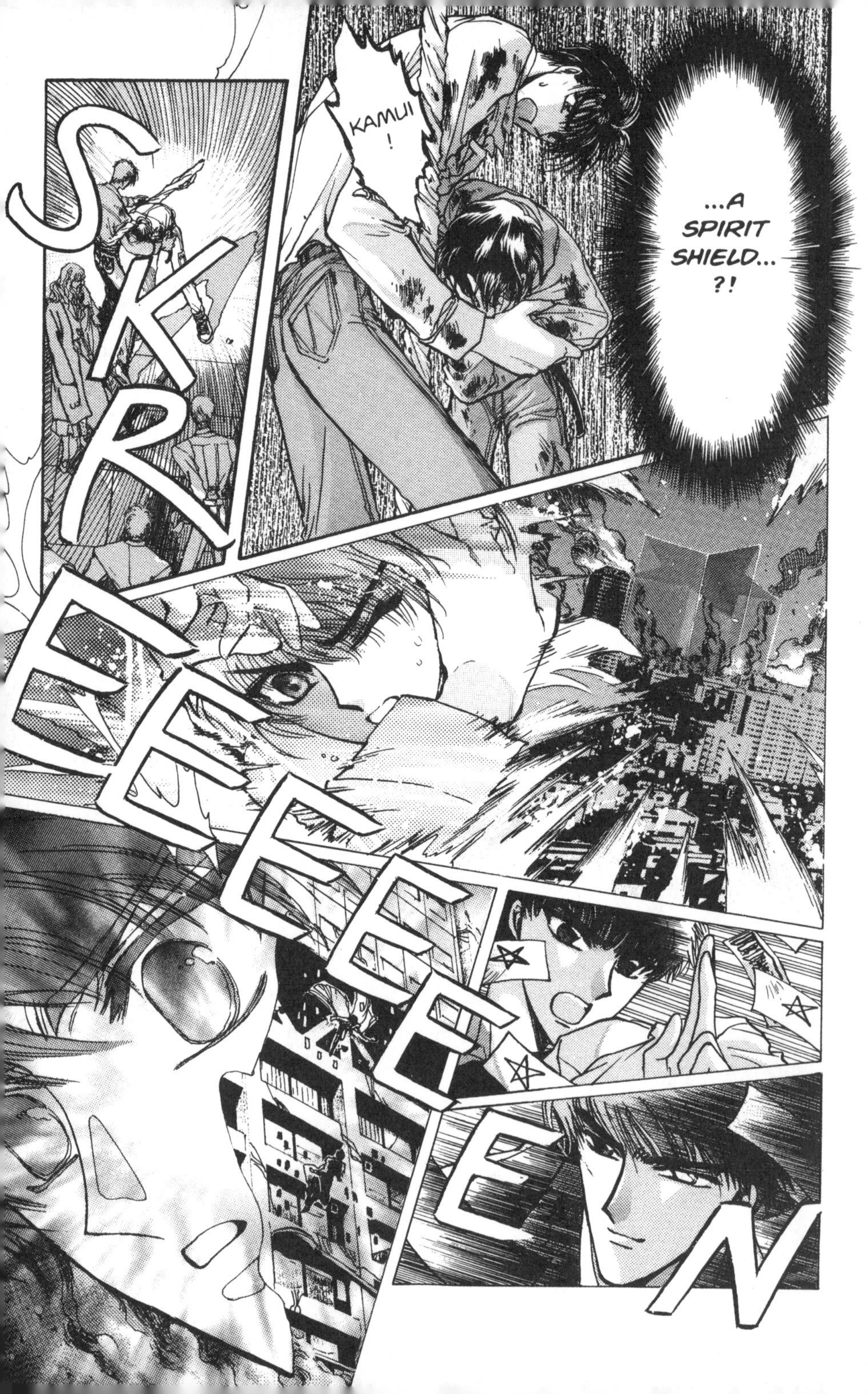

...A SPIRIT SHIELD...?!
KAMUI!
SKREEEEEEN

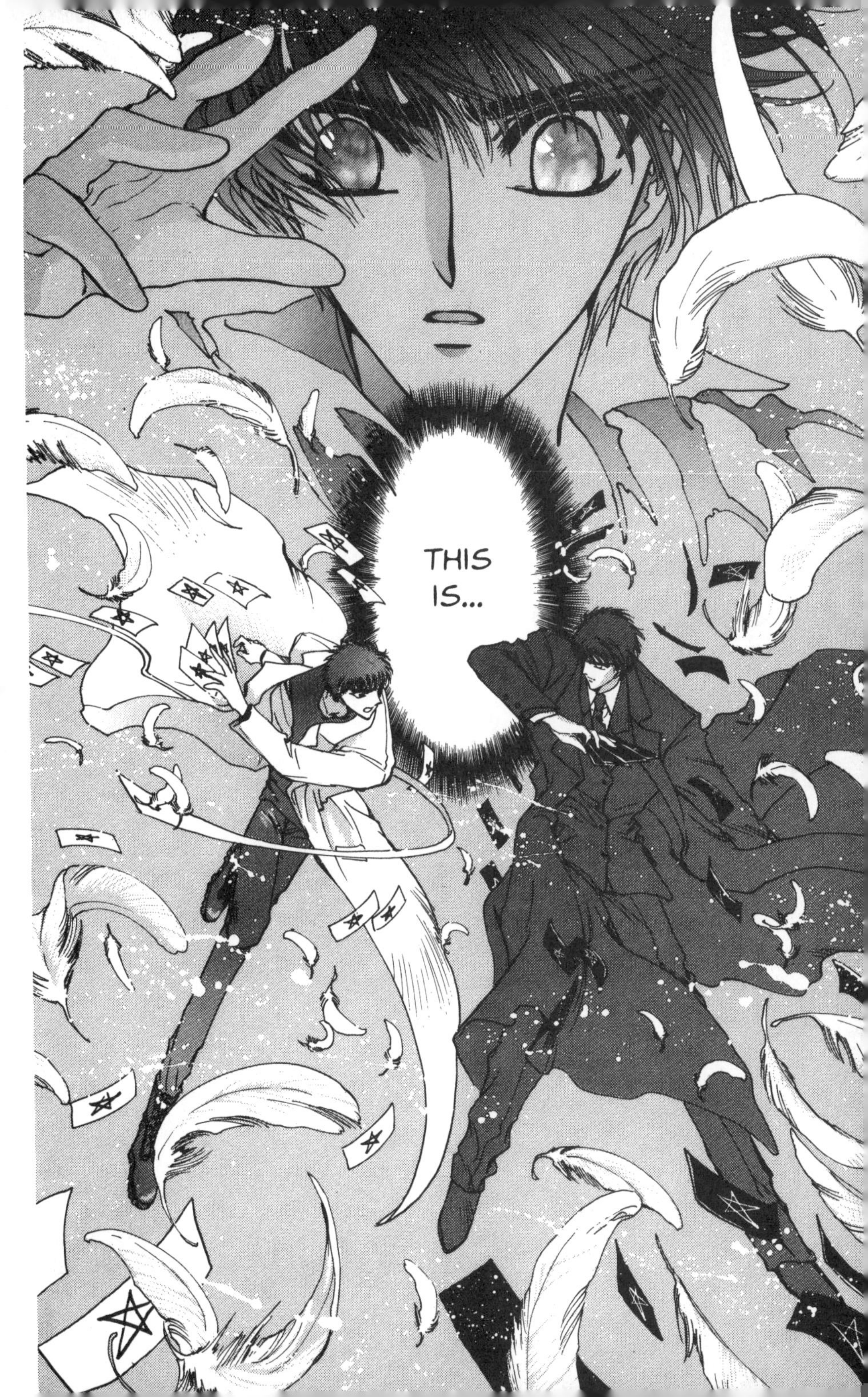
THIS IS...

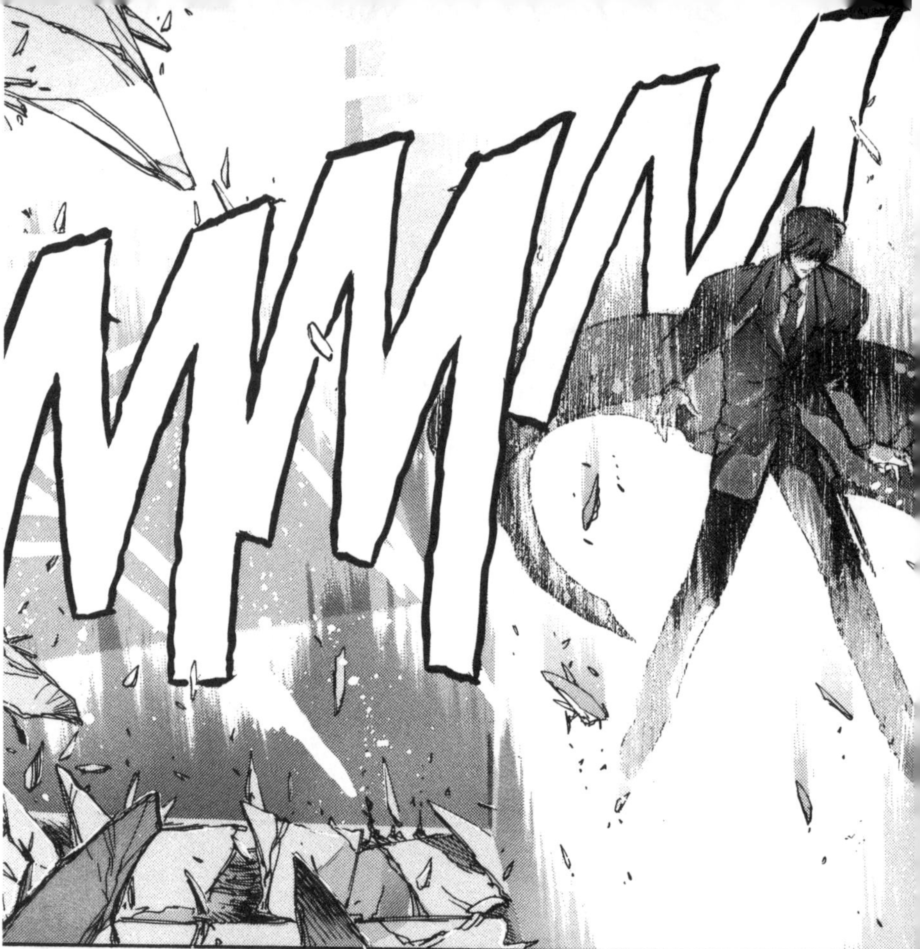
MMMM

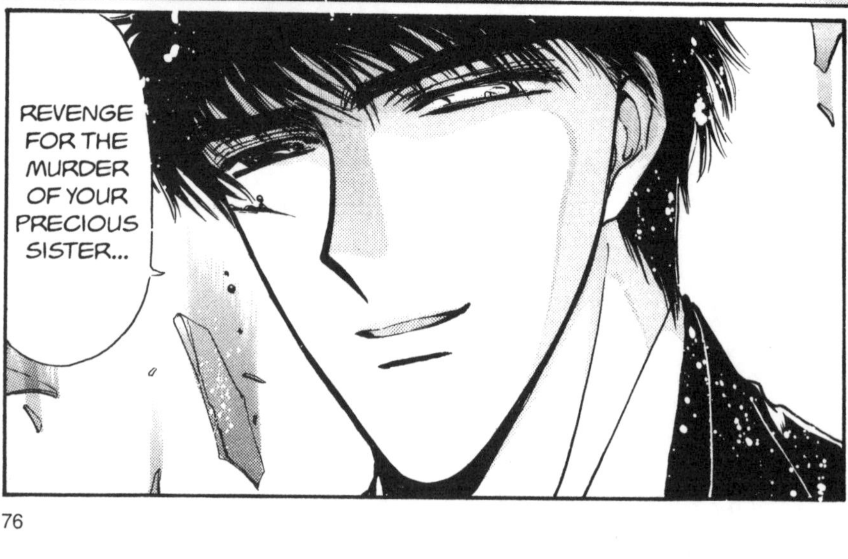
REVENGE FOR THE MURDER OF YOUR PRECIOUS SISTER...

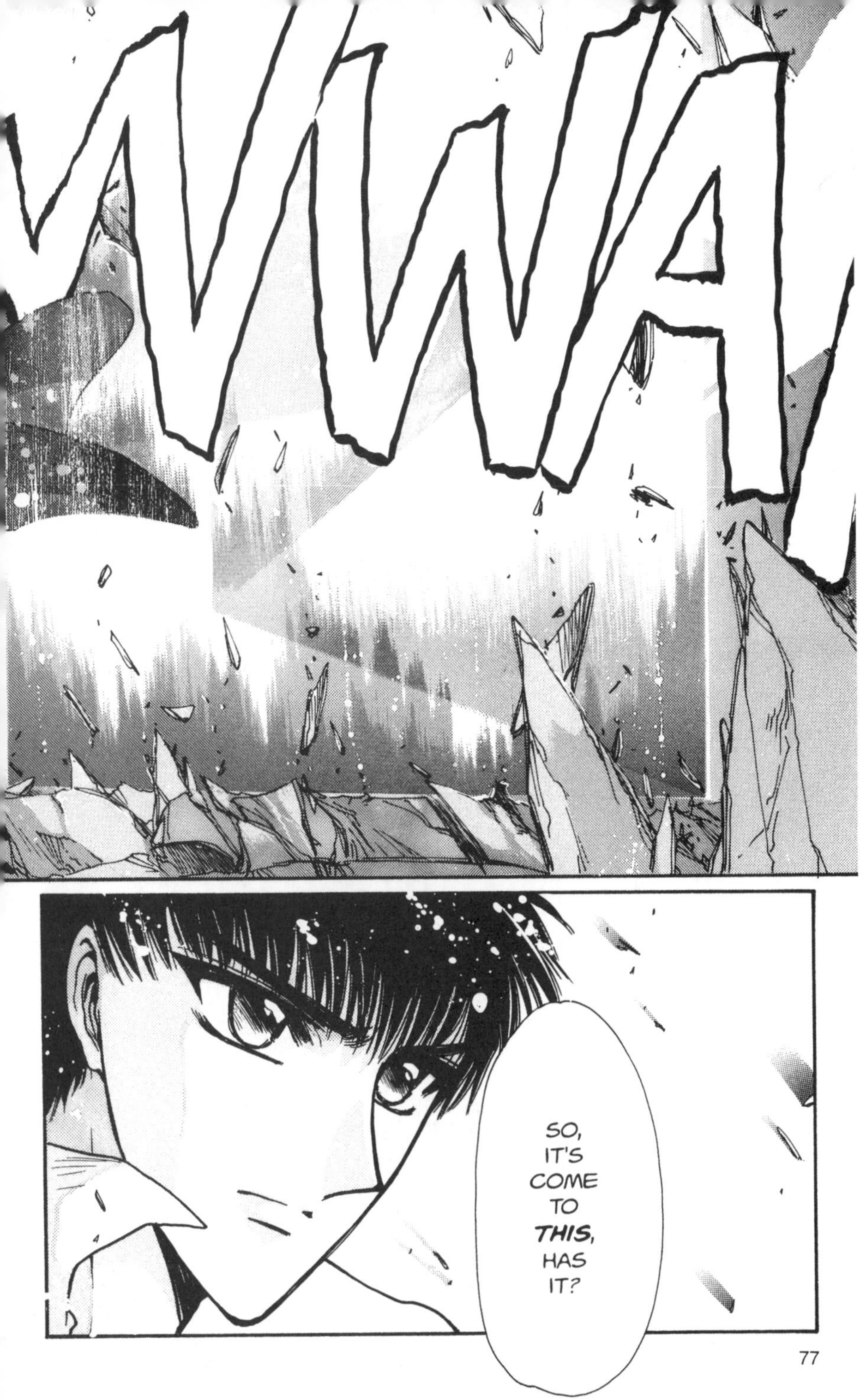
WWA
SO, IT'S COME TO ***THIS***, HAS IT?

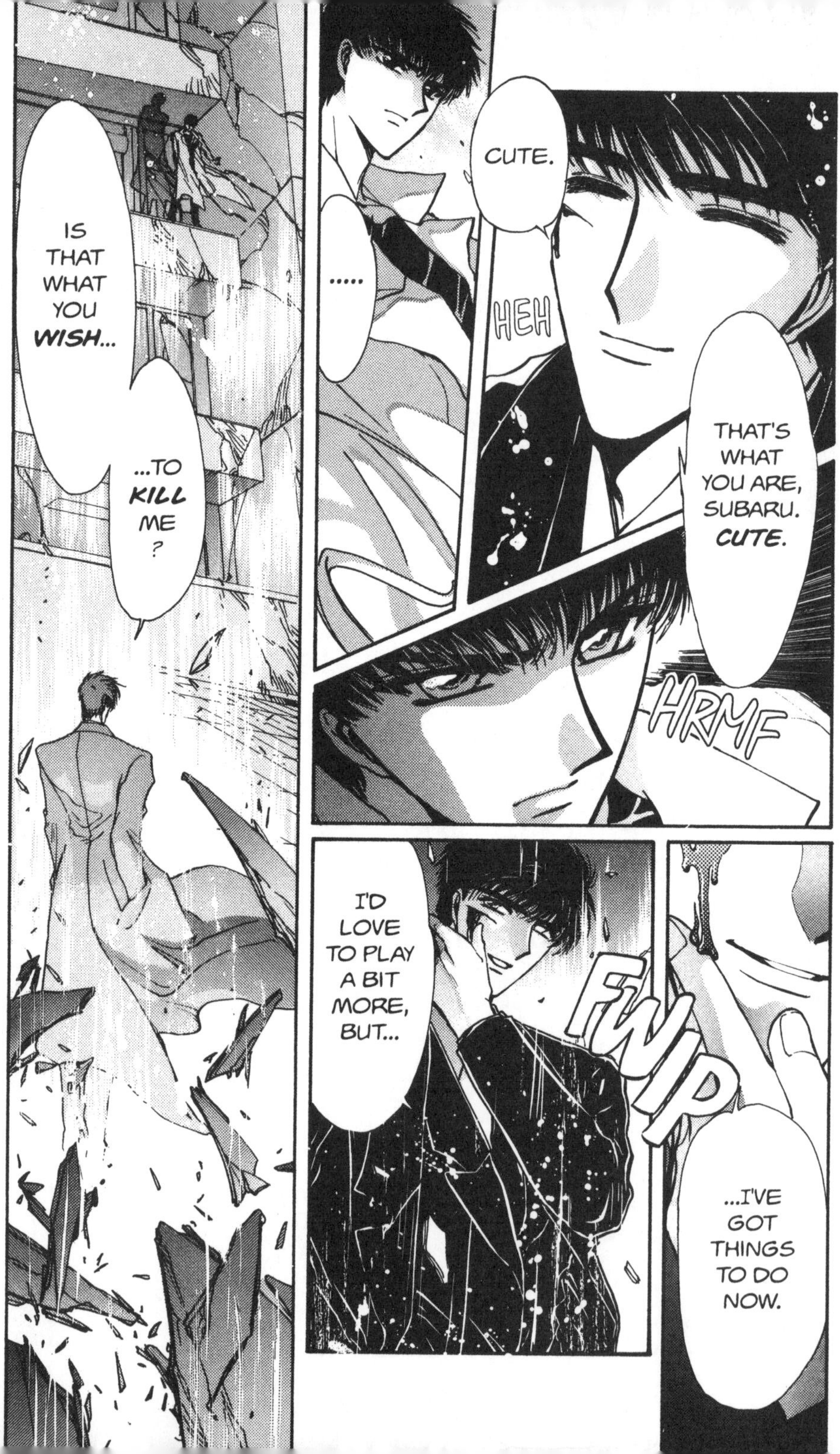
IS THAT WHAT YOU **WISH**...
...TO **KILL** ME ?
.....
CUTE.
HEH
THAT'S WHAT YOU ARE, SUBARU. **CUTE**.
HRMF
I'D LOVE TO PLAY A BIT MORE, BUT...
FWIP
...I'VE GOT THINGS TO DO NOW.

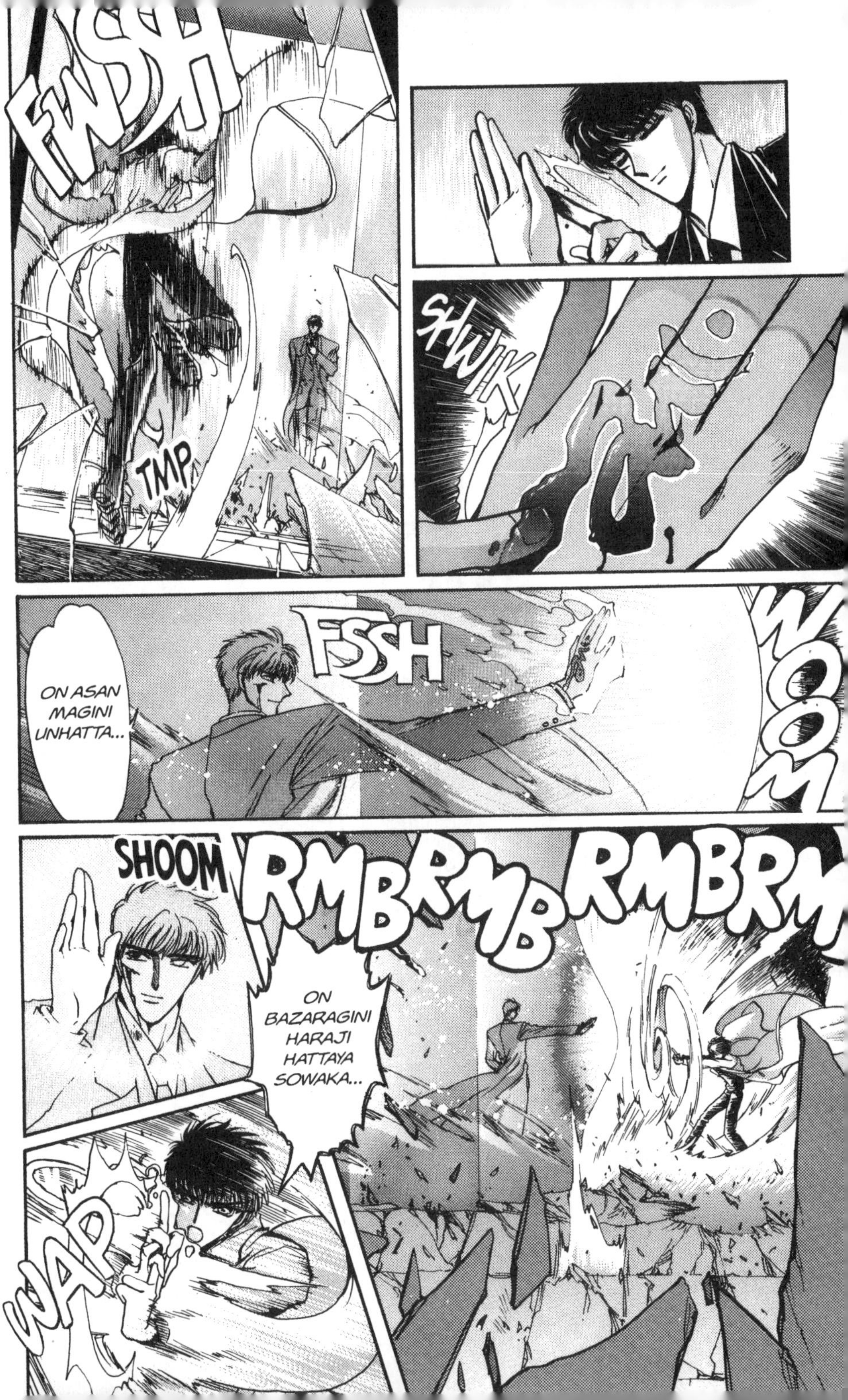
FWSSH
SHWIK
TMP
WOOOM
FSSH
ON ASAN MAGINI UNHATTA...
RMBRMBRMBRMBRM
SHOOM
ON BAZARAGINI HARAJI HATTAYA SOWAKA...
WAP

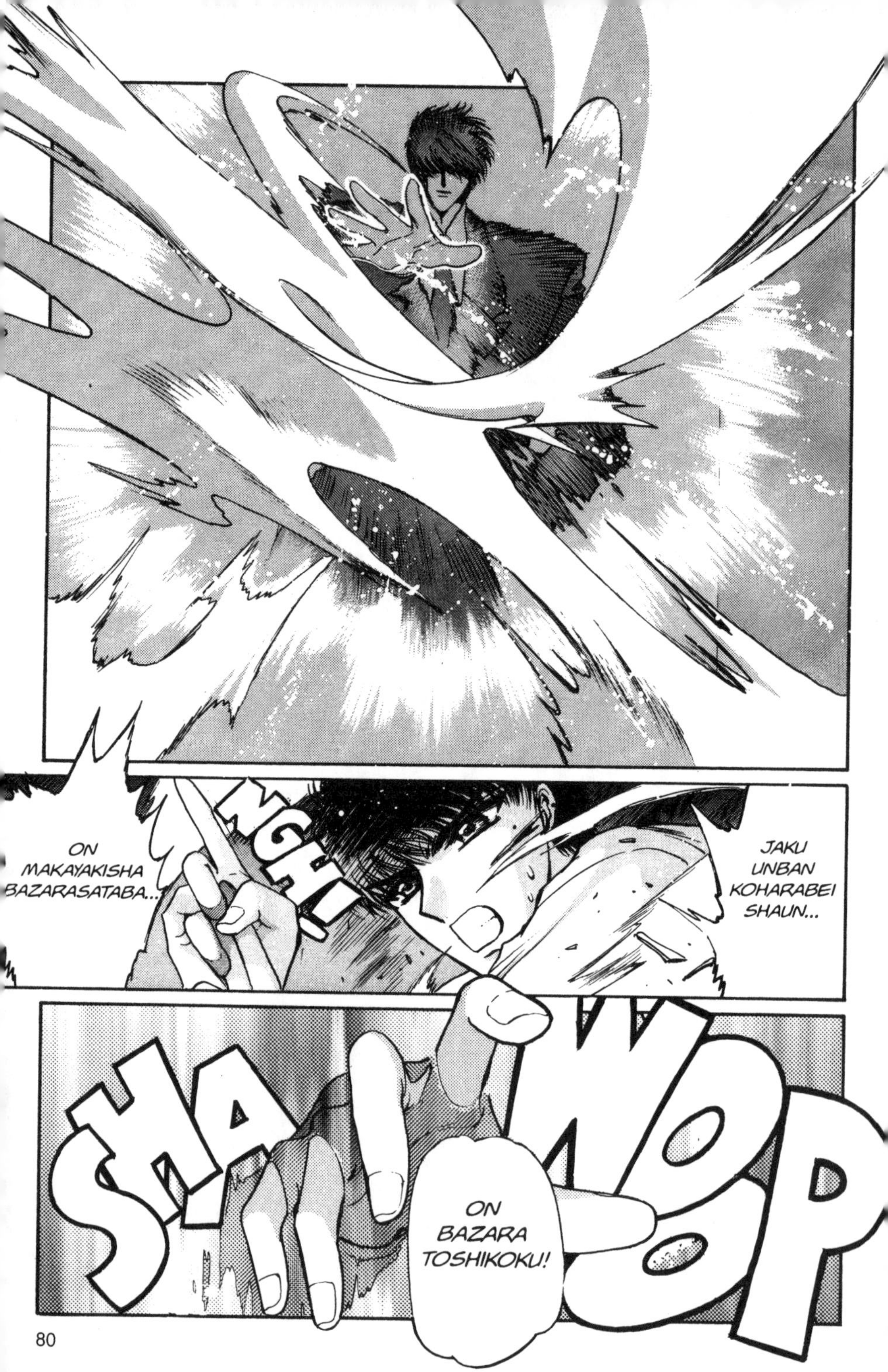
JAKU UNBAN KOHARABEI SHAUN...
NGH!
ON MAKAYAKISHA BAZARASATABA...
SHA WOOP
ON BAZARA TOSHIKOKU!

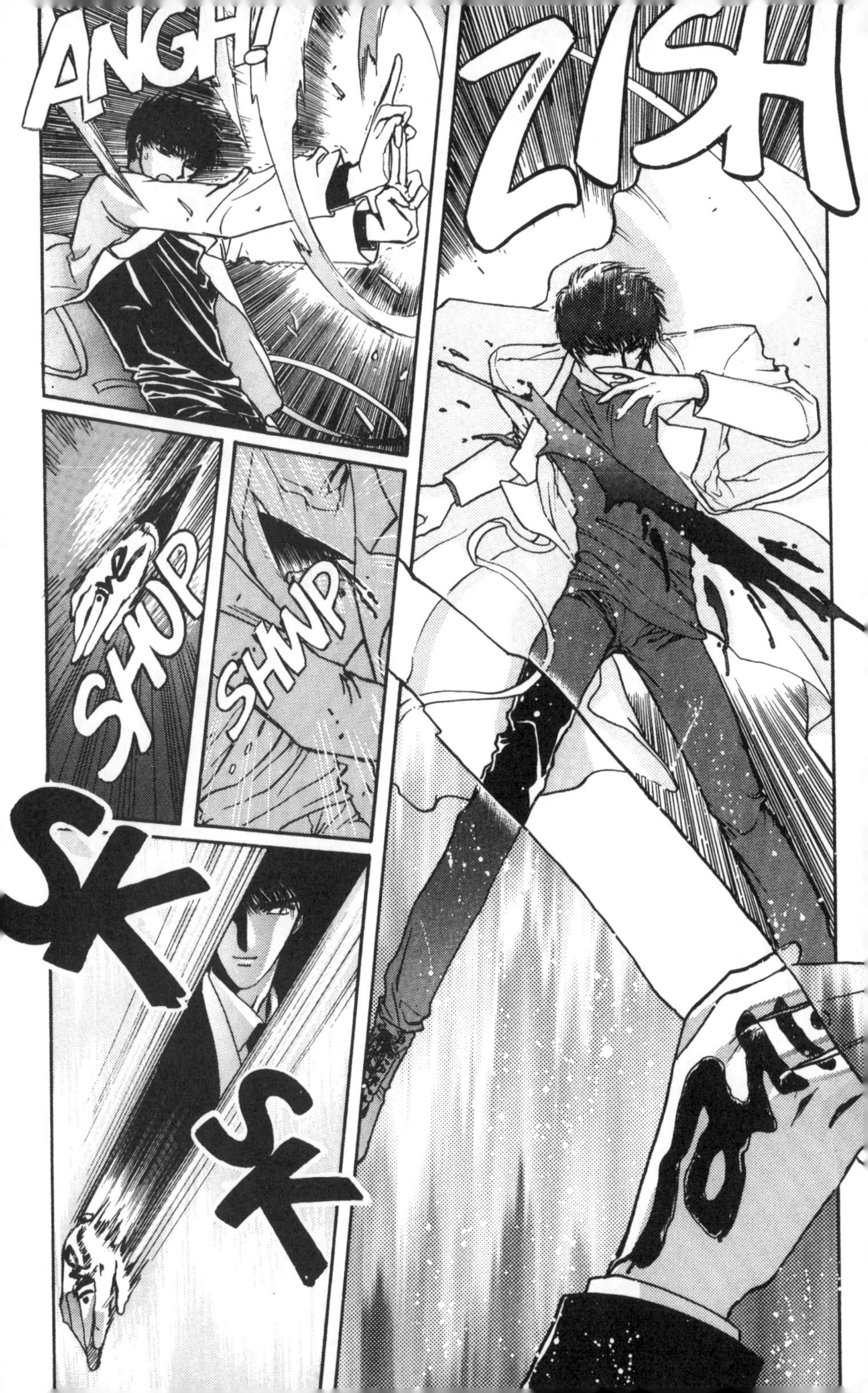
ZISH
ANGH!
SHUP
SHUP
SK
SK

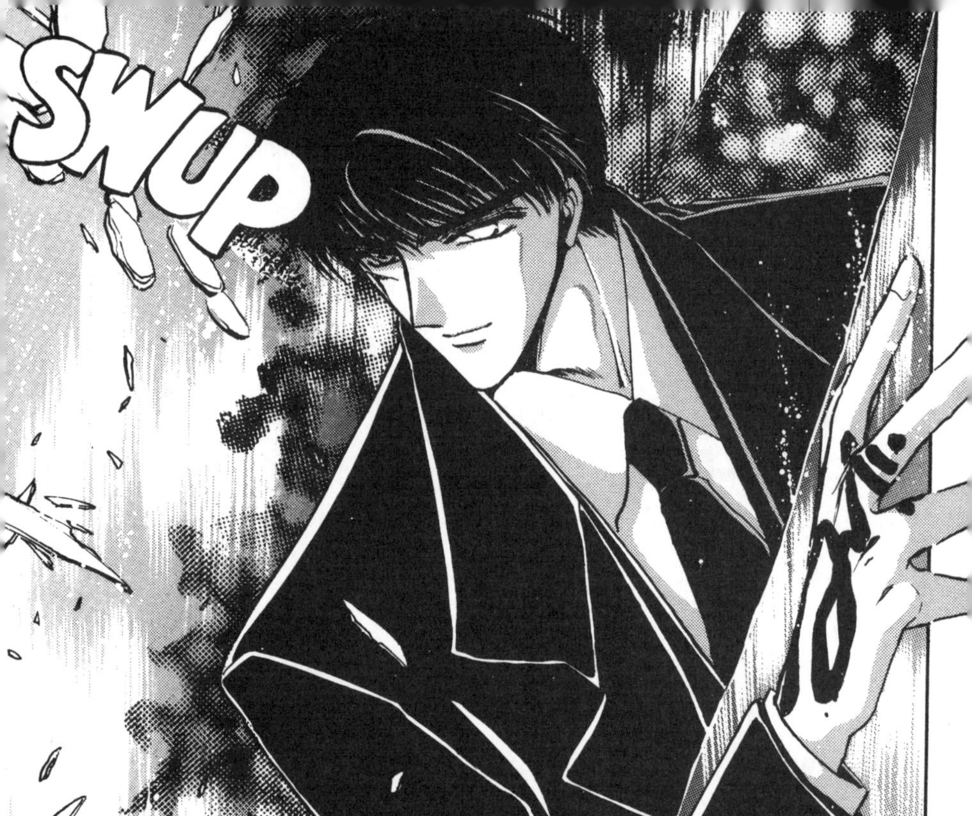
SWUP
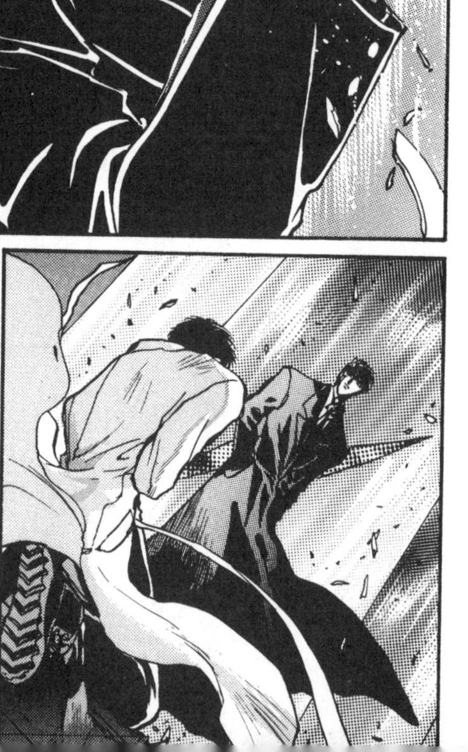
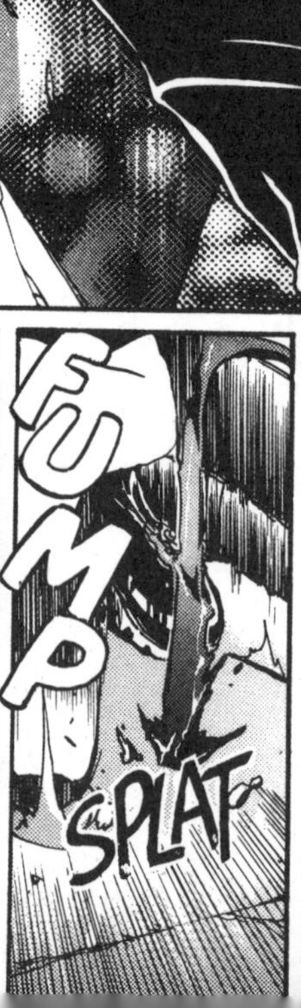
FUMP
SPLAT
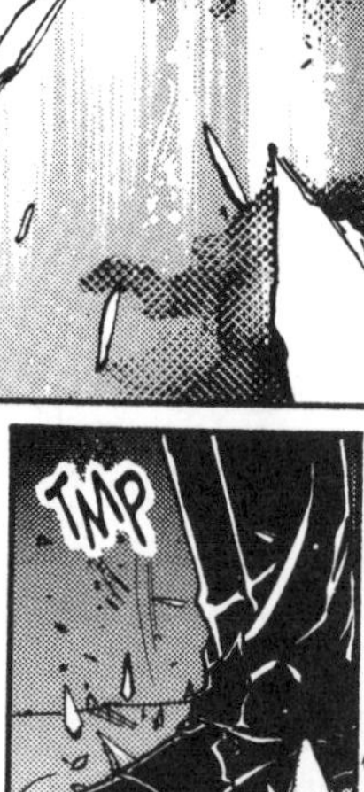
TMP
SKRK

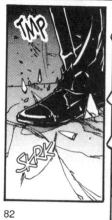

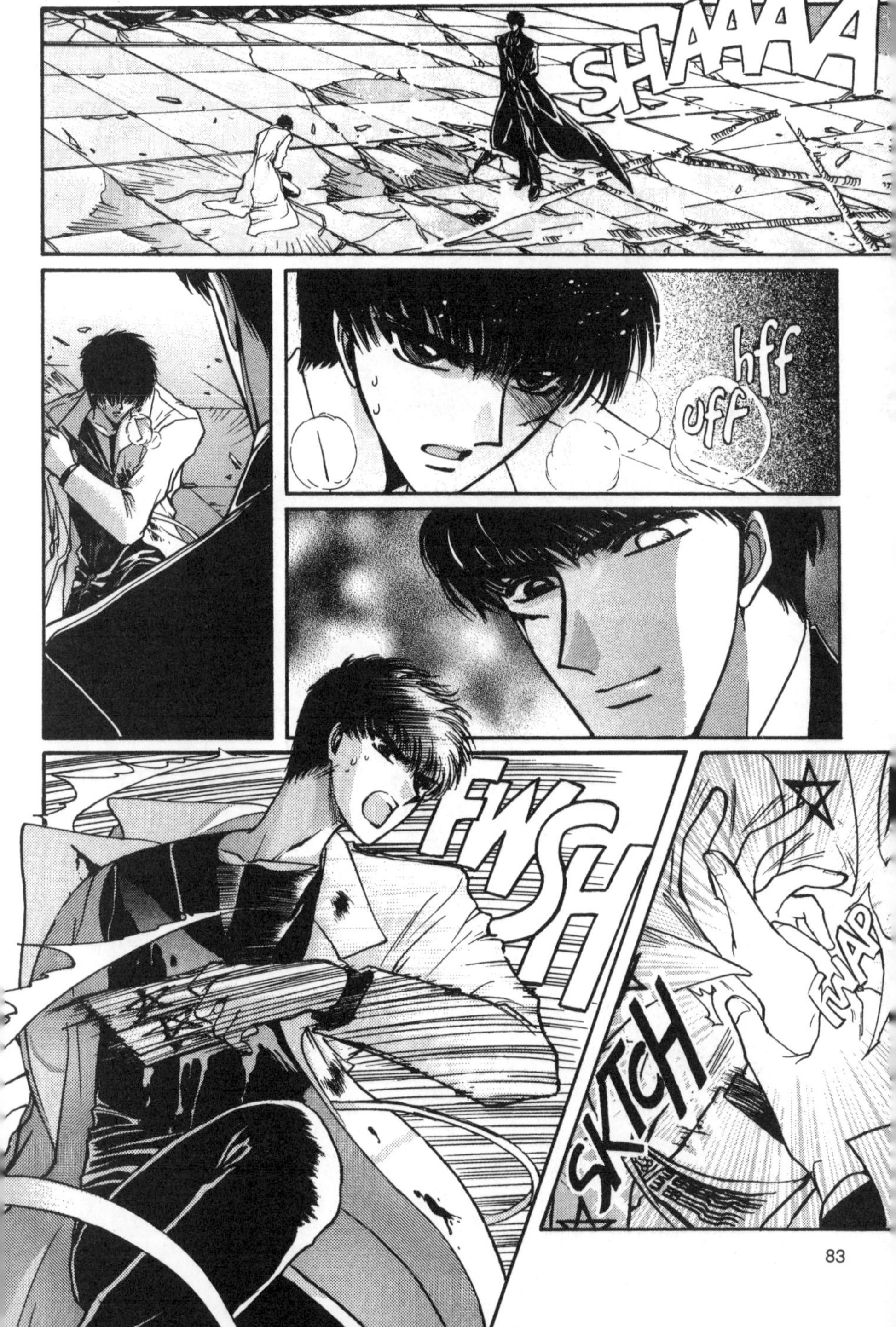
SHAAAAA
hff
uff
FWSH
SKTCH
FWAP

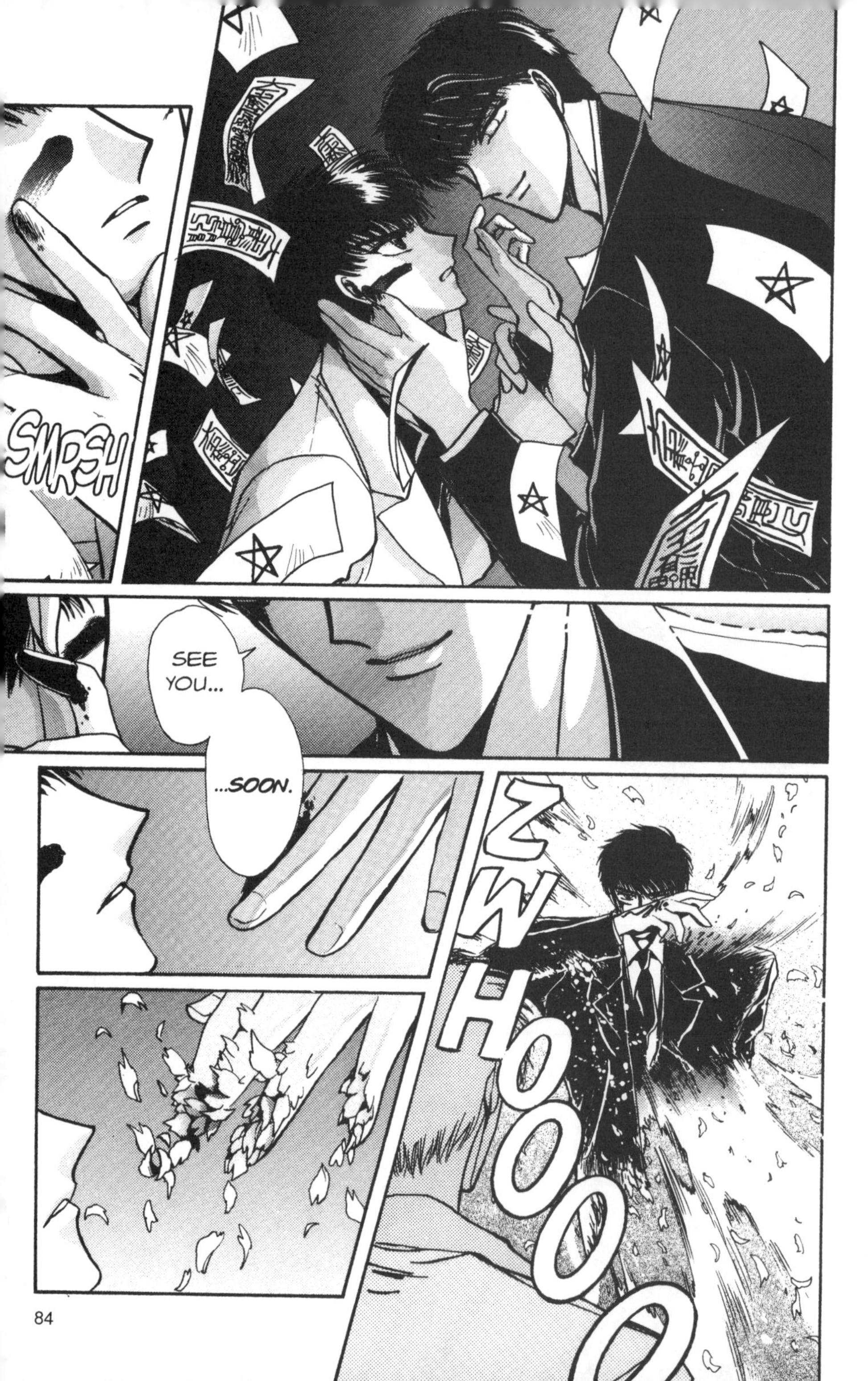
SMASH
SEE YOU...
...SOON.
ZWHOOOOO

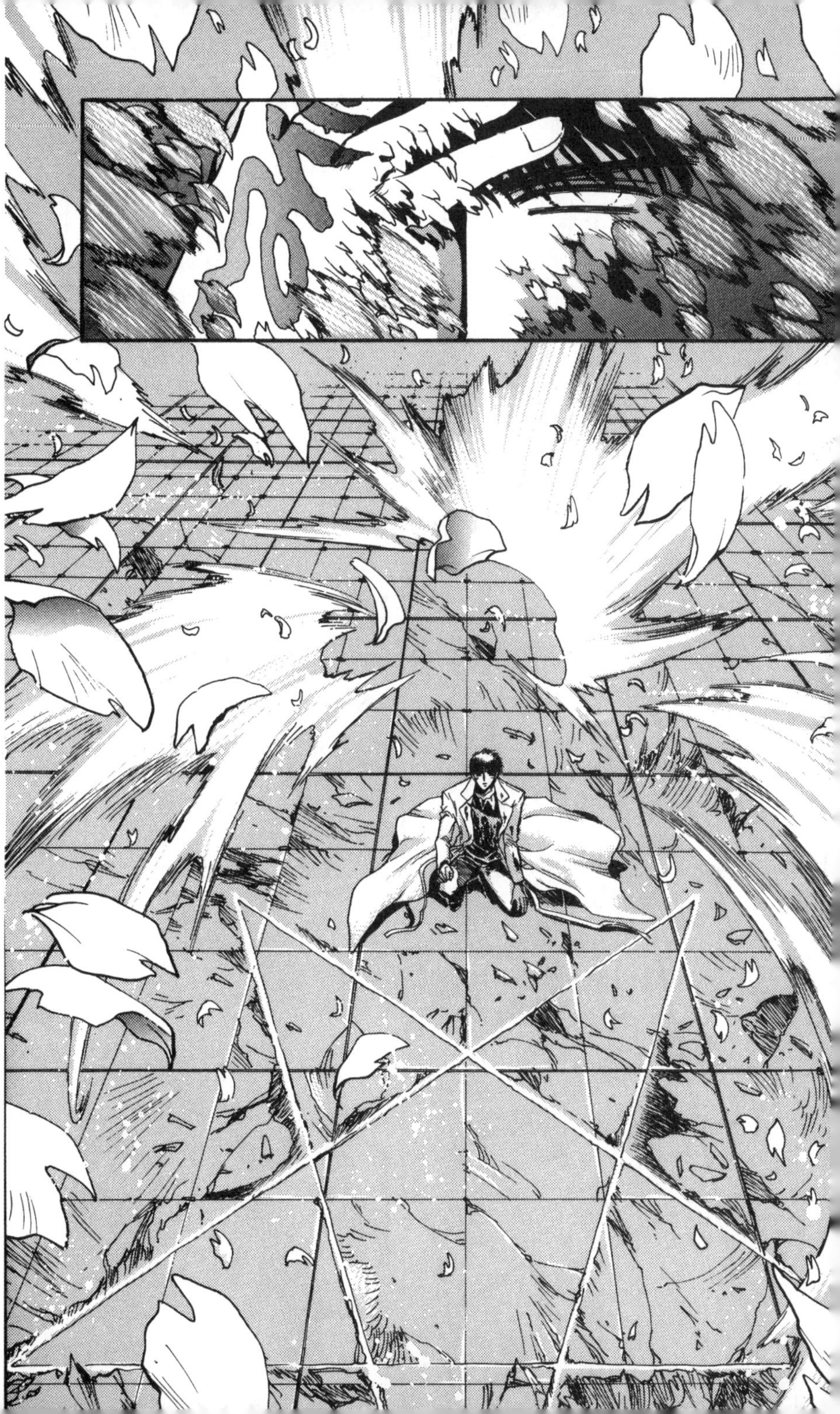

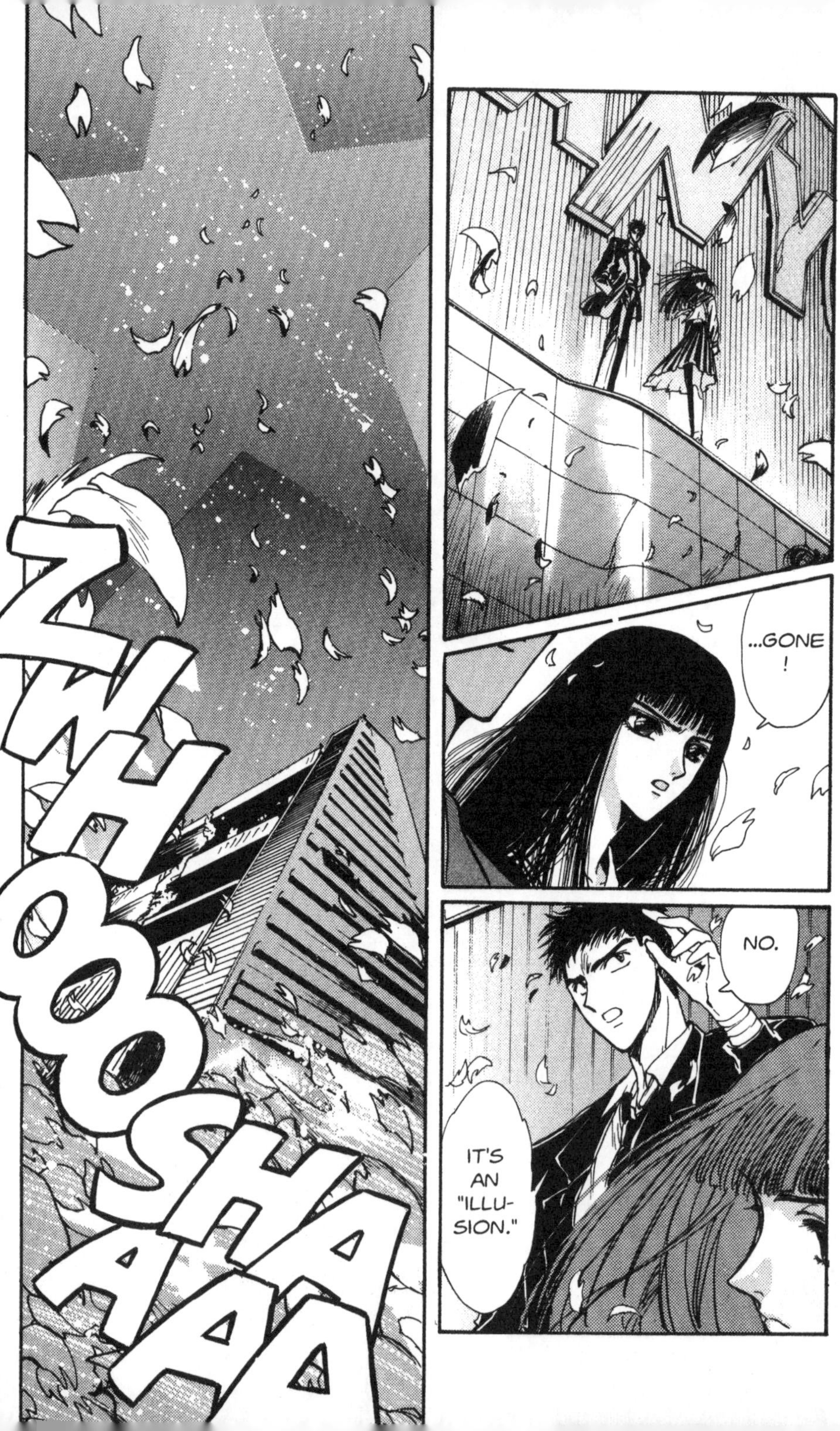
...GONE !
NO.
IT'S AN "ILLUSION."
ZWHOOOSHAAAAA

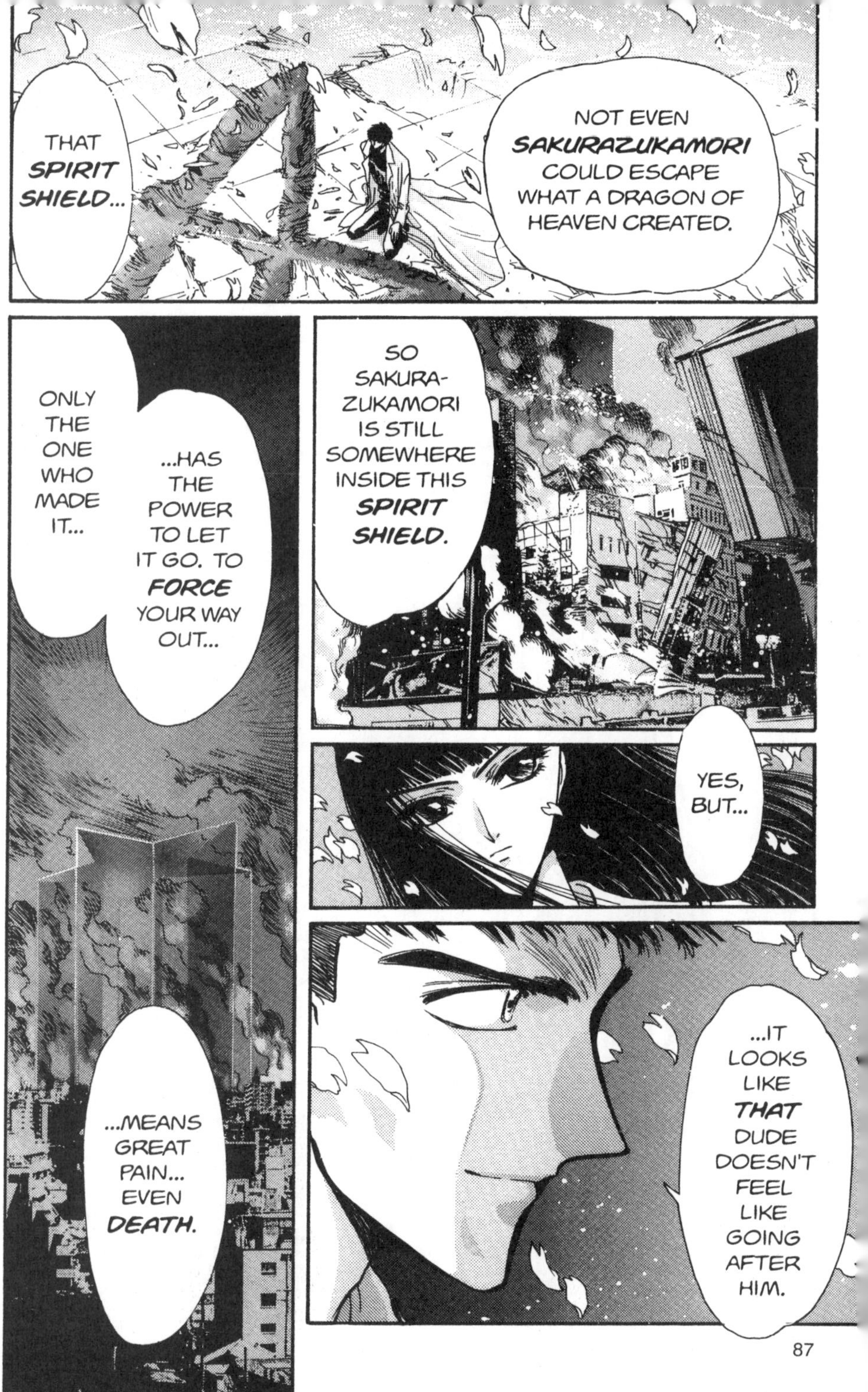
THAT SPIRIT SHIELD...
NOT EVEN SAKURAZUKAMORI COULD ESCAPE WHAT A DRAGON OF HEAVEN CREATED.
ONLY THE ONE WHO MADE IT...
...HAS THE POWER TO LET IT GO. TO FORCE YOUR WAY OUT...
...MEANS GREAT PAIN... EVEN DEATH.
SO SAKURAZUKAMORI IS STILL SOMEWHERE INSIDE THIS SPIRIT SHIELD.
YES, BUT...
...IT LOOKS LIKE THAT DUDE DOESN'T FEEL LIKE GOING AFTER HIM.

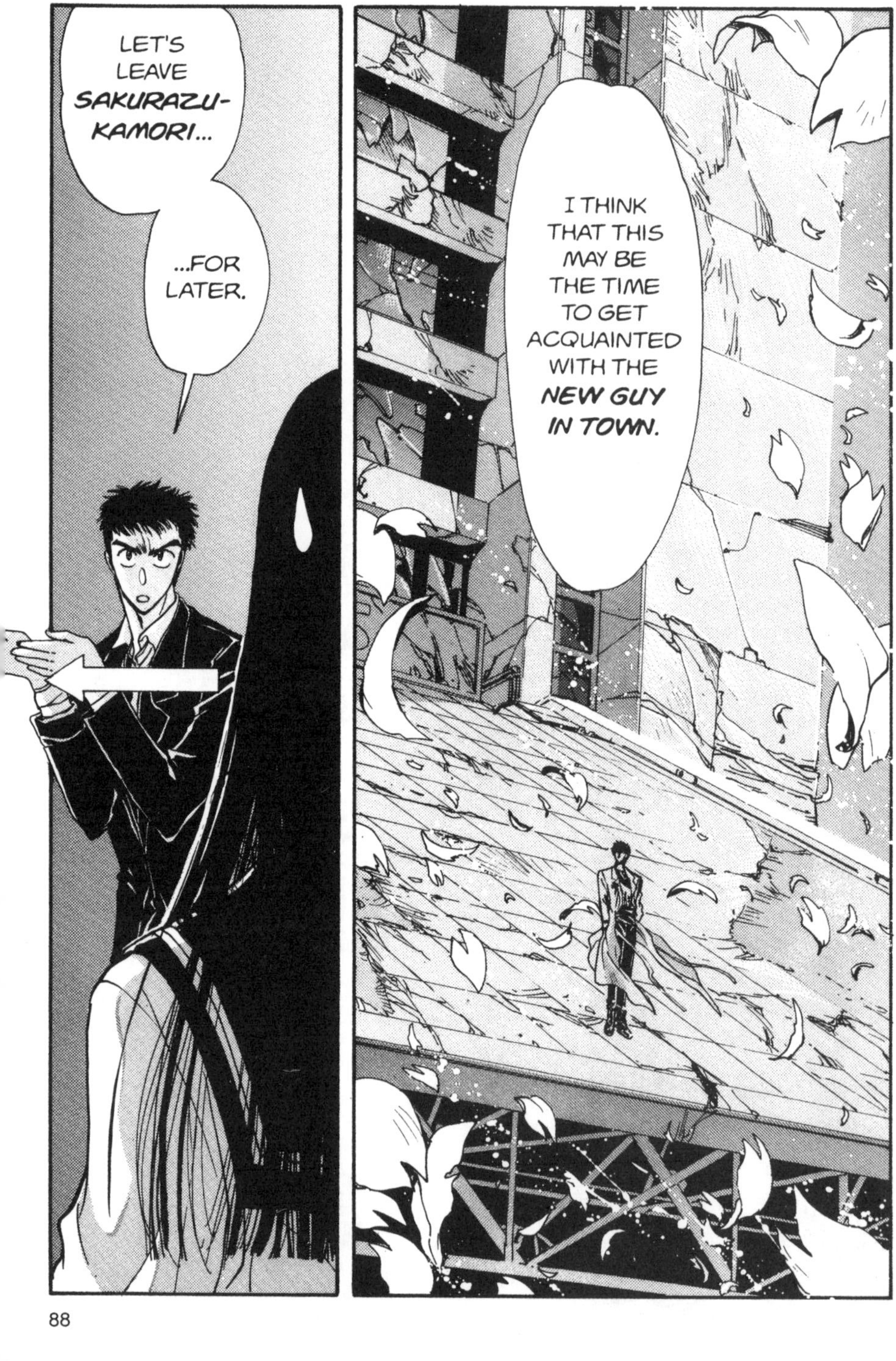
I THINK THAT THIS MAY BE THE TIME TO GET ACQUAINTED WITH THE NEW GUY IN TOWN.
LET'S LEAVE SAKURAZUKAMORI...
...FOR LATER.

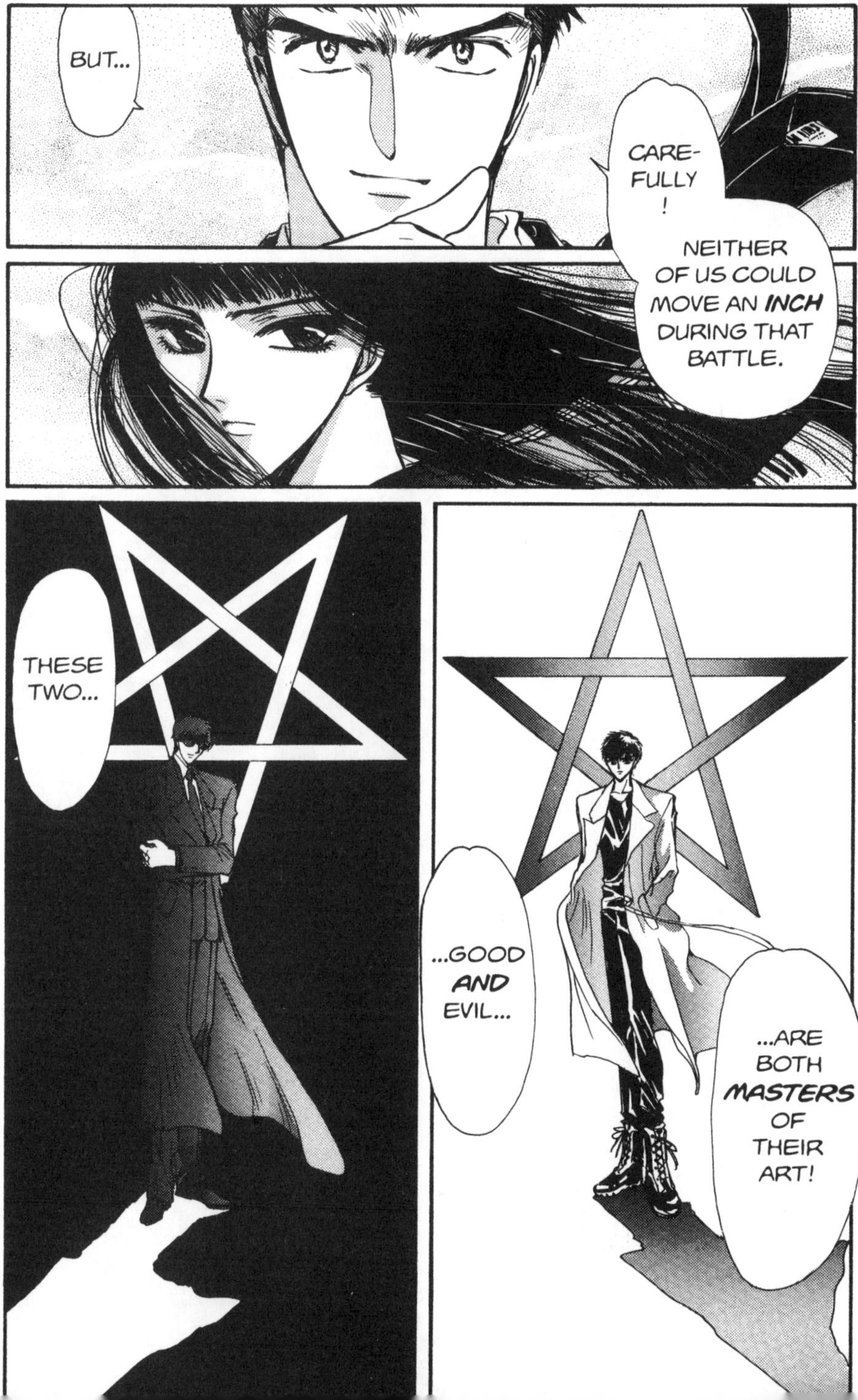
BUT...
CARE-FULLY!
NEITHER OF US COULD MOVE AN INCH DURING THAT BATTLE.
THESE TWO...
...GOOD AND EVIL...
...ARE BOTH MASTERS OF THEIR ART!

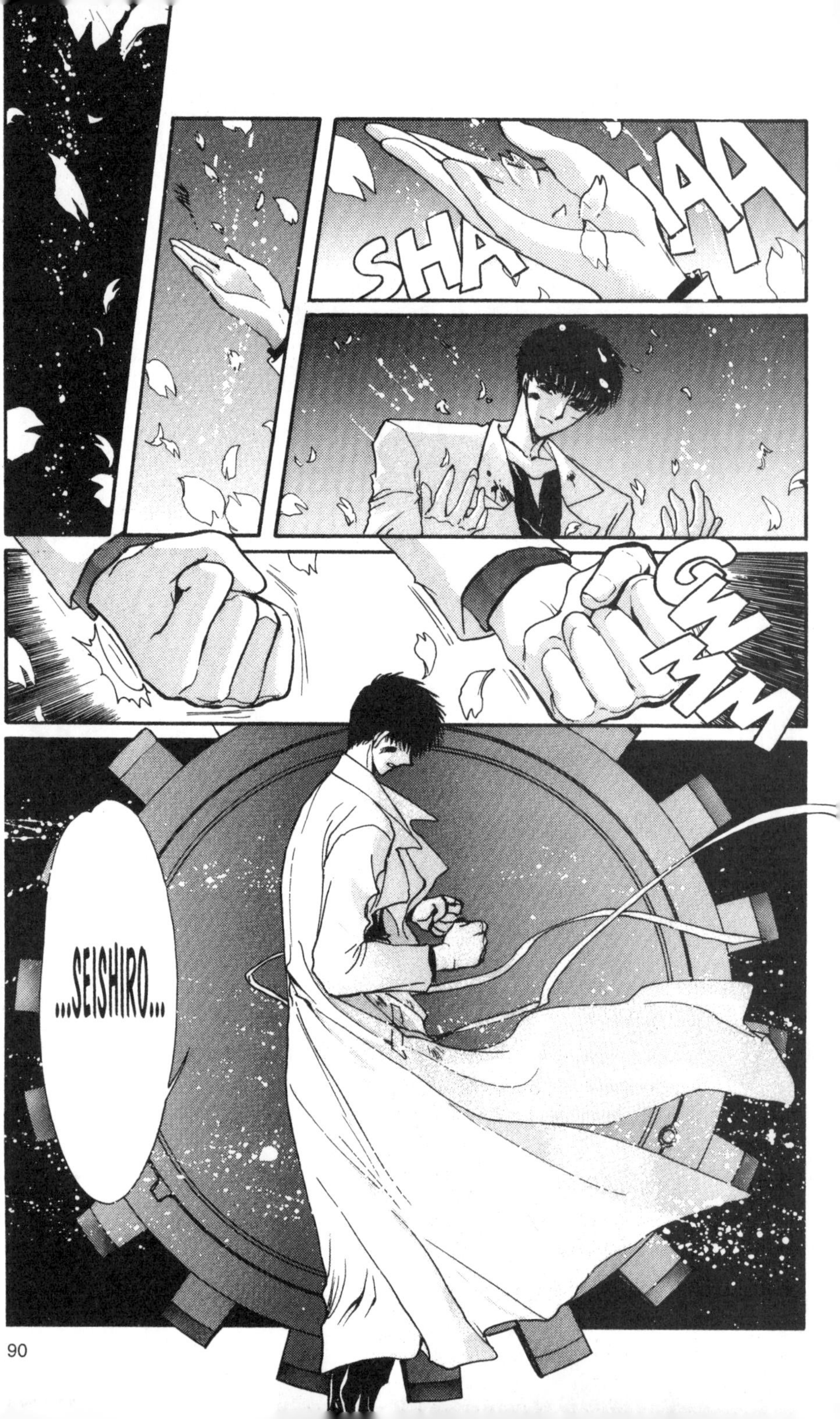
SHAAAA
GWMM
...SEISHIRO...

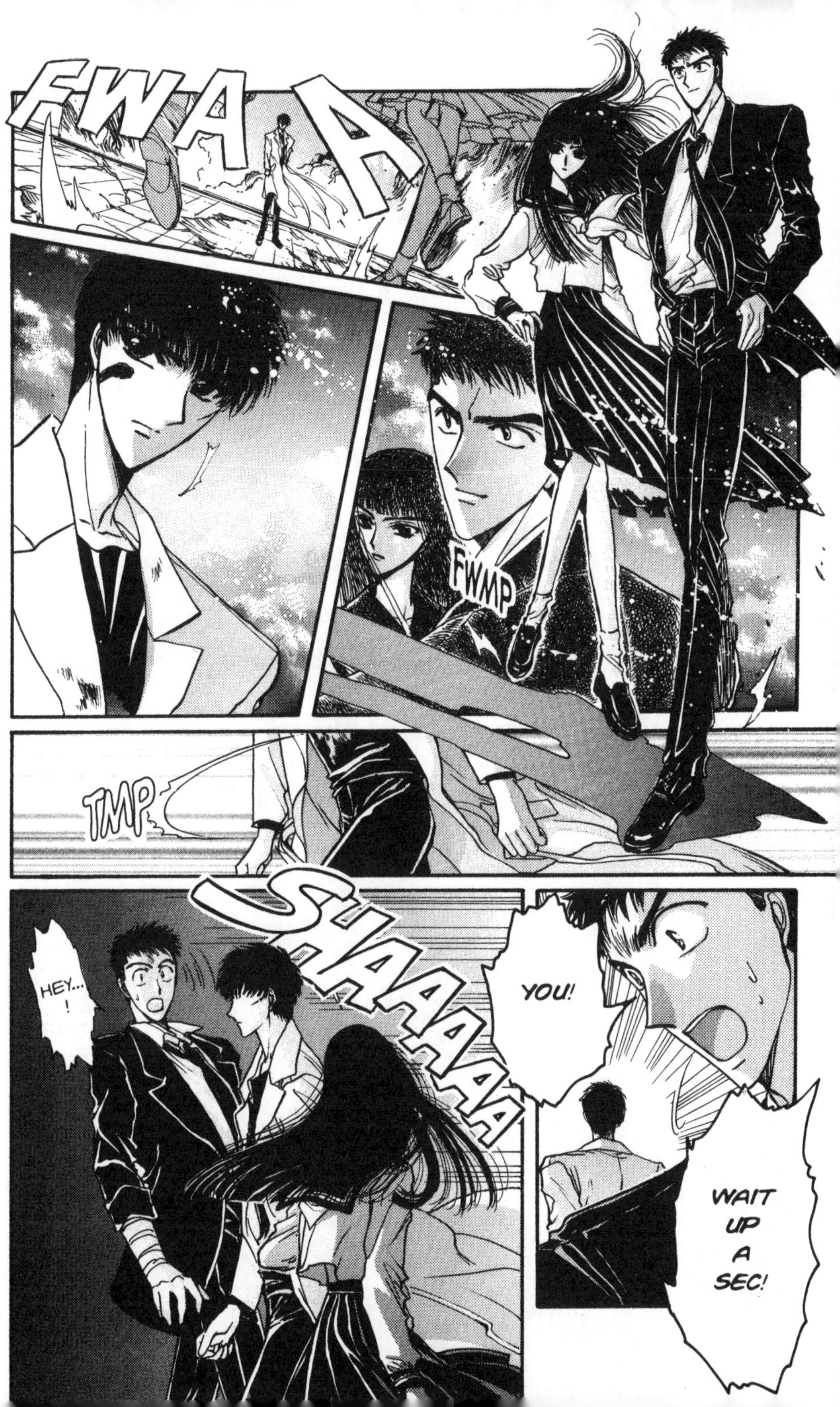
FWAA
FWMP
TMP
YOU!
WAIT UP A SEC!
SHAAAAA
HEY... !

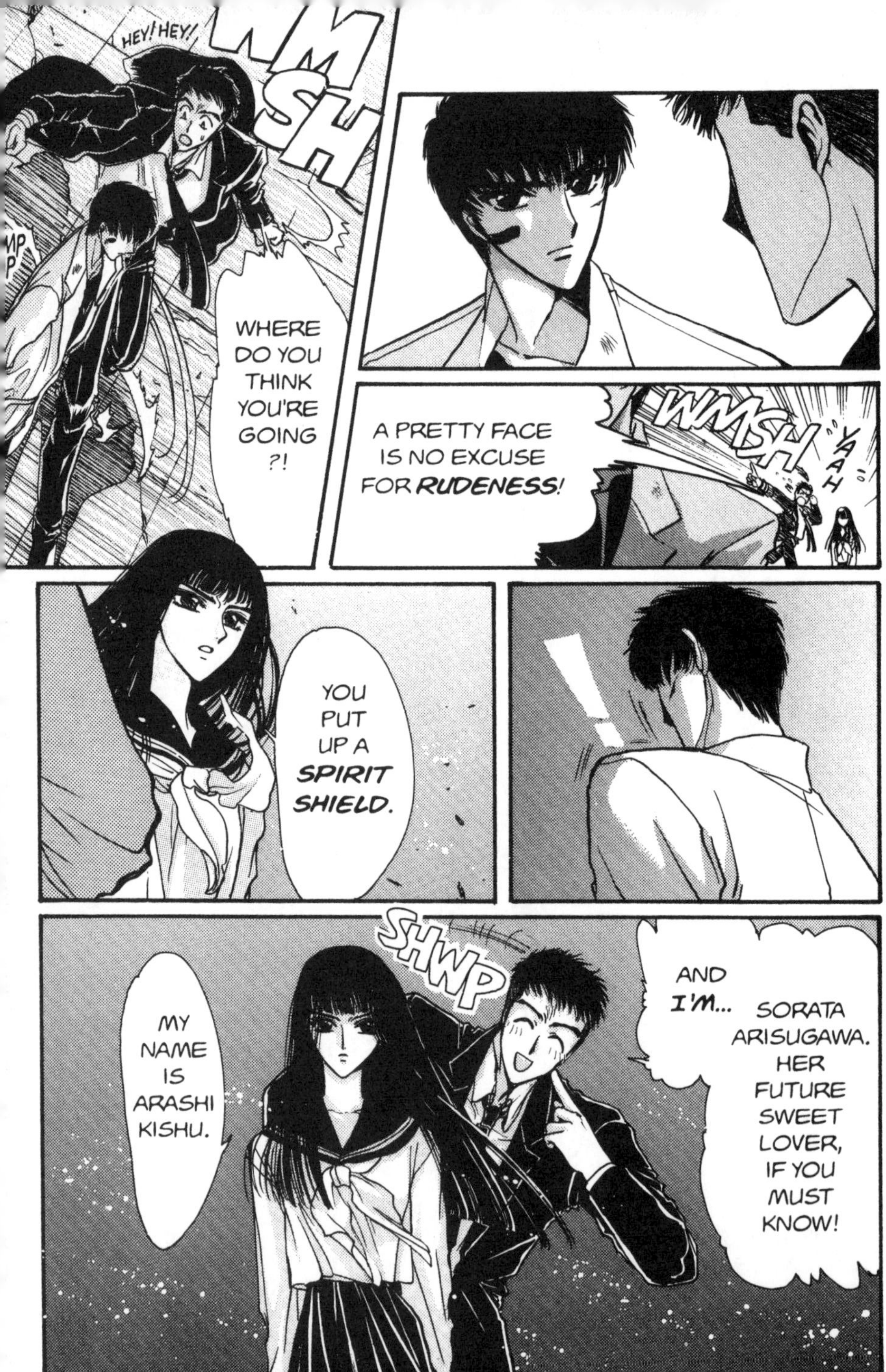
HEY! HEY!
WMMSH
WHERE DO YOU THINK YOU'RE GOING ?!
A PRETTY FACE IS NO EXCUSE FOR **RUDENESS**!
WMSH
YAAAH
YOU PUT UP A **SPIRIT SHIELD**.
!
SHWP
MY NAME IS ARASHI KISHU.
AND **I'M**...
SORATA ARISUGAWA. HER FUTURE SWEET LOVER, IF YOU MUST KNOW!

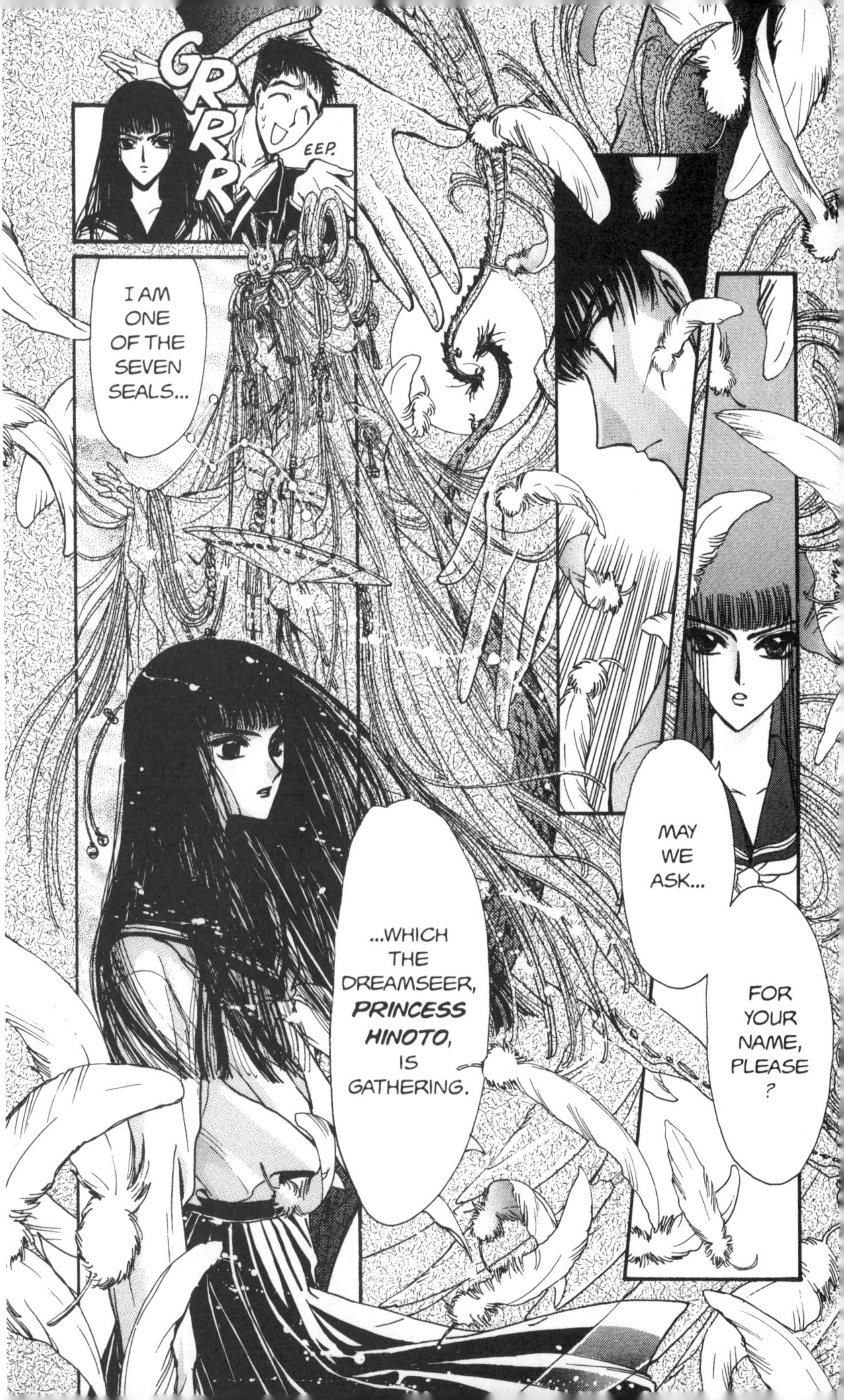
GRRR
EEP.
I AM ONE OF THE SEVEN SEALS...
...WHICH THE DREAMSEER, **PRINCESS HINOTO**, IS GATHERING.
MAY WE ASK...
FOR YOUR NAME, PLEASE ?

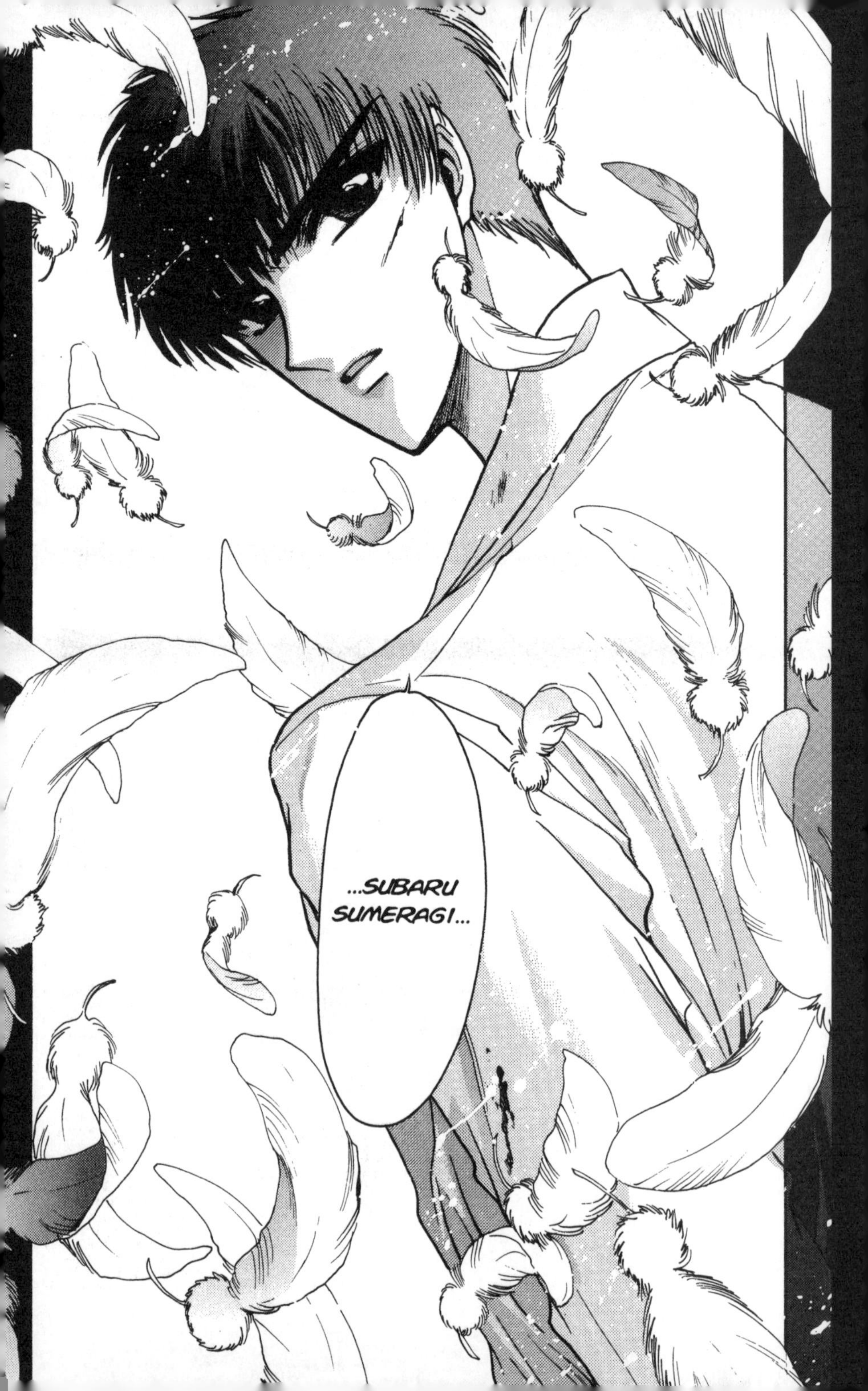
...SUBARU SUMERAGI...

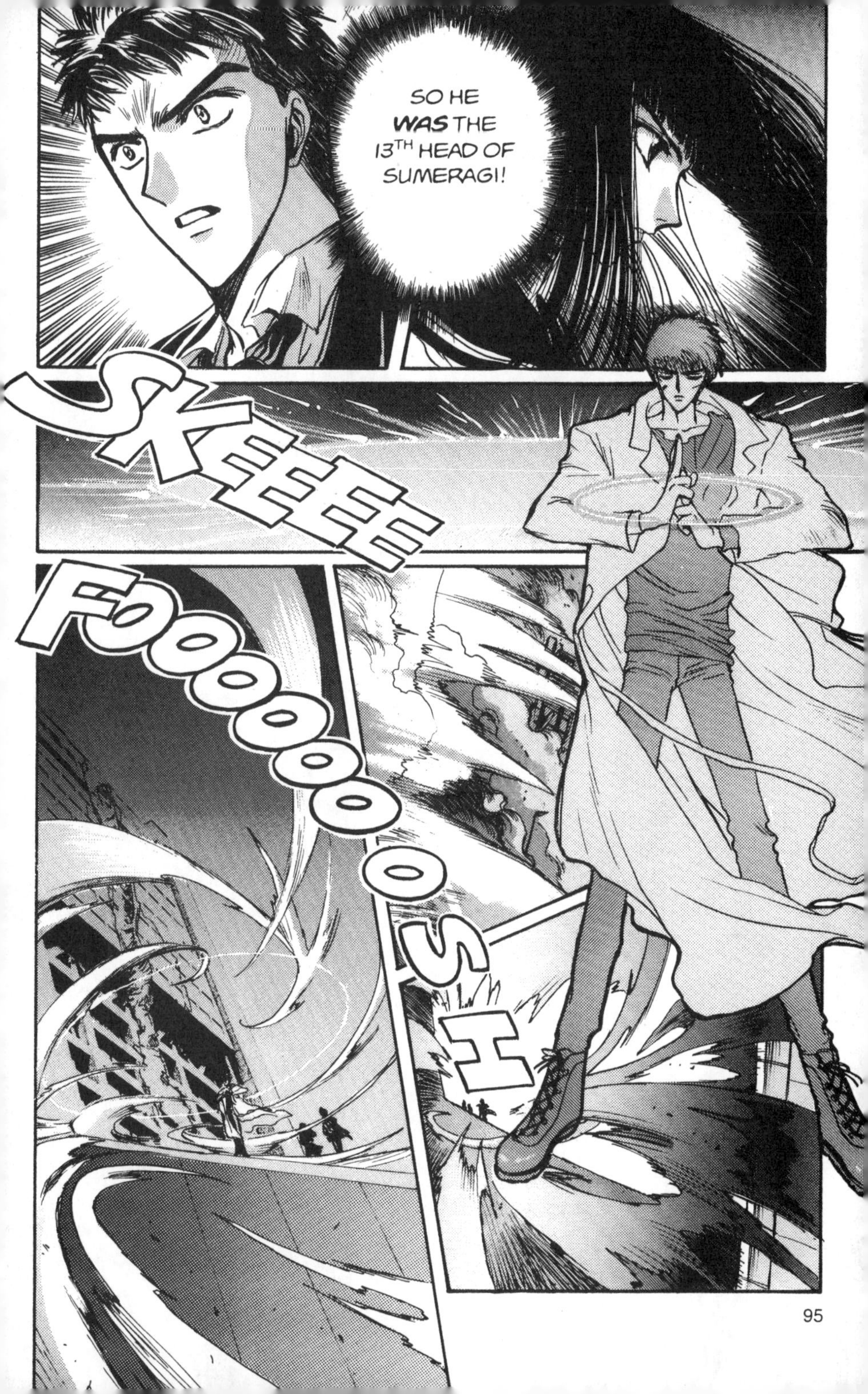
SO HE **WAS** THE 13TH HEAD OF SUMERAGI!
SKEEEE
FOOOOOOOOSH

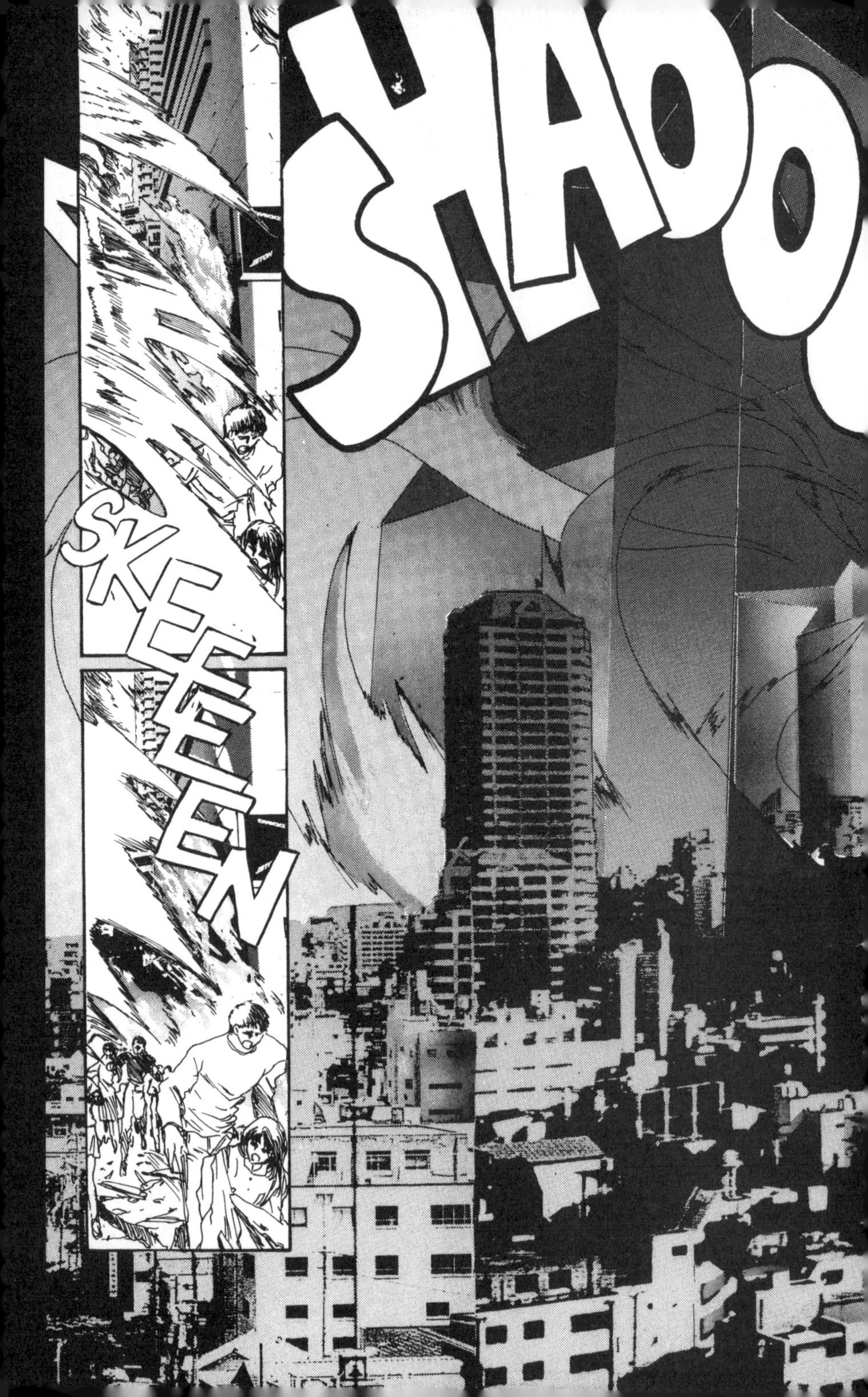
SHAOO
SKEEEEEN

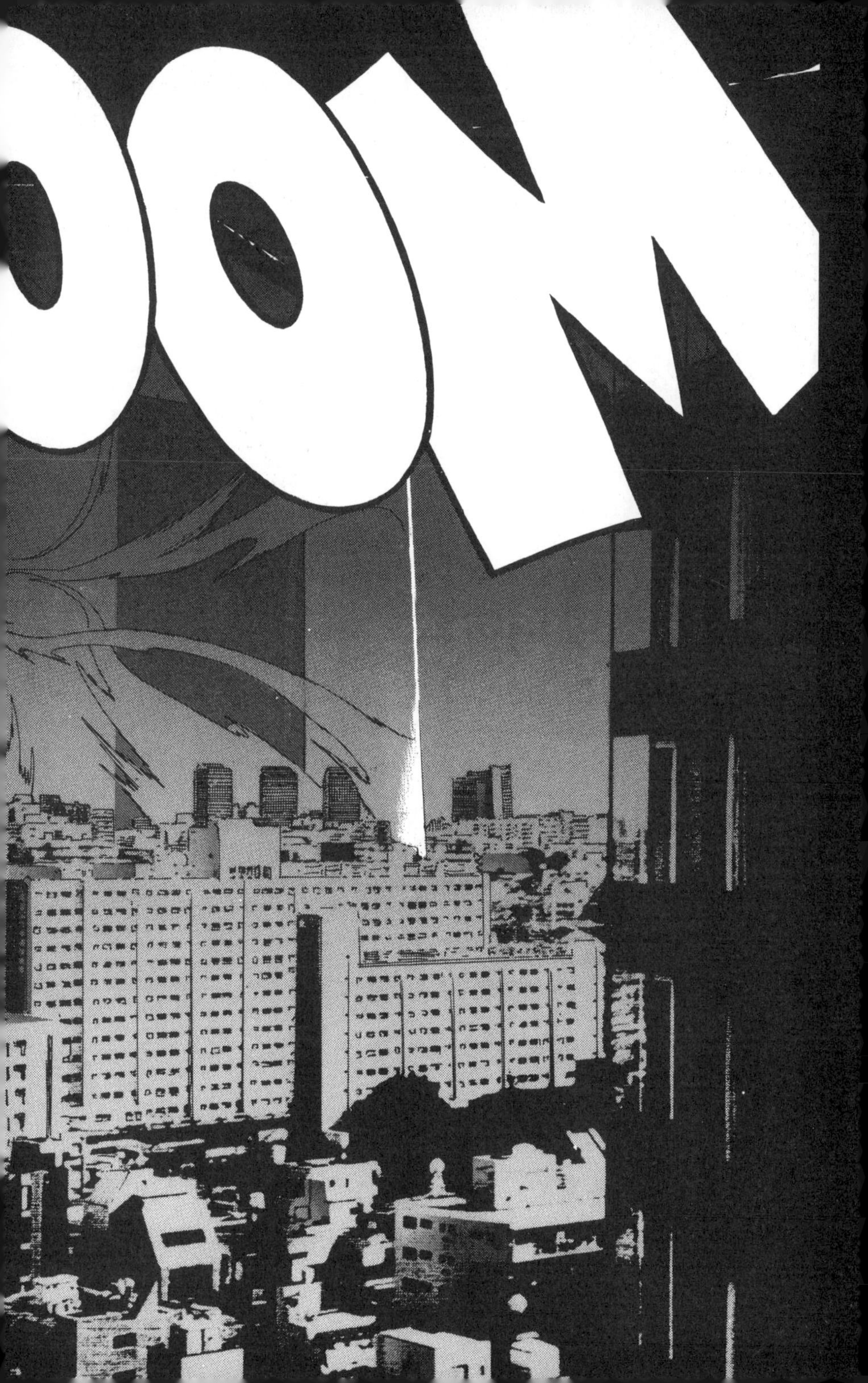
OOM

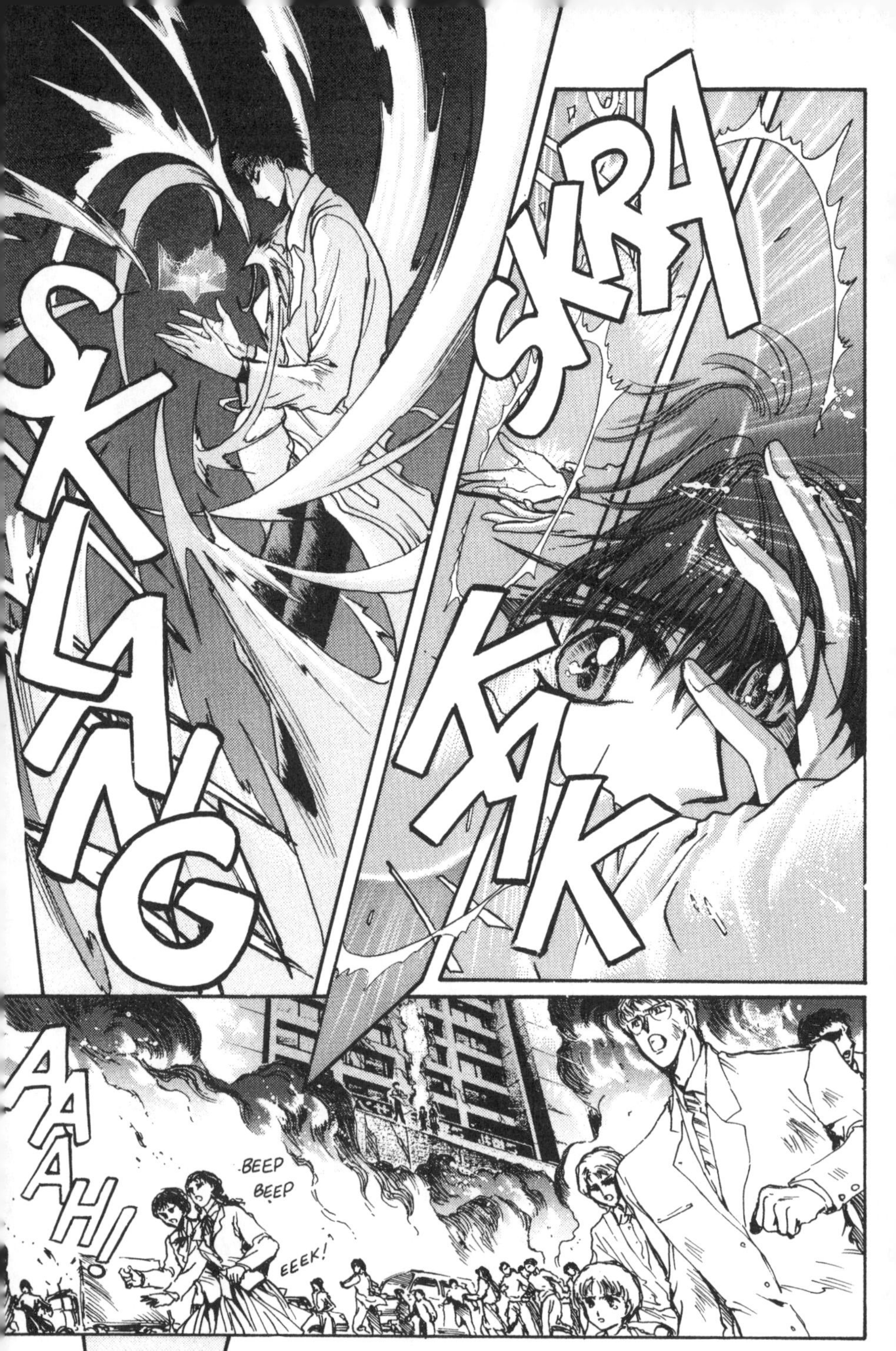
SKRAKAKK
SKLANG
BEEP BEEP
EEEK!
AAAAH!

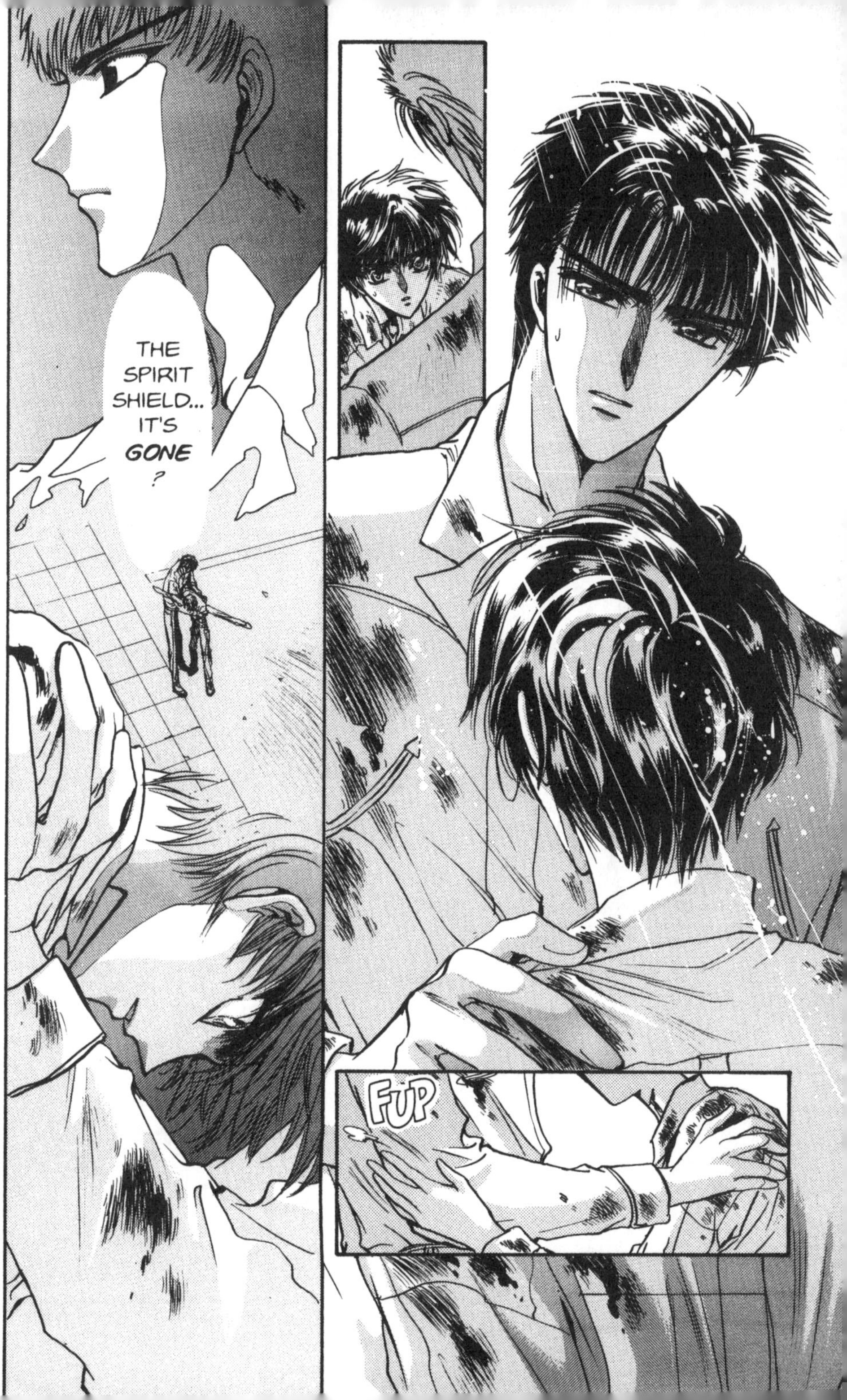
THE SPIRIT SHIELD... IT'S GONE ?
FUP

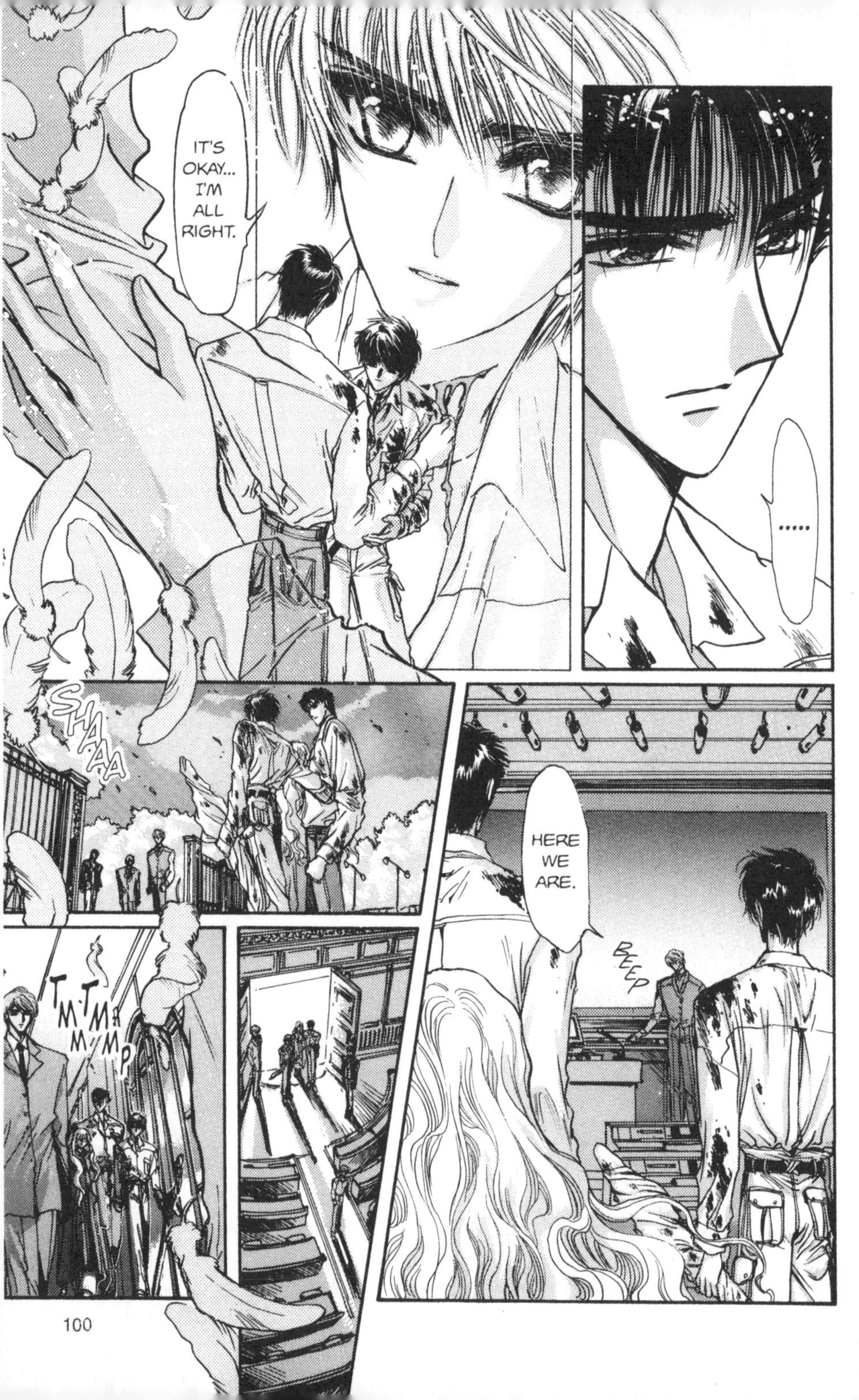
......
IT'S OKAY... I'M ALL RIGHT.
HERE WE ARE.
BEEP
SHAAAA
TMTMTMMMP

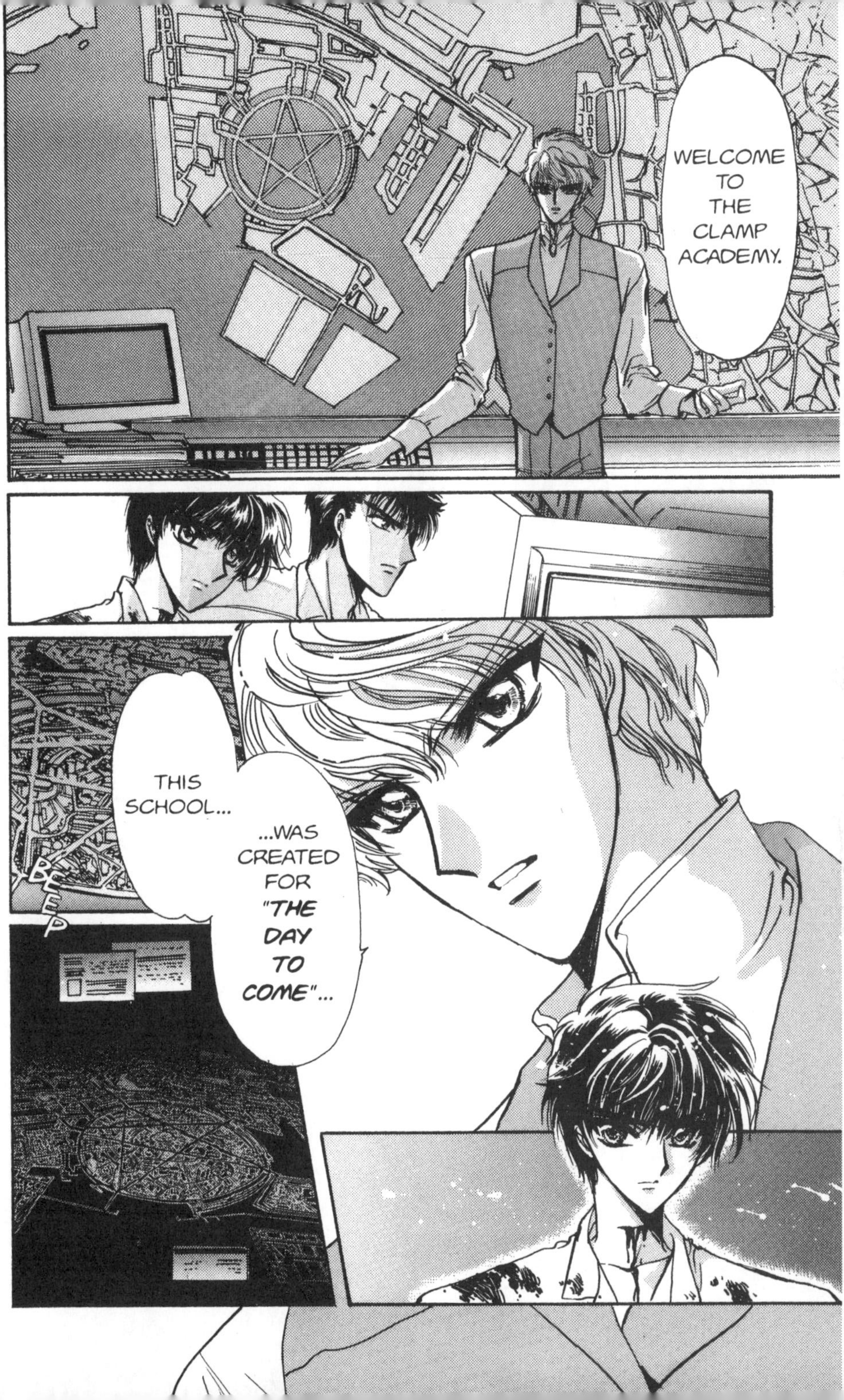
WELCOME TO THE CLAMP ACADEMY.
THIS SCHOOL...
...WAS CREATED FOR "THE DAY TO COME"...
BEEP

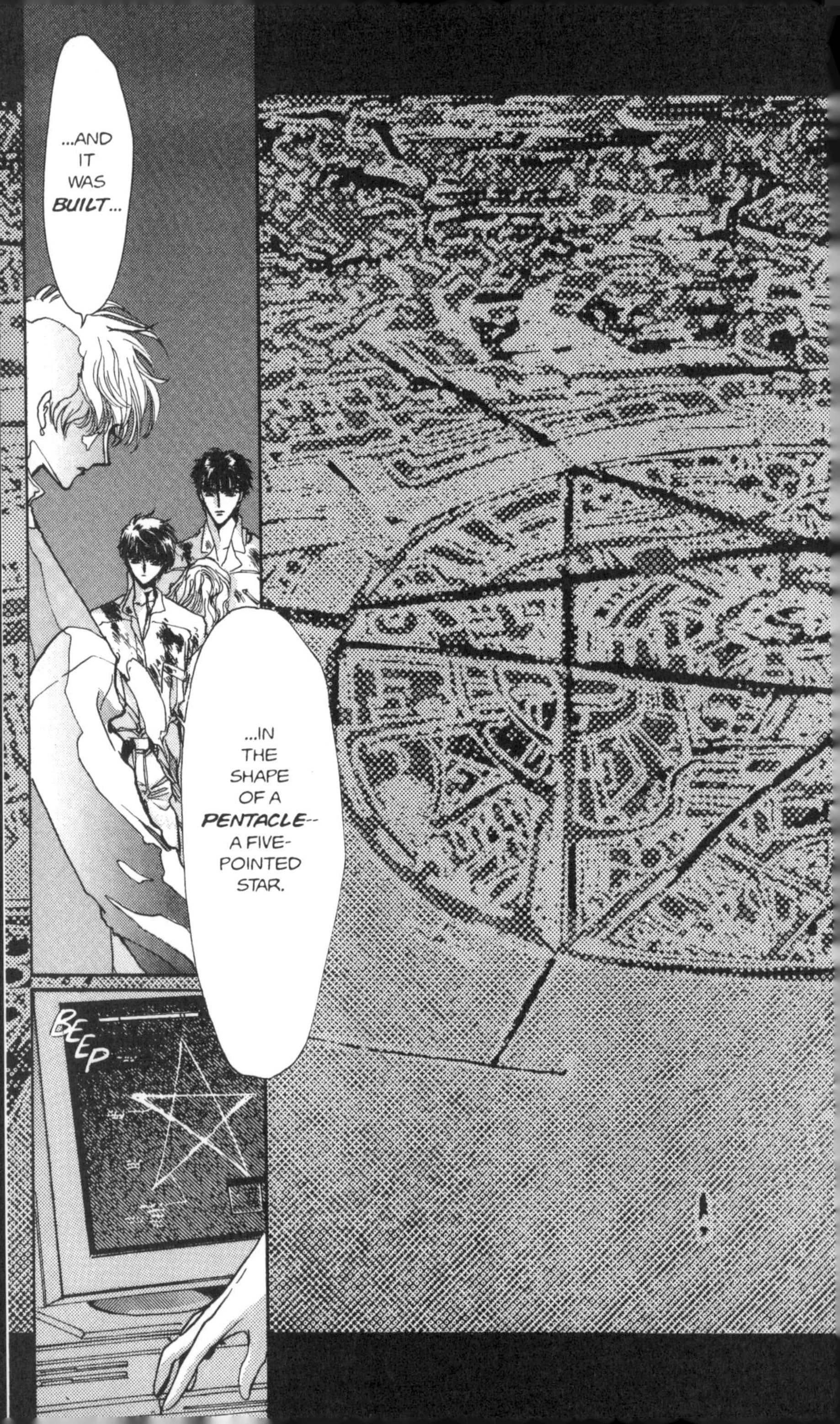
...AND IT WAS **BUILT**...
...IN THE SHAPE OF A **PENTACLE**-- A FIVE-POINTED STAR.
!
BEEP

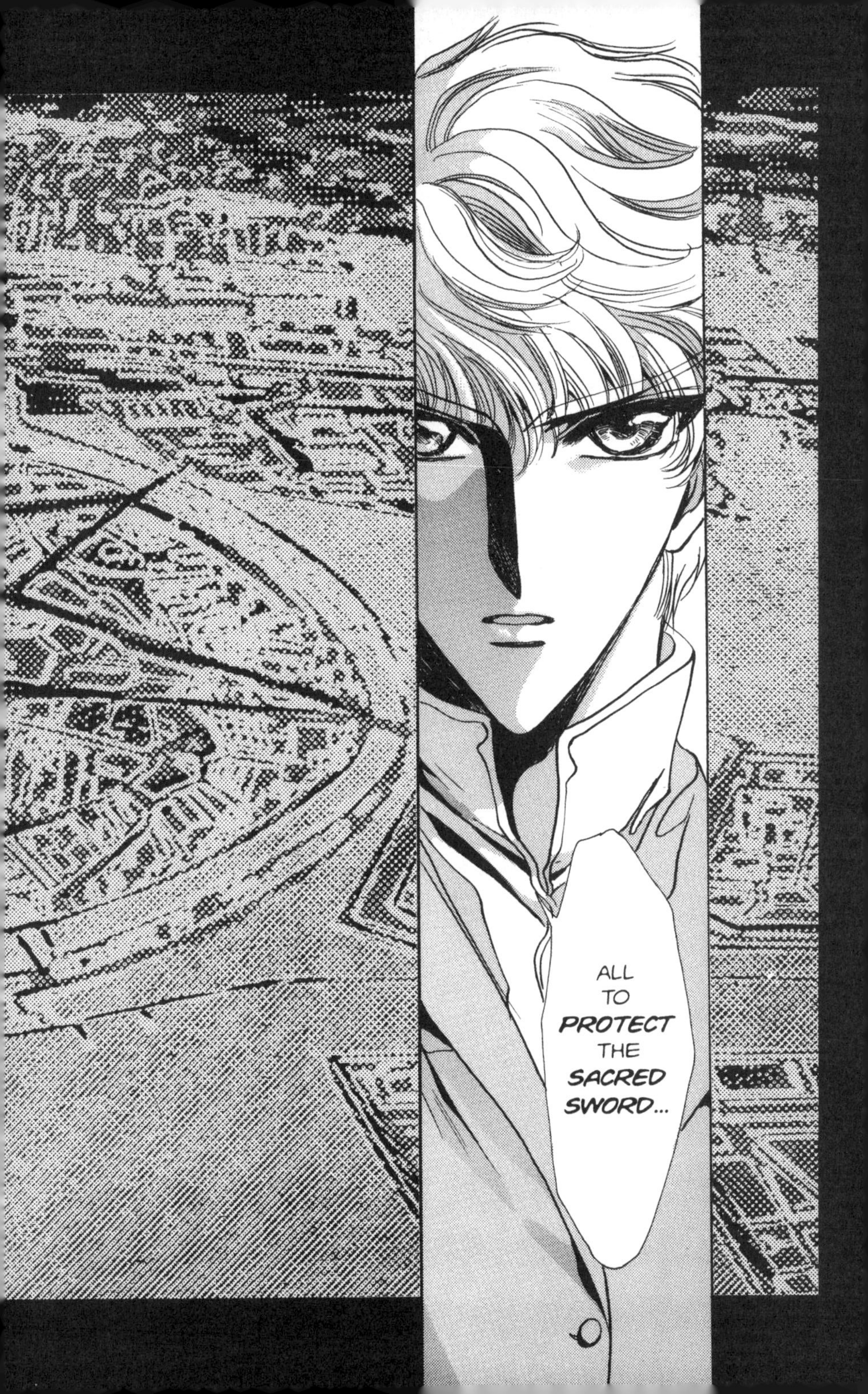
ALL TO **PROTECT** THE **SACRED SWORD**...

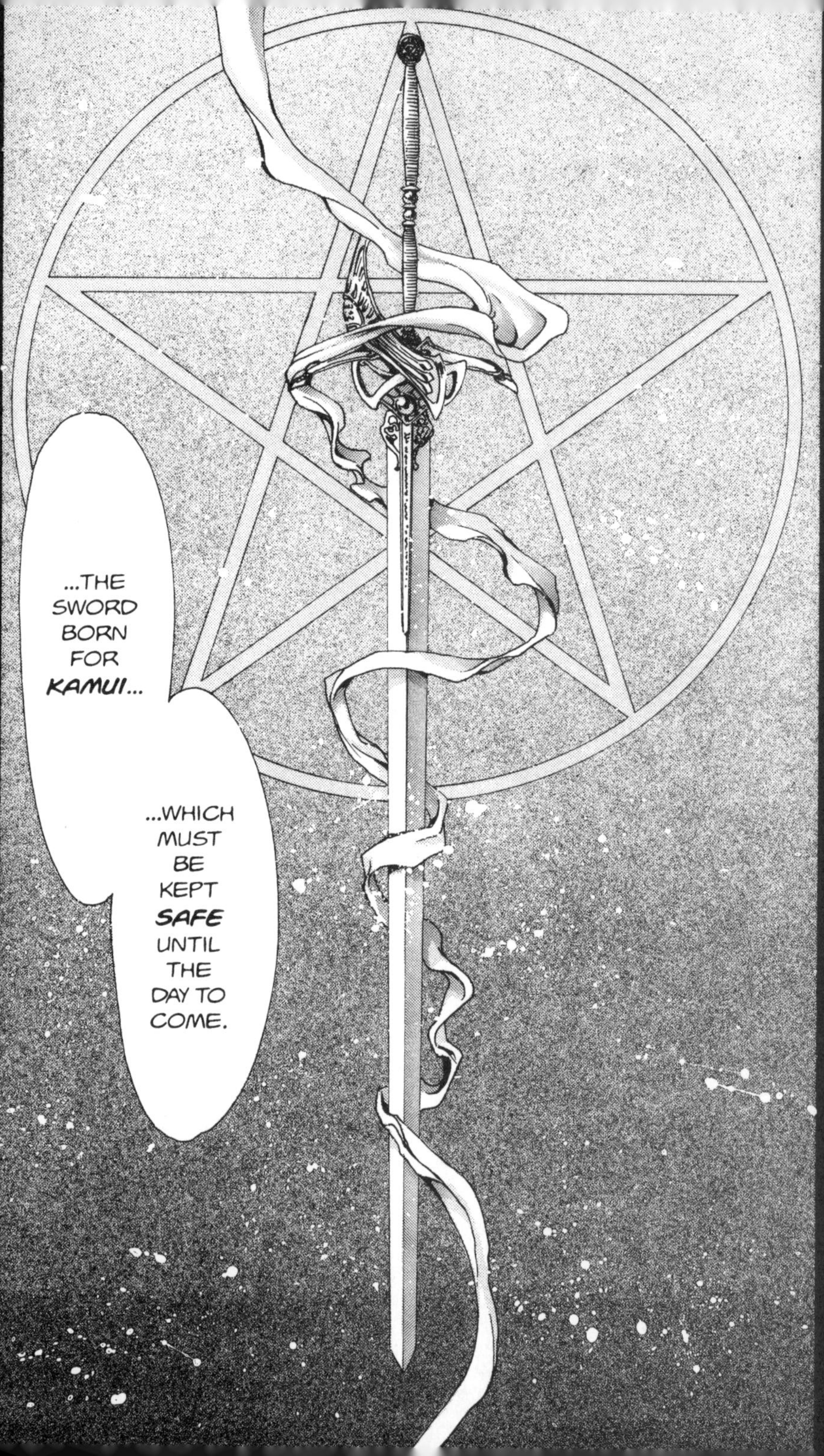
...THE SWORD BORN FOR ***KAMUI...***
...WHICH MUST BE KEPT ***SAFE*** UNTIL THE DAY TO COME.

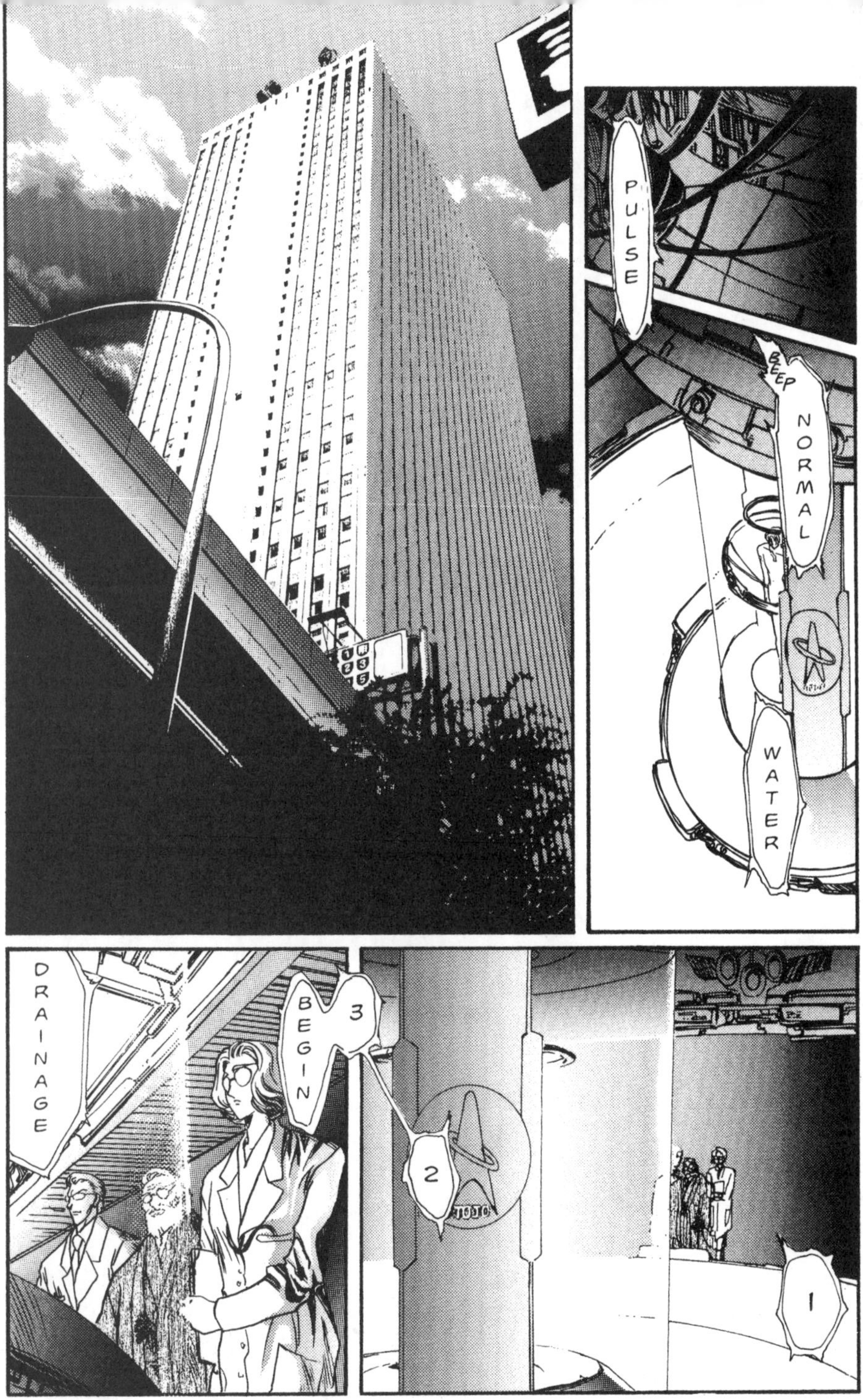
PULSE
BEEP
NORMAL
WATER
1
2
3
BEGIN
DRAINAGE

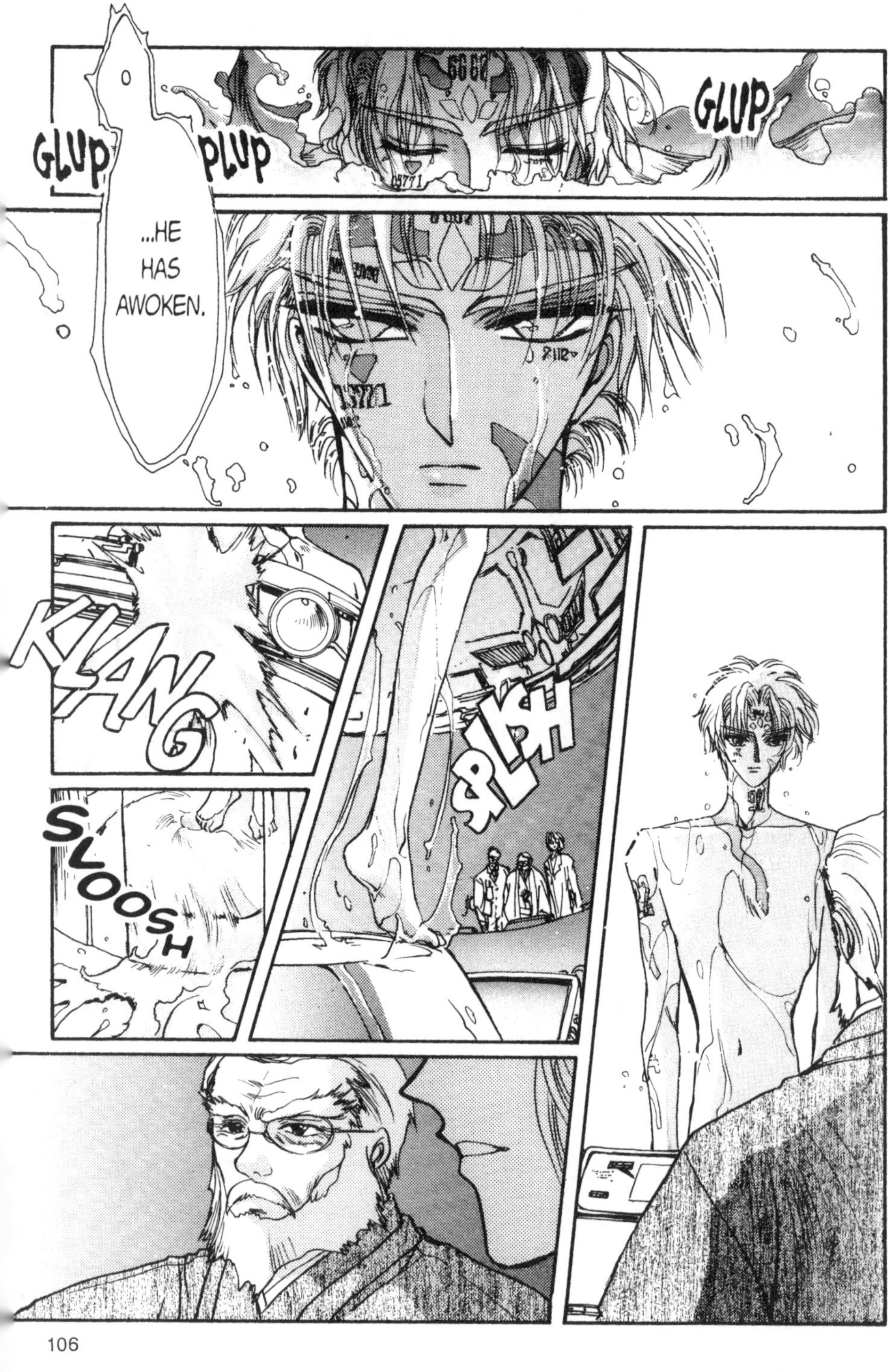
GLUP
GLUP
PLUP
...HE HAS AWOKEN.
KLANG
SPLISH
SLOOSH

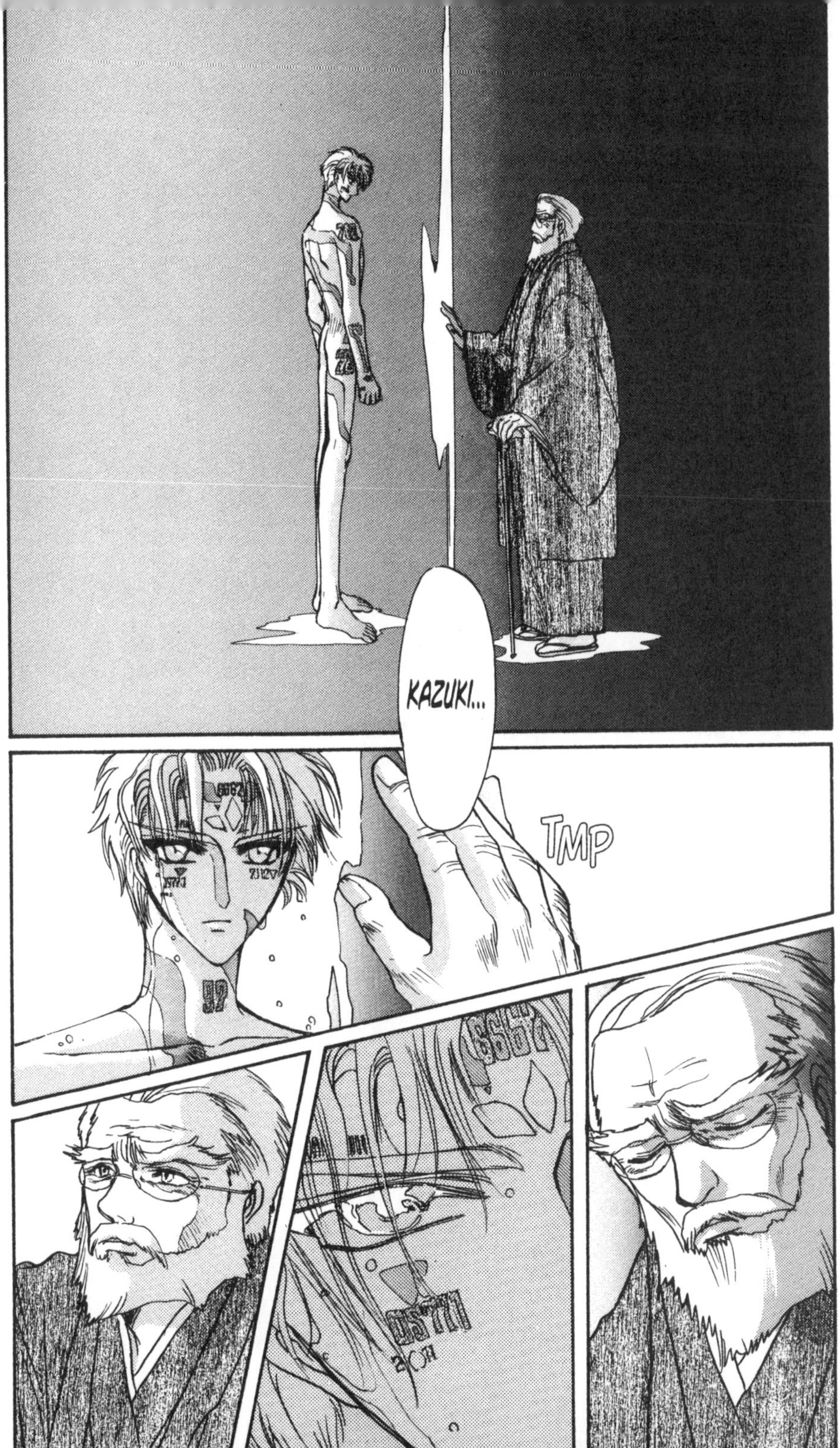
KAZUKI...
TMP

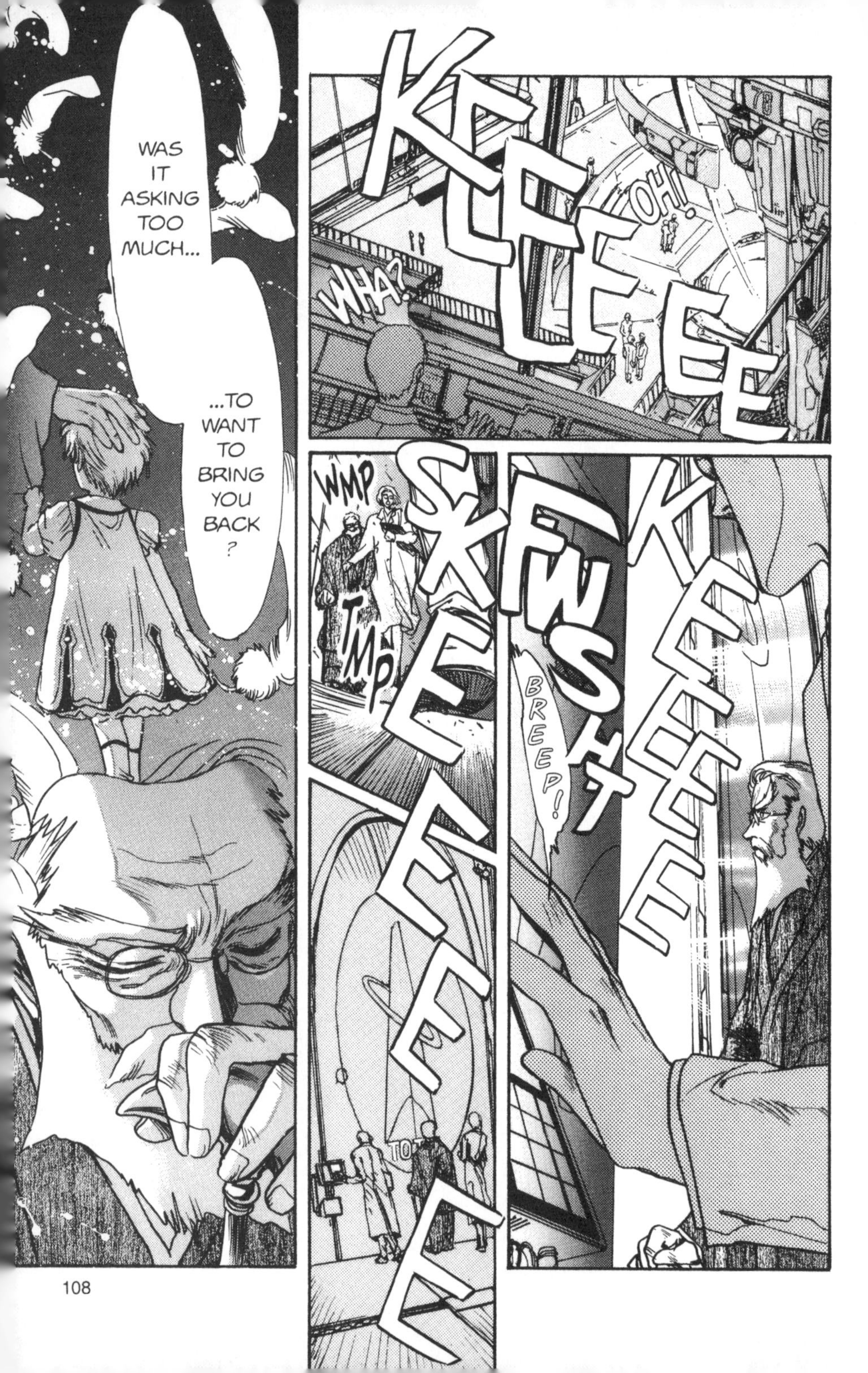
KCLEEEE
OH!
WHA?
KEEEEEE
FWSHT
BREEP!
WMP
TMP
SKEEEEEE
TOT
WAS IT ASKING TOO MUCH...
...TO WANT TO BRING YOU BACK?

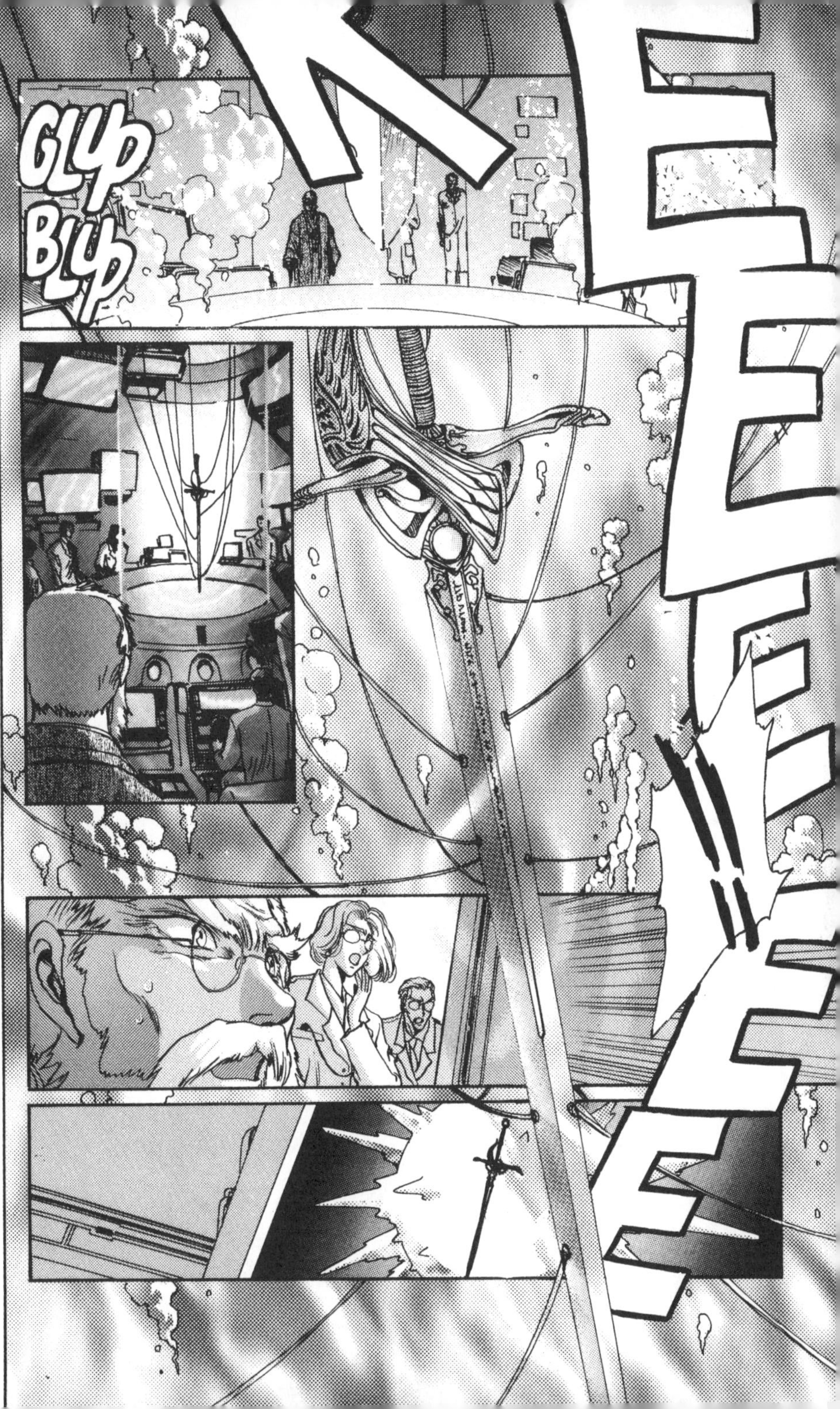
GLUP
BLUP

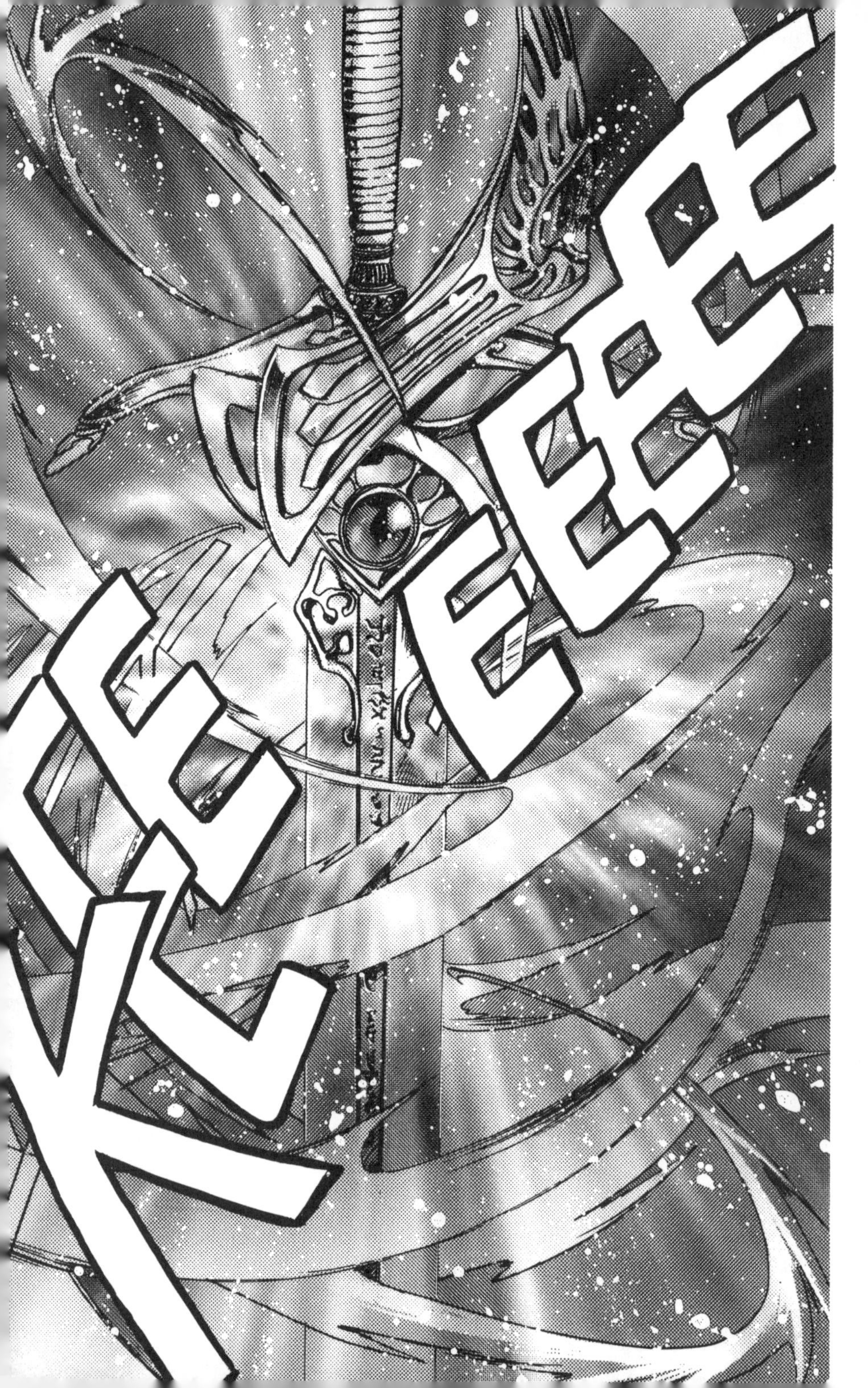

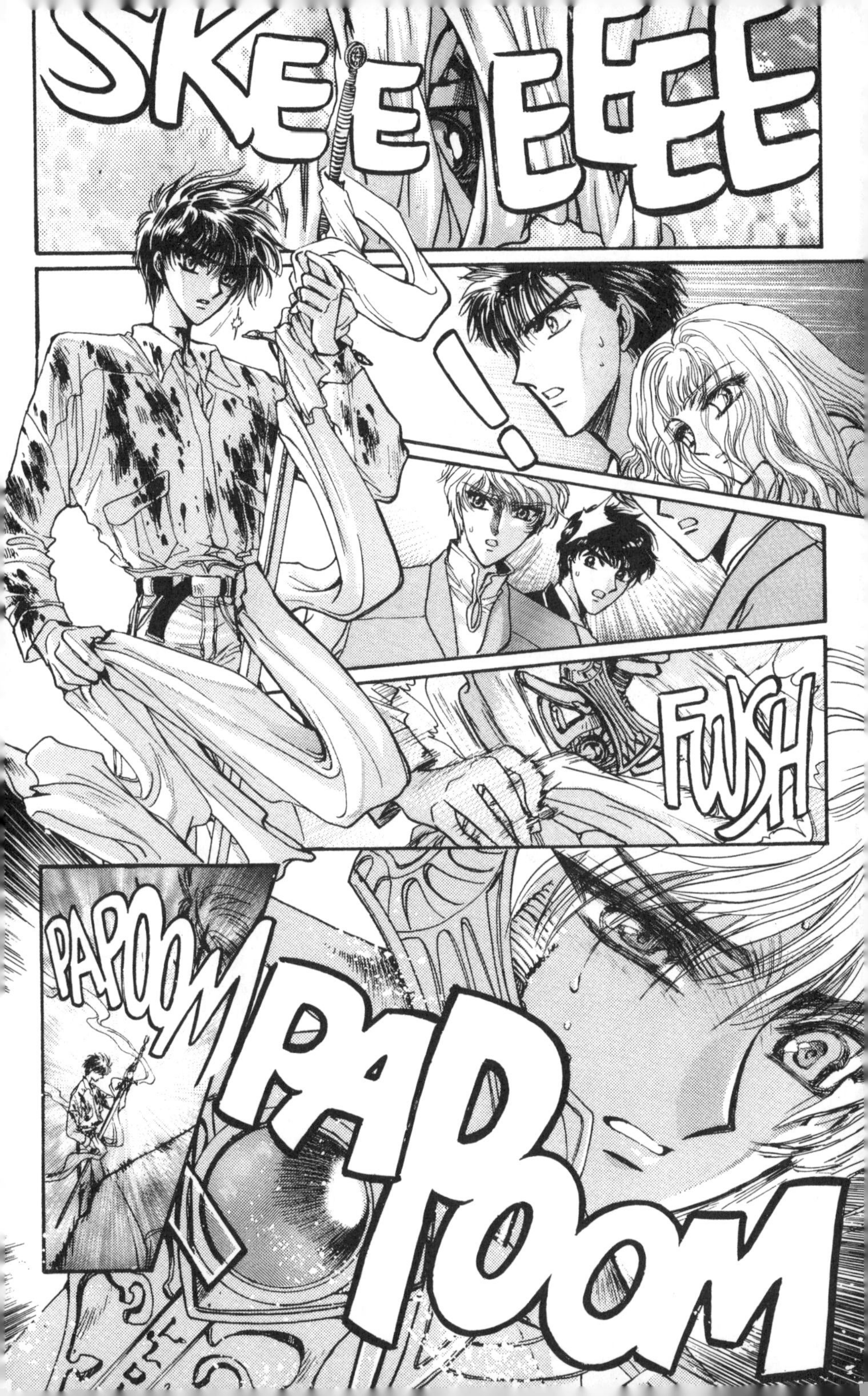
SKEEEEEEE
!
FWSH
PAPOOM
PADOOM

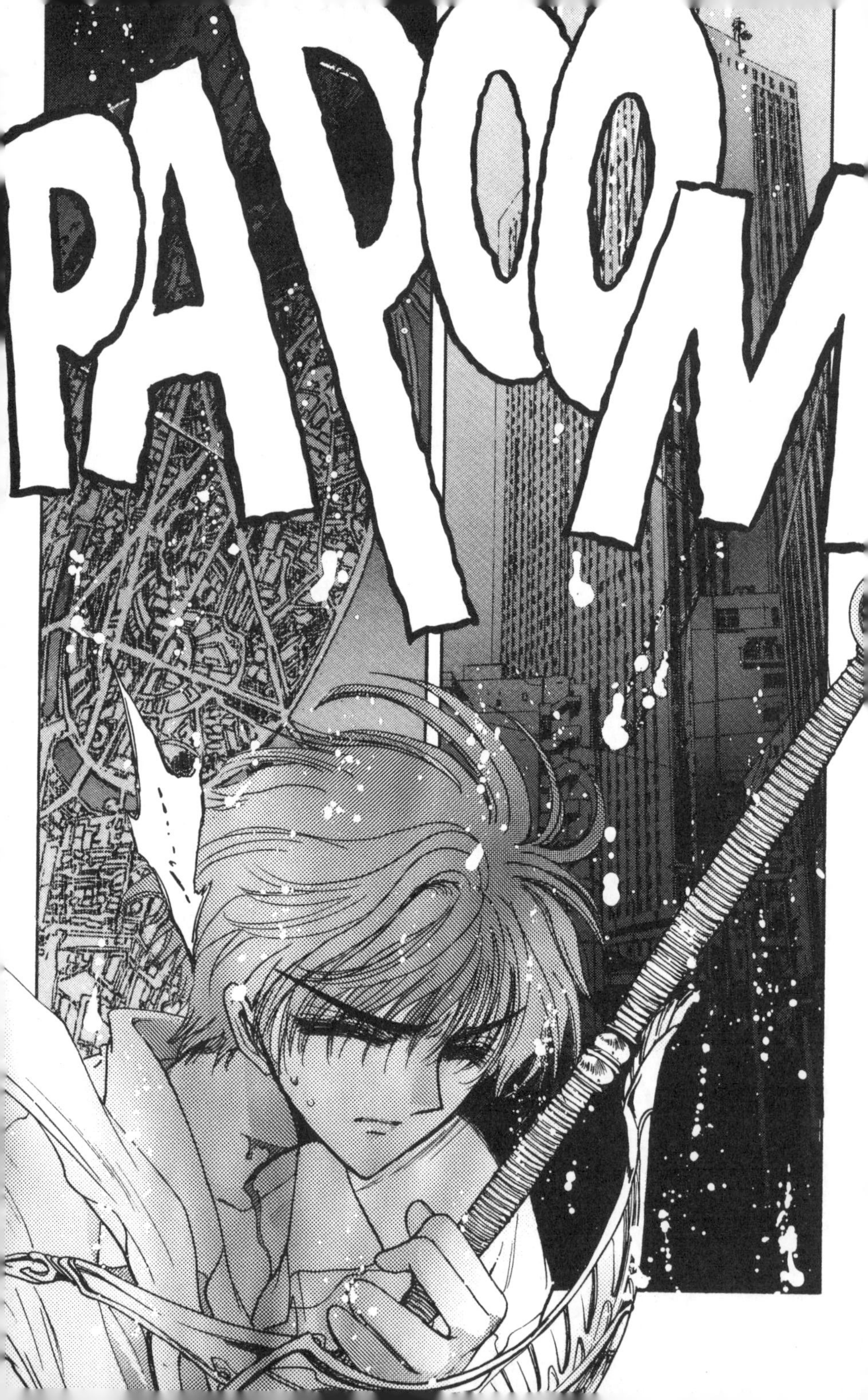
PADOOM
...

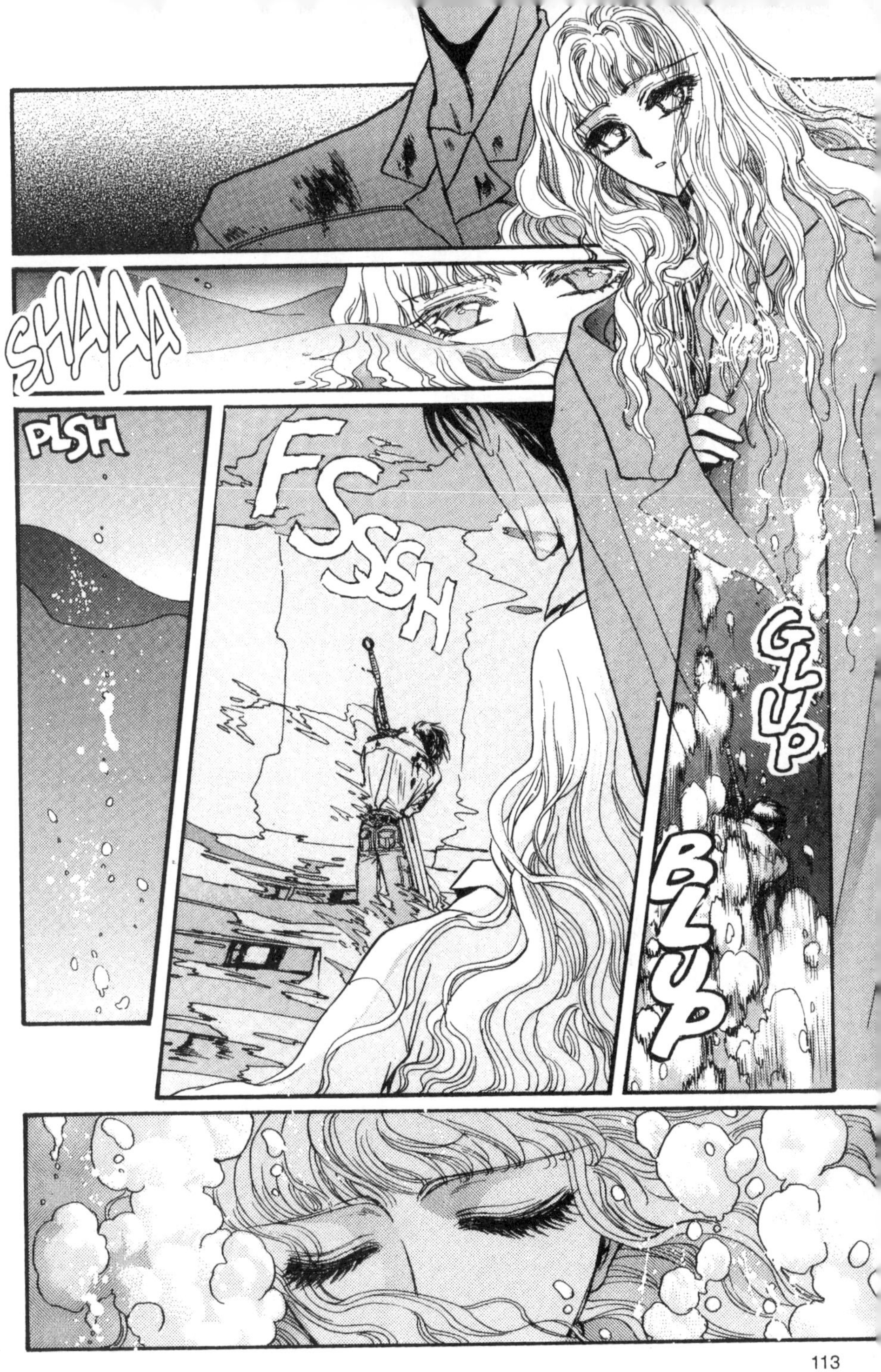
SHAAA
GLUP
BLUP
FSSSH
PLSH

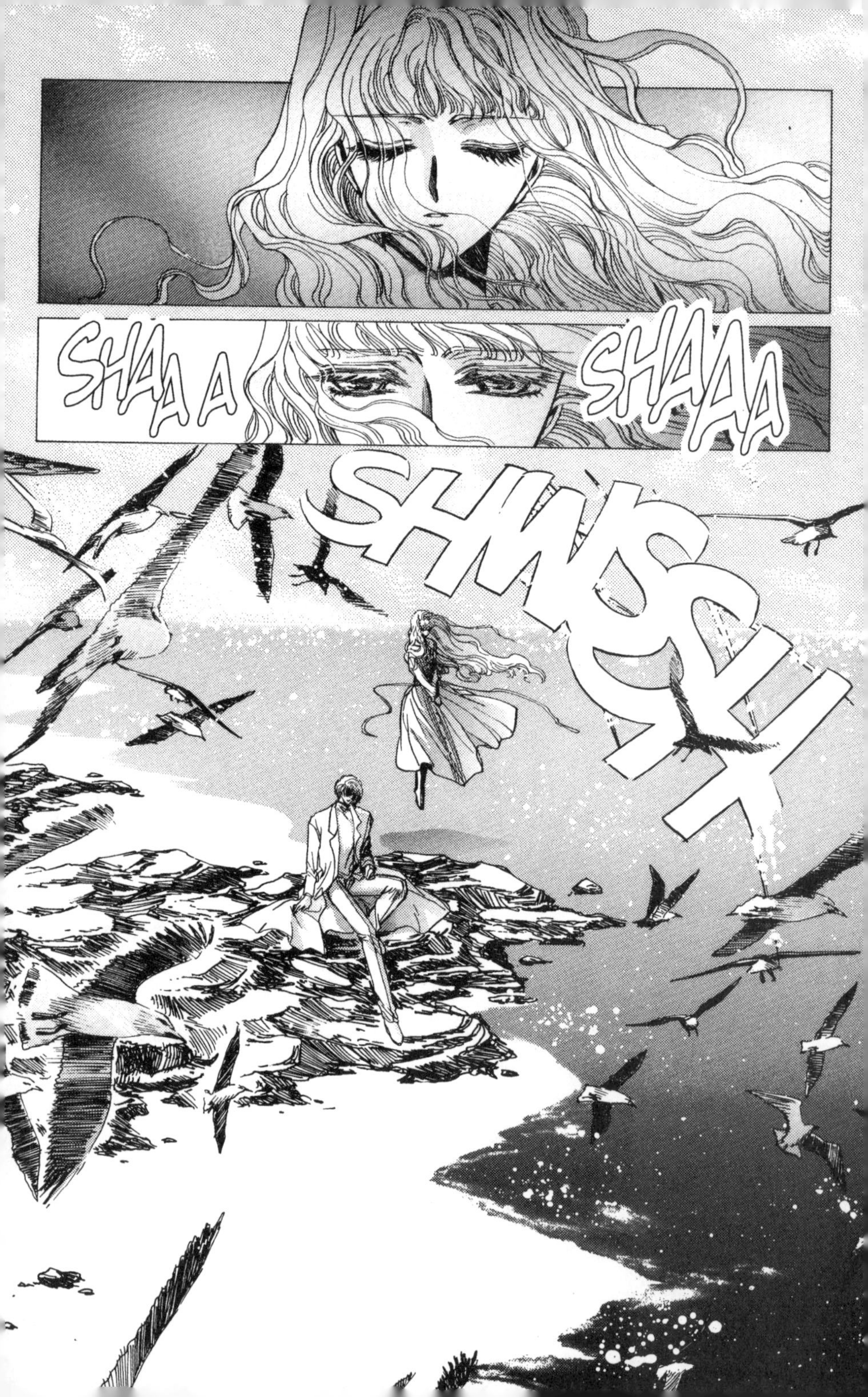
SHAAAA
SHAAA
SHWSSH

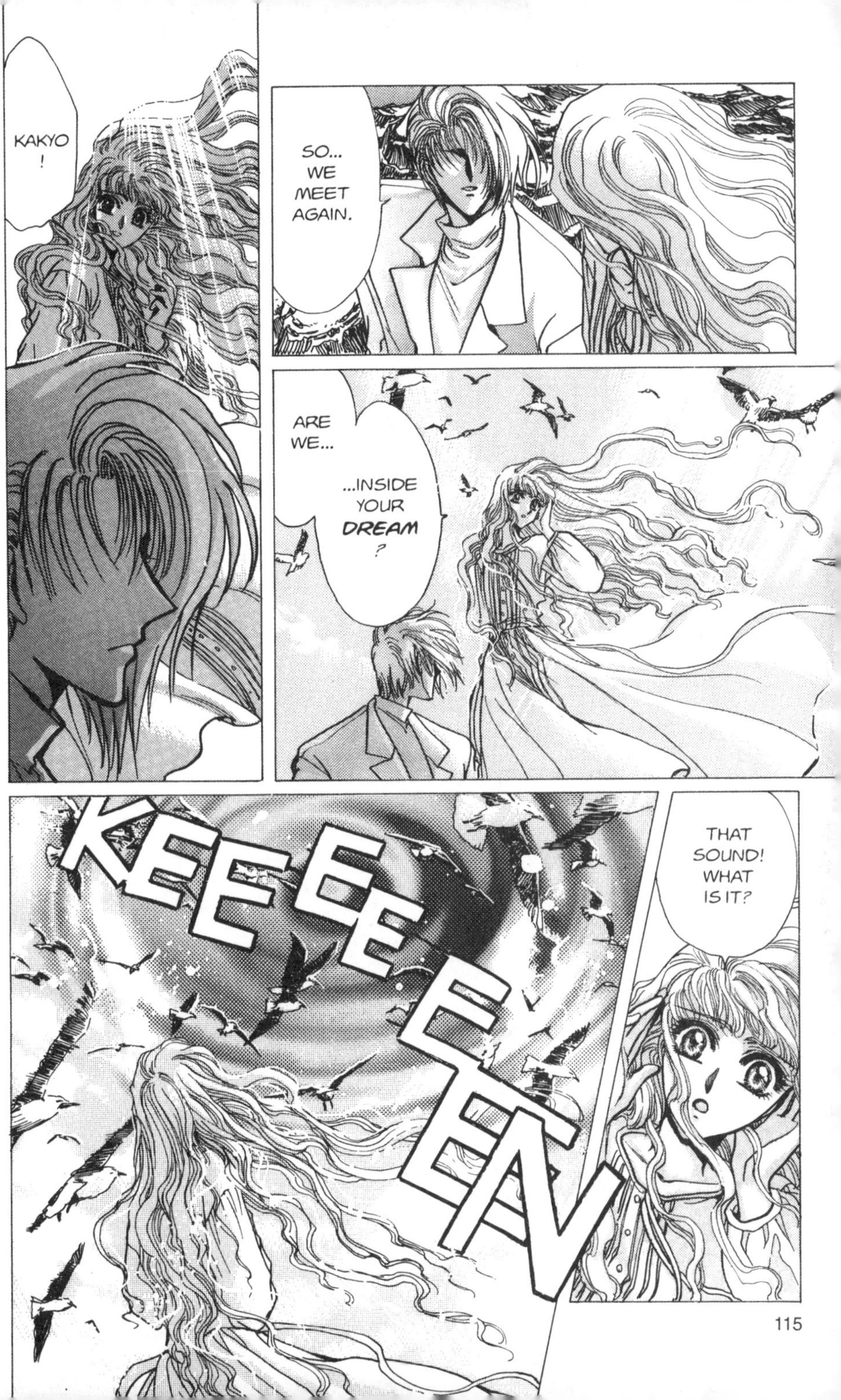
SO... WE MEET AGAIN.
ARE WE...
...INSIDE YOUR DREAM?
KAKYO!
THAT SOUND! WHAT IS IT?
KEEEEEEEN

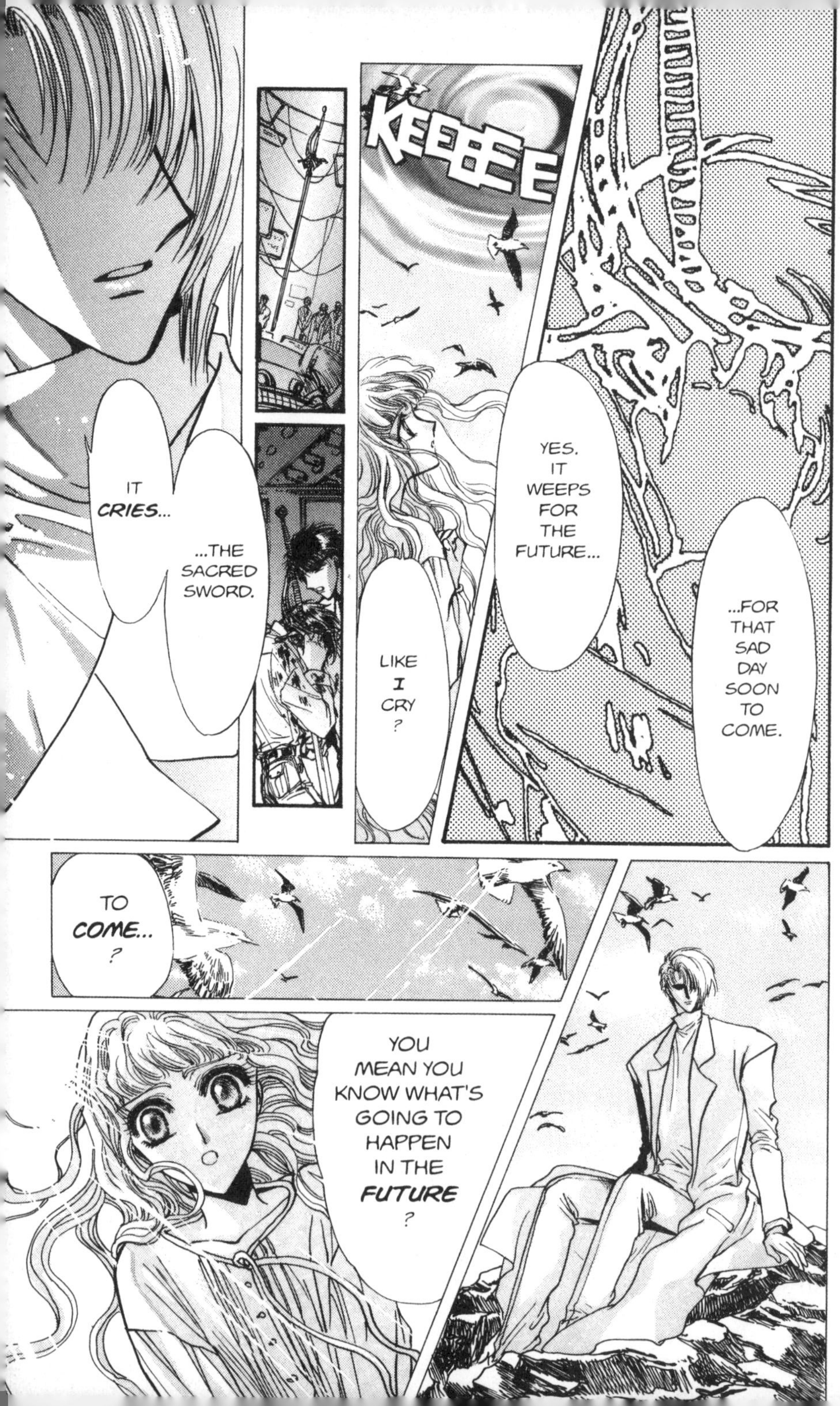
IT CRIES...
...THE SACRED SWORD.
KEEEEE
LIKE I CRY?
YES. IT WEEPS FOR THE FUTURE...
...FOR THAT SAD DAY SOON TO COME.
TO COME...?
YOU MEAN YOU KNOW WHAT'S GOING TO HAPPEN IN THE FUTURE?

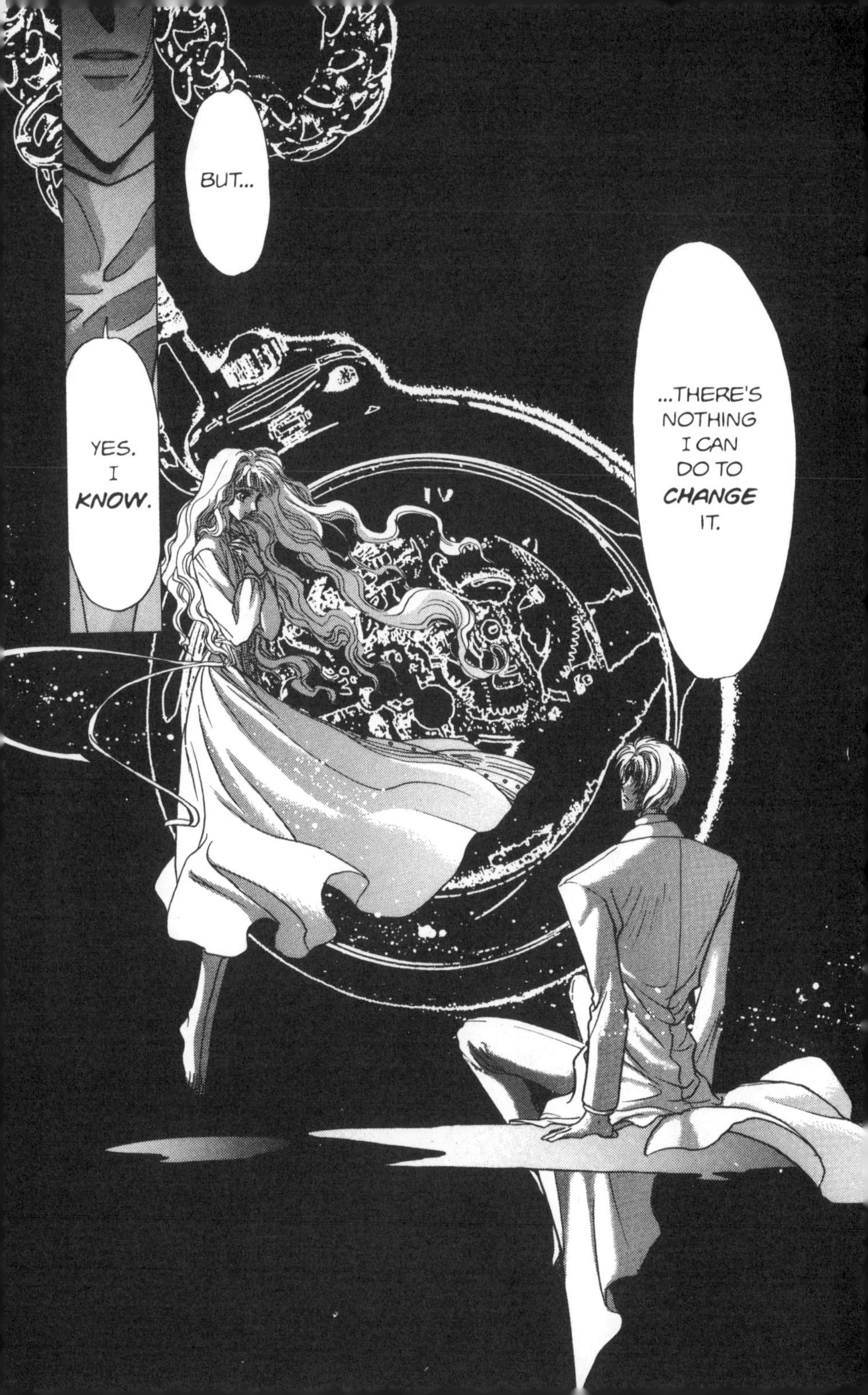
BUT...
...THERE'S NOTHING I CAN DO TO **CHANGE** IT.
YES. I **KNOW**.

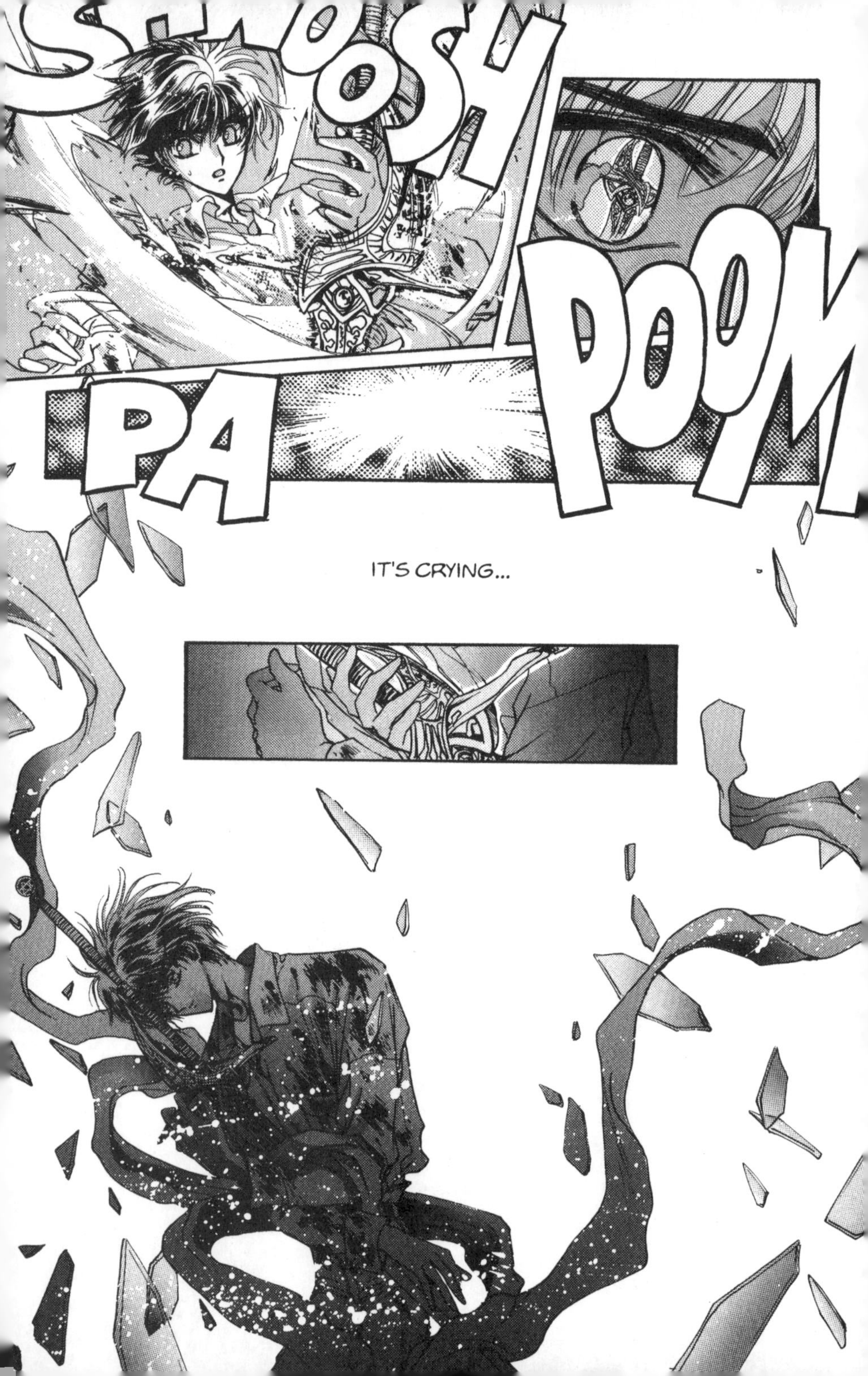
SHOOSH
POOOM
PA
IT'S CRYING...

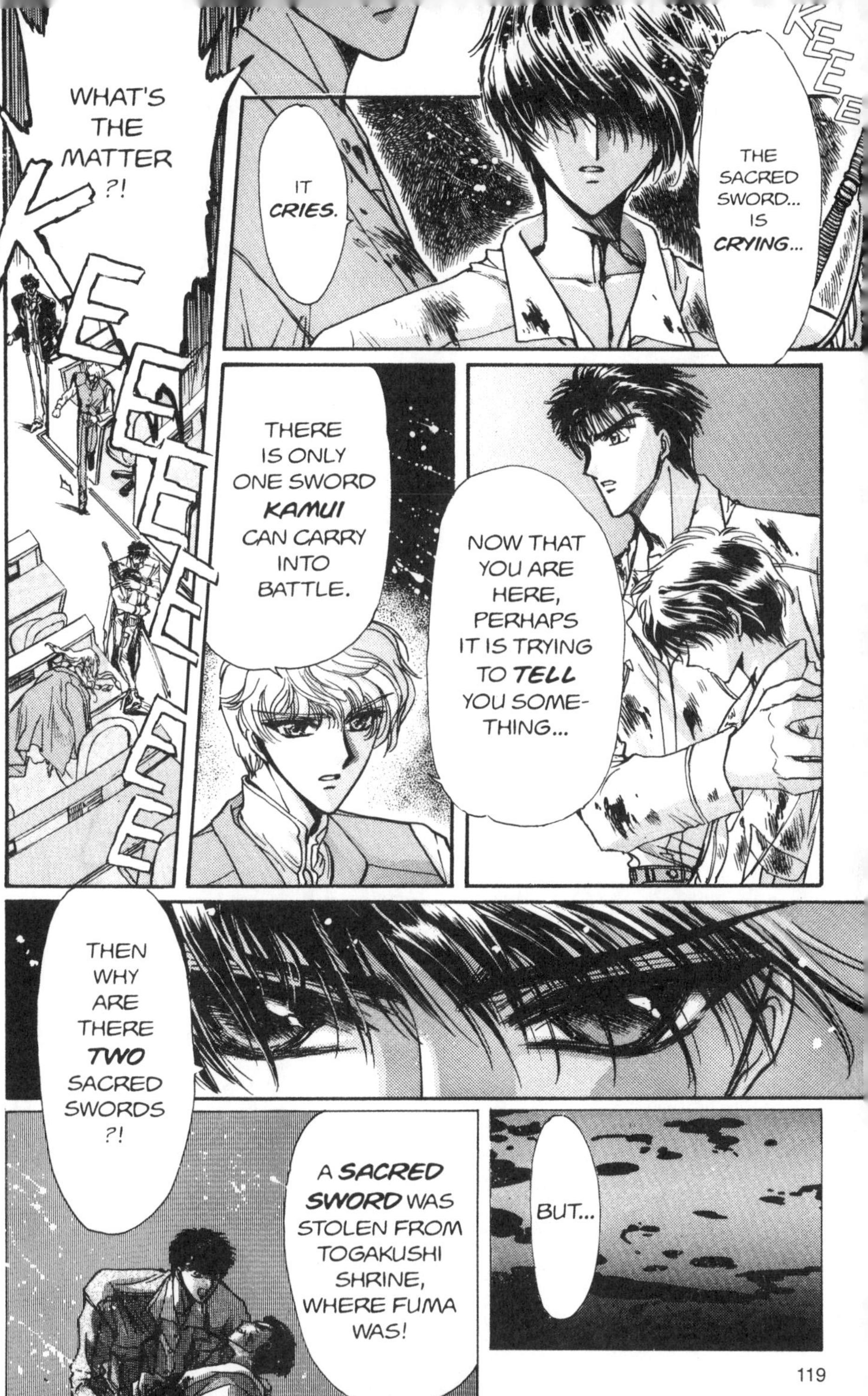
KEEEE
THE SACRED SWORD... IS CRYING...
IT CRIES.
NOW THAT YOU ARE HERE, PERHAPS IT IS TRYING TO TELL YOU SOME-THING...
THERE IS ONLY ONE SWORD KAMUI CAN CARRY INTO BATTLE.
WHAT'S THE MATTER ?!
KEEEEEEE
THEN WHY ARE THERE TWO SACRED SWORDS ?!
BUT...
A SACRED SWORD WAS STOLEN FROM TOGAKUSHI SHRINE, WHERE FUMA WAS!

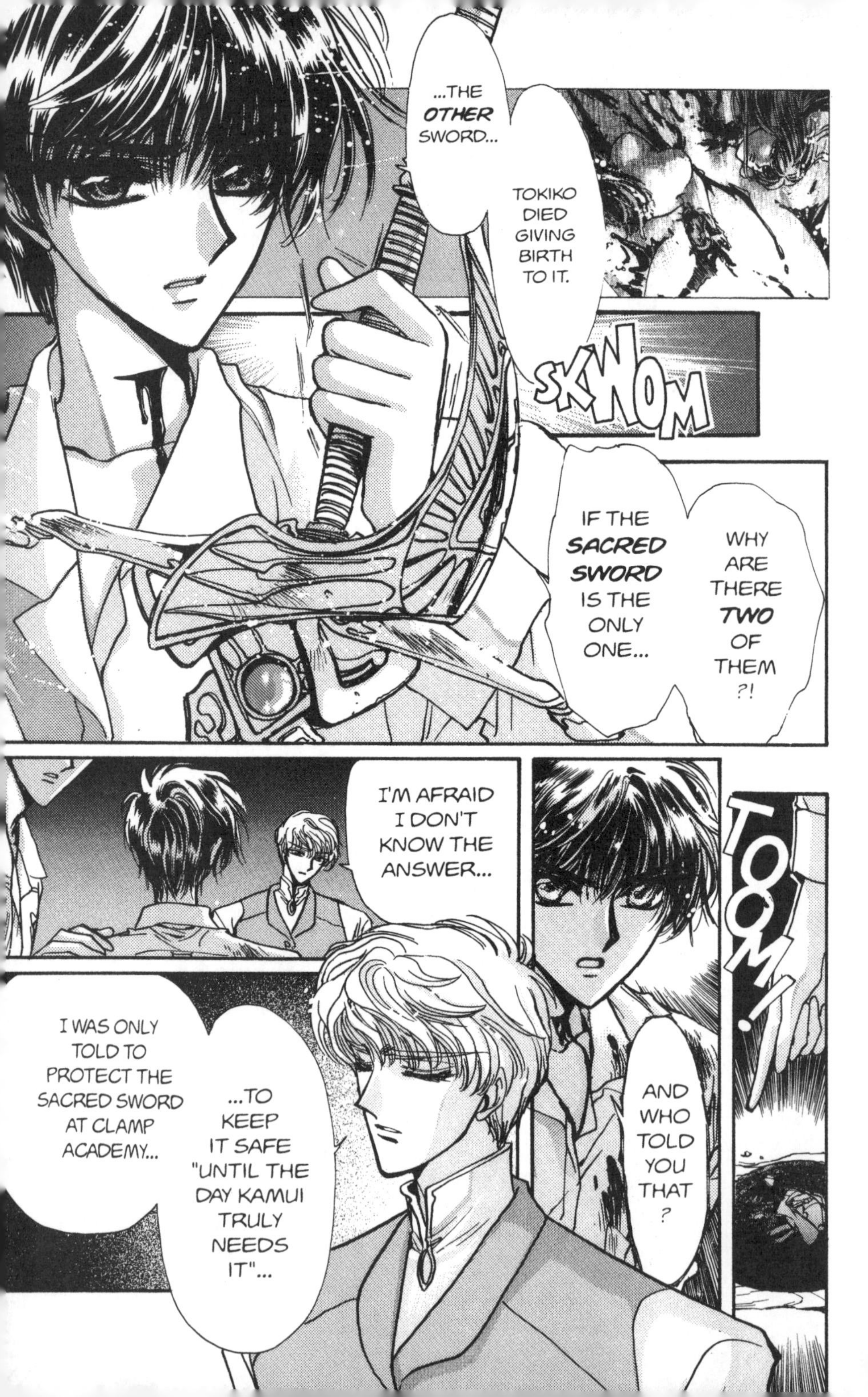
...THE OTHER SWORD...
TOKIKO DIED GIVING BIRTH TO IT.
SKNOM
WHY ARE THERE TWO OF THEM ?!
IF THE SACRED SWORD IS THE ONLY ONE...
TOOM!
I'M AFRAID I DON'T KNOW THE ANSWER...
AND WHO TOLD YOU THAT ?
...TO KEEP IT SAFE "UNTIL THE DAY KAMUI TRULY NEEDS IT"...
I WAS ONLY TOLD TO PROTECT THE SACRED SWORD AT CLAMP ACADEMY...

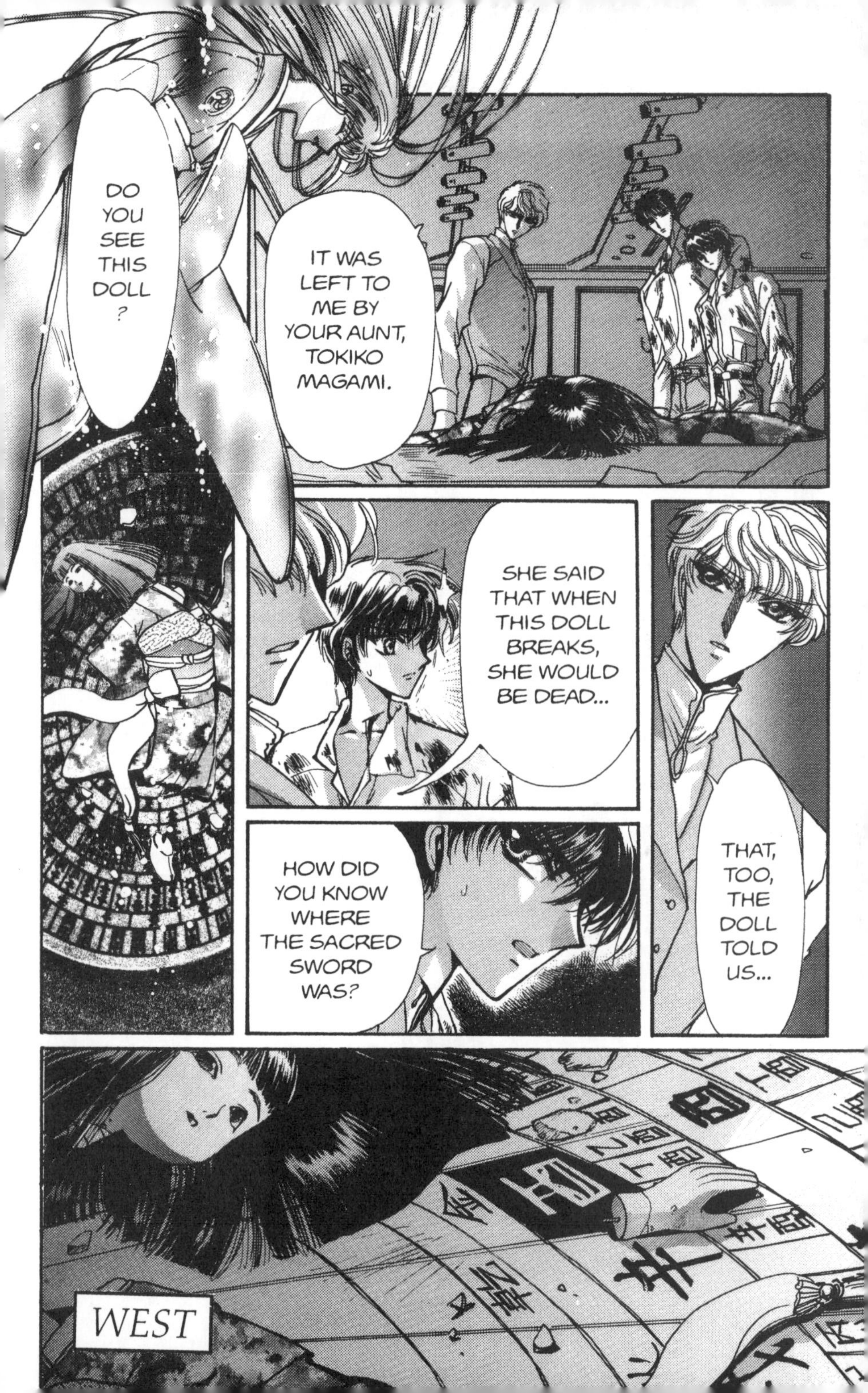
DO YOU SEE THIS DOLL ?
IT WAS LEFT TO ME BY YOUR AUNT, TOKIKO MAGAMI.
SHE SAID THAT WHEN THIS DOLL BREAKS, SHE WOULD BE DEAD...
HOW DID YOU KNOW WHERE THE SACRED SWORD WAS?
THAT, TOO, THE DOLL TOLD US...
WEST

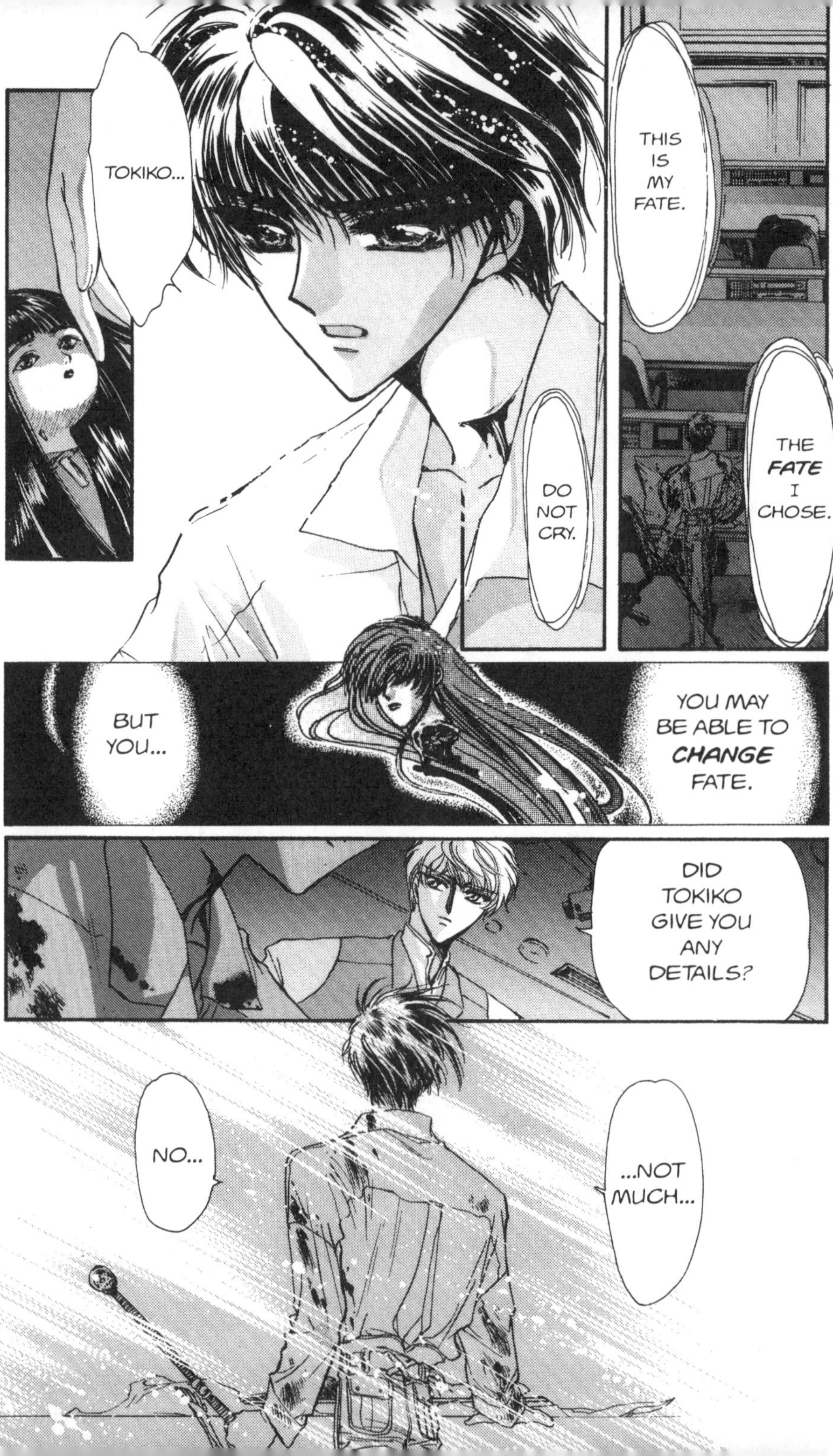
THIS IS MY FATE.
THE FATE I CHOSE.
DO NOT CRY.
TOKIKO...
BUT YOU...
YOU MAY BE ABLE TO CHANGE FATE.
DID TOKIKO GIVE YOU ANY DETAILS?
NO...
...NOT MUCH...

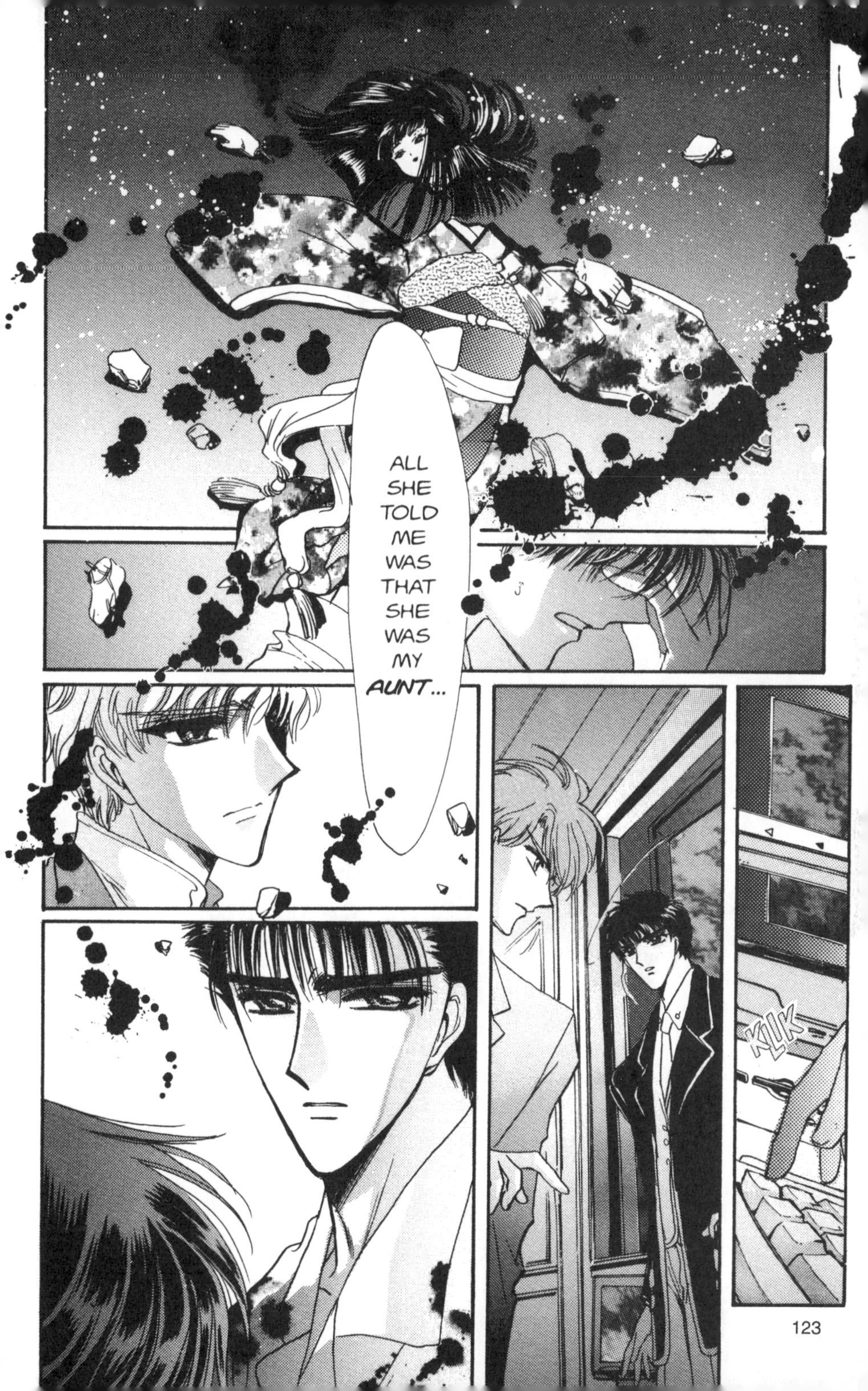
ALL SHE TOLD ME WAS THAT SHE WAS MY *AUNT*...
KLIK

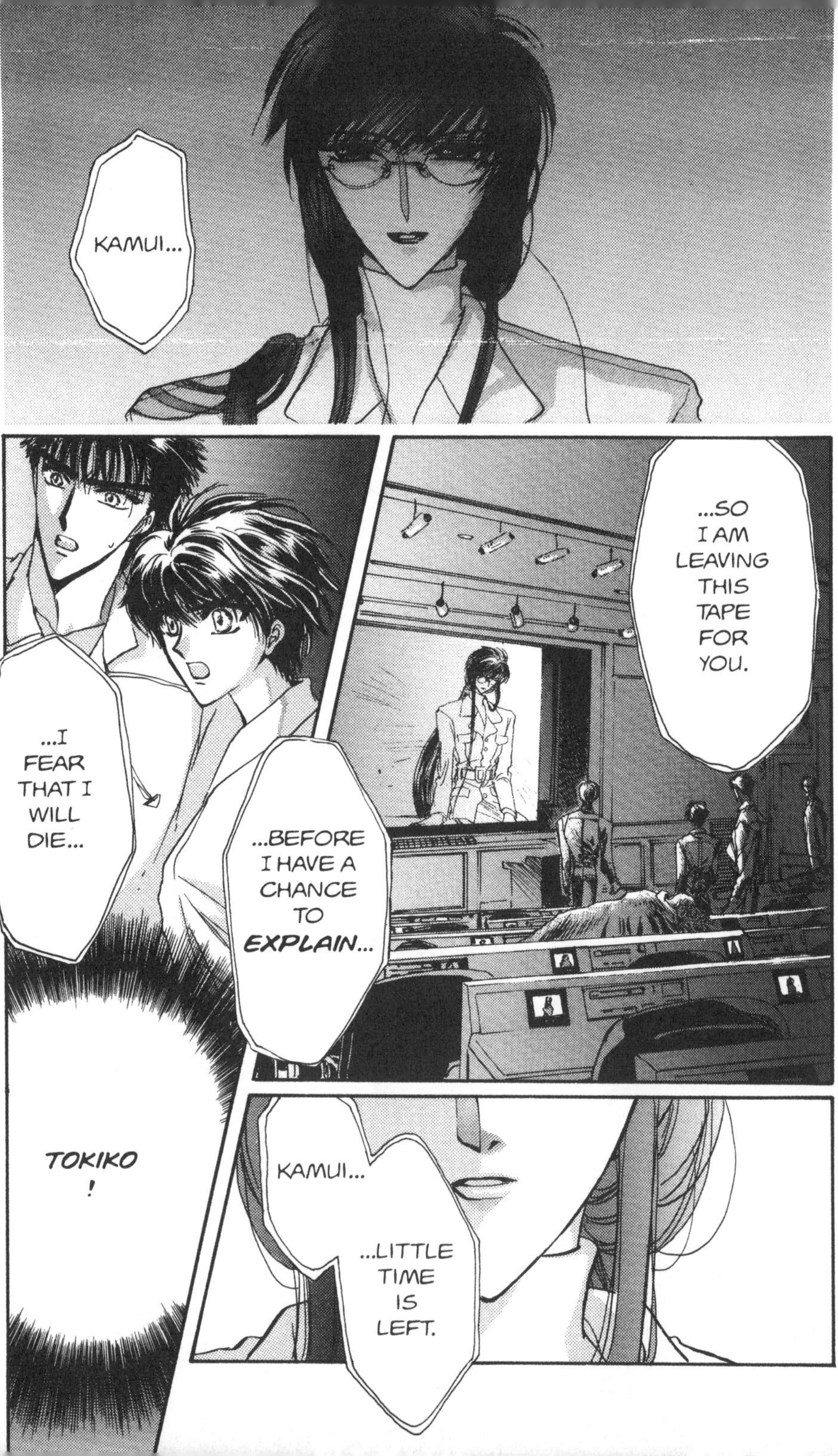
KAMUI...
...SO I AM LEAVING THIS TAPE FOR YOU.
...I FEAR THAT I WILL DIE...
...BEFORE I HAVE A CHANCE TO *EXPLAIN*...
TOKIKO!
KAMUI...
...LITTLE TIME IS LEFT.

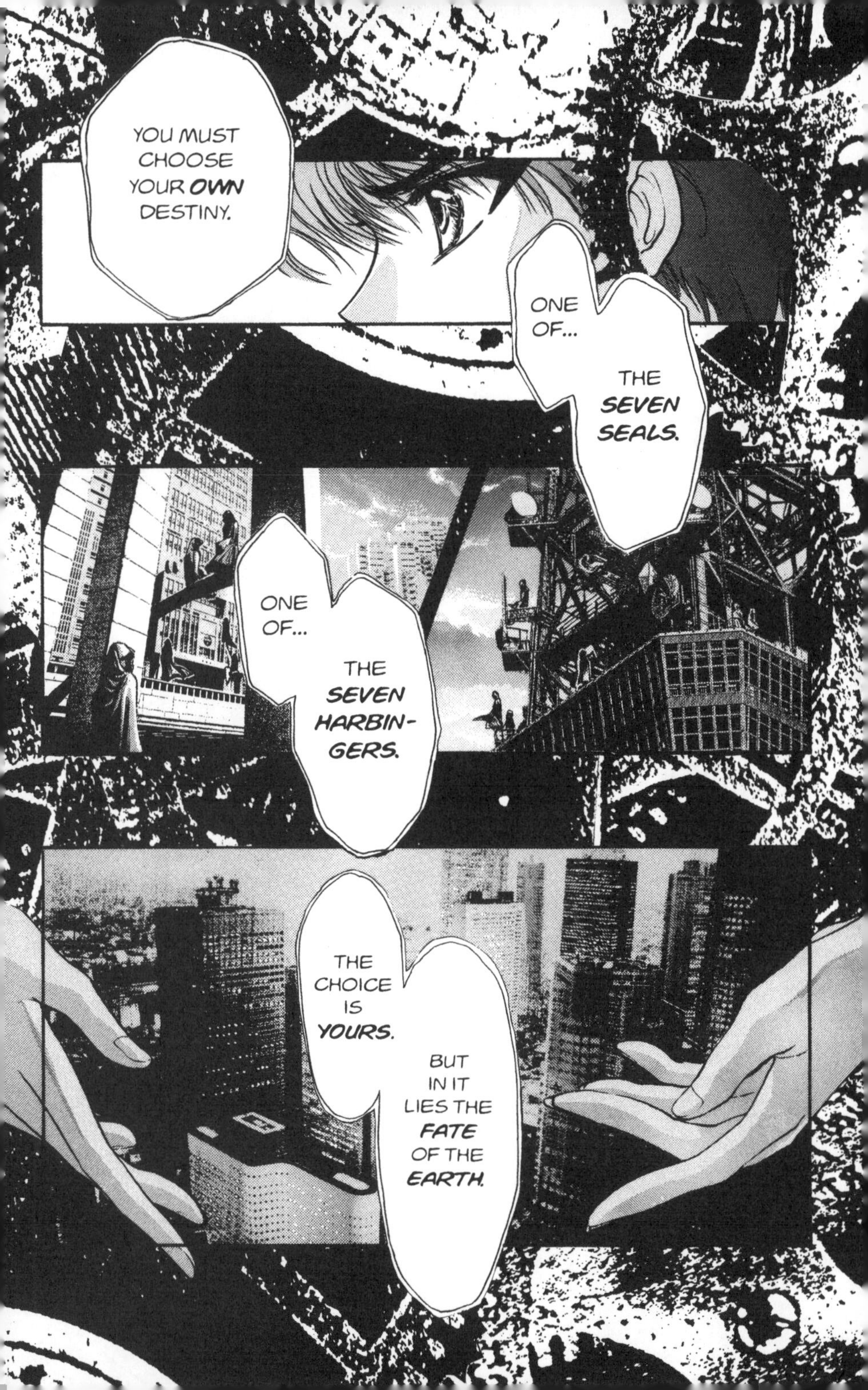
YOU MUST CHOOSE YOUR OWN DESTINY.
ONE OF... THE SEVEN SEALS.
ONE OF... THE SEVEN HARBIN-GERS.
THE CHOICE IS YOURS.
BUT IN IT LIES THE FATE OF THE EARTH.

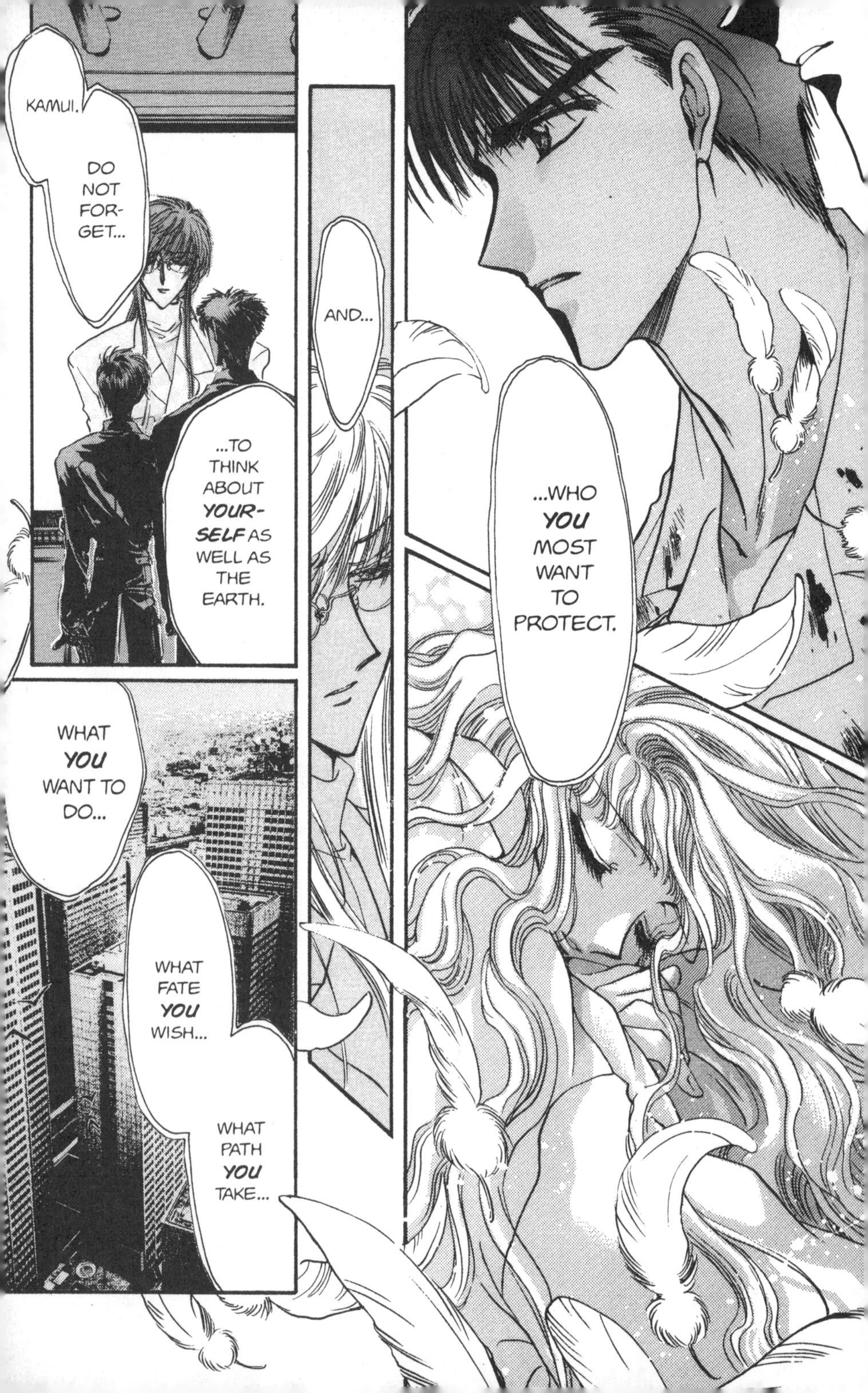
KAMUI.
DO NOT FORGET...
...TO THINK ABOUT YOURSELF AS WELL AS THE EARTH.
WHAT YOU WANT TO DO...
WHAT FATE YOU WISH...
WHAT PATH YOU TAKE...
AND...
...WHO YOU MOST WANT TO PROTECT.

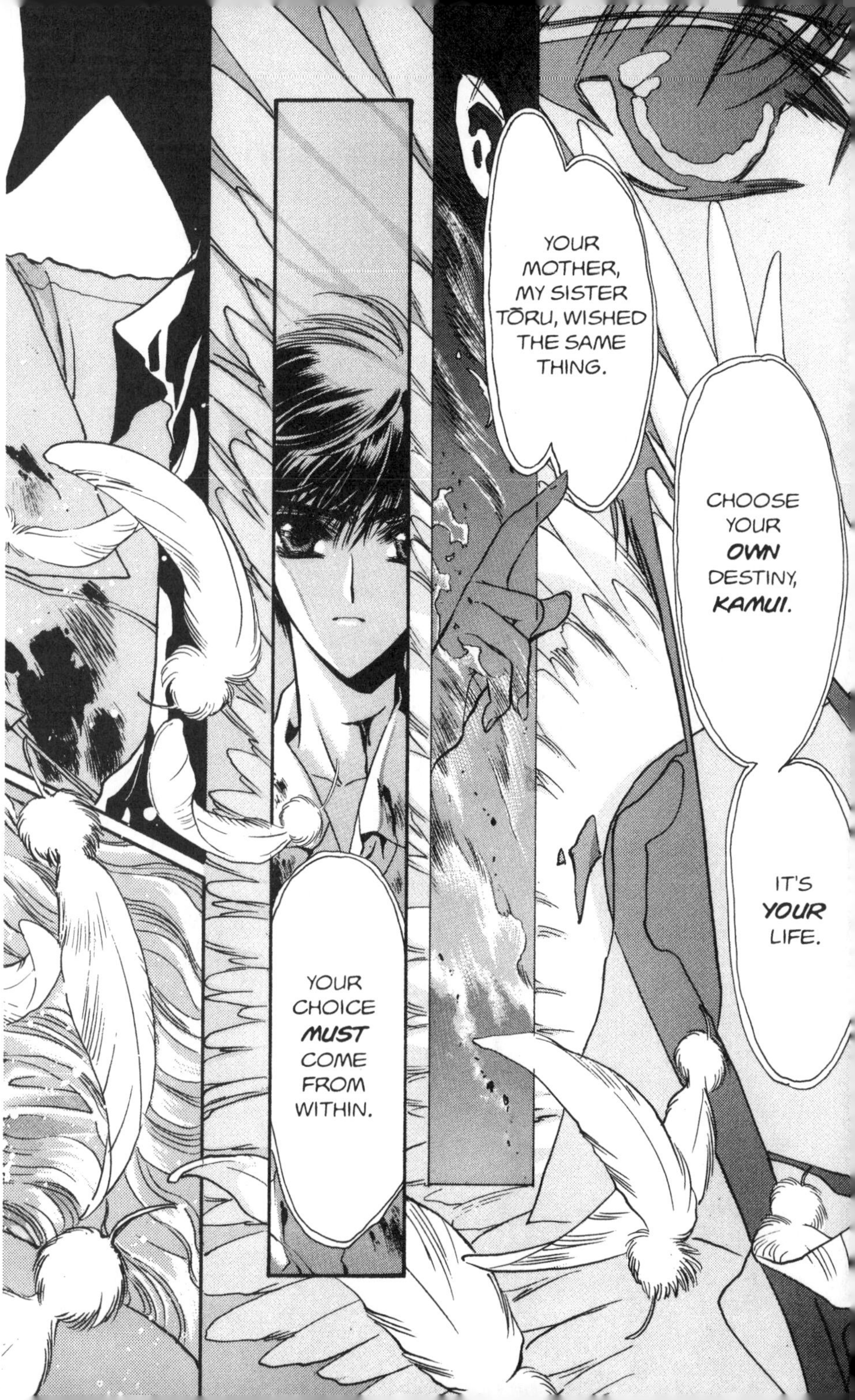
YOUR MOTHER, MY SISTER TŌRU, WISHED THE SAME THING.
CHOOSE YOUR ***OWN*** DESTINY, ***KAMUI.***
IT'S ***YOUR*** LIFE.
YOUR CHOICE ***MUST*** COME FROM WITHIN.

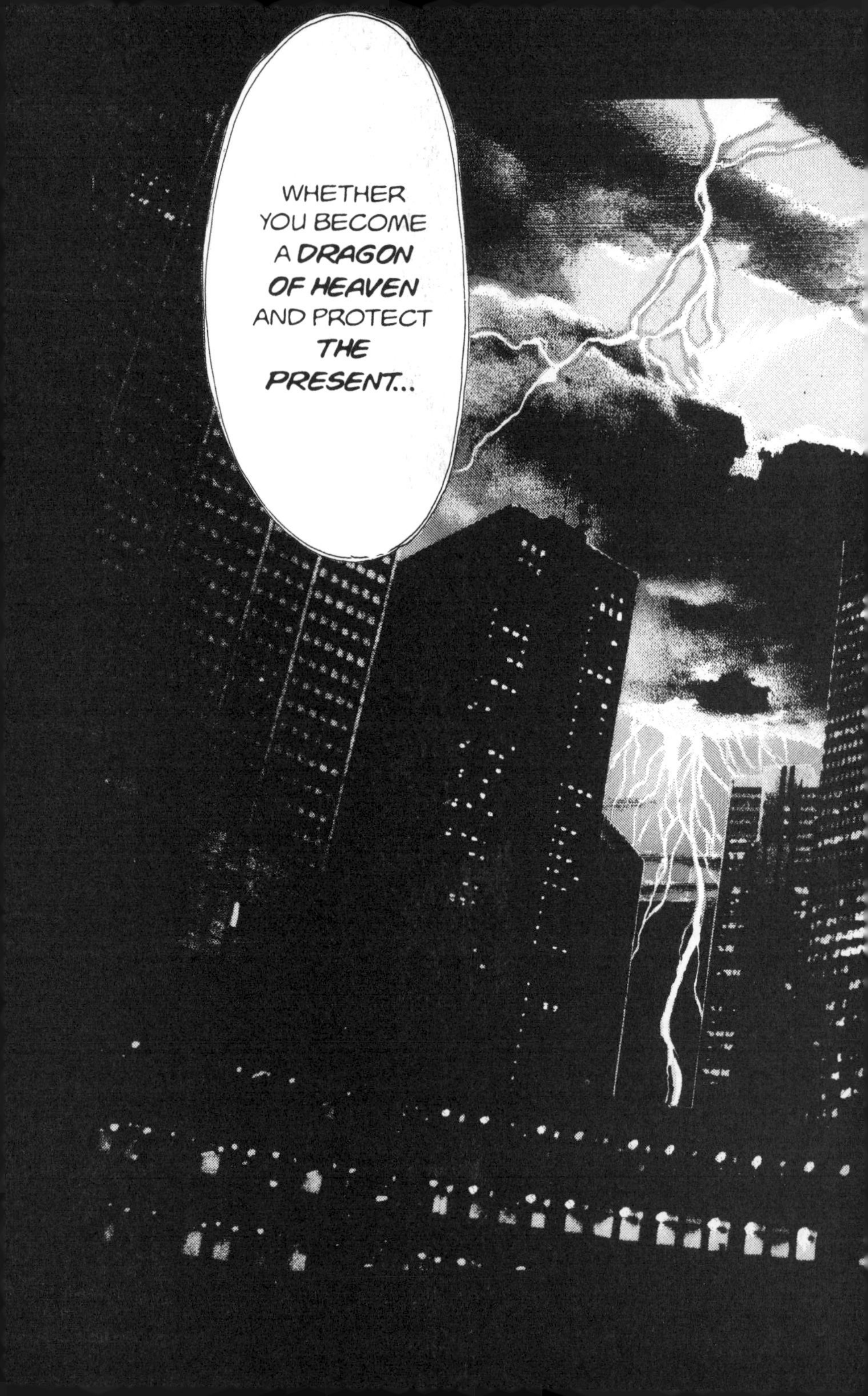
WHETHER YOU BECOME A DRAGON OF HEAVEN AND PROTECT THE PRESENT...

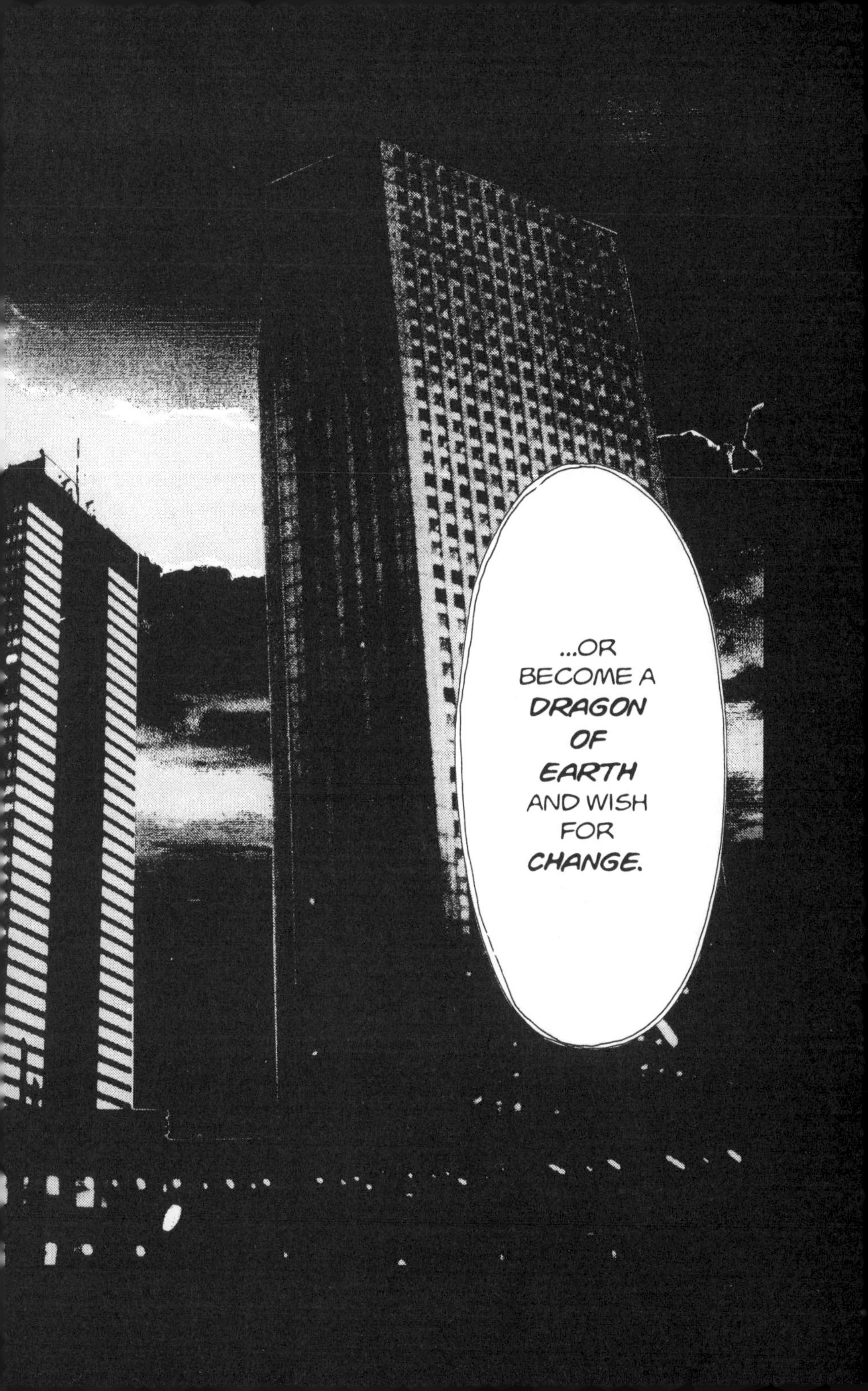
...OR BECOME A DRAGON OF EARTH AND WISH FOR CHANGE.

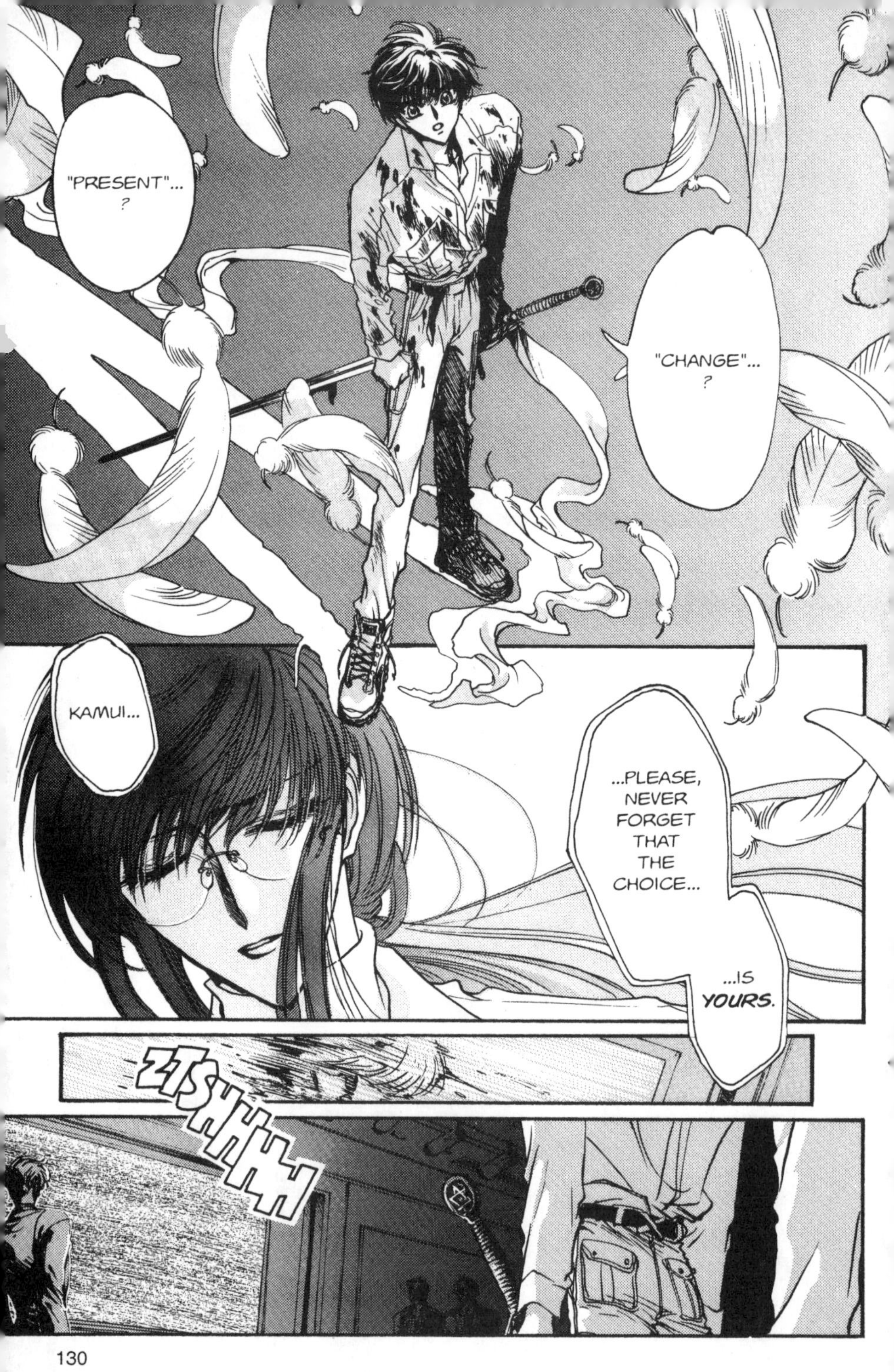
"CHANGE"... ?
"PRESENT"... ?
KAMUI...
...PLEASE, NEVER FORGET THAT THE CHOICE...
...IS YOURS.
ZTSHHHH

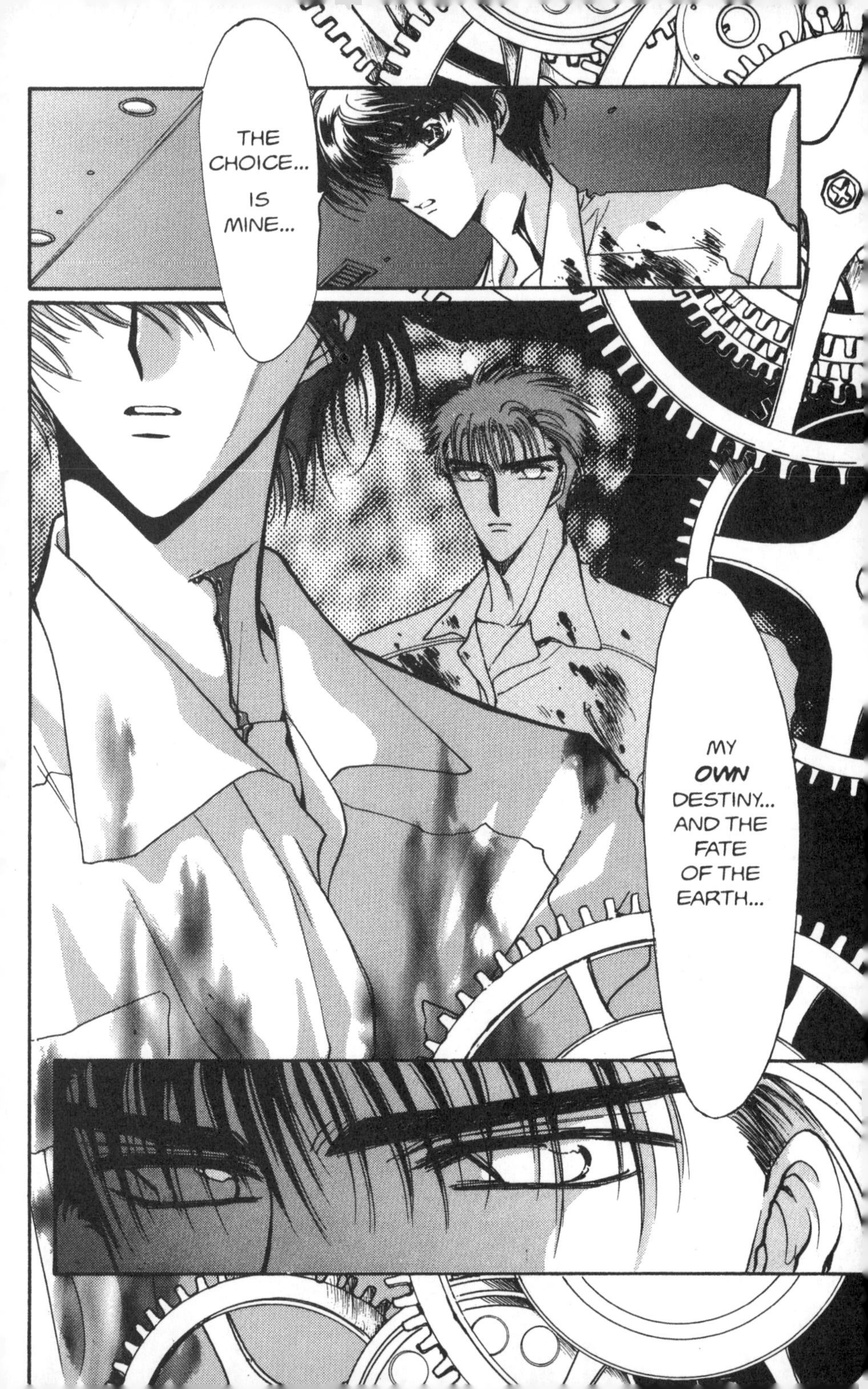
THE CHOICE... IS MINE...
MY OWN DESTINY... AND THE FATE OF THE EARTH...

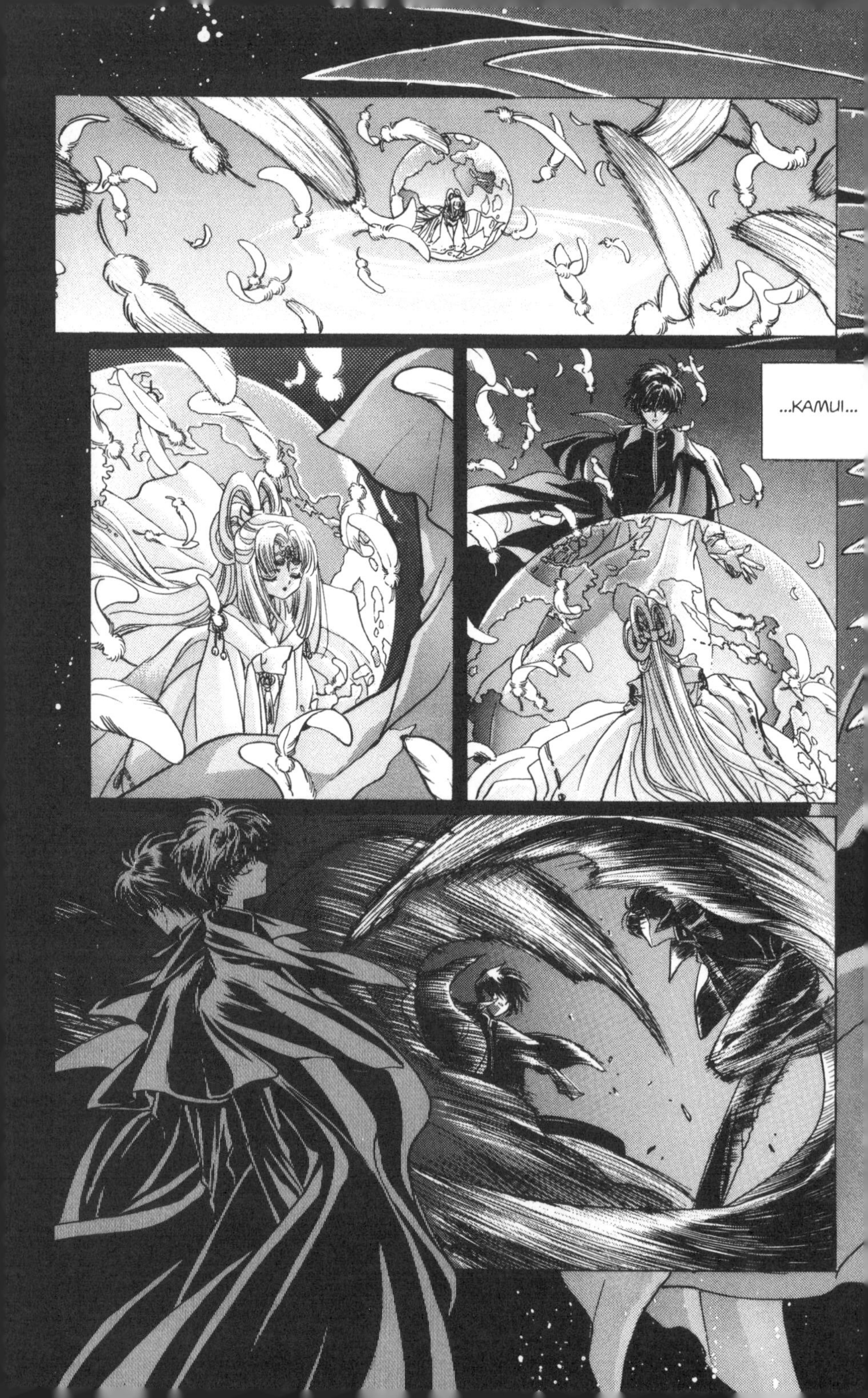
...KAMUI...

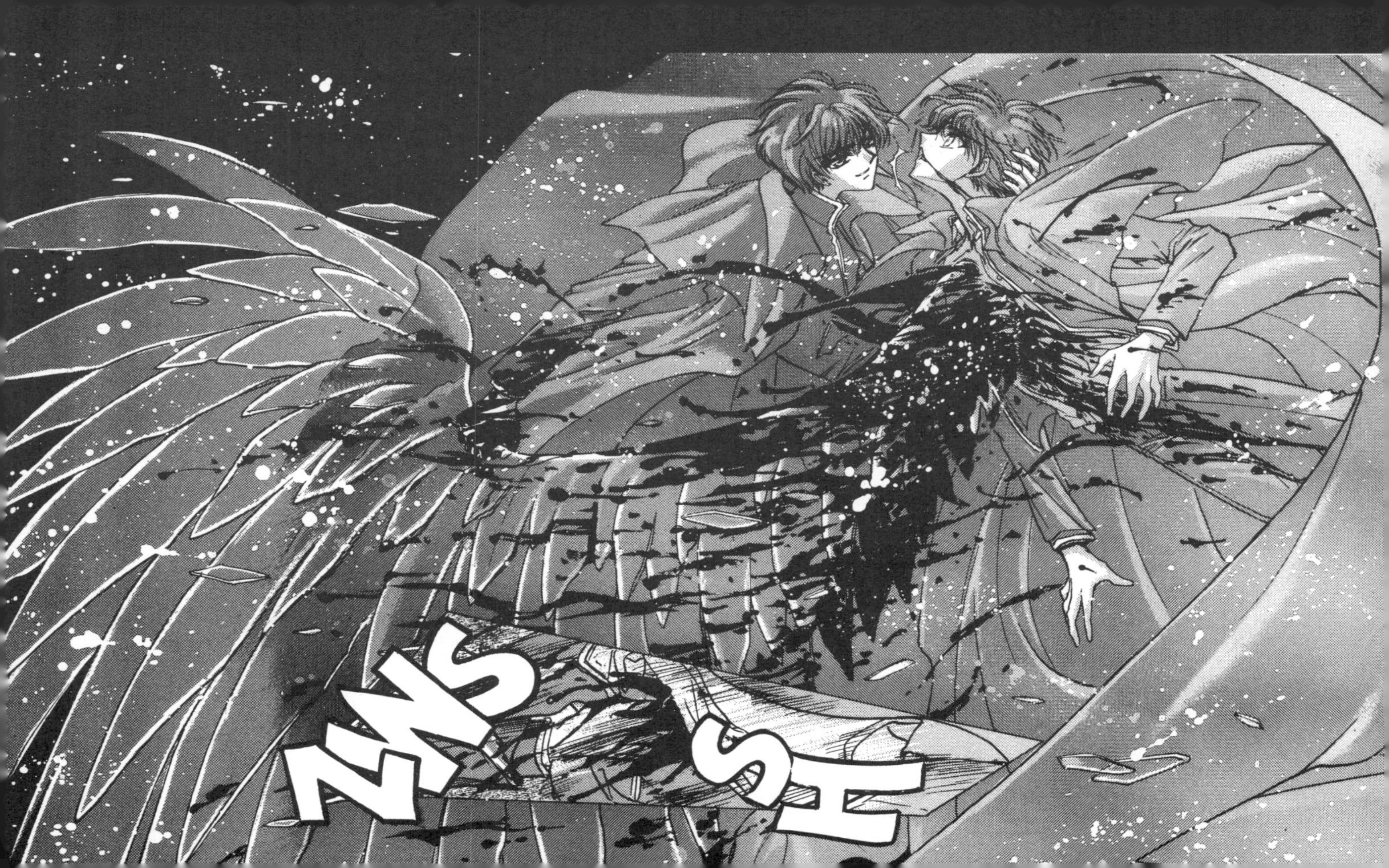
ZWSSH

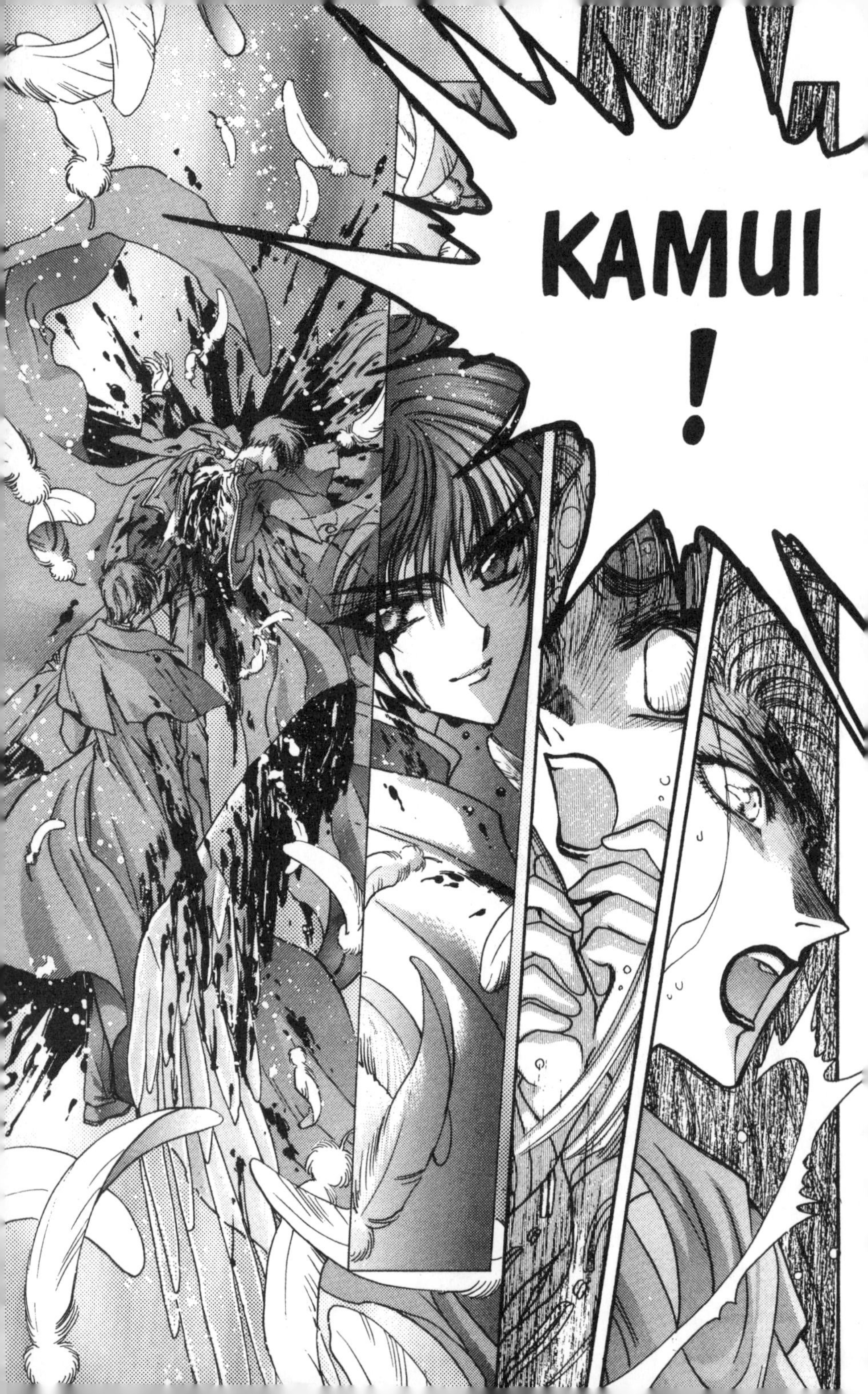
KAMUI
!

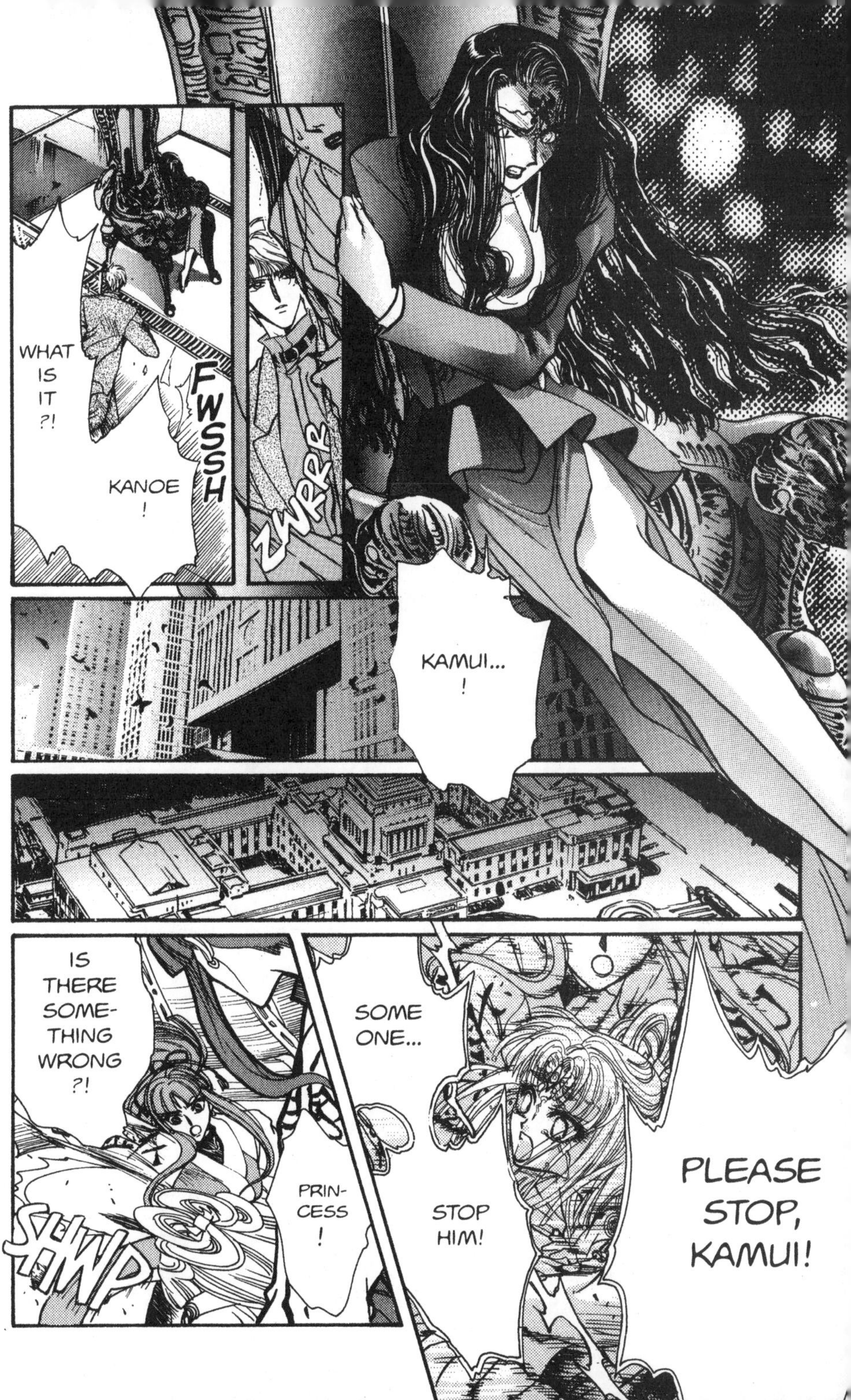
ZWRRR
WHAT IS IT ?!
KANOE !
FWSSH
KAMUI... !
SOME ONE...
STOP HIM!
PLEASE STOP, KAMUI!
IS THERE SOME-THING WRONG ?!
PRIN-CESS !
SHWP

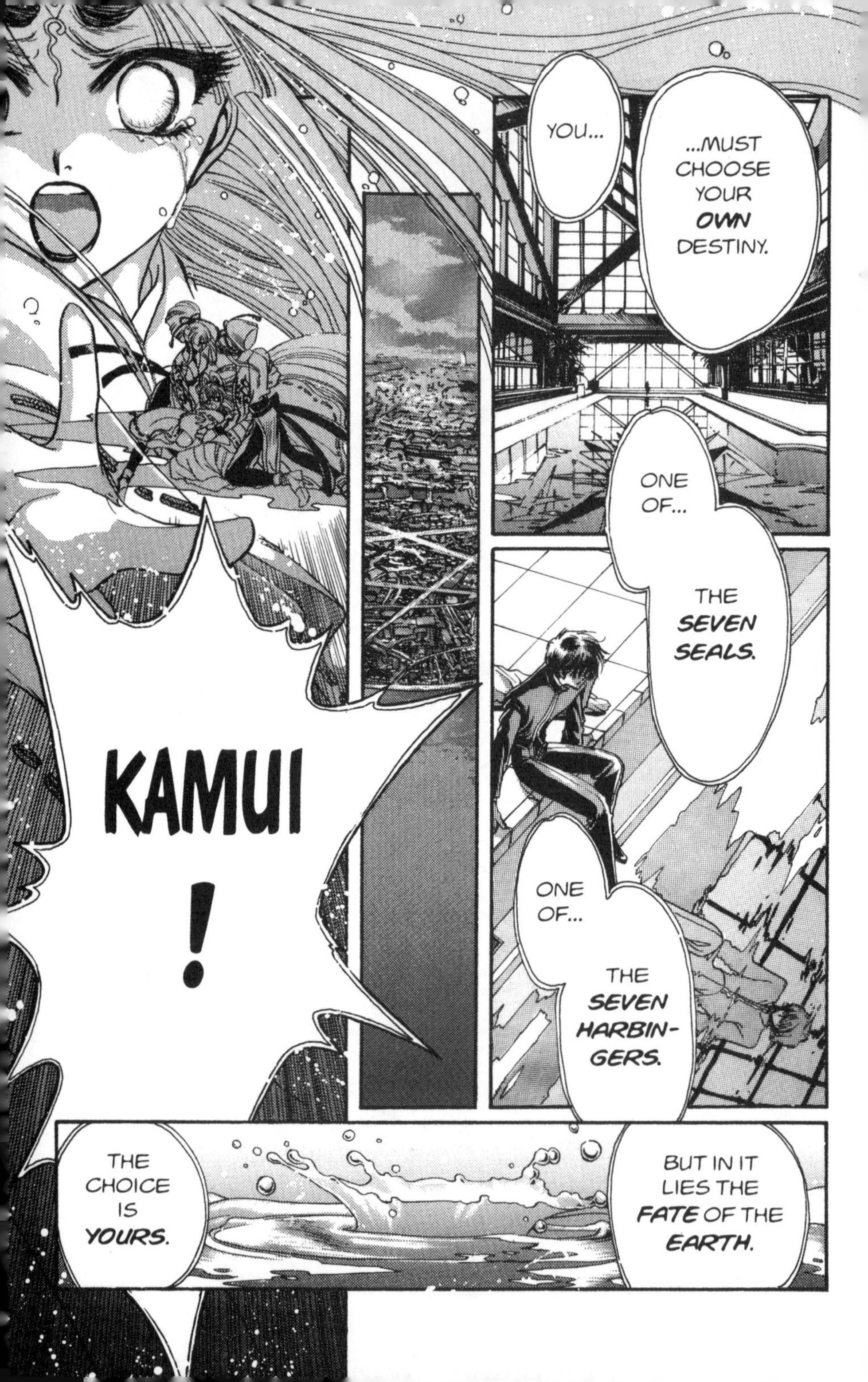
YOU...
...MUST CHOOSE YOUR OWN DESTINY.
ONE OF... THE SEVEN SEALS.
ONE OF... THE SEVEN HARBINGERS.
KAMUI!
BUT IN IT LIES THE FATE OF THE EARTH.
THE CHOICE IS YOURS.

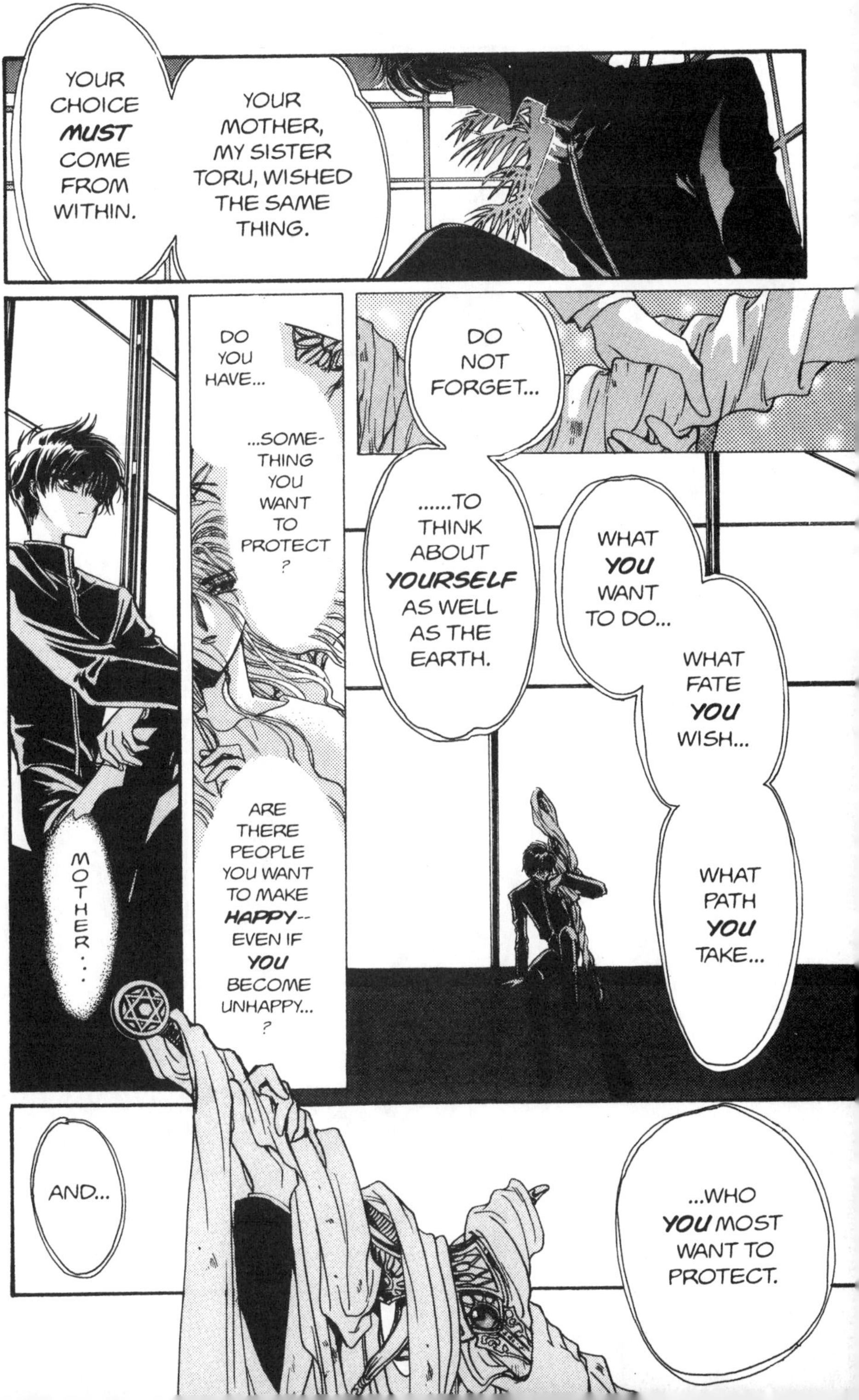
YOUR MOTHER, MY SISTER TORU, WISHED THE SAME THING.
YOUR CHOICE **MUST** COME FROM WITHIN.
DO NOT FORGET...
......TO THINK ABOUT **YOURSELF** AS WELL AS THE EARTH.
WHAT **YOU** WANT TO DO...
WHAT FATE **YOU** WISH...
WHAT PATH **YOU** TAKE...
DO YOU HAVE...
...SOMETHING YOU WANT TO PROTECT?
ARE THERE PEOPLE YOU WANT TO MAKE **HAPPY**-- EVEN IF **YOU** BECOME UNHAPPY...?
MOTHER...
AND...
...WHO **YOU** MOST WANT TO PROTECT.

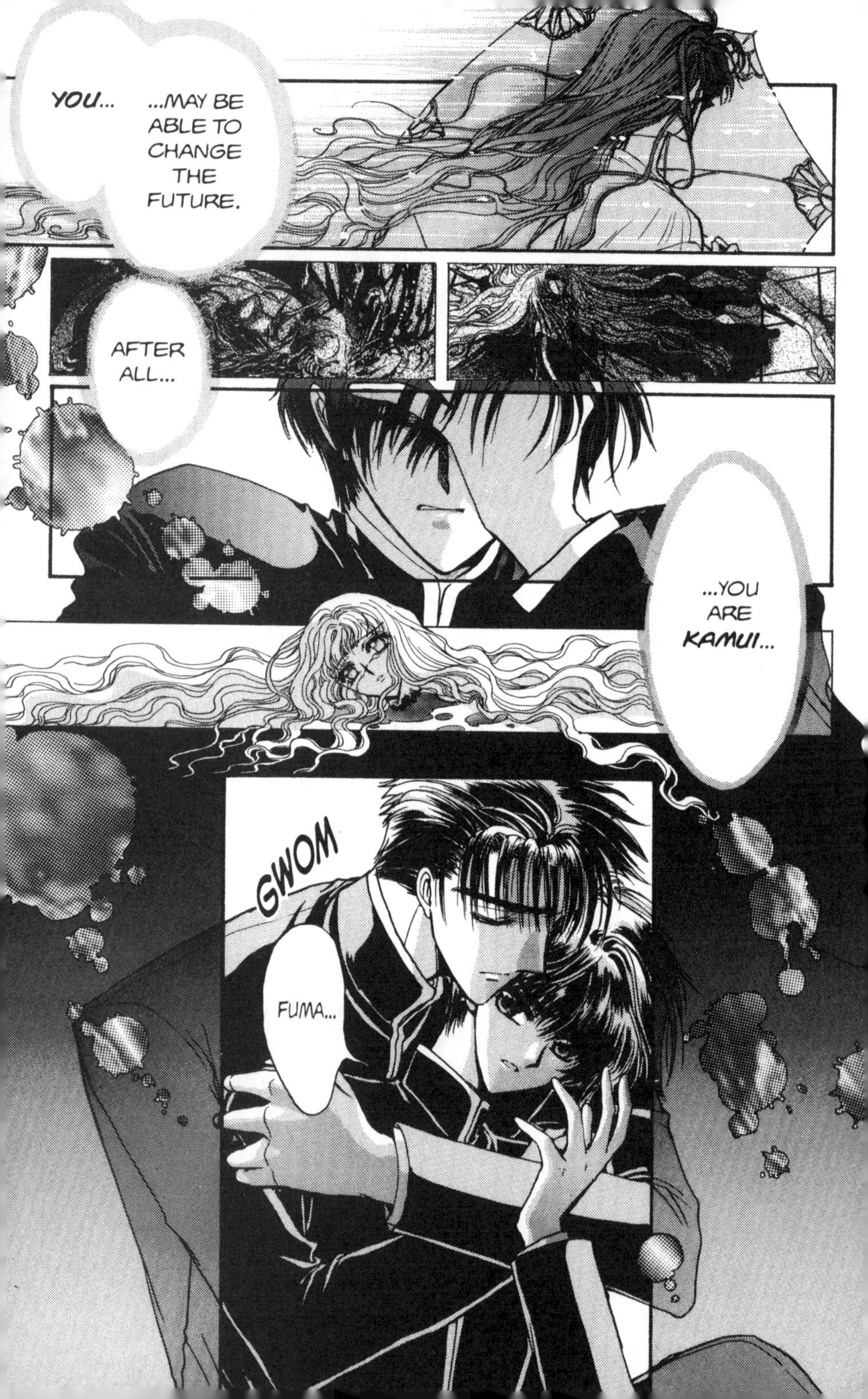
YOU... ...MAY BE ABLE TO CHANGE THE FUTURE.
AFTER ALL...
...YOU ARE KAMUI...
GWOM
FUMA...

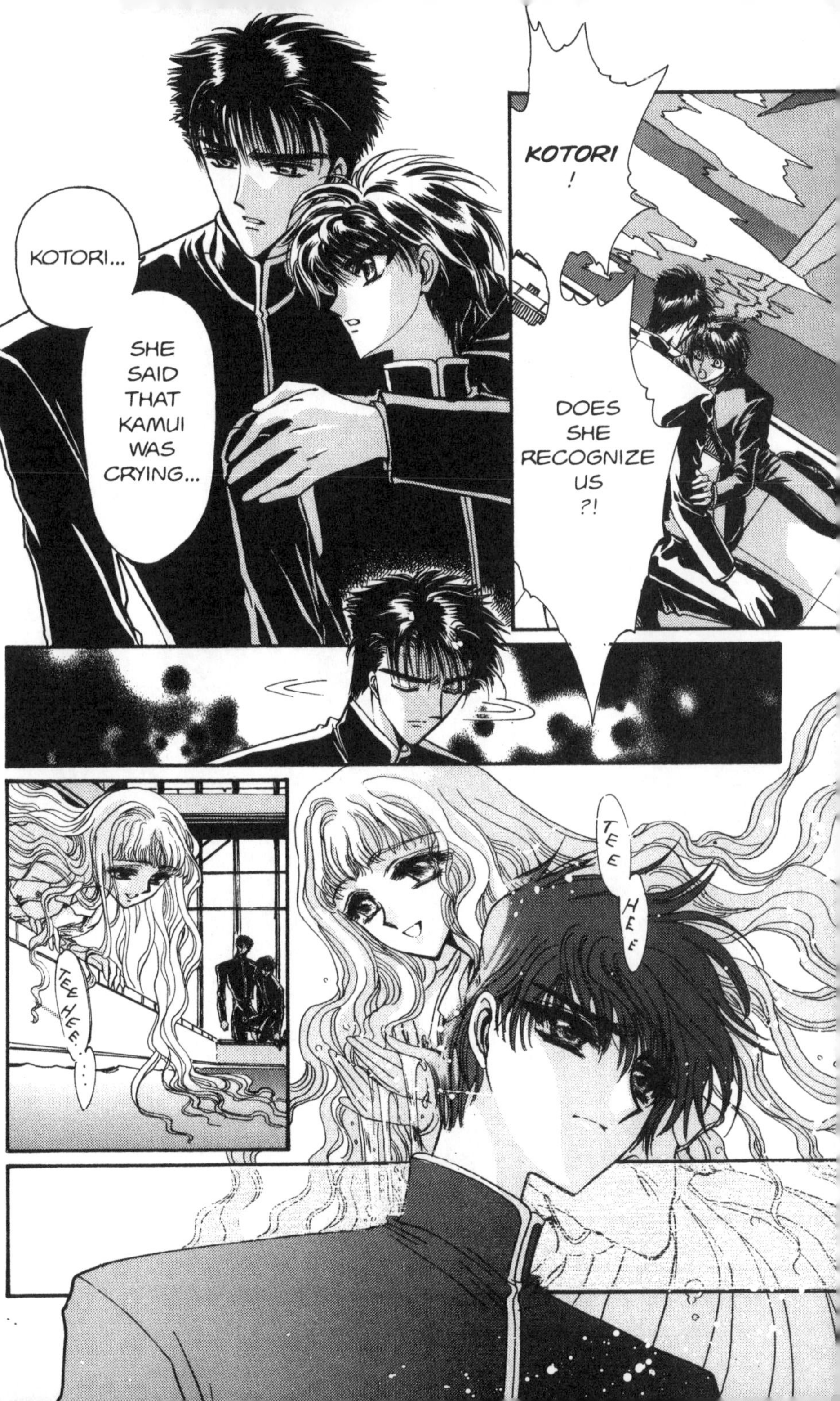
KOTORI!
DOES SHE RECOGNIZE US ?!
KOTORI...
SHE SAID THAT KAMUI WAS CRYING...
TEE HEE
TEE HEE...

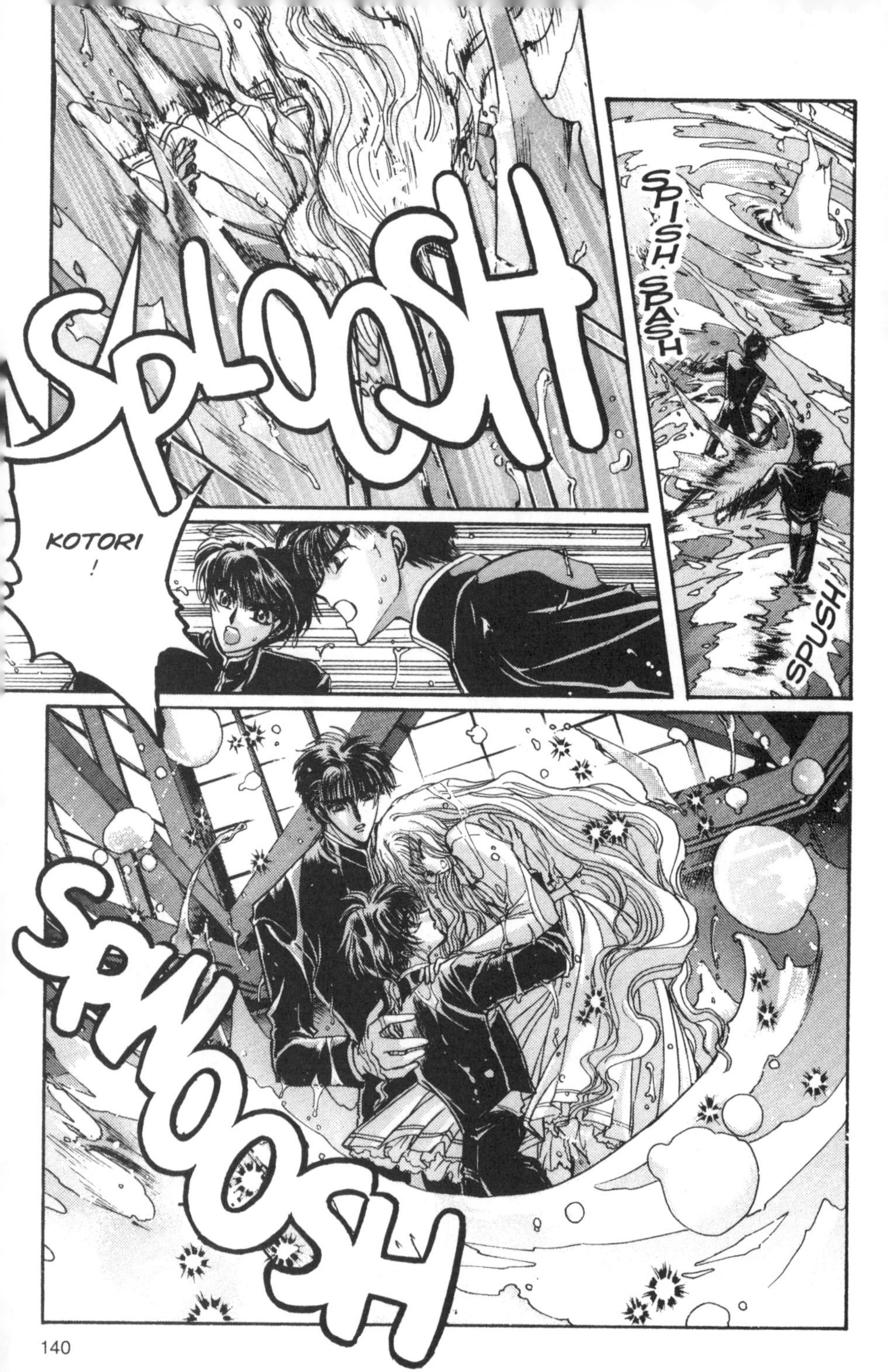
SPISH SPASH
SPUSH
SPLOOSH
KOTORI!
SPLOOOSH

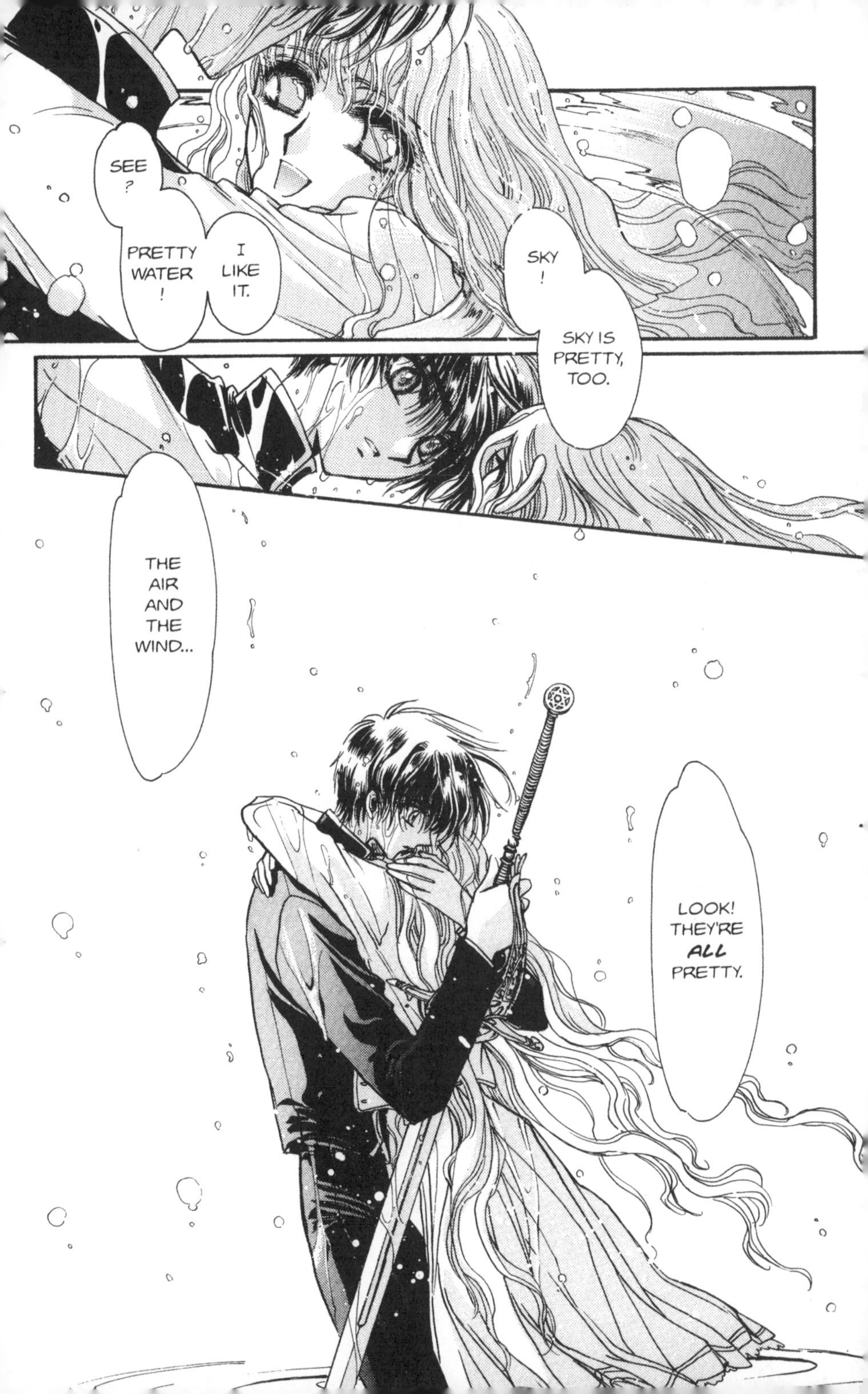
SEE?
PRETTY WATER!
I LIKE IT.
SKY!
SKY IS PRETTY, TOO.
THE AIR AND THE WIND...
LOOK! THEY'RE ALL PRETTY.

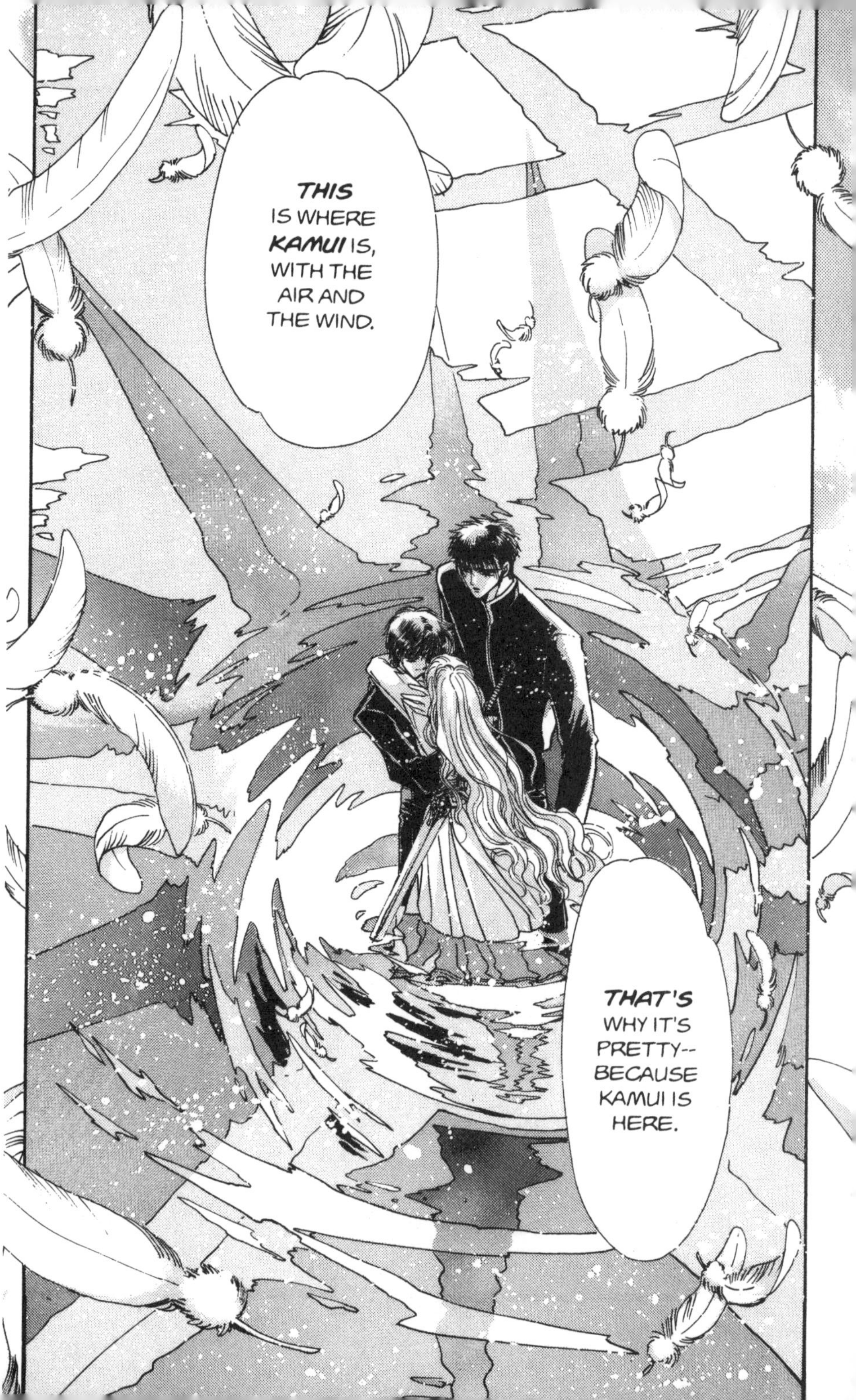
THIS IS WHERE KAMUI IS, WITH THE AIR AND THE WIND.
THAT'S WHY IT'S PRETTY-- BECAUSE KAMUI IS HERE.

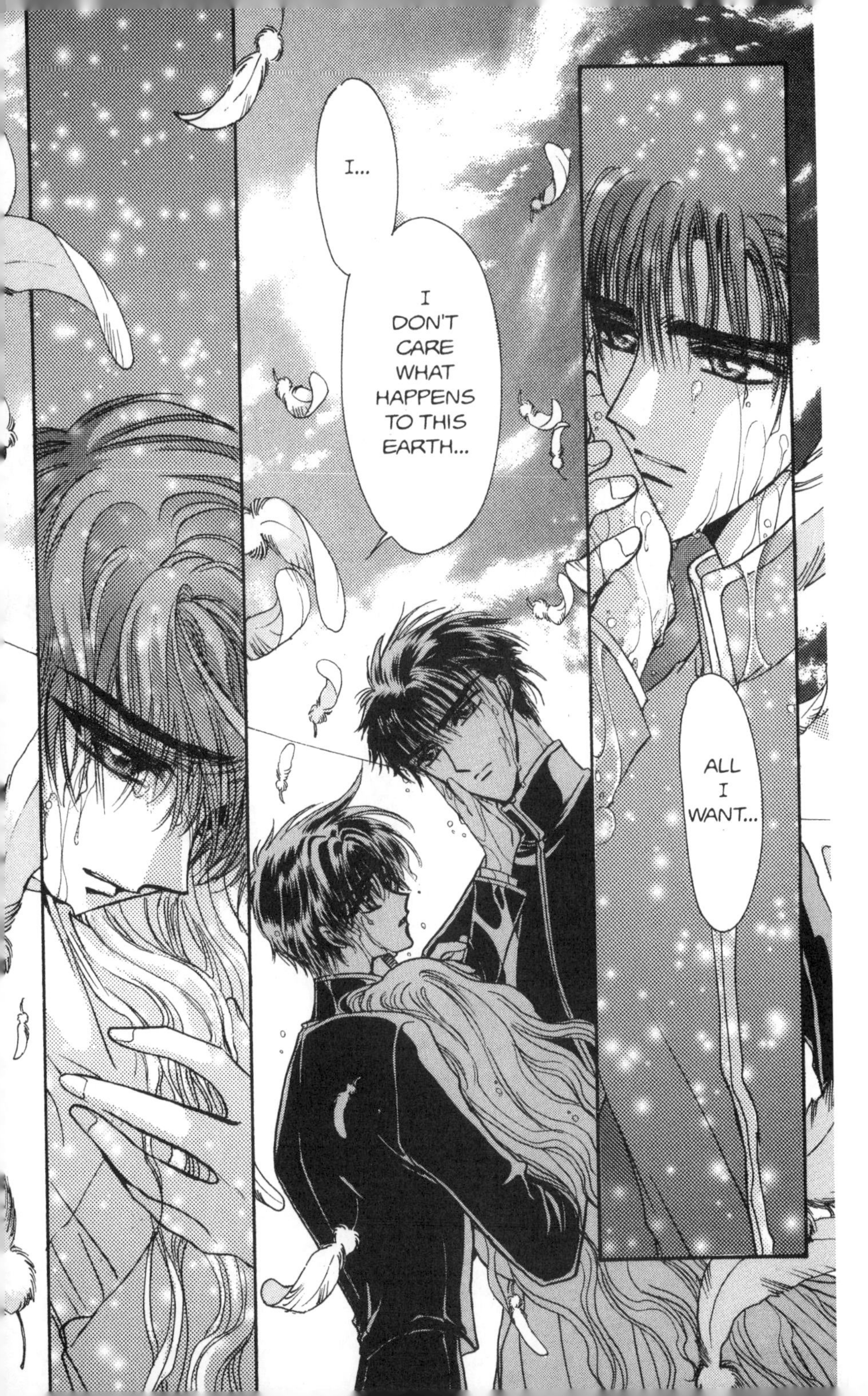
I...
I DON'T CARE WHAT HAPPENS TO THIS EARTH...
ALL I WANT...

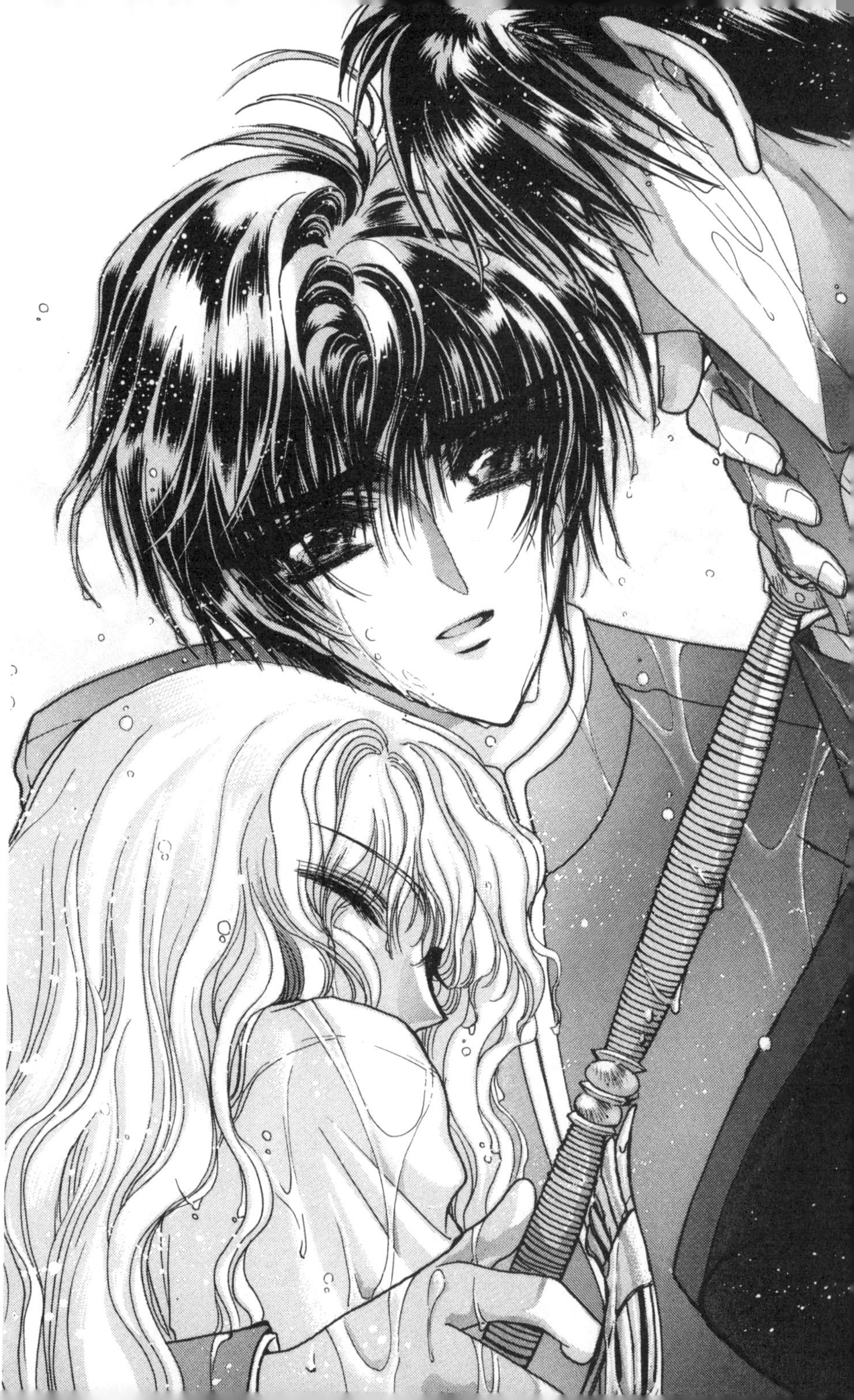

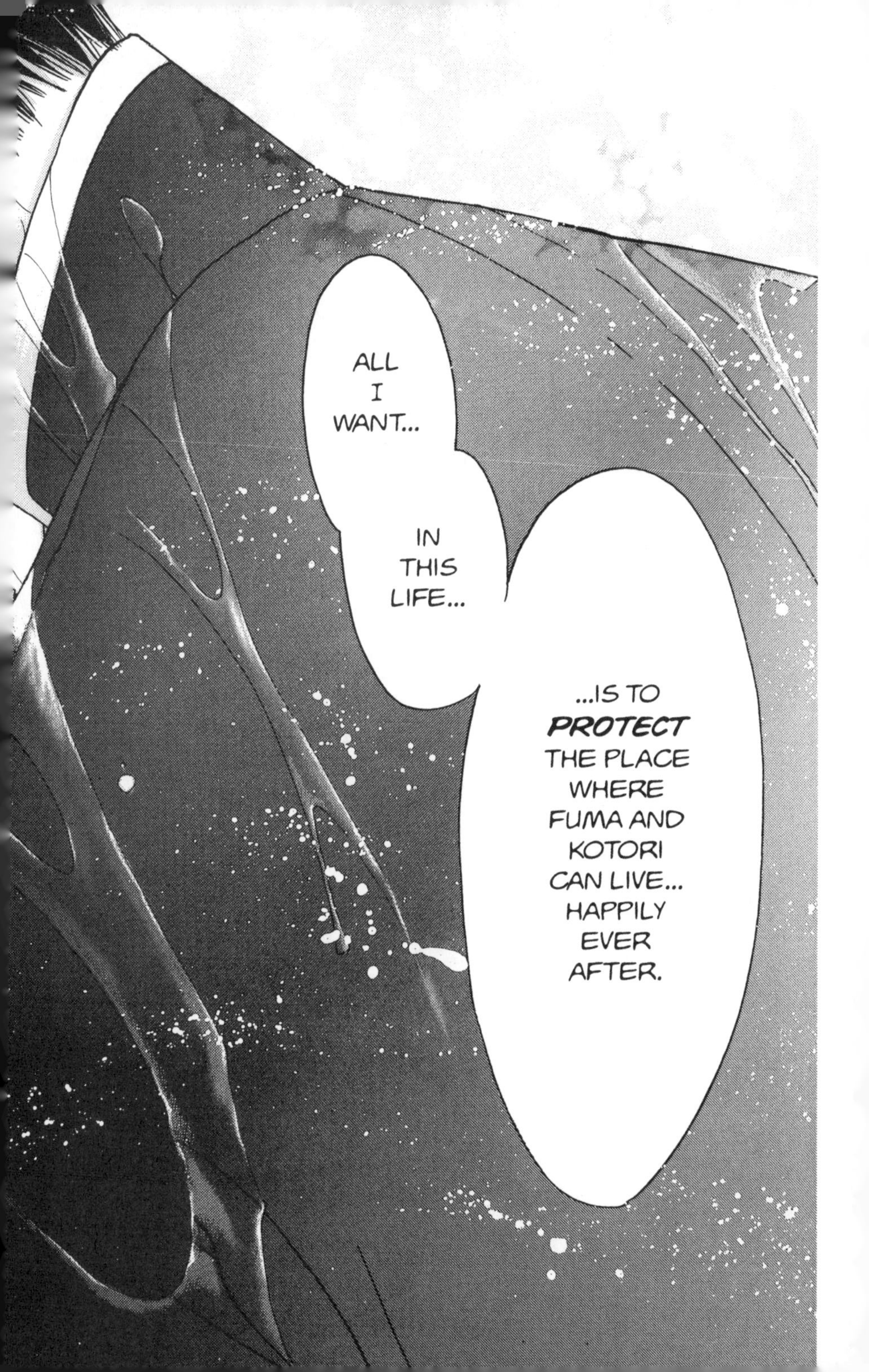
ALL I WANT...
IN THIS LIFE...
...IS TO *PROTECT* THE PLACE WHERE FUMA AND KOTORI CAN LIVE... HAPPILY EVER AFTER.

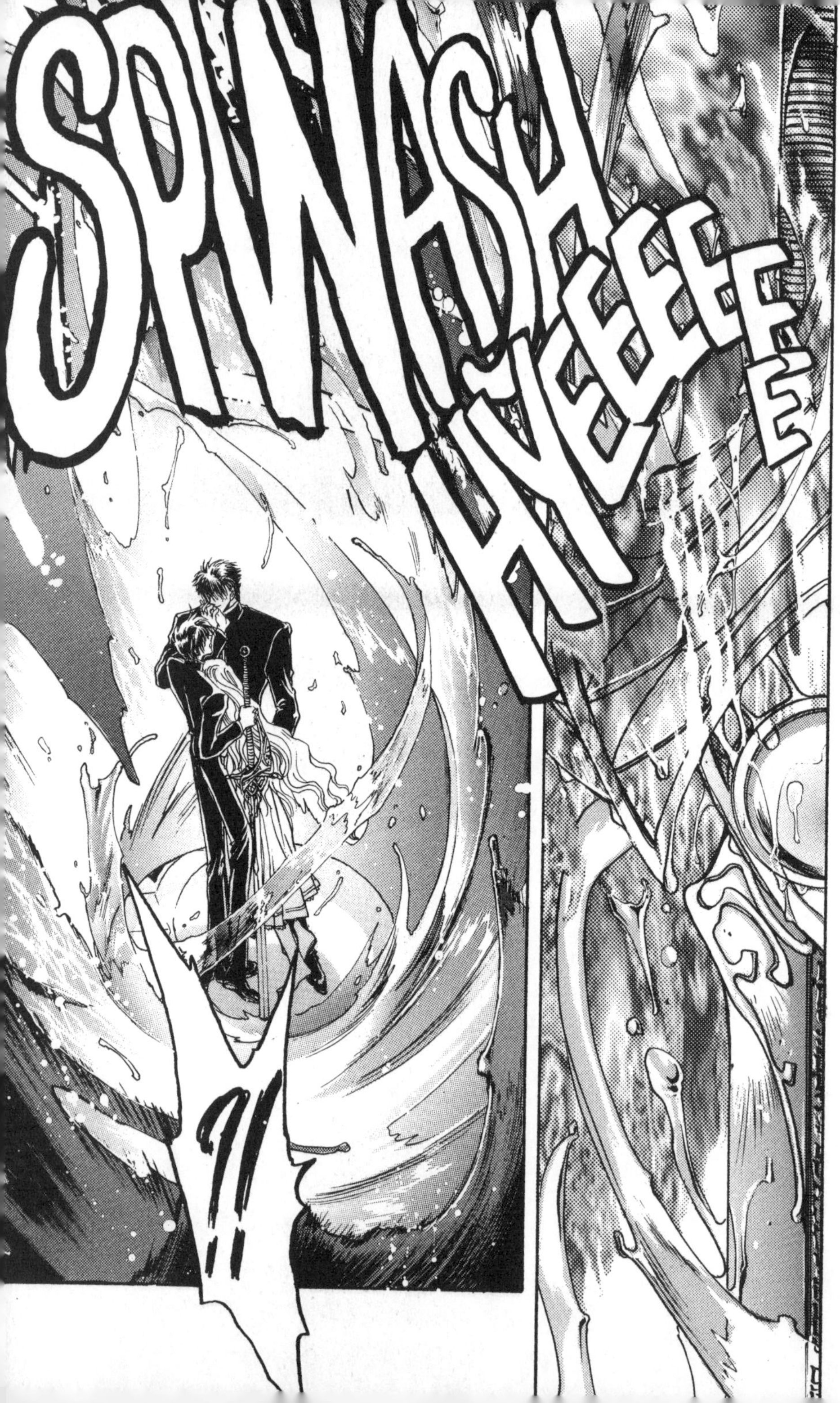
SPLASH
KYEEEEEE

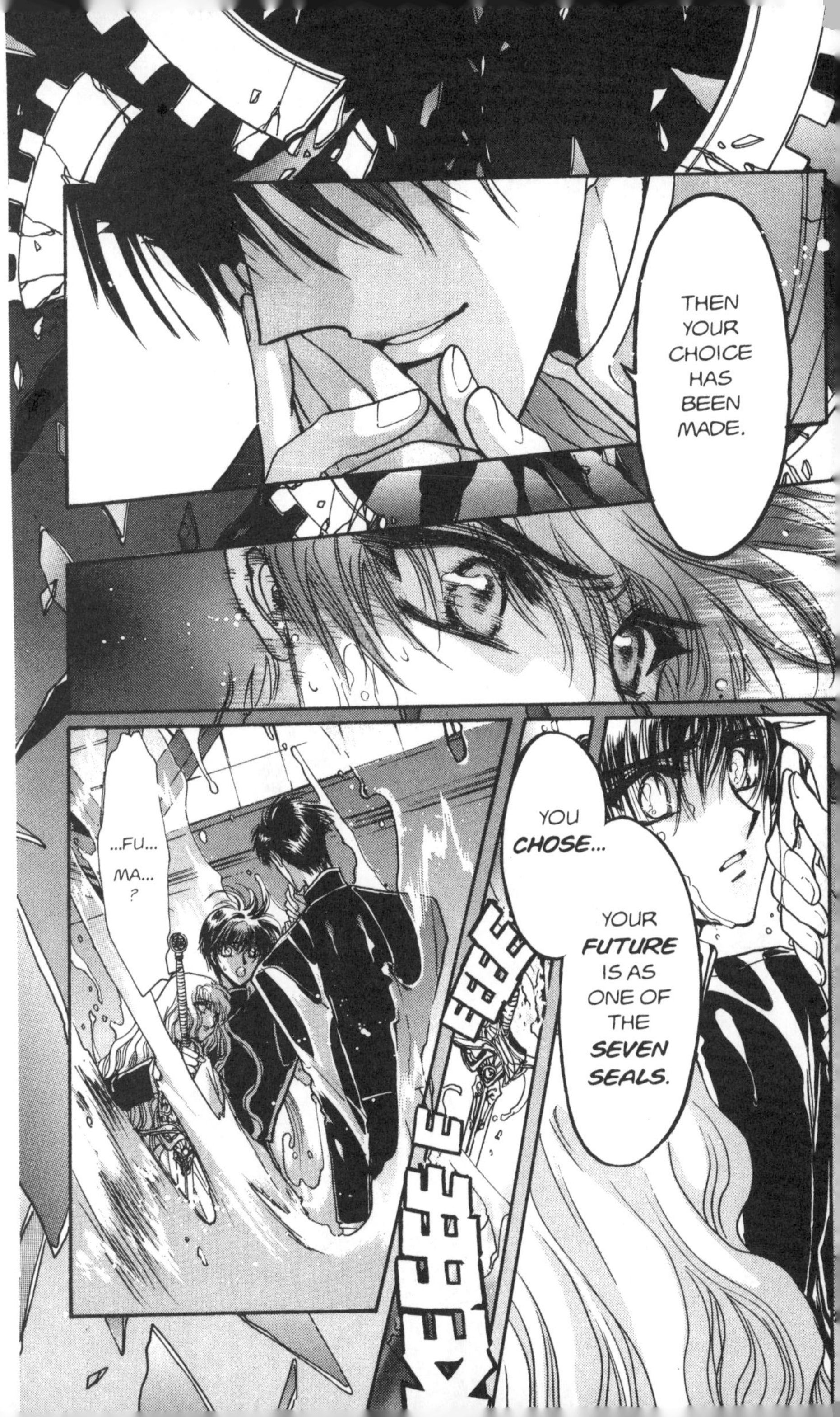
THEN YOUR CHOICE HAS BEEN MADE.
YOU **CHOSE...**
YOUR **FUTURE** IS AS ONE OF THE **SEVEN SEALS.**
...FU... MA... ?

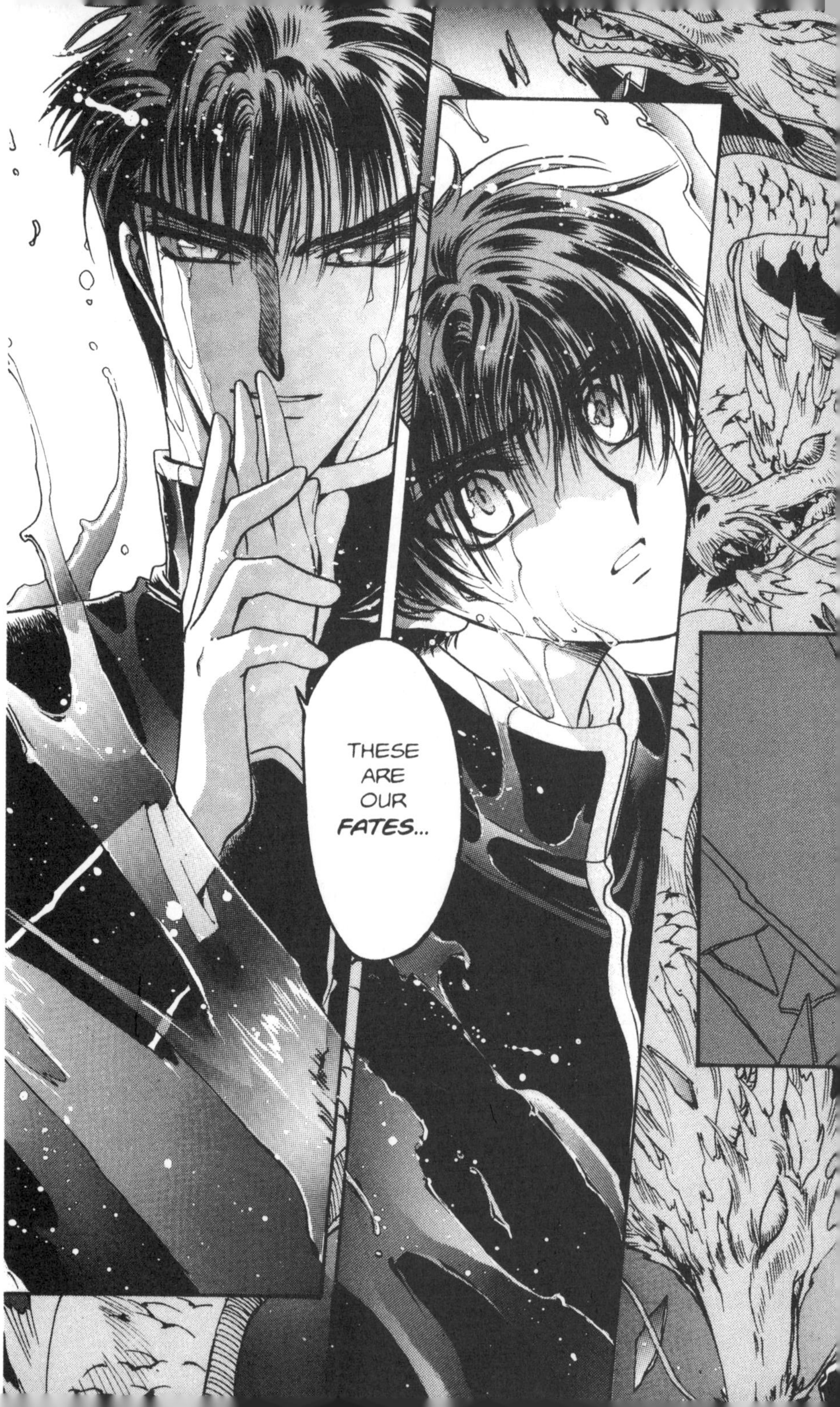
THESE ARE OUR *FATES...*

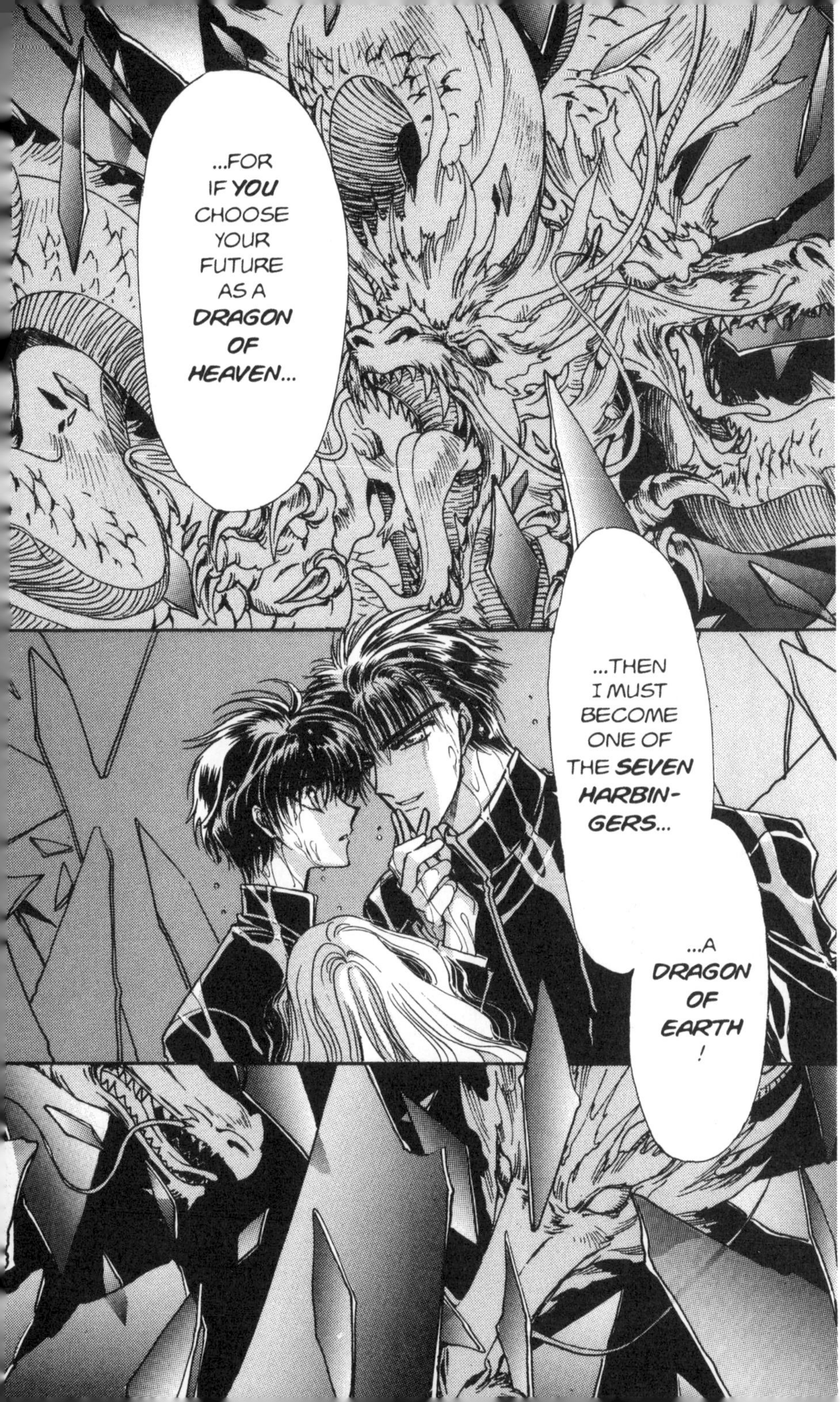
...FOR IF **YOU** CHOOSE YOUR FUTURE AS A **DRAGON OF HEAVEN...**
...THEN I MUST BECOME ONE OF THE **SEVEN HARBIN-GERS...**
...A **DRAGON OF EARTH**!

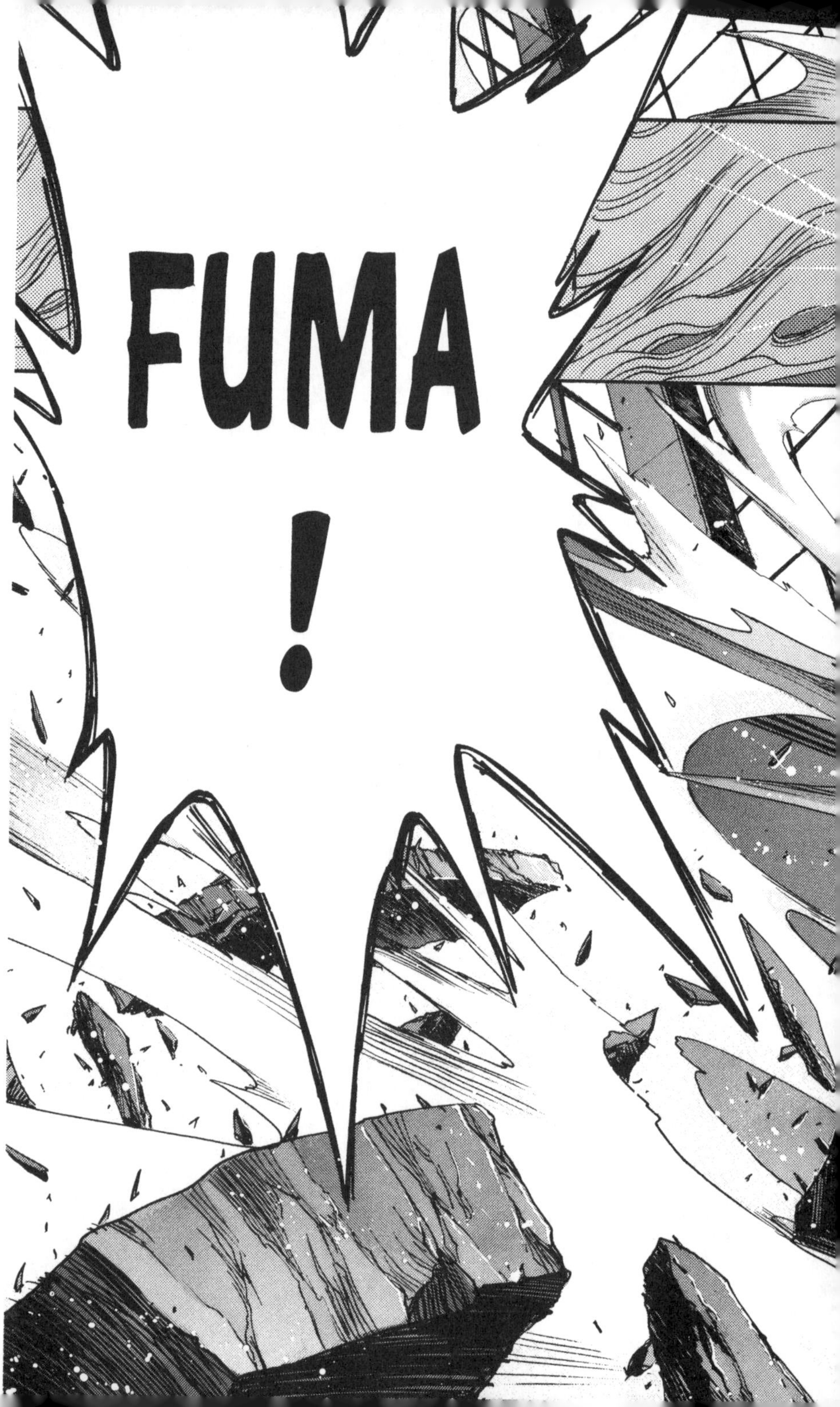
FUMA!

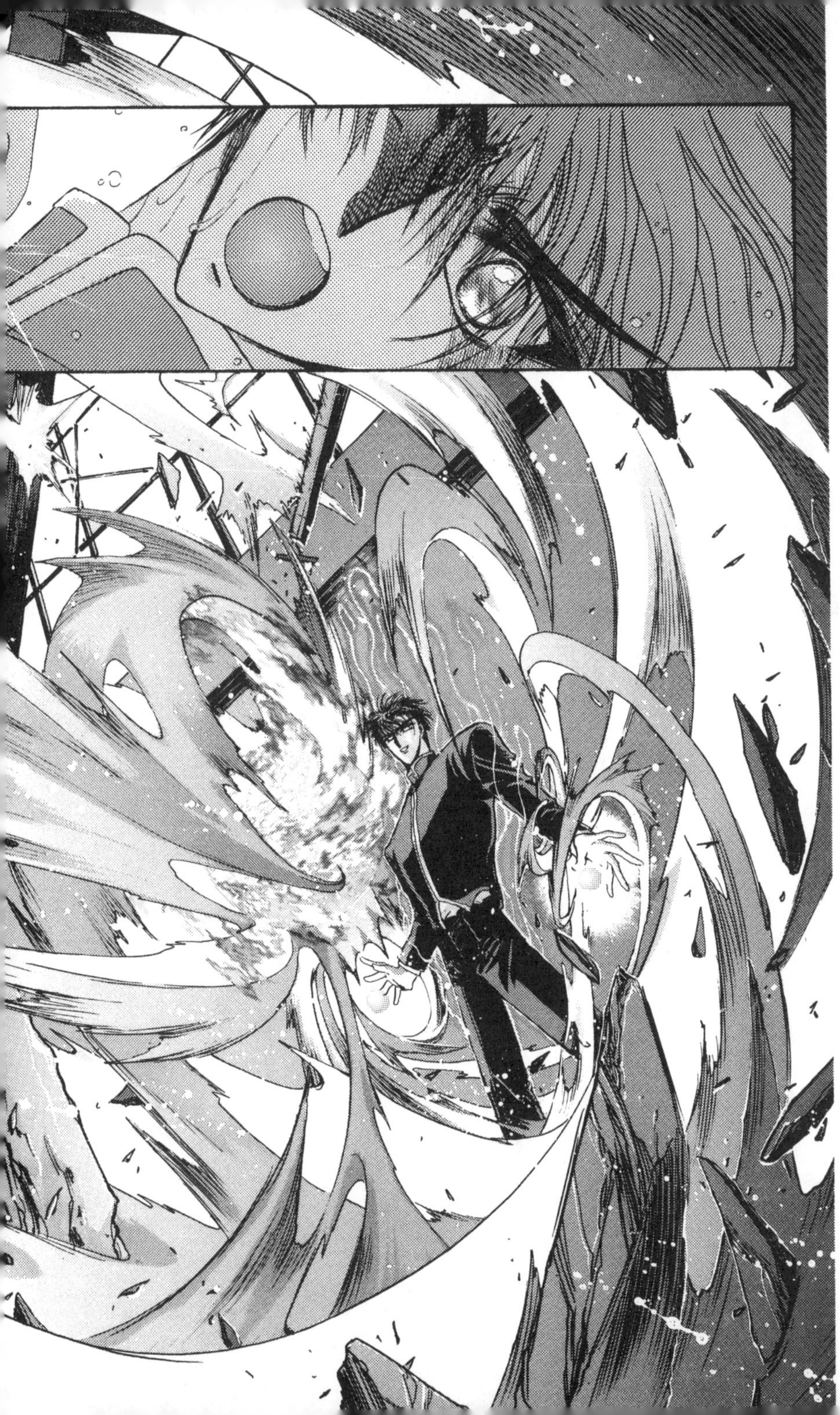

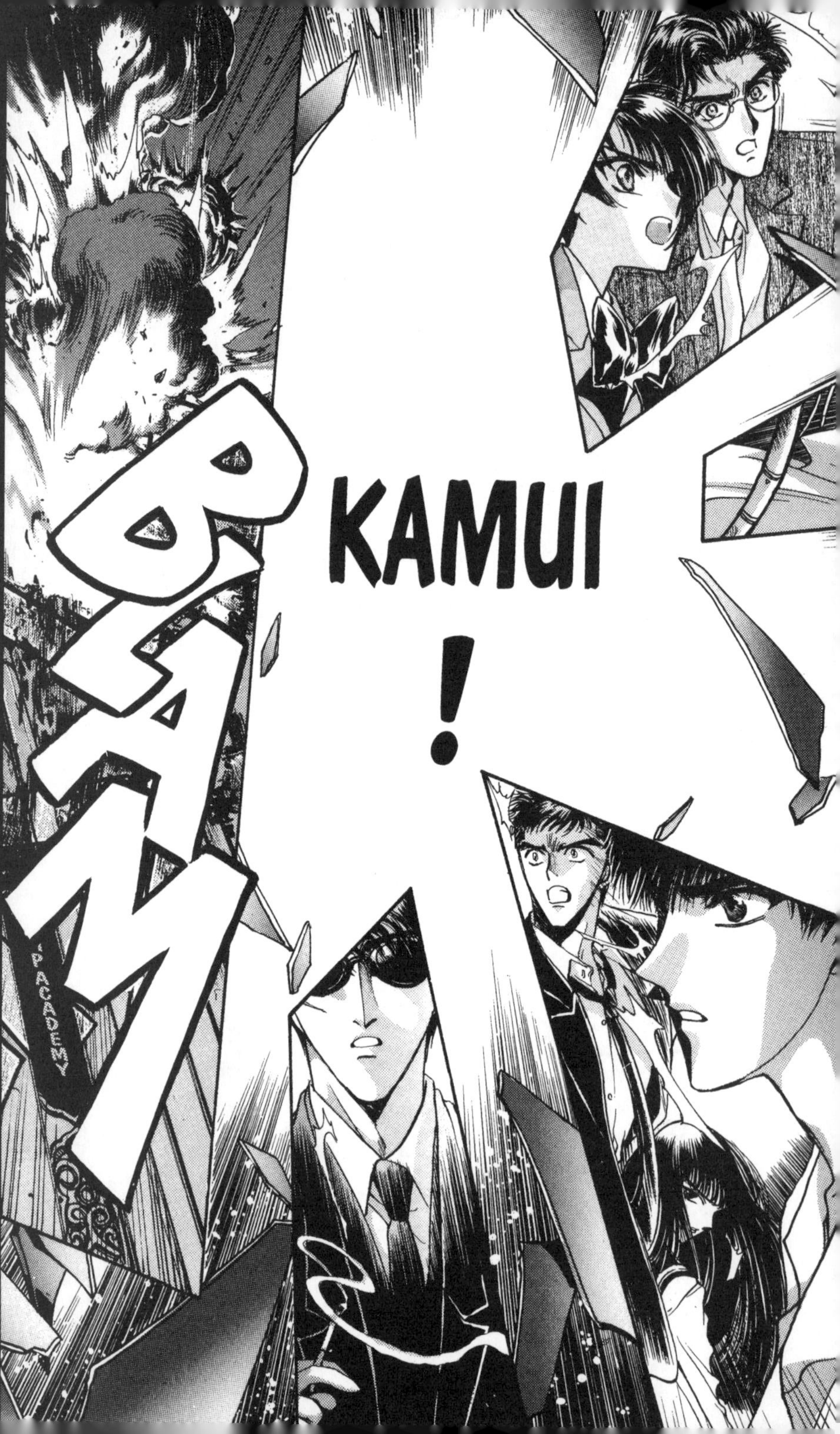

BAM
KAMUI
!
P ACADEMY

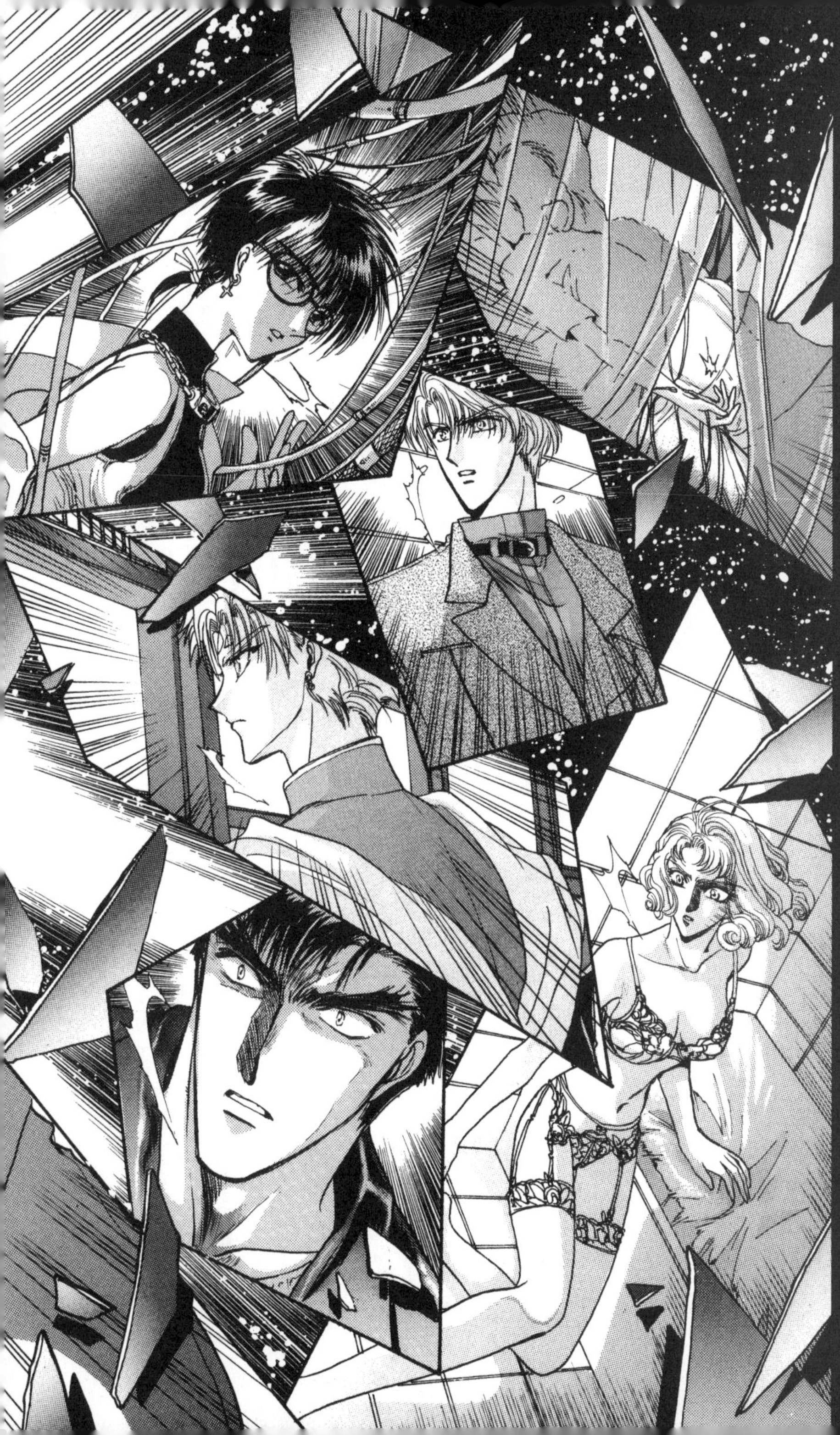

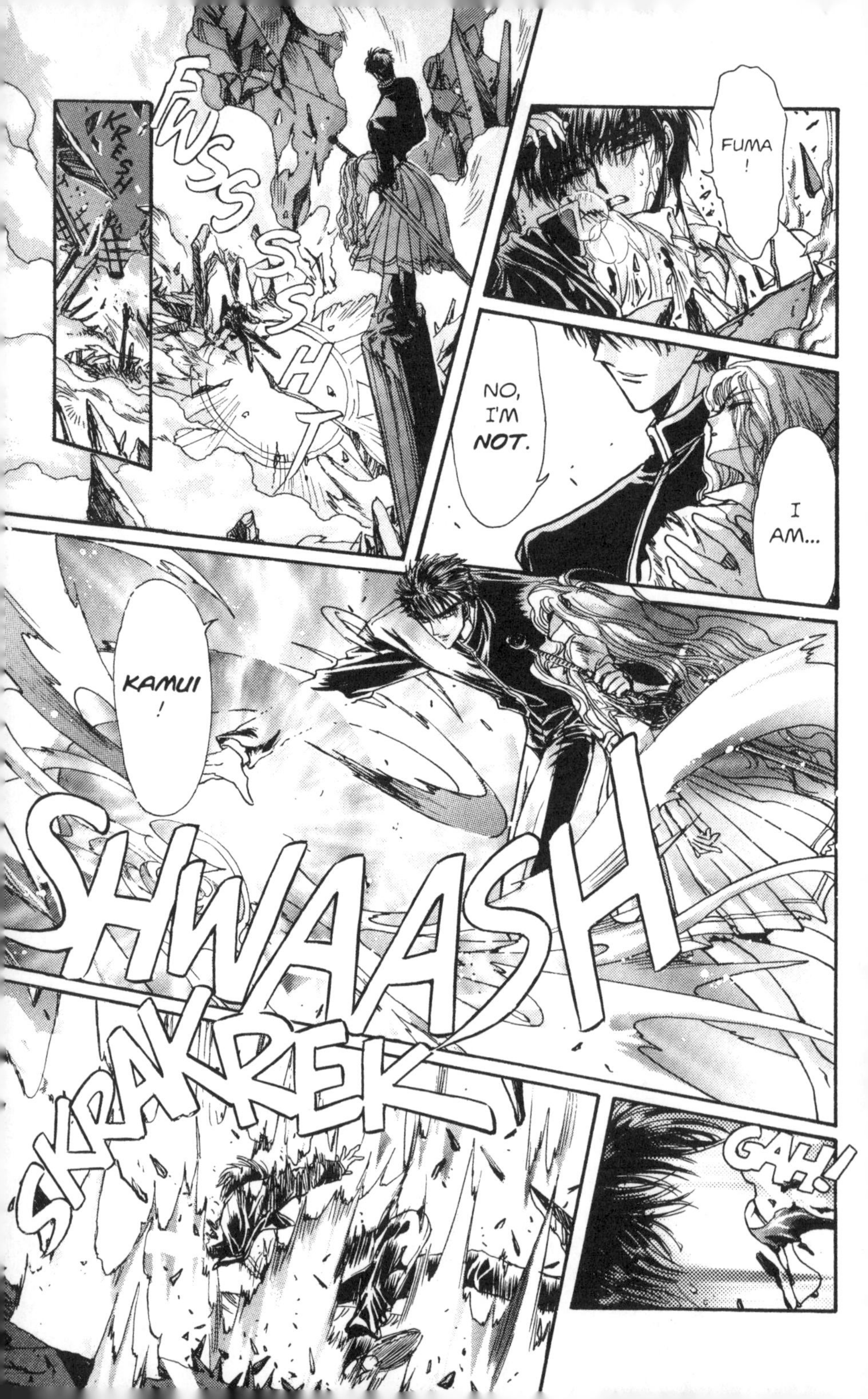
FUMA
!
NO, I'M NOT.
I AM...
FWSSSSHT
KRESH
KAMUI
!
SHWAASH
SKRAKREK
GAH!

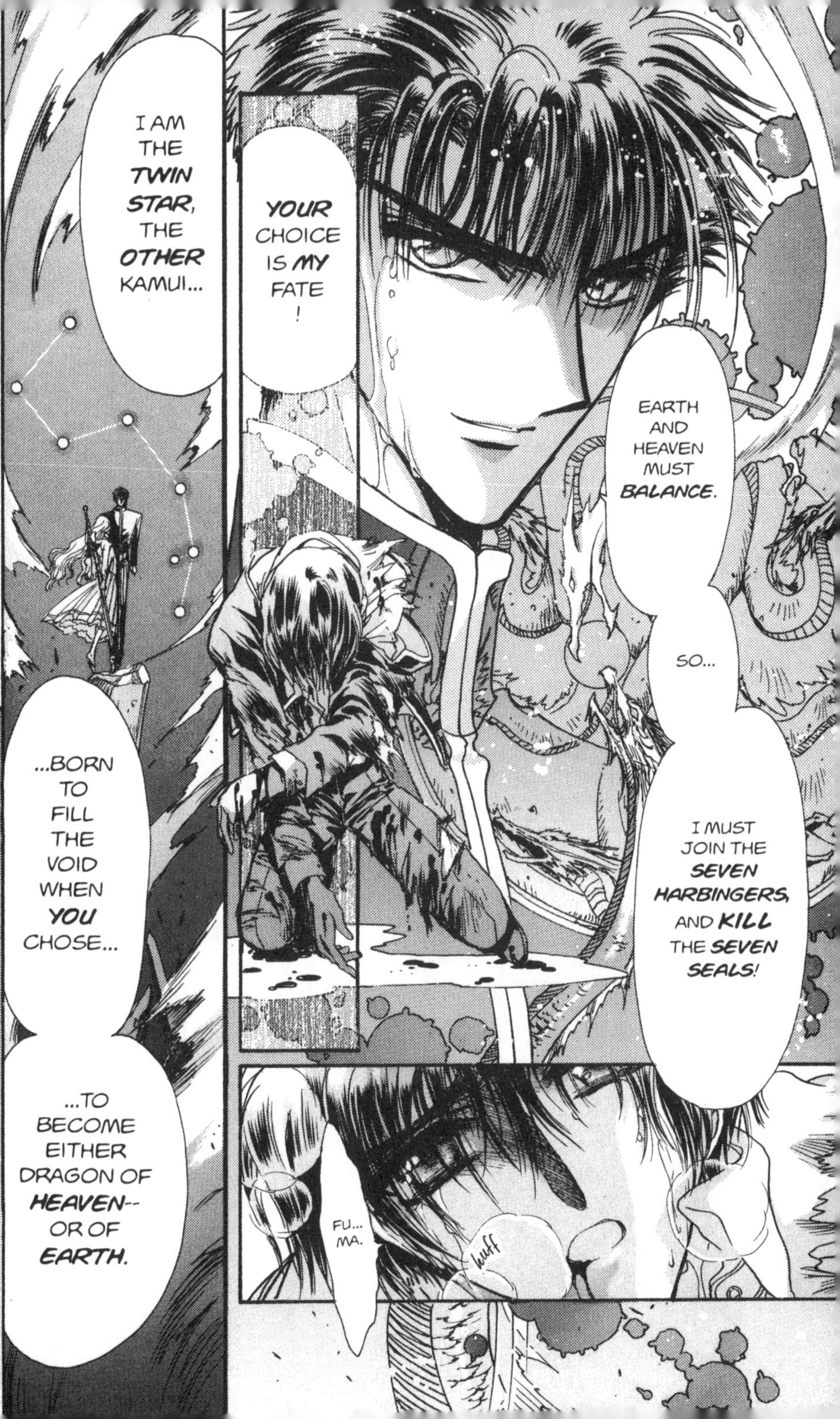
I AM THE TWIN STAR, THE OTHER KAMUI...
...BORN TO FILL THE VOID WHEN YOU CHOSE...
...TO BECOME EITHER DRAGON OF HEAVEN-- OR OF EARTH.
YOUR CHOICE IS MY FATE!
EARTH AND HEAVEN MUST BALANCE.
SO...
I MUST JOIN THE SEVEN HARBINGERS, AND KILL THE SEVEN SEALS!
FU... MA.
huff

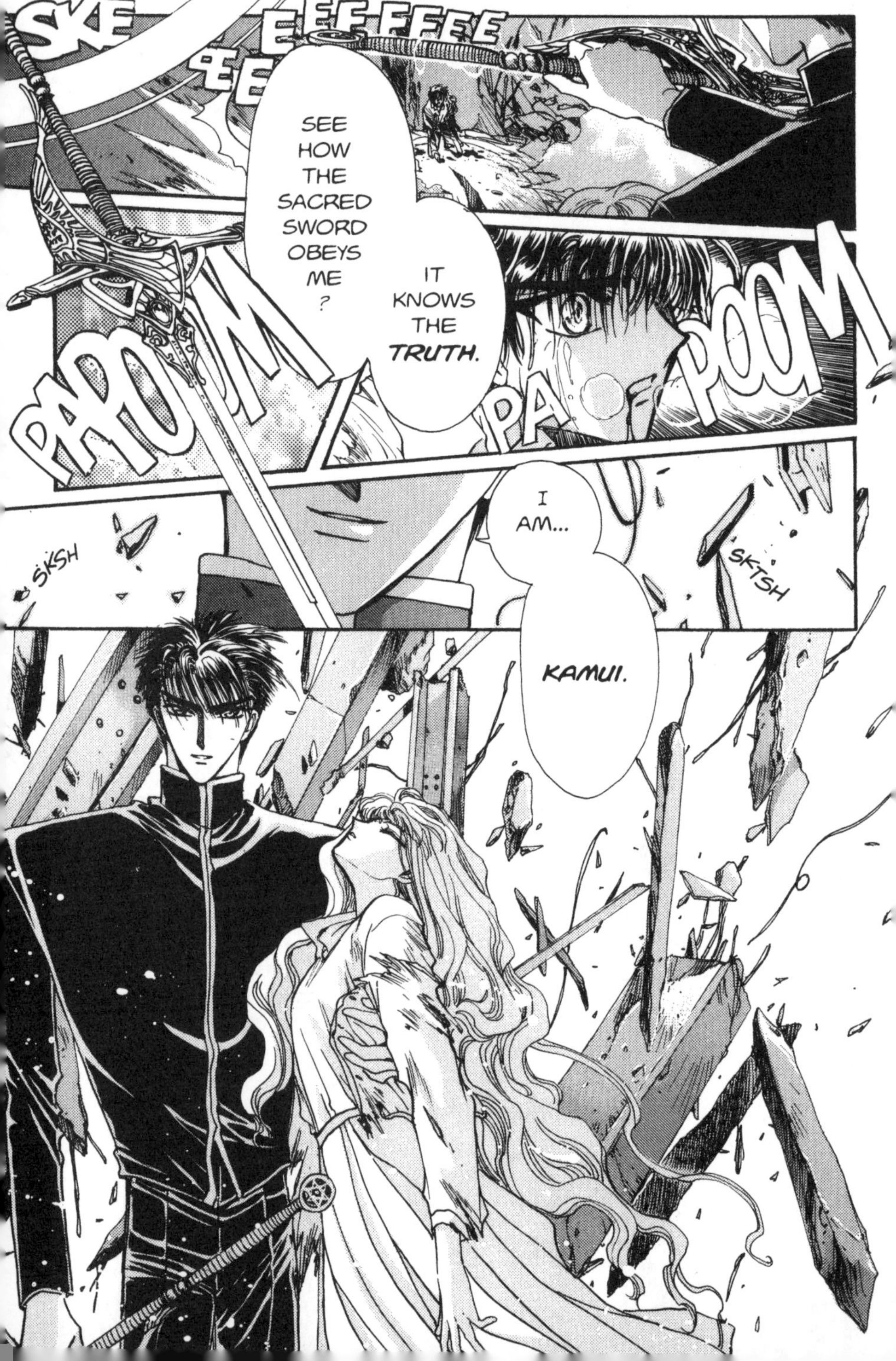
SKEEEEEEEE
SEE HOW THE SACRED SWORD OBEYS ME?
IT KNOWS THE TRUTH.
PAPOOM
PAPOOM
SKTSH
SKSH
I AM...
KAMUI.

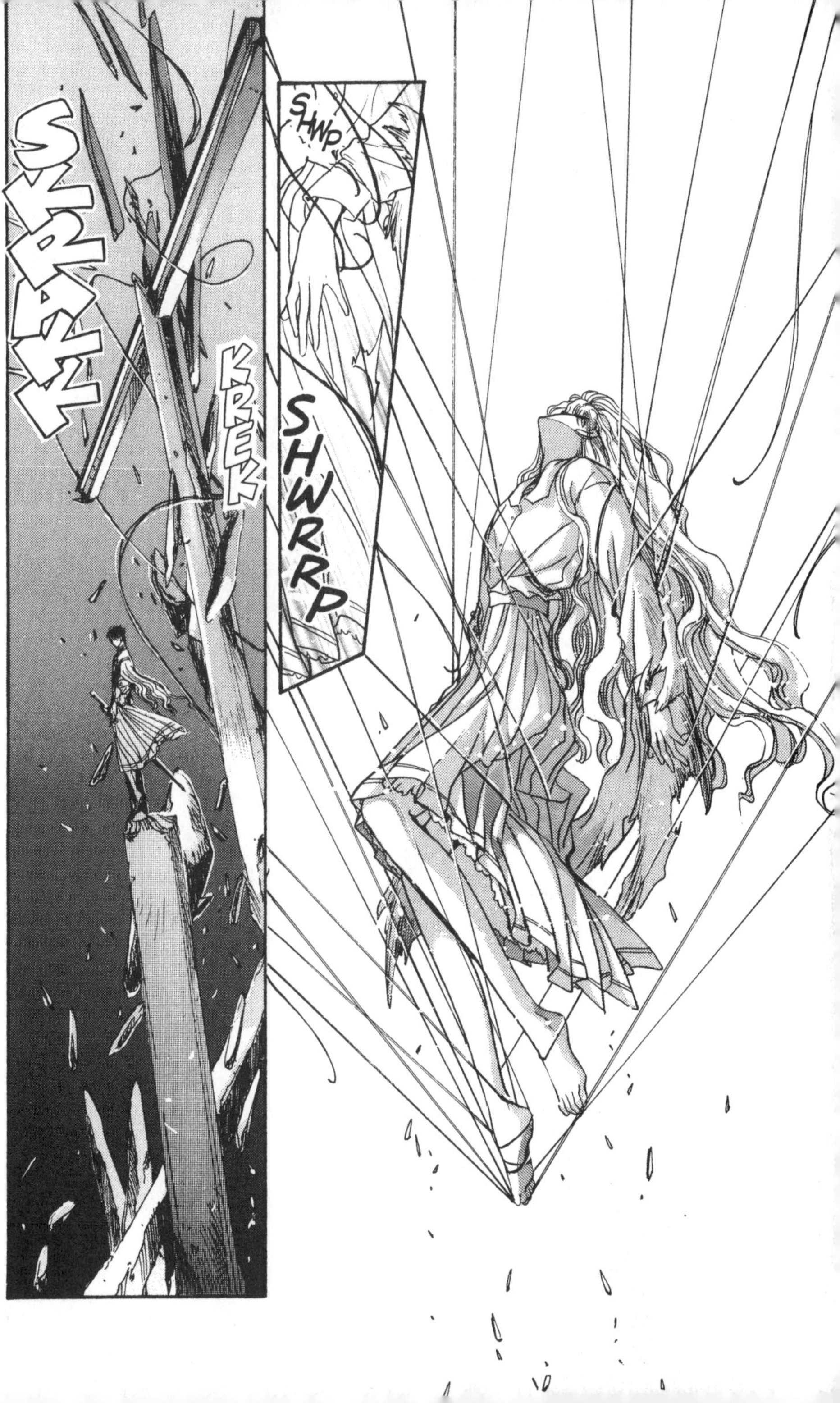
SHWP
SHWRRP
KREK
KRAKS

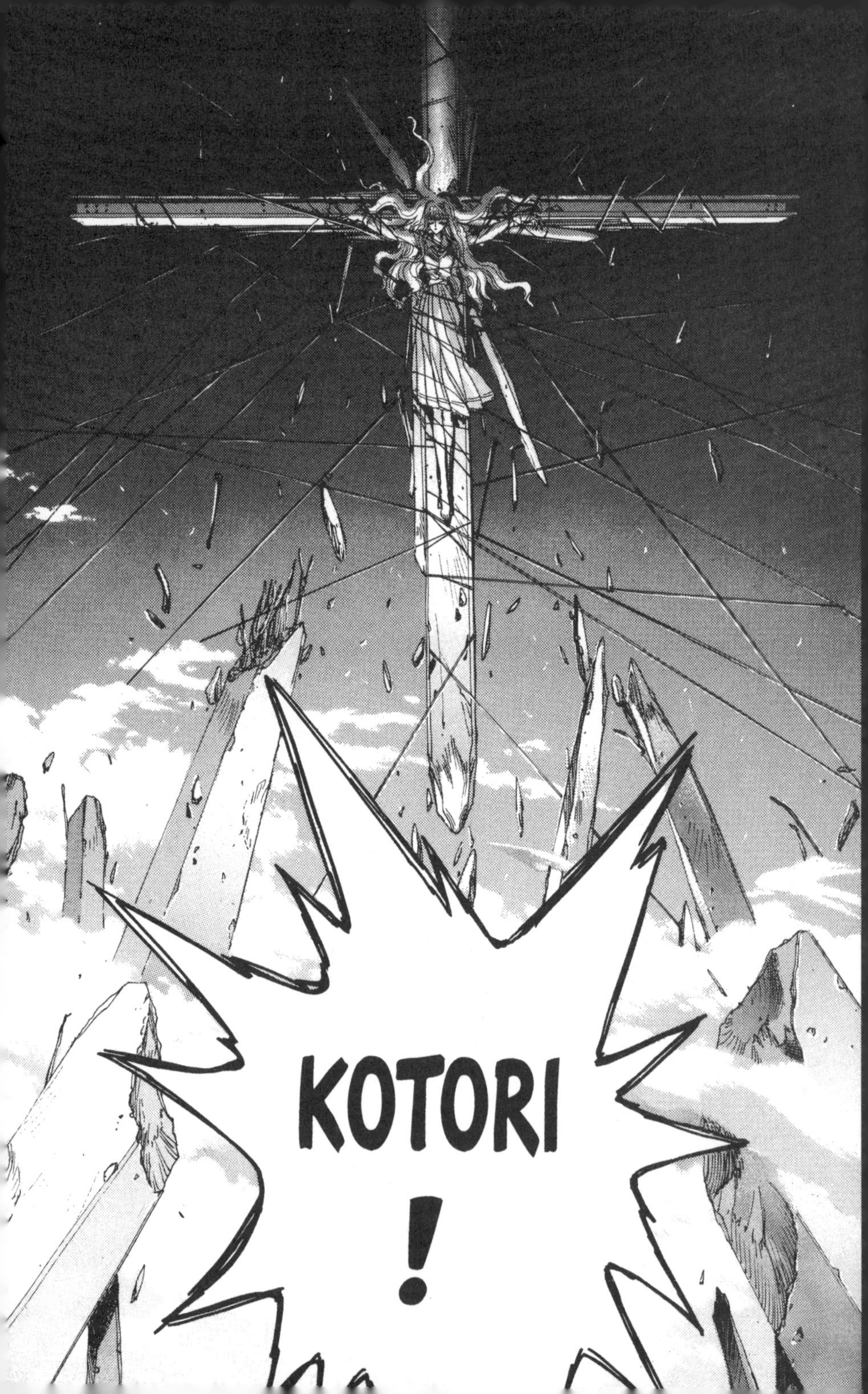
KOTORI
!

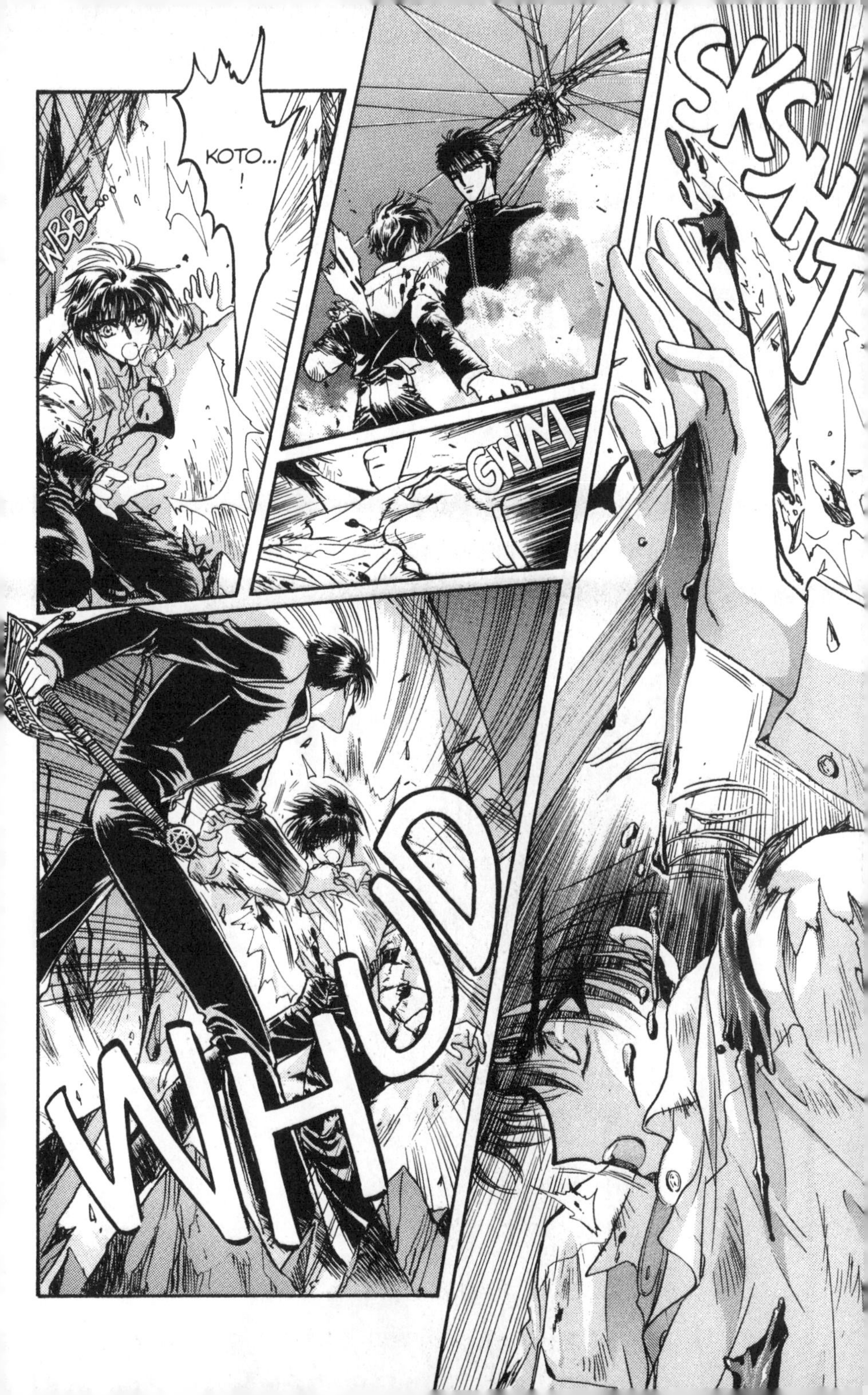
SKSHT
GWM
KOTO... !
WBBL...
WHUD

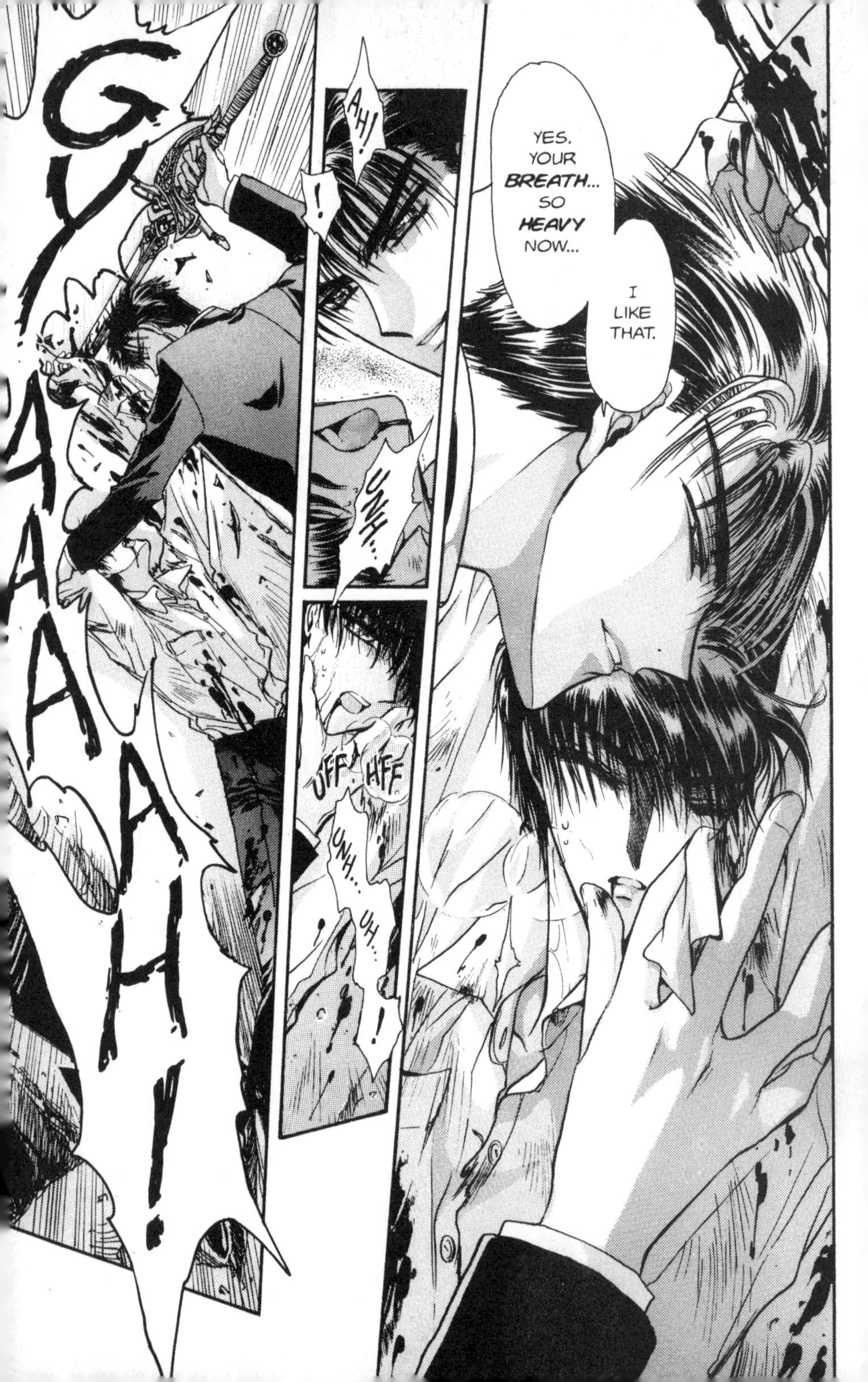
YES. YOUR **BREATH...** SO **HEAVY** NOW...
I LIKE THAT.
AH!
!
UNH...
UFF HFF
UNH... UH...
!
GYAAAAH!

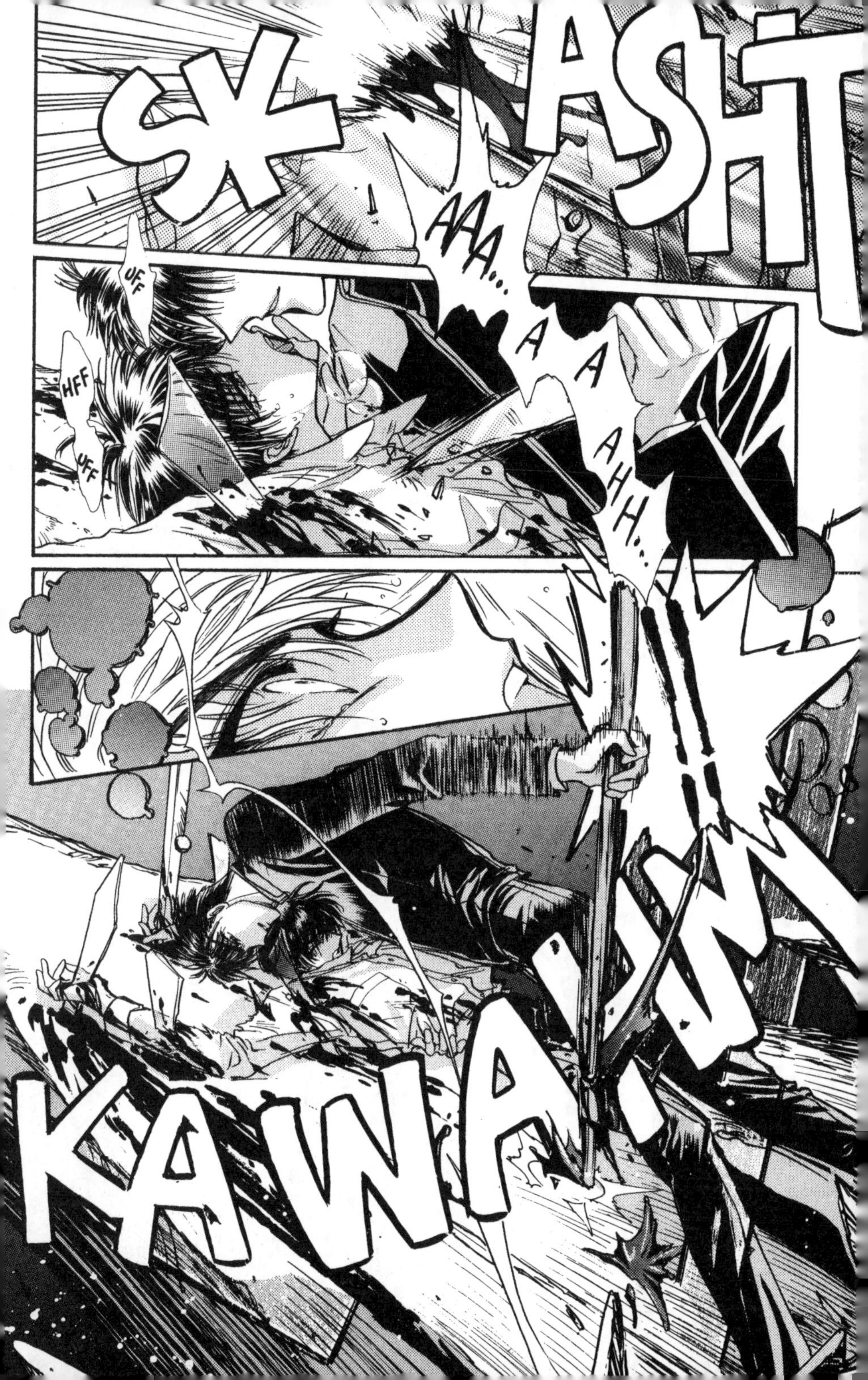
SKLASH
AAAA...
AAAAHH...
UFF
HFF
UFF
KAWAMM

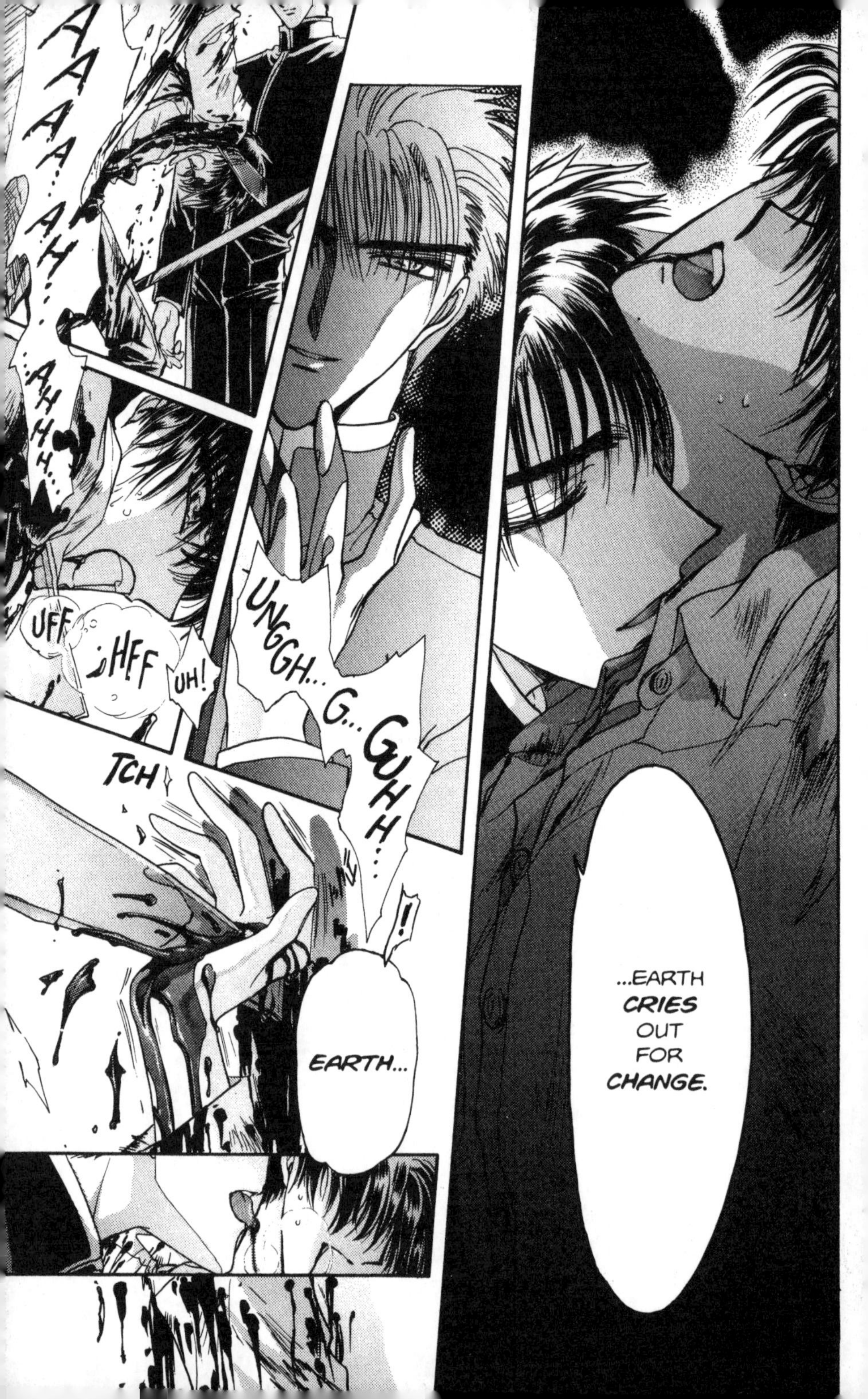
AAAAAAH...AH...AHHHH...
UNGGH...G...GUHH...
UFF
HFF
UH!
TCH
!
EARTH...
...EARTH CRIES OUT FOR CHANGE.

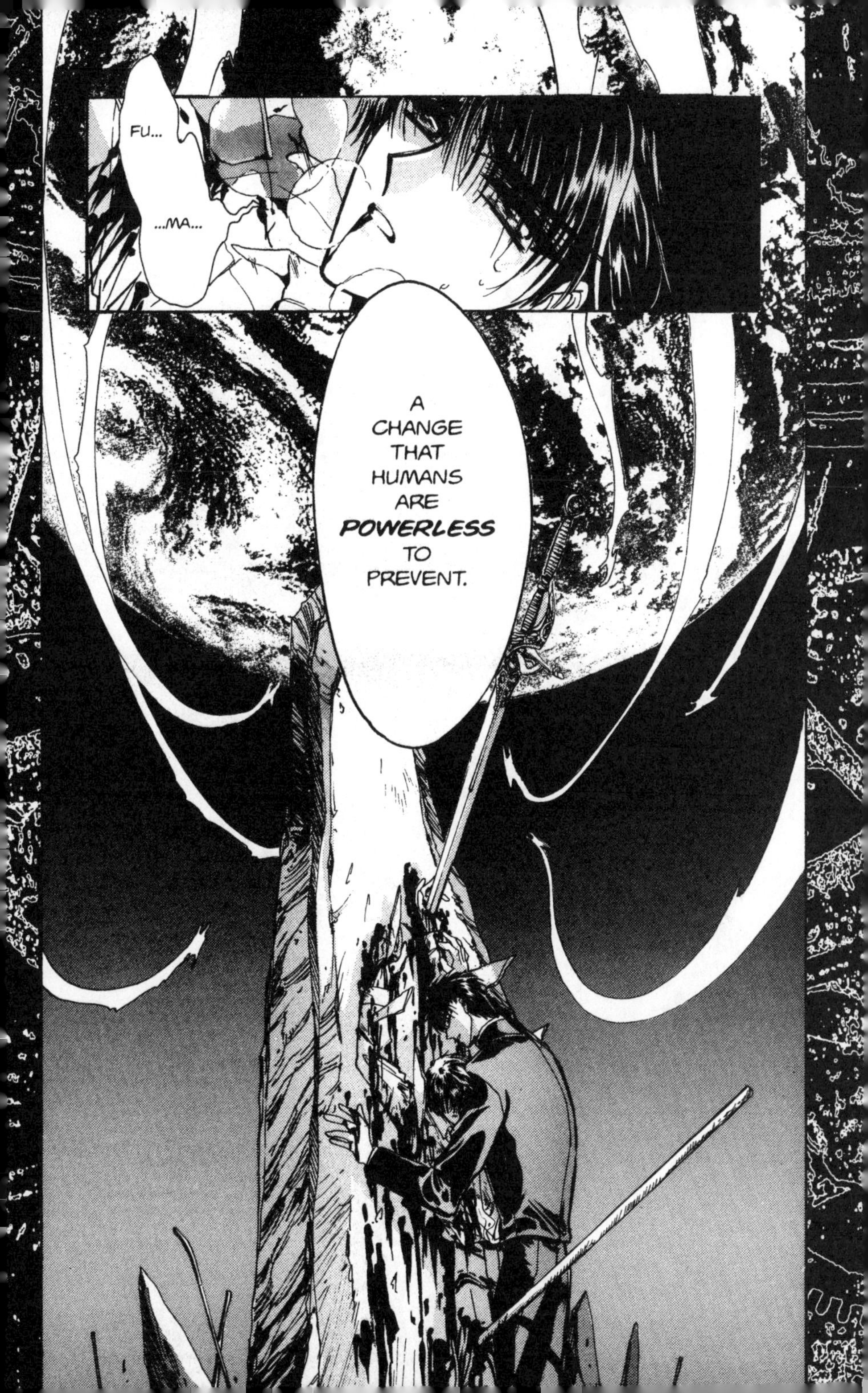
FU...
...MA...
A CHANGE THAT HUMANS ARE **POWERLESS** TO PREVENT.

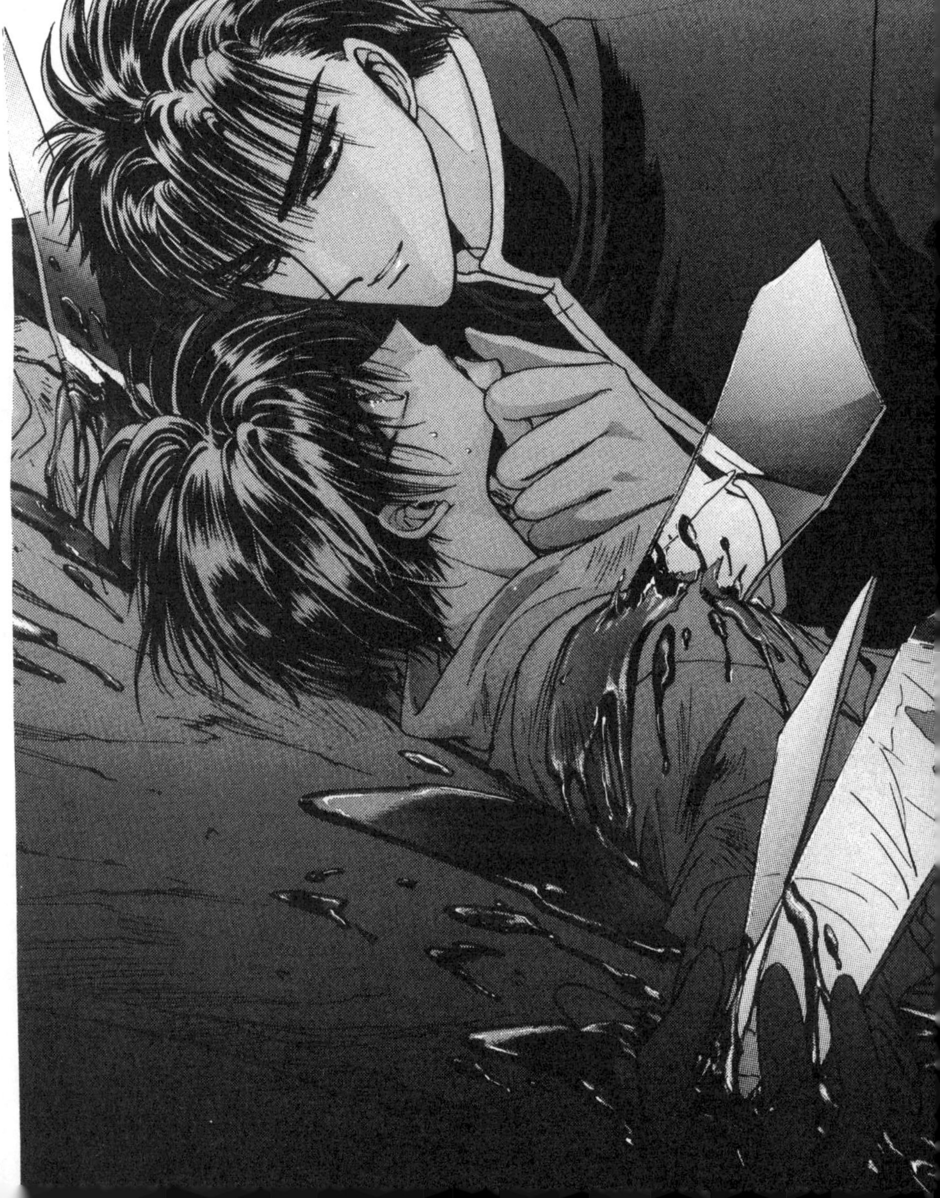

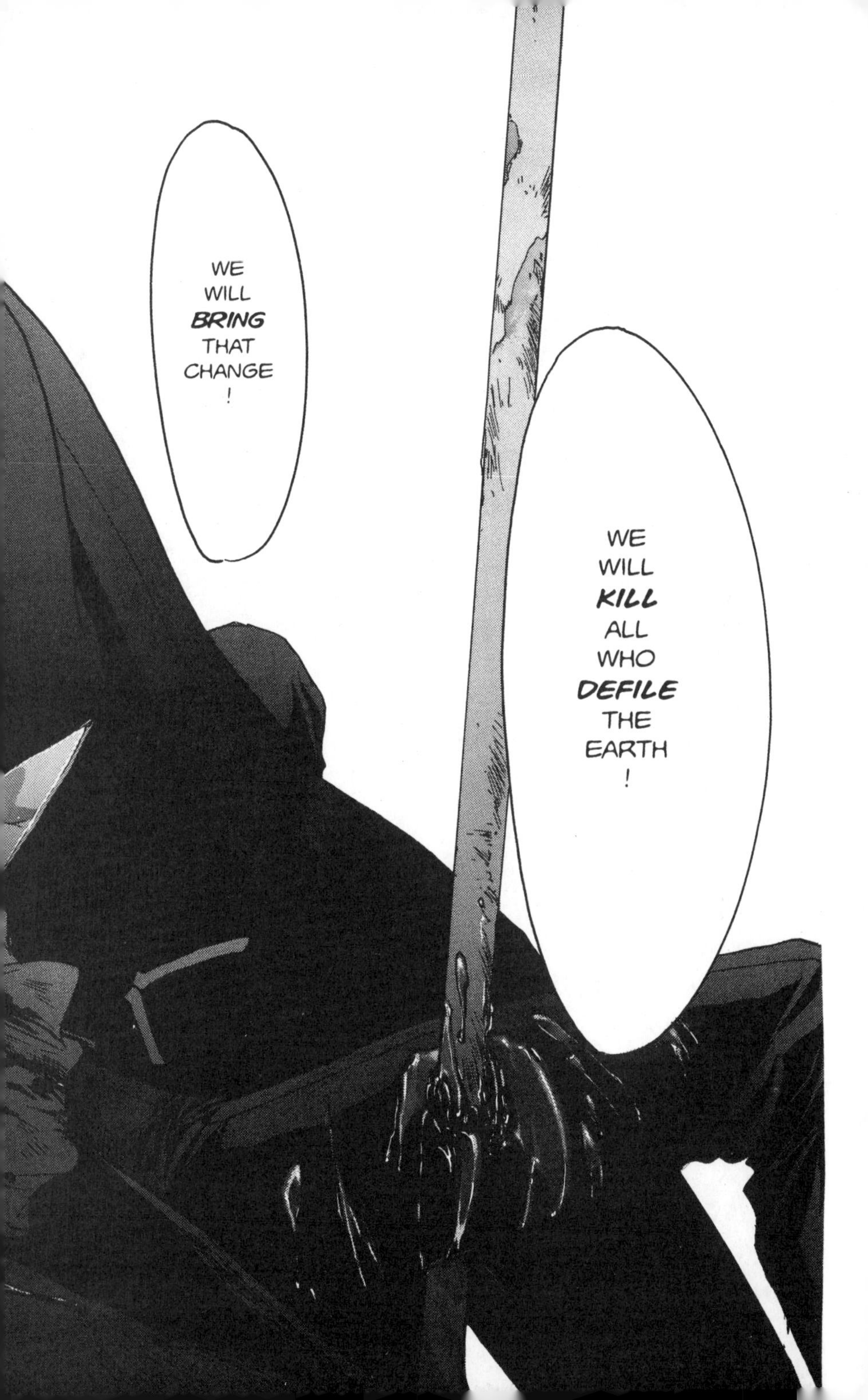
WE WILL **KILL** ALL WHO **DEFILE** THE EARTH!
WE WILL **BRING** THAT CHANGE!

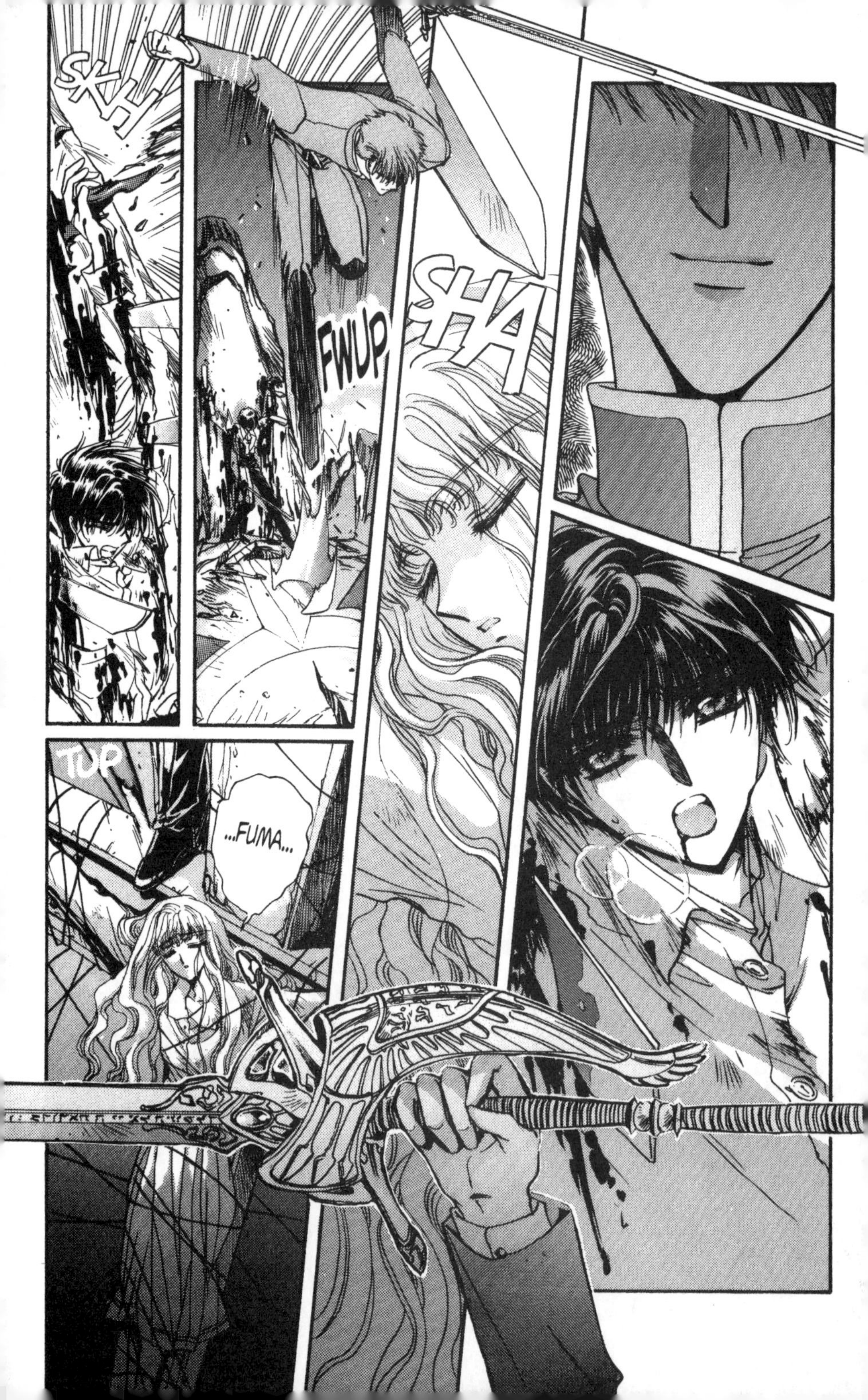
SHA
FWUP
SKH
TUP
...FUMA...

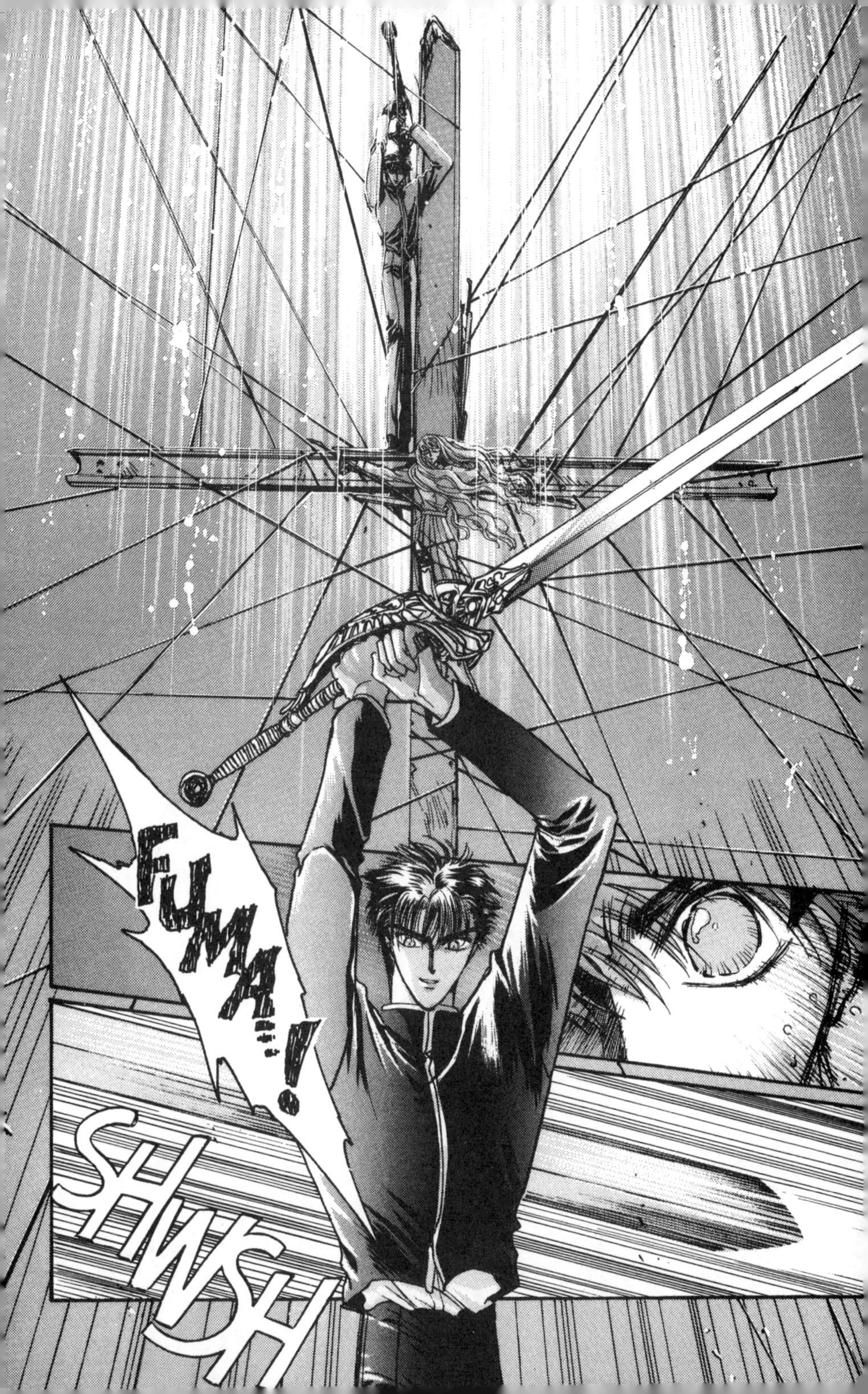
FUMA...!!
SHWSH

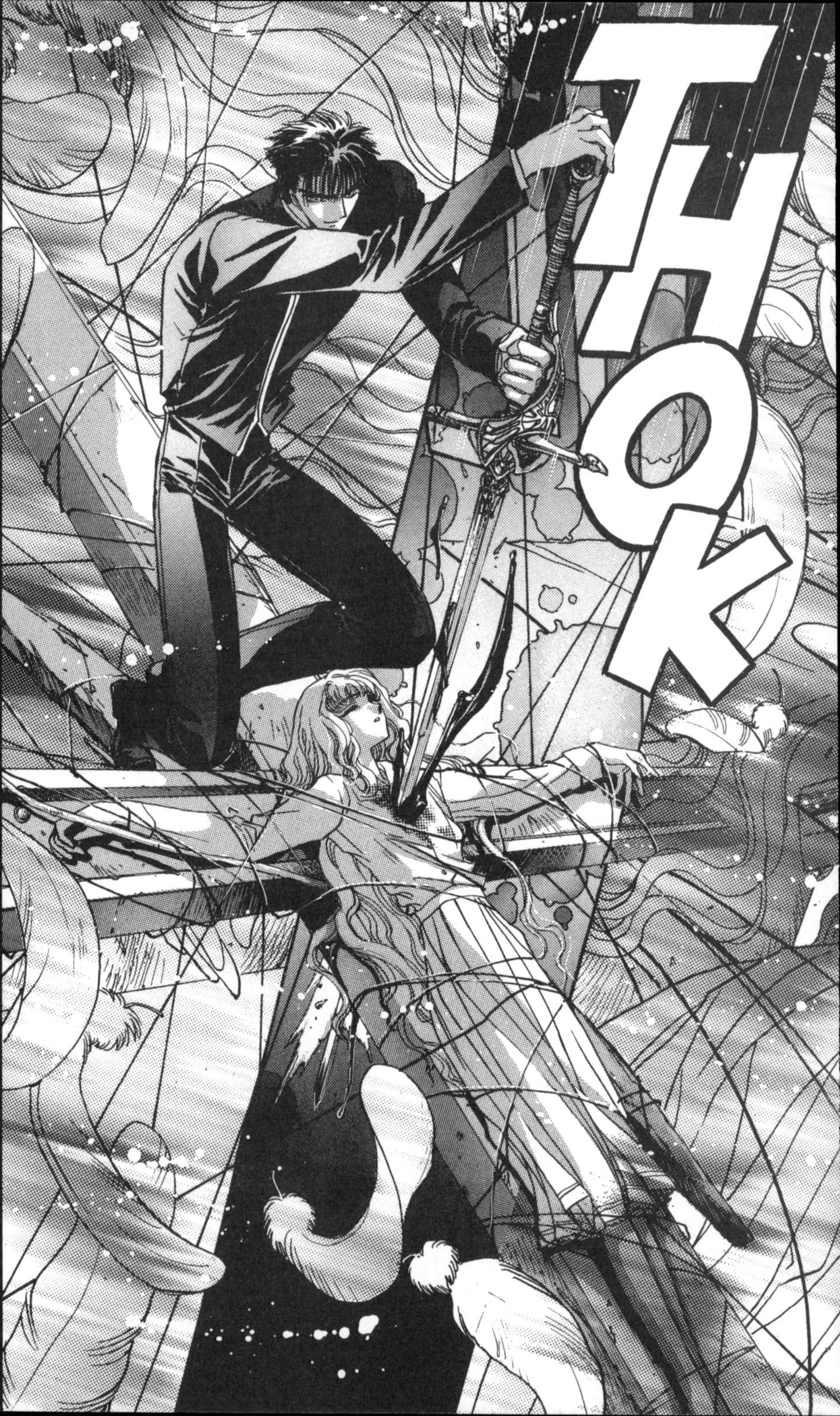
THOK

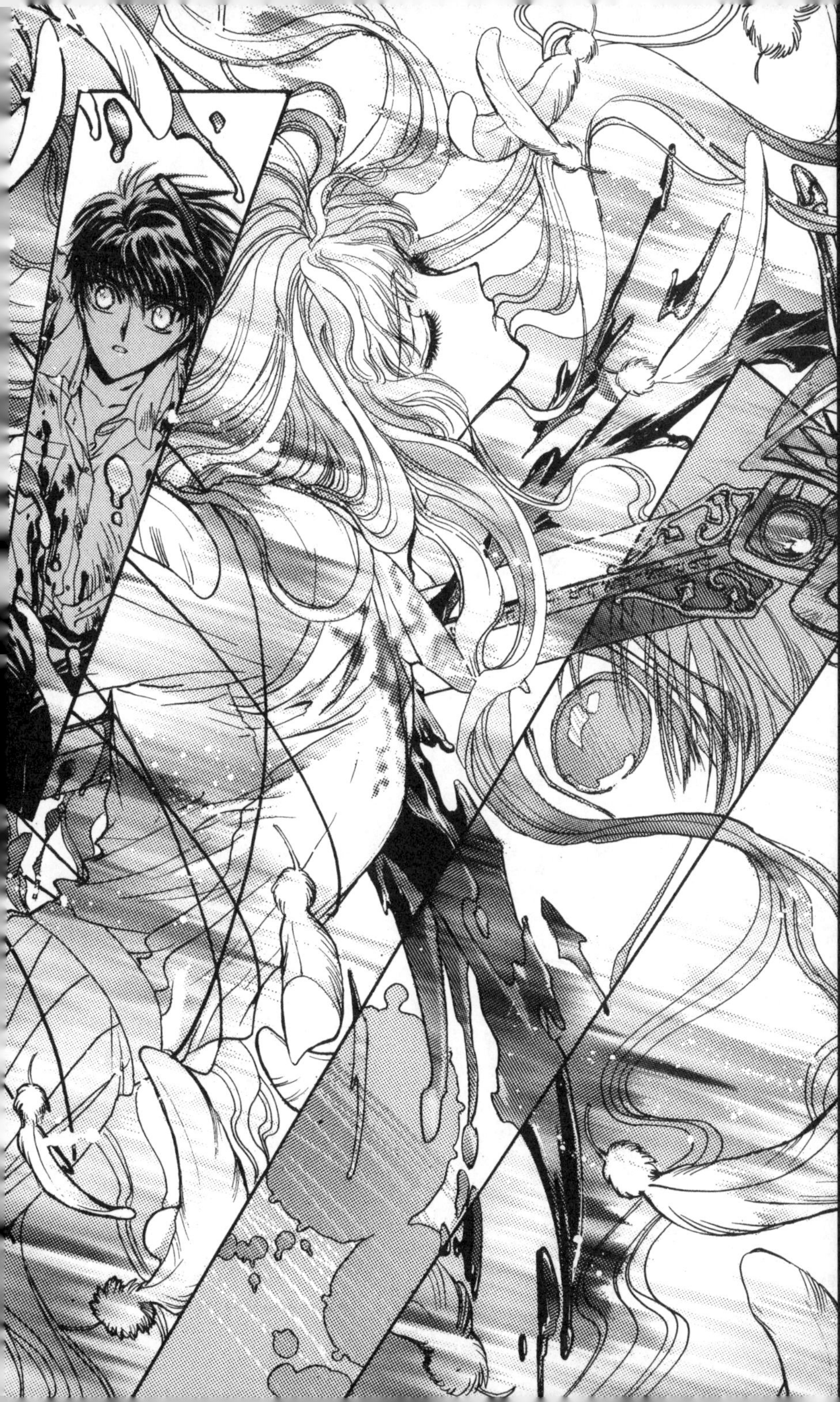

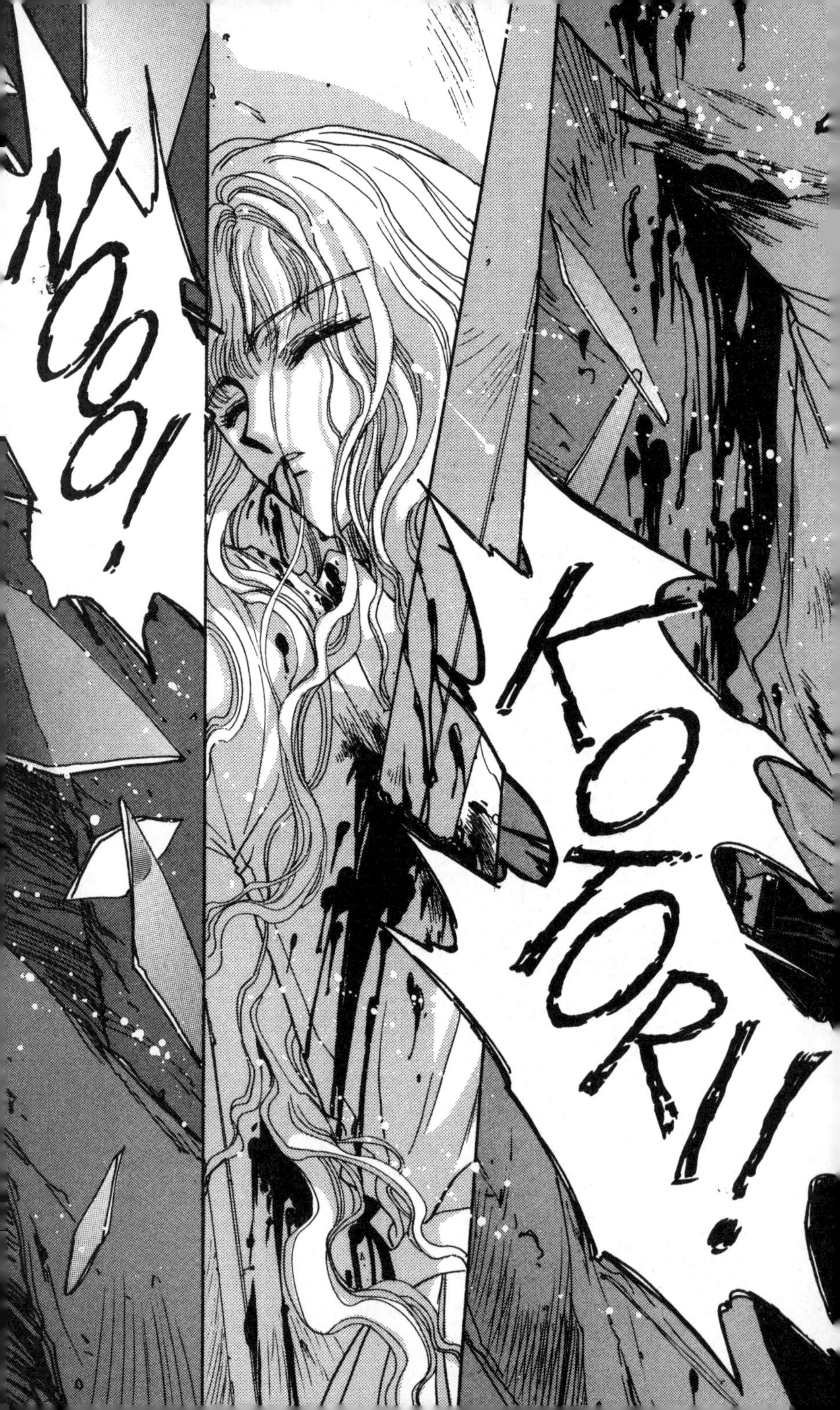
KOTORI!!
NOOO!

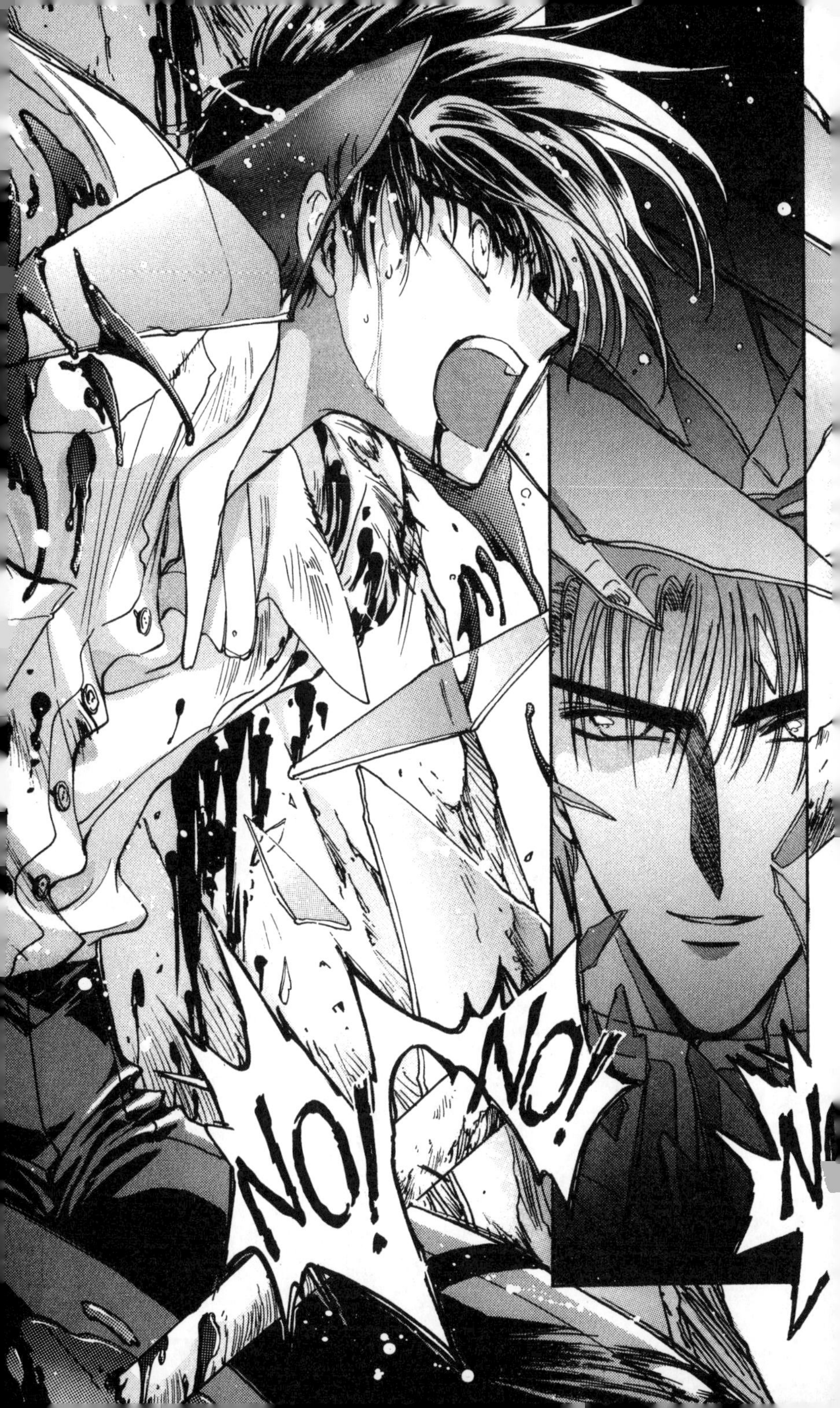
NO!
NO!
NO!
NO

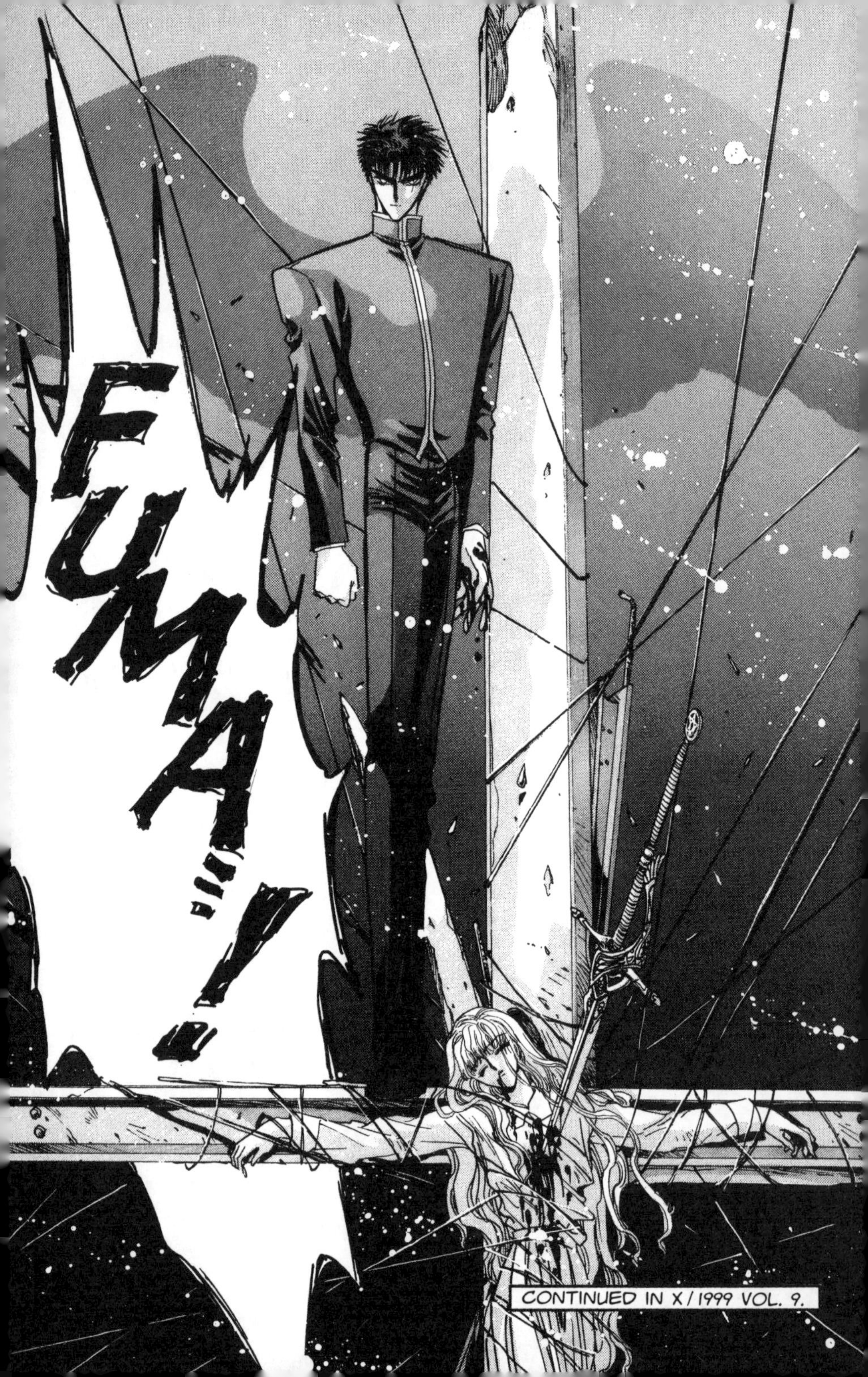
FUMA!!
CONTINUED IN X/1999 VOL. 9.

X

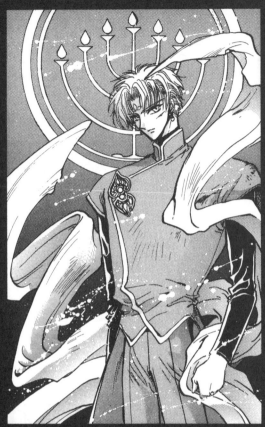

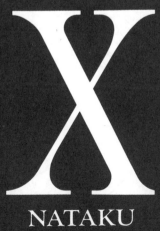

NATAKU

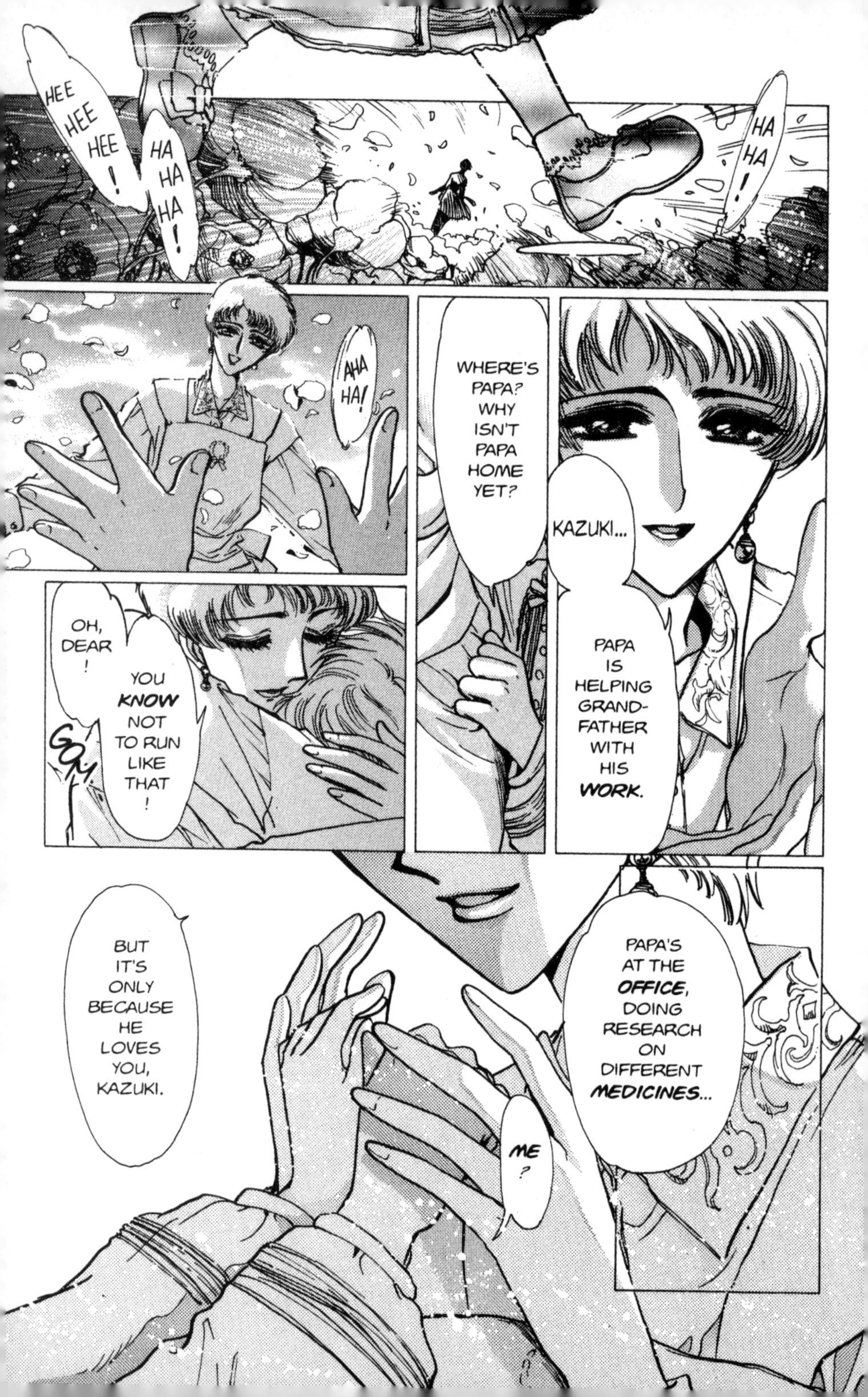

HEE HEE HEE !
HA HA HA !
HA HA !
AHA HA!
OH, DEAR !
YOU *KNOW* NOT TO RUN LIKE THAT !
GOM
WHERE'S PAPA? WHY ISN'T PAPA HOME YET?
KAZUKI...
PAPA IS HELPING GRAND-FATHER WITH HIS *WORK*.
PAPA'S AT THE *OFFICE*, DOING RESEARCH ON DIFFERENT *MEDICINES*...
ME ?
BUT IT'S ONLY BECAUSE HE LOVES YOU, KAZUKI.

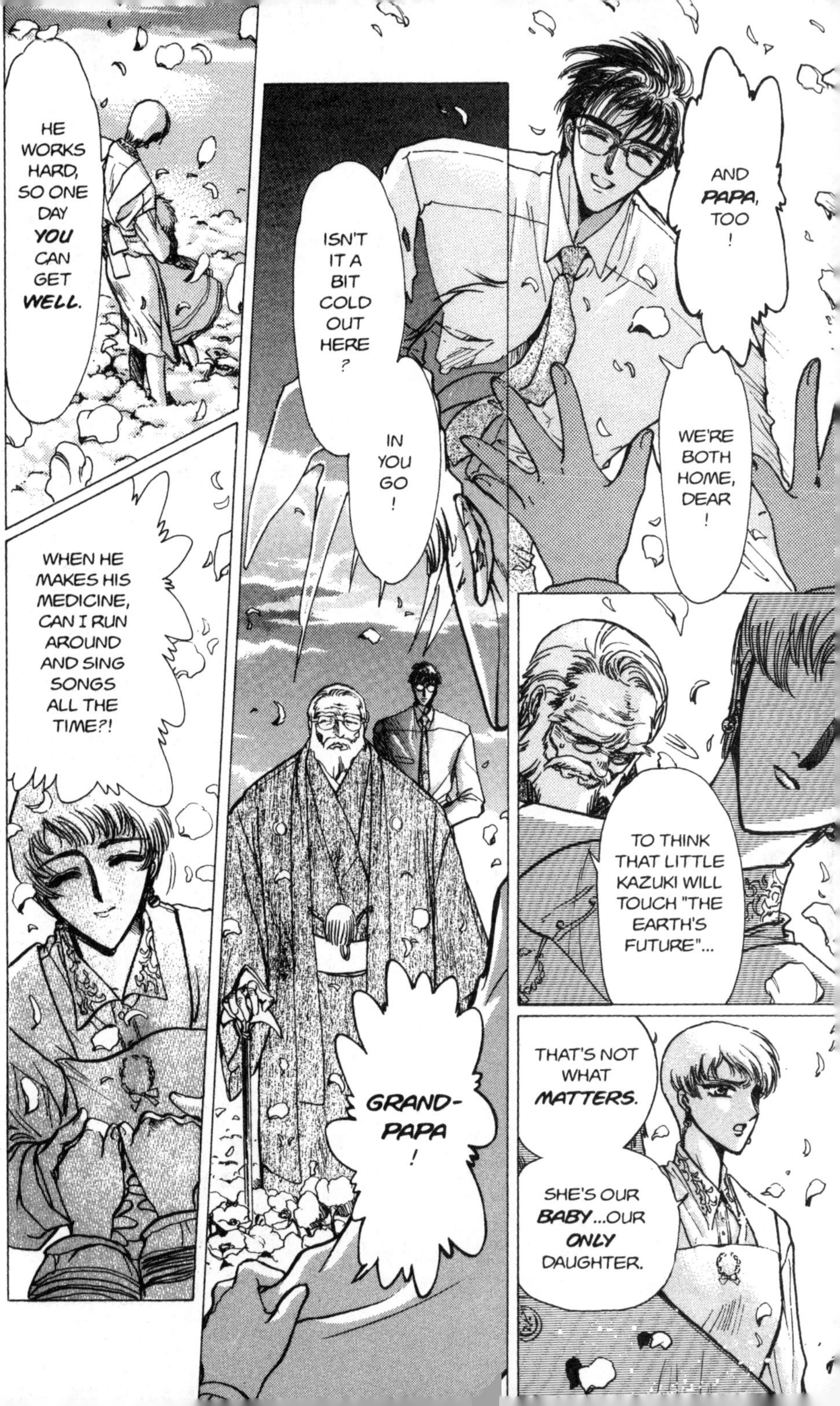
AND PAPA, TOO!
WE'RE BOTH HOME, DEAR!
TO THINK THAT LITTLE KAZUKI WILL TOUCH "THE EARTH'S FUTURE"...
THAT'S NOT WHAT MATTERS.
SHE'S OUR BABY...OUR ONLY DAUGHTER.
ISN'T IT A BIT COLD OUT HERE?
IN YOU GO!
GRANDPAPA!
HE WORKS HARD, SO ONE DAY YOU CAN GET WELL.
WHEN HE MAKES HIS MEDICINE, CAN I RUN AROUND AND SING SONGS ALL THE TIME?!

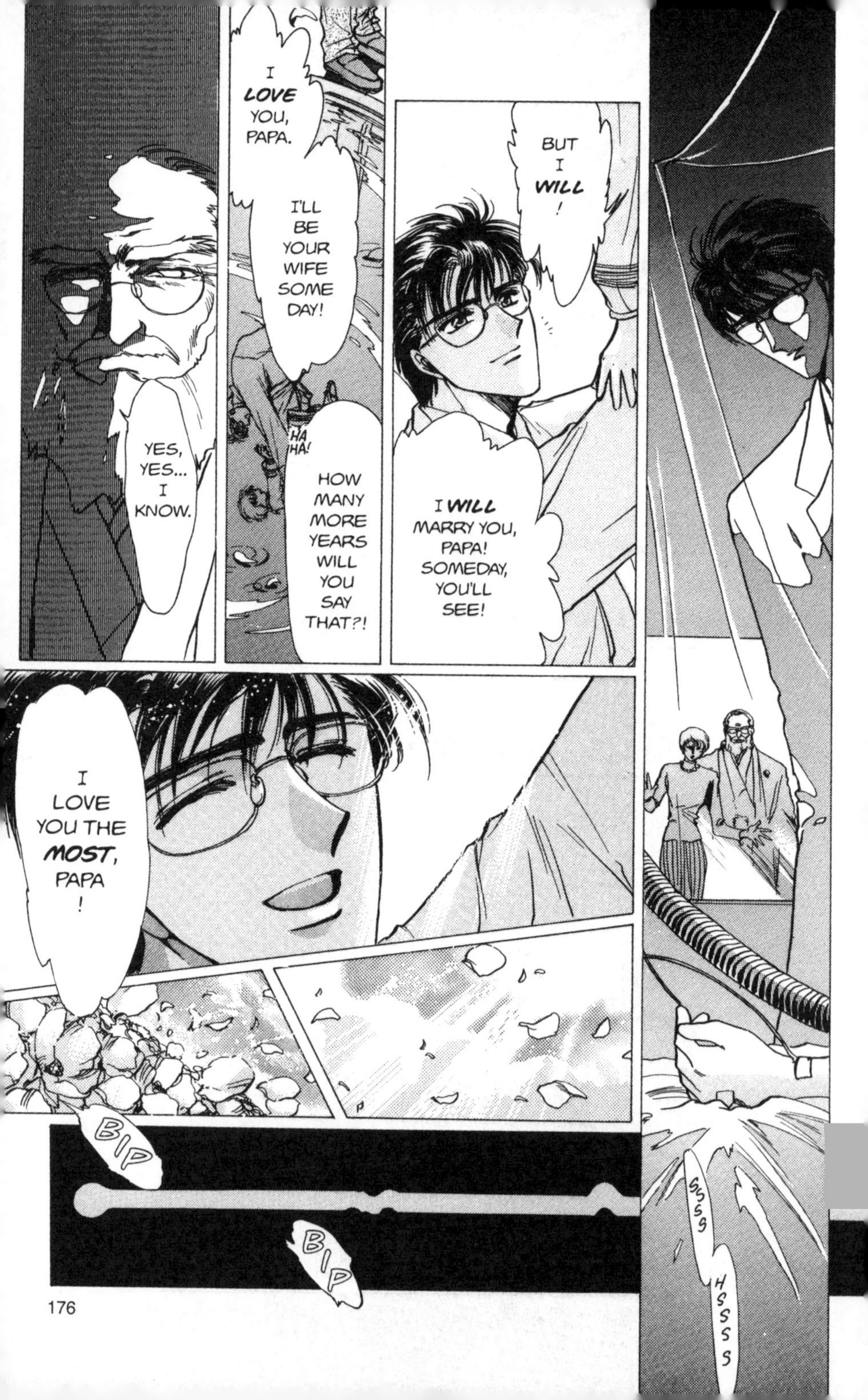

I **LOVE** YOU, PAPA.
I'LL BE YOUR WIFE SOMEDAY!
HA HA!
HOW MANY MORE YEARS WILL YOU SAY THAT?!
BUT I **WILL**!
I **WILL** MARRY YOU, PAPA! SOMEDAY, YOU'LL SEE!
YES, YES... I KNOW.
I LOVE YOU THE **MOST**, PAPA!
BIP
BIP
SSSS
HSSSS

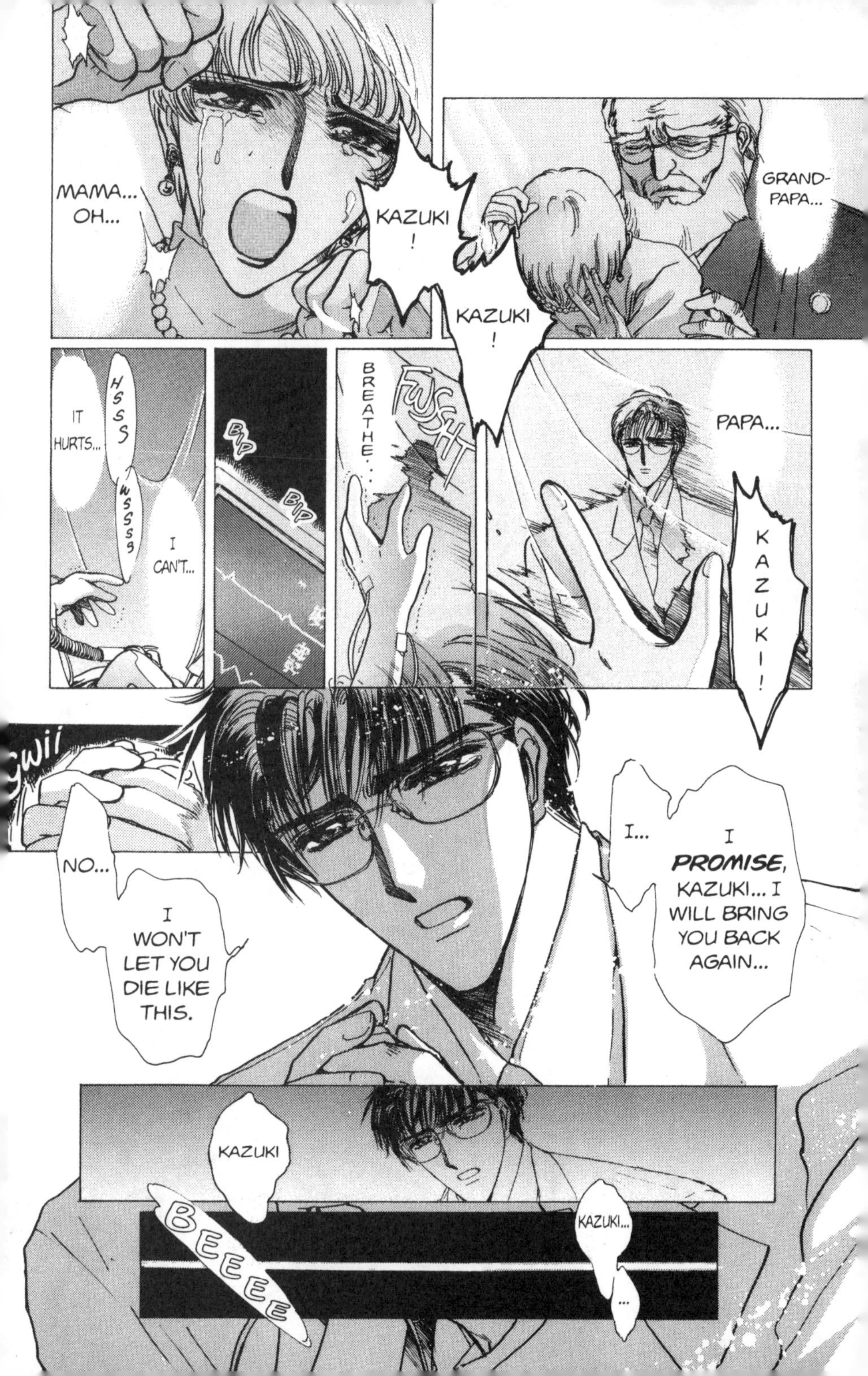
GRAND-PAPA...
KAZUKI!
KAZUKI!
MAMA... OH...
PAPA...
KAZUKI!
BREATHE...
FUSHT
BIP
BIP
HSSS
IT HURTS...
WSSSS
I CAN'T...
I...
I PROMISE, KAZUKI... I WILL BRING YOU BACK AGAIN...
gwii
NO...
I WON'T LET YOU DIE LIKE THIS.
KAZUKI...
...
KAZUKI
BEEEEE

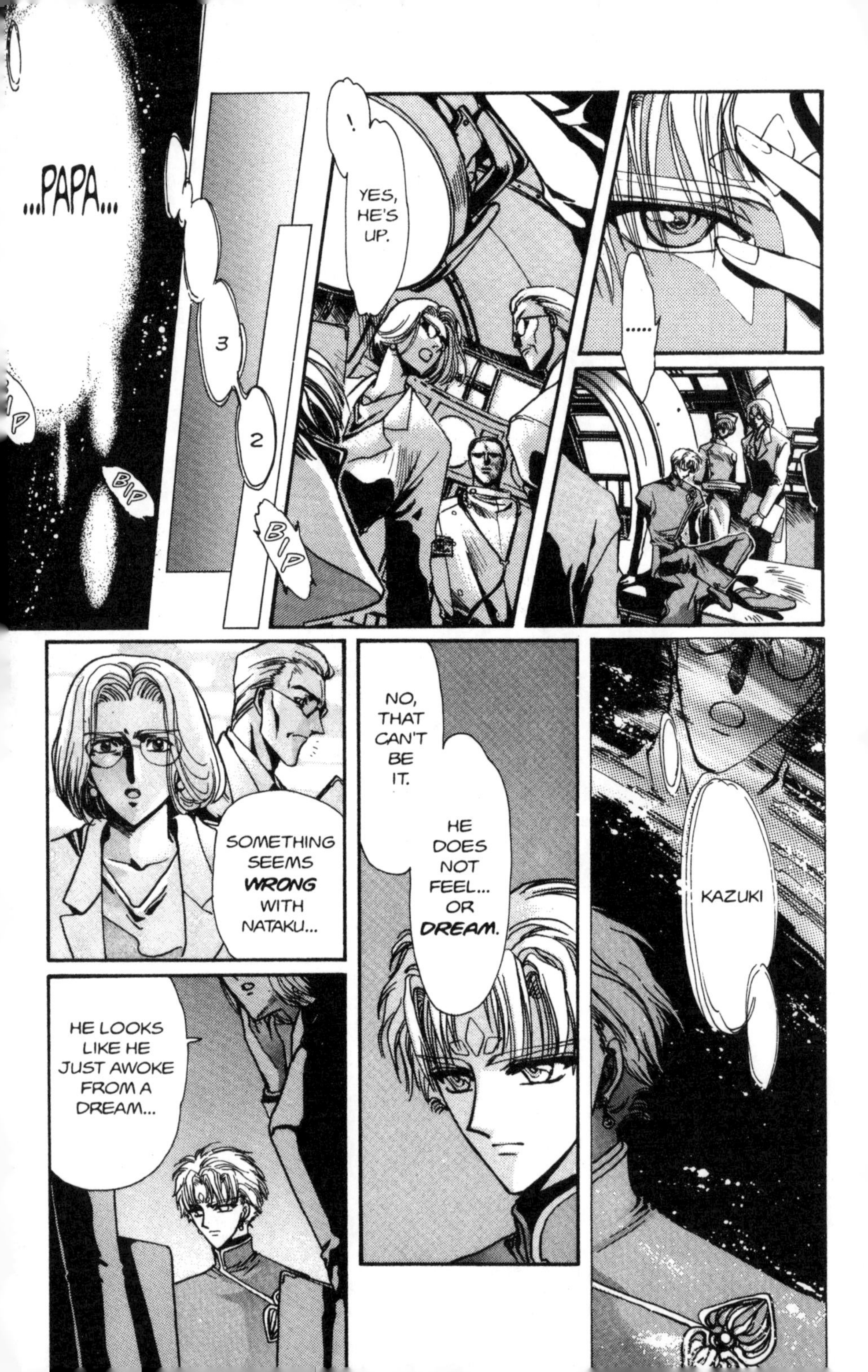
...PAPA...
BIP
3
BIP
2
BIP
!
YES, HE'S UP.
.....
SOMETHING SEEMS **WRONG** WITH NATAKU...
HE LOOKS LIKE HE JUST AWOKE FROM A DREAM...
NO, THAT CAN'T BE IT.
HE DOES NOT FEEL... OR **DREAM**.
KAZUKI

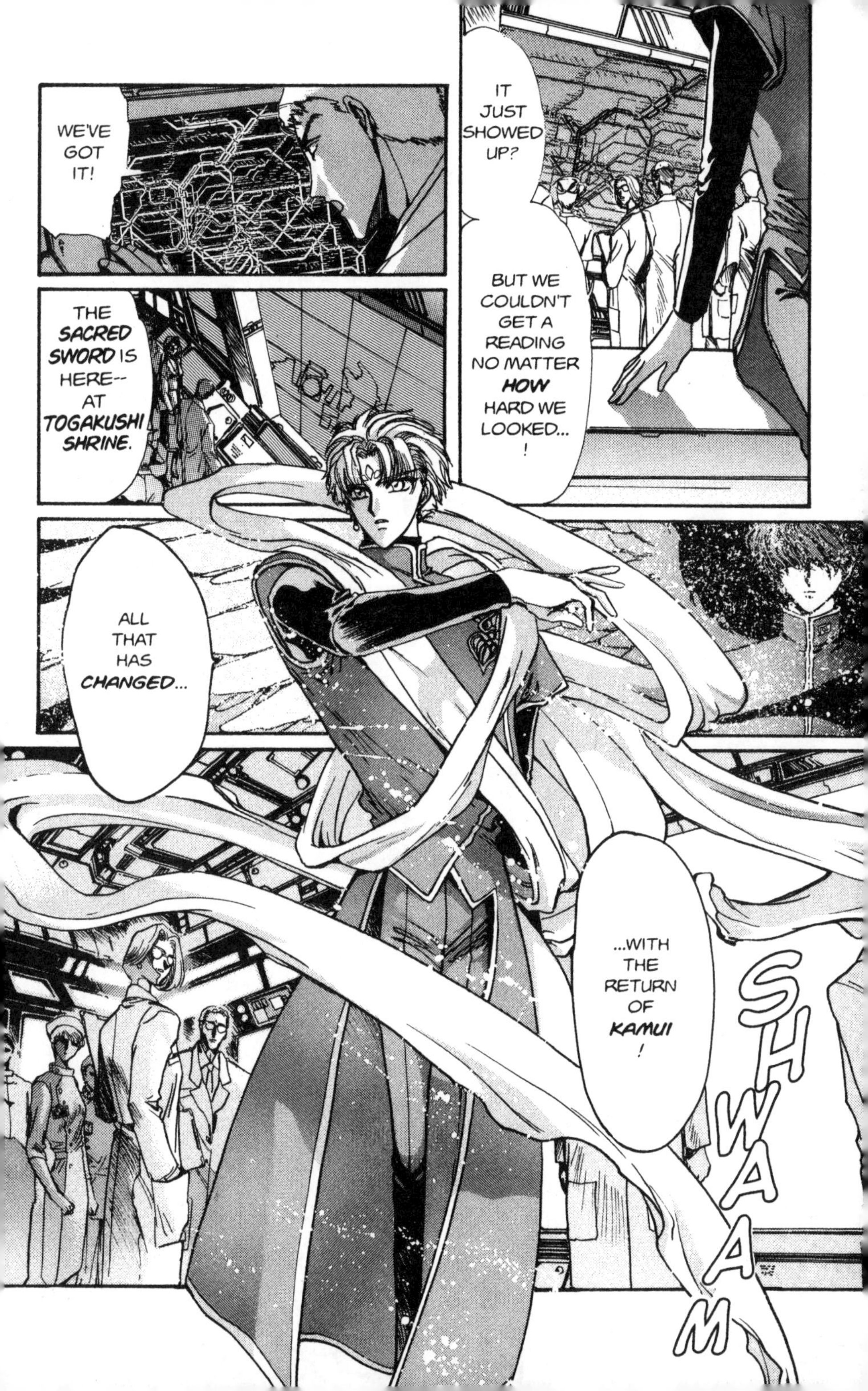
IT JUST SHOWED UP?
BUT WE COULDN'T GET A READING NO MATTER HOW HARD WE LOOKED...!
WE'VE GOT IT!
THE SACRED SWORD IS HERE-- AT TOGAKUSHI SHRINE.
ALL THAT HAS CHANGED...
...WITH THE RETURN OF KAMUI!
SHWAAM

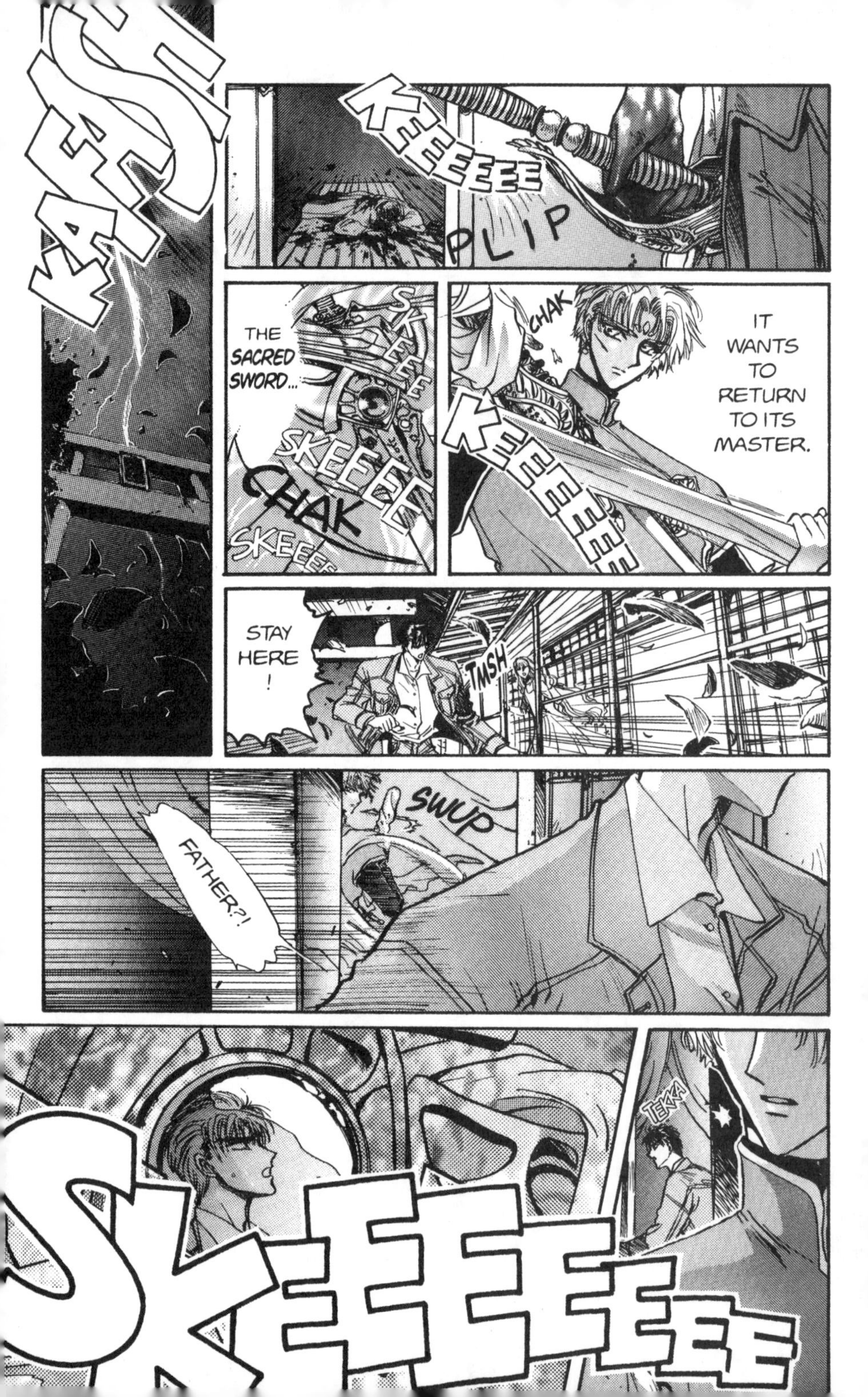
KEEEEEE
PLIP
IT WANTS TO RETURN TO ITS MASTER.
CHAK
KEEEEEEE
THE SACRED SWORD...
SKEEE
SKEEEEE
CHAK
SKEEEE
STAY HERE!
TMSH
KAHSH
SWUP
FATHER?!
TEKKA
SKEEEEEEEE

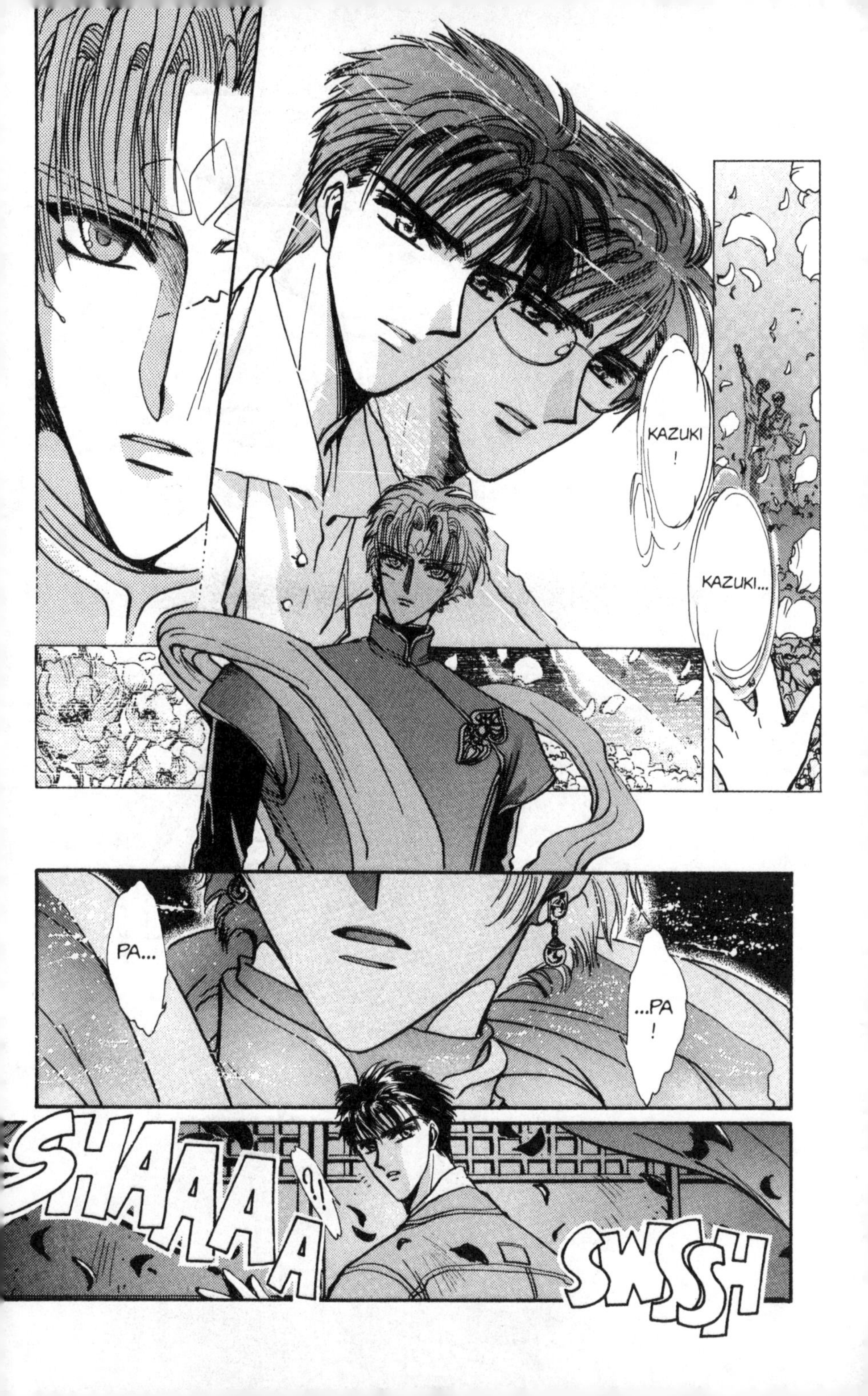
KAZUKI !
KAZUKI...
...PA !
PA...
SWSH
?!
SHAAAAA

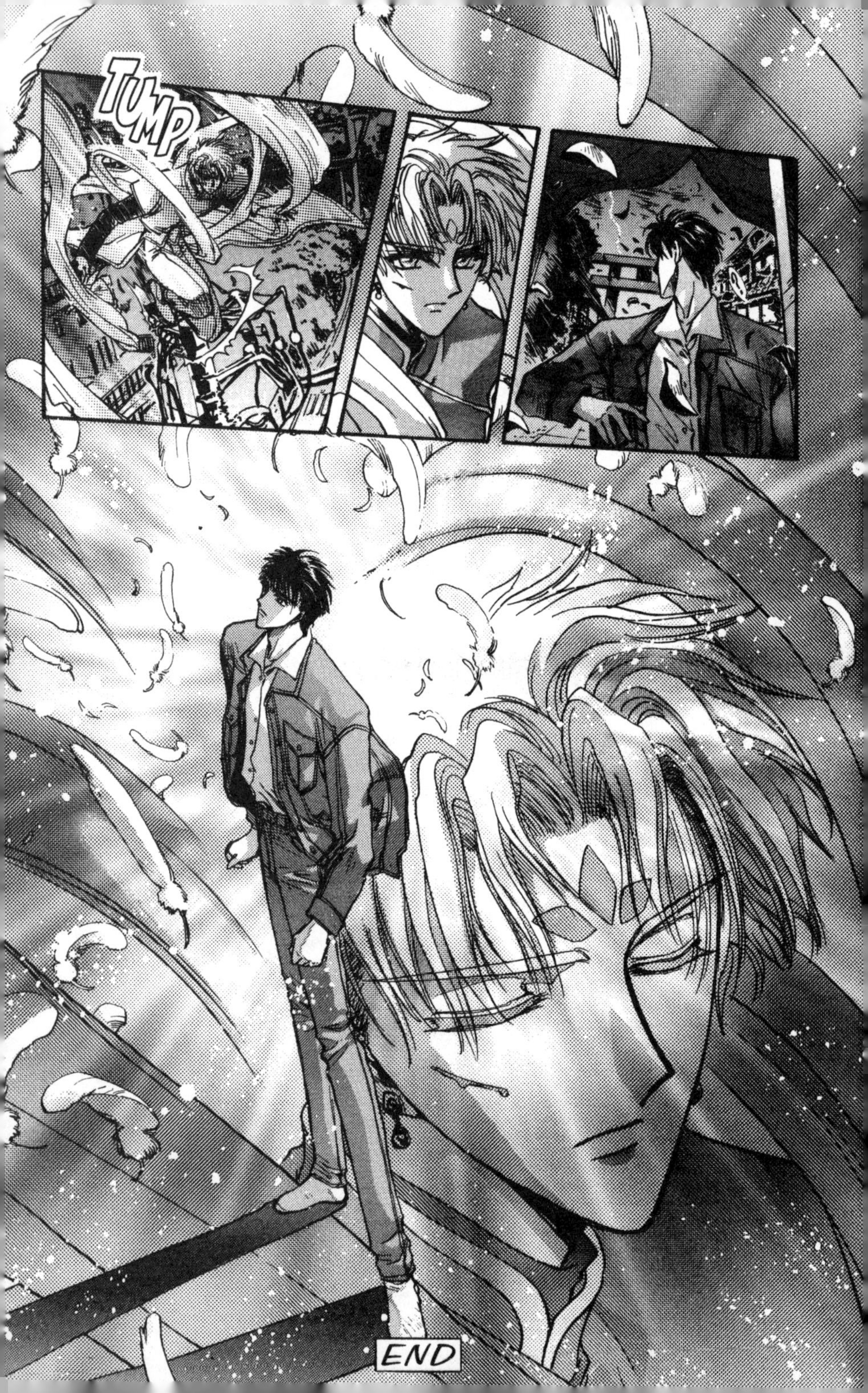
TUMP
END